1,000,000 Books

are available to read at

Forgotten Books

www.ForgottenBooks.com

Read online
Download PDF
Purchase in print

ISBN 978-1-332-96482-6
PIBN 10444074

This book is a reproduction of an important historical work. Forgotten Books uses state-of-the-art technology to digitally reconstruct the work, preserving the original format whilst repairing imperfections present in the aged copy. In rare cases, an imperfection in the original, such as a blemish or missing page, may be replicated in our edition. We do, however, repair the vast majority of imperfections successfully; any imperfections that remain are intentionally left to preserve the state of such historical works.

Forgotten Books is a registered trademark of FB &c Ltd.
Copyright © 2018 FB &c Ltd.
FB &c Ltd, Dalton House, 60 Windsor Avenue, London, SW19 2RR.
Company number 08720141. Registered in England and Wales.

For support please visit www.forgottenbooks.com

1 MONTH OF FREE READING

at

www.ForgottenBooks.com

By purchasing this book you are eligible for one month membership to ForgottenBooks.com, giving you unlimited access to our entire collection of over 1,000,000 titles via our web site and mobile apps.

To claim your free month visit:
www.forgottenbooks.com/free444074

* Offer is valid for 45 days from date of purchase. Terms and conditions apply.

English
Français
Deutsche
Italiano
Español
Português

www.forgottenbooks.com

Mythology Photography **Fiction** Fishing Christianity **Art** Cooking Essays Buddhism Freemasonry Medicine **Biology** Music **Ancient Egypt** Evolution Carpentry Physics Dance Geology **Mathematics** Fitness Shakespeare **Folklore** Yoga Marketing **Confidence** Immortality Biographies Poetry **Psychology** Witchcraft Electronics Chemistry History **Law** Accounting **Philosophy** Anthropology Alchemy Drama Quantum Mechanics Atheism Sexual Health **Ancient History Entrepreneurship** Languages Sport Paleontology Needlework Islam **Metaphysics** Investment Archaeology Parenting Statistics Criminology **Motivational**

MENTAL DEFICIENCY
(AMENTIA)

PLATE I.

TYPES OF BRAIN CELLS·OCCURRING IN AMENTIA.
(Drawn as seen under 1⁄12 inch oil-immersion lens.)

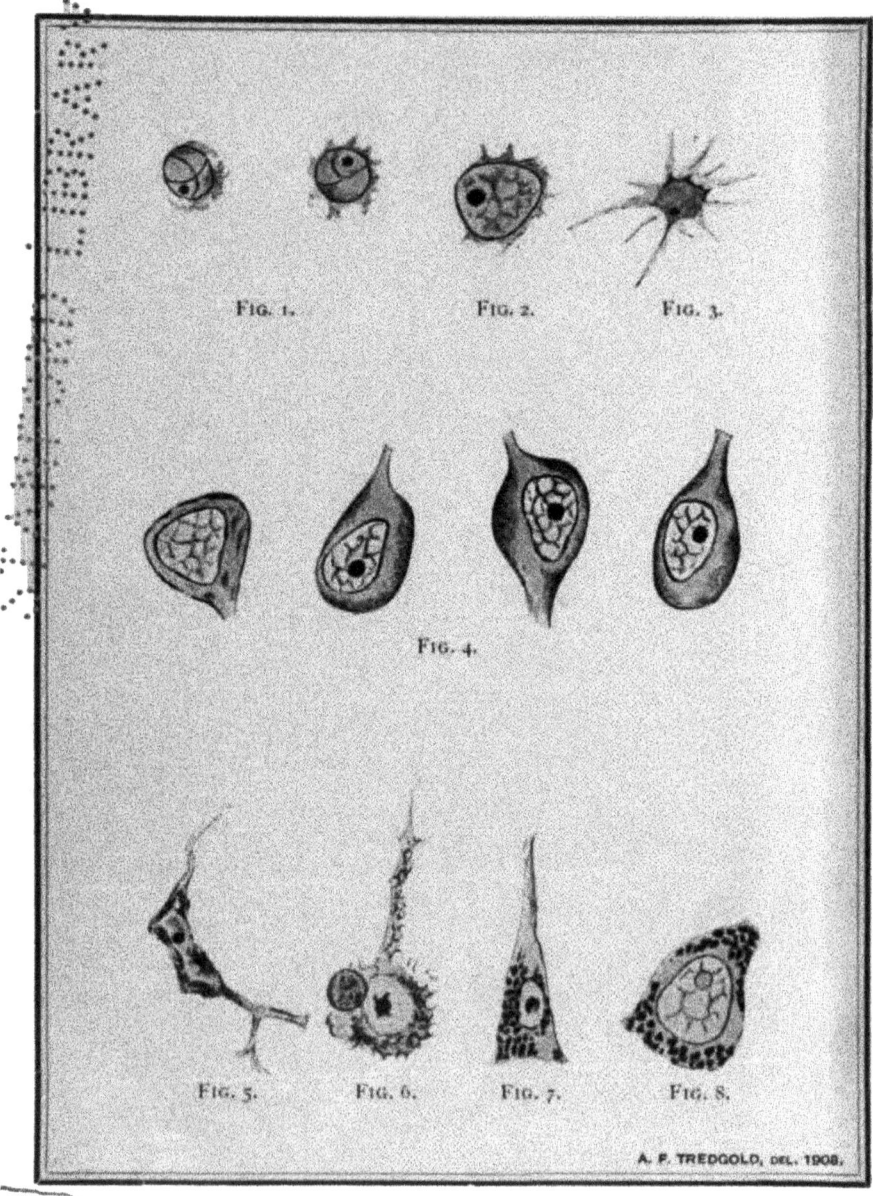

DESCRIPTION OF PLATE I.

FIG. 1.—Incompletely developed nerve cells (neuroblasts), from layer of small pyramids of frontal cortex.

FIG. 2.—Incompletely developed nerve cell, from middle pyramidal layer of motor cortex.

FIG. 3 —Neuroglia cell; from a case of sclerotic amentia.

FIG. 4 —Incompletely developed nerve cells, from layer of middle pyramids of frontal cortex.

FIG. 5.—Atrophied and distorted medium pyramidal nerve cell; from a case of sclerotic amentia.

FIG. 6.—Medium pyramidal cell from frontal cortex, undergoing subacute degeneration; from a case of secondary amentia.

FIG. 7.—Medium pyramidal cell from frontal cortex, undergoing chronic pigmentary atrophy.

FIG. 8.—Pigmented cell of hippocampus; from a case of amentia with epilepsy.

MENTAL DEFICIENCY

(AMENTIA)

BY

A. F. TREDGOLD
L.R.C.P. LOND., M.R.C.S. ENG.

CONSULTING PHYSICIAN TO THE NATIONAL ASSOCIATION FOR THE FEEBLE-MINDED, AND
TO THE LITTLETON HOME FOR DEFECTIVE CHILDREN; MEDICAL EXPERT TO THE
ROYAL COMMISSION ON THE FEEBLE-MINDED; FORMERLY RESEARCH SCHOLAR IN
INSANITY AND NEUROPATHOLOGY OF THE LONDON COUNTY COUNCIL AND
ASSISTANT IN THE CLAYBURY PATHOLOGICAL LABORATORY; LATE RESIDENT
CLINICAL ASSISTANT IN THE NORTHUMBERLAND COUNTY ASYLUM, ETC.

LONDON
BAILLIÈRE, TINDALL AND COX
8, HENRIETTA STREET, COVENT GARDEN
1908

[All rights reserved]

143739

TO

ALL THOSE PERSONS OF SOUND MIND

WHO ARE INTERESTED IN THE WELFARE

OF THEIR LESS FORTUNATE FELLOW-CREATURES

PREFACE

DURING the past few years the subject of mental deficiency has evoked a large amount of attention from many prominent persons interested in social and philanthropic questions. To members of the medical profession in particular it is one of much importance, on account of their responsible duties connected with its diagnosis, with the treatment and training of these patients, and their examination and certification as to fitness for special classes and schools, training-homes, and asylums. And there is no doubt that with new legislation, which cannot now long be delayed, these duties and responsibilities will be considerably increased.

For these reasons I venture to hope that the account which I have attempted to give in these pages regarding the incidence, causation, pathology, mental and physical characteristics, social relationship, diagnosis, prognosis, and treatment of persons suffering from mental deficiency, will be found to justify its publication.

To a great extent this account is based upon observations and researches which I have been making for close on ten years, but I have also made full use of, and frequent reference to, the writings of many other workers in this field. Valuable help, permission to examine cases and make use of notes and illustrations, has been generously accorded me from many quarters. In particular I would like to take this opportunity of gratefully acknowledging my indebtedness to the members of the Asylums Committee of the London County Council; also to Dr. Francis Warner, London; Dr. G. A. Sutherland, London; Dr. John Thomson, Edinburgh; Dr. F. W. Mott, F.R.S., Pathologist to the London County Asylums and Director of the Pathological Laboratory; Dr. R. R. Alexander and Dr. P. Baily, Hanwell Asylum; Dr. W. J. Seward, Colney Hatch Asylum; Dr. J. M. Moody, Cane Hill Asylum; Dr. Robert Jones, Claybury Asylum; Dr. T. W. McDowall, Morpeth Asylum; Dr. F. R. P. Taylor and Dr. C. A. Marsh, formerly of Darenth Asylum; Dr. C. Caldecott, Earlswood Training Institution; and Dr. R. Langdon Down, Normansfield Training Institution.

The greater portion of the microscopical work was carried out in the Claybury Pathological Laboratory, during my two years' tenure of the London County Council Research Scholarship in Insanity and Neuropathology; and to the unequalled advantages which this scholarship afforded for clinical and pathological research in these fields of medicine I desire to pay a grateful tribute.

Finally, I wish to express my indebtedness to the recently issued voluminous Reports of the Royal Commission on the Care and Control of the Feeble-Minded. Of the mass of information contained in these, regarding the number and condition of the mentally deficient population of this country, I have made full use. It is necessary, however, to add a word of explanation with regard to statistics. Under the term "mentally defective" the Commissioners include sane epileptics. Since, in my opinion, these should not rightly be classed as aments, I have considered it advisable to make independent calculations from the original returns—hence the slight discrepancy between the two sets of figures.

A. F. TREDGOLD.

6, DAPDUNE CRESCENT,
   GUILDFORD, SURREY,
      September, 1908.

TABLE OF CONTENTS

	PAGES
PREFACE	vii, viii

CHAPTER

I. INTRODUCTION - - - - - - 1–3

    Mental deficiency. Dementia. Amentia. Variations in "normal" mental capacity. Definition of the "normal" mind. Definition of amentia. Relation of amentia to normal, to dementia and to insanity.

II. INCIDENCE - - - - - - - 4–13

    Difficulty of enumeration. Investigations of the English Royal Commission of 1904. The number of aments in England and Wales. Incidence of the three degrees of amentia. Incidence of amentia relative to insanity. Location of aments in England and Wales. Incidence with regard to sex.

III. CAUSATION - - - - - - 14–50

    A.—INTRINSIC FACTORS (HEREDITY):

    Diseases of the nervous system. Alcoholism. Tuberculosis. Syphilis. Consanguinity. Age of parents.

    B.—EXTRINSIC FACTORS (ENVIRONMENT):

    Acting before Birth.—Abnormal conditions of mother during gestation. Mental. Physical. Illegitimacy. Maternal impressions.
    Acting during Birth.—Abnormalities of labour. Primogeniture. Premature birth.
    Acting after Birth.—Traumatic. Toxic. Epileptic and infantile convulsions. Malnutrition.

    GENERAL CONSIDERATIONS:

    Modus operandi of intrinsic and extrinsic factors. Illustrative family history charts. Factors of causation in regard to local variations of incidence.

Table of Contents

CHAPTER	PAGES

IV. PATHOLOGY — 51–70

The development of the normal brain.

PATHOLOGY OF AMENTIA:
The essential basis of amentia.

HISTOLOGY:
Cells of the cortex cerebri. Fibres. Neuroglia. Vessels. Situation of the cellular changes. The histology of secondary amentia.

MORBID ANATOMY:
Gross developmental anomalies and pathological lesions. Hemiatrophy. Microgyria. Porencephaly. Deficiency of internal structures. Hydrocephalus. Encephalitis and meningo-encephalitis. The skull.

V. CLASSIFICATION — 71–77

Division of amentia into forms, degrees, and clinical varieties.

FORMS:
Primary. Secondary. Delayed primary or developmental.

CLINICAL VARIETIES:
Of primary amentia: Simple, Microcephalic, Mongolian.
Of secondary amentia: Amentia due to cerebral disease, amentia due to defective cerebral nutrition.

DEGREES:
Feeble-mindedness (Children and adults). Imbecility. Idiocy. "Moral Imbecility." Definitions.

TABLE OF CLASSIFICATION.

VI. PHYSICAL CHARACTERISTICS OF AMENTIA — 78–97

Prevalence of physical defects in amentia. Stigmata of degeneracy. Table of anomalies.

ANOMALIES OF ANATOMICAL DEVELOPMENT:
A. Nervous system. B. Special sense organs. C. Osseous. D. Muscular and cutaneous. E. Circulatory and respiratory. F. Alimentary. G. Urinary and generative.

ANOMALIES OF PHYSIOLOGICAL FUNCTION:
Of special organs and of tissue in general. Mortality. Age periods of death. Causes of death, with table.

VII. MENTAL AND NERVOUS CHARACTERISTICS — 98–122

SENSORY:
Vision. Hearing. Taste. Smell. Cutaneous. Muscle. Organic.

Table of Contents

CHAPTER   **PAGES**

MENTAL AND NERVOUS CHARACTERISTICS (*continued*)—

MENTAL :

    Attention. Association and memory. Imagination. Ideation. Judgment and reasoning. Temperament. Emotion and sentiment. Volition.

MOTOR :

    Varieties of movements. Anomalies of quantity and quality. Deficient. Excessive. Inco-ordinate. Speech.

VIII. FEEBLE-MINDEDNESS IN CHILDREN (MENTALLY DEFECTIVE CHILDREN) - - - 123–146

    Introductory account, with early inquiries into number and condition. Definition. Special schools and classes. Inquiries of Royal Commission of 1904. Number. Relative incidence in different areas of the United Kingdom. Relative incidence in town and country. Sex.

DESCRIPTION :

    Physical. Nervous. Mental. Scholastic. The three grades of defect. Mentally defective compared with normal school-children. Varieties of mentally defective children.

DIAGNOSIS :

    Family history. Personal history. Present state. Differential diagnosis from dull and backward children, delayed development, dullness due to ill-health, epilepsy, insanity, and imbecility.

IX. FEEBLE-MINDEDNESS IN ADULTS - - 147–158

    Definition. Number. Sex.

DESCRIPTION :

    Physical and mental characteristics. The " stable " type. The " unstable " type. Examples.

X. IMBECILITY - - - - - - 159–164

    Definition. Number. Sex.

DESCRIPTION :

    Physical. Mental and nervous. Examples.

XI. IDIOCY - - - - - - 165–172

    Definition. Number. Sex.

DESCRIPTION :

    Partial or Incomplete Idiocy.—Physical. Mental and nervous. Apathetic and excitable idiots. Examples.
    Absolute or Complete Idiocy.

DIAGNOSIS OF IDIOCY AND IMBECILITY.

Table of Contents

CHAPTER   **PAGES**

XII. CLINICAL VARIETIES OF PRIMARY AMENTIA - 173–193

Division of primary aments into varieties.

MICROCEPHALICS:

Introductory account and number. Causation. Pathology. Relation of brain weight to intellect. Physical, mental, and nervous condition. Examples.

MONGOLIANS:

Introductory account and number. Causation. Pathology. Description of physical, mental, and nervous characteristics.

THE COMPLICATIONS OF PRIMARY AMENTIA:

Epilepsy. Paralysis. Hydrocephalus. Porencephalus. Sclerosis. Deaf-mutism.

XIII. CLINICAL VARIETIES OF SECONDARY AMENTIA 194–269

Clinical differences between primary and secondary amentia.

SECTION I. AMENTIA DUE TO CEREBRAL DISEASE:

1. Epileptic and eclampsic amentia.
2. Vascular, toxic, and inflammatory amentia: Porencephalic, sclerotic, hydrocephalic.
3. Syphilitic Amentia.
4. Infantile Cerebral Degeneration.

SECTION II. AMENTIA DUE TO DEFECTIVE CEREBRAL NUTRITION.

1. Cretinism: Endemic, sporadic.
2. Amentia due to other nutritional defects.
3. Amentia due to isolation and sense deprivation.

XIV. IDIOTS SAVANTS - - - - - 270–280

Description, with illustrative examples. The mechanical Genius of Earlswood Asylum.

XV. THE AMENT AND SOCIETY—PAUPER AMENTS 281–292

Location of the mentally deficient. The number of aments supported at the public expense. Feeble-minded in receipt of parish relief. Idiots and imbeciles. Vagrants. Aments under inadequate care. Propagation by aments.

XVI. MORAL DEFICIENCY AND CRIMINAL AMENTS 293–309

MORAL DEFICIENCY:

Latent moral defect. Its relation to amentia and to criminality. Habitual criminals and aments.

CRIMINAL AMENTS:

Number. Facile type. Impulsive type. Morally defective or habitual criminal type. Illustrative cases.

CRIMINAL RESPONSIBILITY OF AMENTS:

Conditions of responsibility: Defective knowledge, defective control, delusions. Civil incapacity.

Table of Contents

CHAPTER	PAGES
XVII. INSANE AMENTS	310–323

Sane and insane aments. Predisposition to insanity in aments. Borderland of amentia and insanity. Relative importance of predisposing and exciting factors. Insanity in the mild aments. Mania. Melancholia. Stupor. Alternating insanity. Delusional insanity. Recurrences. Dementia. General paralysis. Epileptic insanity. Insanity in imbeciles and idiots. Illustrative cases.

XVIII. DIAGNOSIS AND PROGNOSIS - - - 324–331

DIAGNOSIS :
In infancy. In childhood. In later years.

PROGNOSIS :
Of the forms, varieties and degrees.

XIX. TREATMENT AND TRAINING - - - 332–356
MEDICAL AND SURGICAL TREATMENT.

EDUCATION :
The general principles of education. Home training. School training. The senses, movement, intelligence, speech and scholastic. Industrial training. Moral training.

XX. CONCLUSION - - - - - 357–362
The necessity for training. Supervision and after-care. Prevention of propagation. Sterilization. Marriage. Eradication.

APPENDIX I. A TABLE OF NORMAL DEVELOPMENTAL DATA - - - - - - - 364, 365

APPENDIX II. METHOD OF ESTIMATING THE TOTAL NUMBER OF AMENTS IN ENGLAND AND WALES 366–369

APPENDIX III. THE LAW OF ENGLAND CONCERNING AMENTIA, WITH THE RECOMMENDATIONS OF THE ROYAL COMMISSION (1904) - - - - - 370–376

INDEX - - - - - - - - 377

LIST OF TABLES

TABLE		PAGE
I.	Showing the Total Number of Aments, and of Idiots, Imbeciles, and Feeble-Minded, per 1,000 Population, in Certain Districts of the United Kingdom	6
II.	Showing the Relative Incidence of Amentia in Certain Areas of the United Kingdom	7
III.	Approximate Estimation of the Total Number of Aments, and of the Respective Degrees, existing in England and Wales on January 1, 1906	9
IV.	Showing the Relative Incidence of the Degrees of Amentia in Certain Districts of the United Kingdom	10
V.	The Location of All Aments in Eleven Selected Areas of England and Wales	12
VI.	Showing the Condition of 150 Aments with their Brothers and Sisters	39
VII.	Classification of Amentia	77
VIII.	Anatomical and Physiological Anomalies associated with Amentia	82
IX.	Relative Mortality of Aments and Non-Aments	92
X.	Showing Age Periods of 1,000 Consecutive Deaths in Earlswood Asylum	92
XI.	Showing the Percentage of Deaths to the Number of Patients in Residence at Earlswood Asylum over a Period of Seventeen Years	93
XII.	Showing the Cause of Death in 1,000 Consecutive Deaths in Earlswood Asylum	94
XIII.	Consonantal Defects in Amentia	121
XIV.	Showing the Percentage of Mentally Deficient Children to the Public Elementary School Population in Certain Districts of the United Kingdom	126
XV.	Showing the Relation of Epilepsy to Amentia	197
XVI.	Showing the Location of Feeble-Minded Persons in Urban and Rural Areas respectively	286
XVII.	The Number of Aments inadequately cared for	287
Appendix I.	A Table of Normal Developmental Data	364

LIST OF FAMILY HISTORY CHARTS

CHART		PAGE
I.	SHOWING GOOD HEREDITY CONTAMINATED BY SLIGHT ALCOHOLIC HEREDITY AND TOWN LIFE	41
II.	SHOWING GOOD HEREDITY CONTAMINATED BY MORBID HEREDITY	41
III.	SHOWING GOOD HEREDITY CONTAMINATED BY INSANE HEREDITY	42
IV.	SHOWING THE EFFECT OF INSANE + PHTHISICAL HEREDITY	42
V.	SHOWING THE EFFECT OF ALCOHOLIC AND INSANE INHERITANCE + PHTHISICAL INHERITANCE	43
VI.	SHOWING THE EFFECT OF DOUBLE MORBID HEREDITY	43
VII.	SHOWING THE EFFECT OF DOUBLE MORBID HEREDITY	44
VIII.	SHOWING THE EFFECT OF A DOUBLE INSANE INHERITANCE + SYPHILIS	44
IX.	SHOWING THE EFFECT OF CONSANGUINITY WITH A TENDENCY TO VASCULAR LESIONS OF THE BRAIN	45

LIST OF ILLUSTRATIONS

PLATE	FIGS.		PAGE
I.	1-8.	Types of Brain Cells occurring in Amentia	*Frontispiece*
II.	9.	Diagrammatic Sections of Frontal Cortex in Amentia, Dementia, and the Normal Brain	63
	10.	Schema for taking Cranial Measurements	85

			TO FACE PAGE
III.	11-16.	Mentally Defective School-Children	128
IV.	17-18.	Primary Amentia, Feeble-Mindedness, Mentally Stable Type (Males)	150
V.	19-20.	Primary Amentia, Feeble-Mindedness, Mentally Unstable Type (Females)	154
VI.	21-22.	Primary Amentia, Imbecility, Mentally Unstable Type (Males)	160
VII.	23-24.	Primary Amentia, Imbecility (Females)	162
VIII.	25-26.	Primary Amentia, Imbecility (Males)	164
IX.	27.	Primary Amentia, Imbecility	166
	28.	Primary Amentia, Idiocy with Sclerosis	166
X.	29-30.	Primary Amentia, Idiocy, Excitable Type	168
XI.	31-32.	Primary Amentia, Microcephalic Variety	176
XII.	33-34.	Primary Amentia, Mongolian Variety	184
XIII.	35-36.	Primary Amentia, Mongolian Variety, Children	186
XIV.	37-38.	Primary Amentia, Mongolian Variety, Children	188
XV.	39.	Secondary Amentia due to Epilepsy	200
	40.	Secondary Amentia due to Cerebral Lesion	200
XVI.	41.	Secondary Amentia with Paralysis and Convulsions due to Infantile Lesion	214
	42.	Secondary Amentia with Paraplegia due to Vascular Lesion at Birth	214
XVII.	43.	Secondary Amentia with Epilepsy due to Encephalitis in Infancy	218
	44.	Secondary Amentia due to Encephalitis in Infancy	218
XVIII.	45.	Secondary Amentia due to Sclerosis (so-called "Hypertrophy of the Brain")	232

PLATE	FIG.		TO FACE PAGE
XVIII.	46.	Hydrocephalic and Microcephalic Imbeciles	232
XIX.	47.	Secondary Amentia due to Hydrocephalus, Child 1½ Years Old	236
	48.	Female Microcephalic Aged 4¾ Months	236
XX.	49–50.	Secondary Amentia due to Syphilis	246
XXI.	51–52.	Secondary Amentia, Cretinism	254
XXII.	53.	Secondary Amentia due to Congenital Blindness	266
	54.	Secondary Amentia due to Deafness (the Genius of Earlswood Asylum)	266
XXIII.	55.	Diagrammatic Life History of the Genius of Earlswood Asylum	276
XXIV.	56.	A Crayon Copy of the Picture "Bolton Abbey"	278
	57.	A Fully Rigged Man-of-War	278
XXV.	58.	A Page of the Patient's Private Memorandum Book	280
	59.	The "Great Eastern" Steamship	280
XXVI.	60.	Criminal Ament	296
	61.	Insane Ament	296
XXVII.	62–63.	Insane Aments	312
XXVIII.	64–65.	Insane Aments	314
XXIX.	66–67.	Insane Aments	316

MENTAL DEFICIENCY

CHAPTER I

INTRODUCTION

LITERALLY, the term " mental deficiency " is just as applicable to a decay as to a non-development of the mental powers, to the dotage of old age or disease as to idiocy from birth, and it is still often used indiscriminately of either of these conditions. There is, however, a great difference between them. Mental defect occurring subsequently to mental development may be compared to a state of bankruptcy, and is more fittingly described as *dementia* (*de*, down, from ; *mens*, mind) ; whilst the person whose mind has never attained normal development may be looked upon as never having had a banking account, and this state is designated *amentia* (*a*, without ; *mens*, mind). In both of these, of course, there is literally mental deficiency ; but in view of the convenient and growing tendency to restrict this term to the latter class, I shall in this book use it in a specific sense as synonymous with " amentia."

Mental deficiency, or amentia, then, is that state in which the mind has failed to attain normal development. But the question at once arises, What is " normal " mental development ? for there is probably no quality in which human beings differ so much as the degree of their mental capacity. All civilized nations are composed of men of very varying grades of intellect, ranging from the genius of a Bacon, Newton, Kepler, Copernicus, Shakespeare, Plato, or Galileo, to the rustic simplicity of an agricultural Hodge ; and all of these come within the compass of the normal Mind. Corresponding differences are present amongst barbarians and savages, and probably have always existed. What, then, is to be considered the standard, and how and where are we to draw a line which shall divide the normal from the abnormal, the least intellectually gifted members of normal mankind from the population which is mentally deficient?

It is not easy to do this, but I think that our best definition of the " normal " mind must be a degree of intellectual capacity sufficient to enable its possessor to perform his duties as a member of society in that position of life to which he is born.

Fortunately for human progress, the mental capacity of many persons suffices for this, and more; but where there is any falling short of this irreducible minimum, then I think we must say that the bounds of normal variation have been overstepped, and that a condition of incomplete development, or amentia, is present. We may thus define amentia as *a state of mental defect from birth, or from an early age, due to incomplete cerebral development, in consequence of which the person affected is unable to perform his duties as a member of society in the position of life to which he is born.*

It is not, however, to be assumed that amentia is merely a subtraction in varying degree from the normal. Although the contrary might be thought, nevertheless the two conditions do not merge into one another, and between the lowest normal and the highest ament a great and impassable gulf is fixed. Whilst the former is heavy, stolid, and uniformly dull-witted, he has yet sufficient common sense to look after his interests and hold his own in that environment in which Nature has placed him. The mildest ament, on the other hand, may show no apparent dullness; he may even be bright and vivacious, and in some of his abilities immeasurably superior to the clodhopper. But the other faculties of his mind are not present in like proportion. Instead of harmonious working there is discord, and in the possession of that essential to independent existence—common sense—he is lacking, and the want can never be supplied.

The difference has been well described by Sir J. Batty Tuke,[*] who says: " Where in theory the morbid and the healthy types might be supposed to approach each other, we find in practice

[*] Article " Insanity," " Encyclopædia Britannica."

that no such debatable ground exists. The uniformity of dullness in the former stands in marked opposition to the irregularity of mental conformation in the latter."

The fact is that amentia is not merely a mental subtraction, but a distinct pathological condition which is produced by disease. The cerebral tissues concerned in Mind do not suffer from a uniform arrest of their development at a point which is inadequate for the needs of everyday life, but their whole growth and development is irregular. Even the function of the parts laid down is often imperfect and perverted, the total result being not only mental defect, but mental discord.

The two other chief forms of mental disease are dementia and insanity. The former of these has already been referred to, and is the result of neuronic degeneration; whilst "insanity" is the clinical manifestation of a disturbance or perversion of neuronic function, which may or may not terminate in degeneration, and which, as we shall subsequently see, is by no means incompatible with neuronic deficiency or amentia.

The subject of amentia, therefore, whilst presenting many interesting problems to the physician, the pathologist, and the psychologist, has also a much wider interest and importance. Since in Man the predominant feature is Mind, and since it is by the development of this faculty that human progress has taken, and must take, place, it is clear that the question of its disease, and particularly of its defect, is one of supreme importance to the statesman, the sociologist, and the philosopher.

CHAPTER II
INCIDENCE

THE enumeration of the mentally deficient population of any country is an extremely difficult matter, and there can be no doubt that most official inquiries, particularly those by means of the ordinary census, fall very far short of the truth. The reasons for this are numerous, the chief being the inability or unwillingness of parents to recognize mental abnormality, their total incapacity to distinguish between its various forms, and their not unnatural reluctance to proclaim its presence on a census paper. The milder forms of defect, which are at once the most important from a sociological aspect, and the most frequent, cannot possibly be detected by such means. For these reasons I am of opinion that the official returns of any country respecting the number of its aments are so unreliable and incomplete that no useful purpose would be served by quoting them.

Investigations of the Royal Commission of 1904.

In this country, however, an enumeration has recently been made on quite another basis. In the year 1904 a Royal Commission was appointed to consider the existing methods of dealing with these persons, and the Commissioners decided that, before any practical scheme of administration could be formulated, it was imperative that they should obtain approximately accurate information as to the number and condition of the class. With this object, a series of personal investigations were instituted on a considerable scale, and this is the first systematic attempt which has been made to obtain reliable data. It is not too much to say that these inquiries have added enormously to our knowledge regarding the condition, manner of living, and environment of the aments of this country, besides making it possible to calculate their total number with a degree of accuracy hitherto unattainable.

The method adopted by the Royal Commission consisted of a series of elaborate and searching inquiries by a number of medical men, to each of whom a selected area was assigned. The investigator was instructed to visit personally all public elementary schools, poor-law institutions, charitable establishments, training-homes, reformatories, common lodging-houses, prisons, idiot asylums, hospitals, and, indeed, any establishment likely to harbour the mentally abnormal. Further, he was to see persons in receipt of out-door relief, to apply to the clergy, medical practitioners, the police, charity organization societies, and similar agencies, and, in short, to make use of any and every channel which might help him to make the enumeration complete.

It was not found practicable to investigate the whole of the country in this way, but, in order that conclusions applicable to the entire country might be drawn, a selection of certain typical areas was made. Altogether, there were examined nine areas in England, two in Wales, one in Scotland, and four in Ireland, having an aggregate population of 3,873,151.

I shall again allude to many facts revealed by this inquiry in subsequent chapters; but in this place some statistics regarding the ascertained number of aments may be quoted.

The total number of aments varies in the different areas examined, and although to a slight extent this may be due to different personal equations, in many cases the difference is so great that it can only be regarded as the result of a real difference of incidence. This is shown in the following table :

TABLE I.*

SHOWING THE TOTAL NUMBER OF AMENTS, AND OF IDIOTS, IMBECILES, AND FEEBLE-MINDED RESPECTIVELY PER 1,000 POPULATION, IN CERTAIN DISTRICTS OF THE UNITED KINGDOM, ACCORDING TO THE INVESTIGATIONS OF THE ROYAL COMMISSION, 1904.

		Idiots.	Imbeciles.	Feeble-minded. Adults.	Feeble-minded. Children.	Total Aments.
Urban	Manchester	0·05	0·32	1·20	2·10	3·74
	Birmingham	0·09	0·27	1·70	1·60	3·76
	Hull	0·02	0·20	0·55	0·58	1·35
	Glasgow	0·07	0·23	0·32	1·00	1·68
	Dublin	0·19	0·57	1·20	2·10	4·14
	Belfast	0·13	0·63	0·70	0·97	2·45
Industrial	Stoke-on-Trent	0·21	0·45	2·10	1·10	3·96
	Durham	0·02	0·34	0·56	0·56	1·48
	Cork	0·07	0·32	0·16	0·54	1·10
Mixed Industrial and Agricultural	Nottinghamshire	0·30	0·66	1·50	1·20	3·81
	Carmarthenshire	0·59	0·65	0·51	1·20	3·05
Agricultural	Somersetshire	0·18	1·00	2·10	1·10	4·54
	Wiltshire	0·35	0·69	2·20	0·90	4·25
	Lincolnshire	0·44	0·98	1·40	1·70	4·68
	Carnarvonshire	0·24	0·58	2·10	0·94	3·96
	Galway	0·13	1·00	1·00	2·20	4·40

It will be seen from this Table that, whilst the mean average incidence of total amentia in the sixteen areas is 3·28 per 1,000 population, the variation ranges from a minimum of 1·1, in the case of Cork, to a maximum of 4·68 in the case of Lincolnshire. The following table shows the areas grouped according to the prevalence of amentia :

* The figures in this table slightly underestimate the true incidence for the reason that they do not include a small proportion of cases certified under the Lunacy Act.

TABLE II.

SHOWING THE INCIDENCE OF RELATIVE AMENTIA IN CERTAIN AREAS OF THE UNITED KINGDOM.

Low Incidence (under 3 per 1,000 Population).	Mean Average Incidence (3 to 4 per 1,000 Population).	High Incidence (over 4 per 1,000 Population).
Hull	Manchester	Dublin
Glasgow	Birmingham	Somersetshire
Belfast	Stoke-on-Trent	Wiltshire
Durham	Nottinghamshire	Lincolnshire
Cork	Carmarthenshire	Galway
	Carnarvonshire	

It is thus seen that the incidence of amentia in this country is far from being uniform ; that, in fact, great differences exist between areas in which there is little difference in physical, social, and industrial features. By means of the annual reports of the Lunacy Commissioners I have ascertained that the same applies to the incidence of insanity, and that, on the whole, there is a tolerably close correspondence between the relative extent of the two conditions (amentia and insanity). The cause of this differing prevalence of mental disease is not clear, and its investigation would probably necessitate very minute inquiries into the social, industrial, and hereditary condition of the people over a long period. Since, however, it relates rather to mental disease in general than to amentia in particular, it is beyond the scope of this work to do more than allude to it.

The Number of Aments in England and Wales.

If the incidence of amentia were tolerably uniform throughout the country, it would be a very simple matter to calculate the total number of affected persons from the figures revealed by this inquiry ; but, as we have seen, the incidence is very far from being uniform. It would also be quite easy could it be shown that the proportion of low to high prevalent areas in those examined were relatively the same as obtains in the whole country—if, in fact, we could be certain that we were dealing with a fair sample—but there is no *a priori* evidence that this is so. Consequently the estimation is a somewhat complicated one. I believe, however, that by using the incidence of insanity as a standard we may arrive at a result which is approximately correct. All insane persons are not, of course, certified, but the returns of the Lunacy Commissioners regarding the number of the certified pauper insane may be accepted as a sufficiently accurate indication of the *relative* prevalence of insanity in the various union districts of England and Wales. The incidence of amentia, as already remarked, is, on the whole, directly proportionate to the incidence of insanity. Now, if we calculate the proportion per 1,000 population of the certified pauper insane in the eleven areas of England and Wales investigated by the Royal Commission of 1904, it works out at 3·15 ; but if we calculate the proportion per 1,000 of the certified pauper insane throughout the country (using in each case the returns of the Lunacy Commission* and the population according to the 1901 census†), it works out at 3·42. So that the mean average incidence of insanity, and consequently of amentia, in these areas is less than the mean average for the entire country, and this can only be due to the fact that the eleven areas examined contain a greater relative proportion of districts of low incidence.

The actual number of aments in the country is therefore expressed by the equation :

$$\underbrace{\text{Aments : certified insane}}_{\text{in areas examined}} :: \underbrace{\text{aments : certified insane}}_{\text{in England and Wales}}$$

From which it follows that the total number of aments in England and Wales on January 1, 1906, was approximately 138,529 persons, equivalent to (with an estimated population on that date of 34,349,435, according to the Registrar-General) 4·03 persons per 1,000, or 1 in every 248.‡

---

* Total pauper certified insane in England and Wales on January 1, 1906, according to the Sixtieth Report of Lunacy Commissioners = 111,256. Total pauper insane in the areas investigated, as obtained from Table I., Appendix B, of same report = 7,328.

† Population of England and Wales, according to 1901 census = 32,525,716. Population of the eleven areas examined, according to 1901 census = 2,321,567.

‡ For further particulars and corrections, see " Appendix II.

Incidence

The Number of Persons suffering from Each of the Three Degrees of Amentia in England and Wales.

This may be calculated in a similar manner to the foregoing, and the results arrived at are shown in the following table :

TABLE III.

APPROXIMATE ESTIMATION OF THE TOTAL NUMBER OF AMENTS, AND OF THE RESPECTIVE DEGREES, EXISTING IN ENGLAND AND WALES ON JANUARY 1, 1906.

(Estimated Total Population according to Registrar-General, 34,349,435.)

Idiots	8,654	persons, or 0·25	per 1,000 population.
Imbeciles	25,096	,, 0·73	,, ,,
Feeble-minded { Adults	54,114*	,, 1·57	,, ,,
Feeble-minded { Children	50,665	,, 1·47	,, ,,
Total	138,529	,, 4·03	,, ,,

(or 1 person in every 248)

The Relative Incidence of the Three Degrees of Amentia.

It is seen from Table III. that *idiots* are decidedly the least numerous of the three degrees of amentia ; that *imbeciles* occur next in frequency, being nearly three times as plentiful ; whilst the number of the *feeble-minded* is more than three times as great as the idiots and imbeciles combined. In other words, taking the country as a whole, there are *in every* 100 *aments* :

Idiots.	*Imbeciles.*	*Feeble-minded.*	
		Adults.	Children.
6	18	39	37

Or, *in every* 10,000 *population* there are (taking the nearest whole numbers) :

Idiots.	*Imbeciles.*	*Feeble-minded.*		*Insane.*
		Adults.	Children.	
—	.	15	14	36

* It seems probable that the excess of adult over juvenile feeble-minded is due to the inclusion in the former group of 4,450 patients in asylums. The majority of these belong to the mildest type of mental defect, and are detained on account of insanity or epilepsy. If seen during the school period, they would probably be looked upon as doubtful, and given the benefit accordingly. Their condition becomes obvious when competition with the outside world has to be faced.

There are, however, certain variations in the relative incidence of these degrees of amentia which seem to be referable to the environment, and to these brief allusion must be made. It is found that the severer degrees of defect (idiots and imbeciles) are both relatively and absolutely much more numerous in agricultural than in urban and industrial areas, whilst in the case of the juvenile feeble-minded (mentally defective children) the results are reversed, these being both relatively and absolutely more numerous in urban than in agricultural areas. The actual figures will be seen by reference to Tables I. and IV.

TABLE IV.

SHOWING THE RELATIVE INCIDENCE OF THE DEGREES OF AMENTIA IN CERTAIN DISTRICTS OF THE UNITED KINGDOM. CALCULATED FROM THE RETURNS OF THE ROYAL COMMISSION, 1904.

			In Every 100 *Aments* there are—			
					Feeble-minded.	
			Idiots.	Imbeciles.	Adults.	Children
Urban		Manchester	1·5	8·6	31·0	57·0
		Birmingham	2·5	7·2	45·0	44·0
		Hull	1·5	7·8	44·0	46·0
		Glasgow	4·3	13·7	19·4	62·6
		Dublin	4·6	14·0	30·0	51·3
		Belfast	5·3	25·9	29·0	39·5
Industrial		Stoke-on-Trent	5·3	11·4	53·0	30·0
		Durham	1·5	23·0	37·0	38·0
		Cork	6·7	29·0	15·0	49·0
Mixed Industrial and Agricultural		Nottinghamshire	8·1	17·0	41·0	32·0
		Carmarthenshire	14·0	22·0	18·0	44·0
Agricultural		Somersetshire	4·0	23·0	47·0	25·0
		Wiltshire	8·3	15·0	52·0	23·0
		Lincolnshire	9·5	21·0	31·0	37·0
		Carnarvonshire	6·0	14·0	55·0	24·0
		Galway	2·9	22·8	23·7	50·5

Incidence

Inasmuch as the inquiries from which these statistics are compiled excluded all persons certified under the Lunacy Act, there is a slight fallacy in these figures. In order to ascertain the extent of this, I made a special investigation as to the *total* number of aments (certified and uncertified) in a few of the areas examined. The results show that the proportion excluded does not appreciably alter the relative incidence as shown in Table IV. The cause of this difference of relative incidence will be discussed in a subsequent chapter.

Incidence of Amentia relative to Insanity.

It has been stated that the incidence of amentia is directly proportionate to that of insanity, and on the whole this is true; for it is found that where insanity is rife amentia is also prevalent, and, conversely, where there is little insanity there is little amentia. The inquiries of the Royal Commission show, however, that the relative incidence of these two forms of mental disease is subject to slight variations according to the environment, and, generally speaking, amentia would appear to be relatively more prevalent in rural, and insanity in urban, districts.

The aments are a slightly more numerous class than the insane, for a calculation of the total number of the latter (uncertified as well as certified) shows that the approximate number of this class in England and Wales on January 1, 1906, was 125,827, corresponding to 3·66 per 1,000 population, or to 1 person in every 273.

The approximate total number of persons suffering from all forms of pronounced mental disease (amentia, insanity, and dementia) in England and Wales is, therefore, 264,356, equivalent to 7·69 per 1,000, or 1 person in every 130.

Location.

In order to give a general idea as to the location of these aments I append the following table (V.), which shows the situation of the 8,079 persons revealed by the inquiries of the

Royal Commission, together with those not so included on account of being certified under the Lunacy Act :

TABLE V.

LOCATION OF ALL AMENTS IN ELEVEN SELECTED AREAS OF ENGLAND AND WALES. MAINLY BASED UPON THE INQUIRIES OF THE ROYAL COMMISSION, 1904.

	Feeble-minded.		Imbe-ciles.	Idiots.	Totals.	
	Juvenile.	Adult.			Persons.	Per Cent.
(a) In institutions :						
Poor Law	83	1,387	152	47		
Charitable*	34	115	—	—		
Idiot asylums	3	22	60	15	2,866	32·5
Lunatic asylums	—	366	276	92		
Prisons	—	197	—	—		
Inebriate homes	—	17	—	—		
(b) In receipt of outdoor relief	10	358	237	103	708	8·0
(c) Not receiving relief :						
1. Friends able to make partial or full permanent provision	50	234	138	72	494	5·6
2. Friends unable to make permanent provision	217	926	434	147	1,724	19·5
(d) In public elementary or special schools	2,936	11	74	—	3,021	34·2
Totals	3,333	3,633	1,371	476	8,813	

* Charitable institutions are composed as follows :

Institutions for the blind, deaf, crippled, epileptic, and defective, 21 persons.
Training and rescue homes, penitentiaries, etc., 128 persons.

Incidence with Regard to Sex.

The sex of the 12,120 aments discovered in sixteen areas of the United Kingdom is as follows :

	Idiots.	Imbeciles.	Feeble-minded.		Totals.
			Children.	Adults.	
Males	303	959	3,244	2,179	6,685
Females	282	848	2,193	2,112	5,435

It is thus seen that, considered either in regard to each degree or collectively, there is a slight preponderance of the male sex, the relative proportion of males to females being practically as 6 to 5. It is probable that of all aments born a considerably greater proportion than this are of the male sex ; but that the number of these is subsequently diminished by a relatively higher infantile mortality.

That a greater number of aments are to-day resident in institutions than was the case a generation back is, I think, incontestable, and the exigencies of modern life must undoubtedly lead to an increase of this number in years to come ; but as to whether the condition is or is not more prevalent than formerly, or as to the relative incidence in different countries, we have no data upon which to form an opinion. It is quite clear, however, from the statistics here given, that even on account of its present prevalence the condition is one deserving of the gravest consideration.

CHAPTER III

CAUSATION

AMENTIA has been defined as mental deficiency due to imperfect or arrested cerebral development, and in the investigation of its causes we have to inquire into all the influences concerned in embryonic development, as well as those affecting the growth of the brain after birth. In other words we must ascertain as completely as possible the family and the early personal history of these afflicted persons. Now such an inquiry is by no means easy; it requires not only a considerable amount of special knowledge in order rightly to interpret the accounts furnished by unscientific and often ignorant persons, but it also demands much patience and tact. The not unnatural reluctance evinced by the majority of persons to admit the presence of mental unsoundness in the family often leads to the deliberate withholding of information, whilst a strongly prejudiced view of the importance of some one particular factor may cause all others to be ignored, and so greatly mislead the investigator. I do not think there is any disease in which, in the minds of parents and relatives, the *post hoc ergo propter hoc* opinion figures more largely.

Nevertheless a very large number of cases have now been examined, and although the opinions of inquirers differ slightly as to their relative importance, there is a very general agreement as to the main influences which are responsible for the imperfect condition of the brain cells.

It would be too large a task to refer to all the work which has been done in this direction, even in this country alone; and as I have myself devoted much time to the subject, and have investigated the antecedents of a large number of these patients, I propose to give my own results, alluding where necessary to the points upon which they differ from those of other inquirers. My reason for doing this is that the question of causation not only involves the ascertainment of facts, but the careful analysis and consideration of such facts in conjunction with the clinical features of the patients, and I feel more competent to do this with data personally collected than with those obtained by other persons. My investigations* embrace patients seen in the asylums of the London County Council, the special institutions at Darenth and Earlswood, the Littleton Home for Defective Children, and my own private practice, and they include every grade and variety of amentia. This point is important, because the type of case varies much in different institutions, and statistics, however numerous, which are confined to any one institution are apt, on that account, to be misleading.

In dealing with this subject, it has been the usual custom for writers to divide the cases into two groups—" congenital " and " acquired." Such a division is open to the objection that what would be termed a congenital condition may really be due to a factor of the environment, and acquired *in utero*. The real question is the relative parts played by heredity and environment. Accordingly, I have thought it better to use the terms *intrinsic* and *extrinsic*. Intrinsic factors are hereditary influences which modify the germinal plasm before conception takes place, and the form of amentia so produced may be termed *primary*. Extrinsic factors are those conditions of the environment which affect the development of the brain (and body) either whilst yet within or without the uterus, and in this case the amentia may be termed *secondary*. The various etiological factors will, therefore, be discussed in the following order :

(A) Intrinsic—Heredity.

1. Disease of the Nervous System.
2. Alcoholism.
3. Tuberculosis.
4. Syphilis.
5. Consanguinity.
6. Age of Parents.

---

* An analysis of 150 of these was given in my article on " Amentia " in Mott's " Archives of Neurology," vol. i. Nearly another hundred have since been investigated, with practically identical results.

(B) **Extrinsic—Environment.**

(a) *Before Birth* { 1. Abnormal Conditions of the *Mother* during Pregnancy—(1) Mental, (2) Physical.
2. Injuries to the *Fœtus*.

(b) *During Birth* { 1. Abnormalities of Labour.
2. Primogeniture.
3. Premature Birth.

(c) *After Birth* { 1. Traumatic.
2. Toxic.
3. Epileptic and Infantile Convulsions.
4. Malnutrition.

(A) **Causes Inherent in the Germinal Plasm—Heredity.**

1. DISEASE OF THE NERVOUS SYSTEM.

It is agreed by all who have studied this question, that the most frequent cause of amentia is some ancestral pathological condition—morbid heredity. It is also agreed that the commonest form of morbid heredity is disease of the nervous system. In a small proportion of cases the antecedent nervous disease consists of cerebral hæmorrhages, paralysis, or various neuroses; but in the great majority it is insanity, dementia, or epilepsy. My own inquiries showed that over 80 per cent. of persons suffering from the severer grades of amentia were the descendants of a pronounced neuropathic stock. In 64 per cent. the heredity was in the form of insanity or epilepsy; whilst in 18 per cent. it consisted of a marked family tendency to paralysis, cerebral hæmorrhages, or various neuroses and psychoses. Somewhat similar results, showing the great prevalence of this factor, have been obtained by other investigators. For instance, in *England* it was found by Beach and Shuttleworth* that insanity, epilepsy, and allied neuroses were well marked in the ancestors of 42 per cent. of the patients they examined; but Dr. Caldicott considers that 70 to 75 per cent. have neuropathic antecedents. In *America* a Commission appointed by the Legislature of Connecticut *found neuropathic heredity to be the undoubted cause in 43 per cent. In *Germany* Koch† came to the conclusion that it accounted for

---

* Beach and Shuttleworth, Clifford Allbutt's "System of Medicine," vol. vii.

† J. L. A. Koch, " Zur Statistik der Geisterkrankheiten in Würtemberg, und der Geisterkr. überhaupt." Stuttgart, 1878.

60 per cent. of cases. In *Switzerland* (Canton of Berne) the census of 1893 showed that heredity was present in 55 per cent. of idiots; whilst in *Norway* Ludwig Dahl found it to occur in 50 per cent. of cases.

It is seen that my own results are considerably higher than those obtained by most other observers, and it is necessary to explain the discrepancy. I believe it to be entirely a question of the method adopted. Most statistics relating to this subject have been compiled from case-books or official returns, and although by this means an immense amount of material is available, the details must necessarily be lacking in the accuracy and completeness obtainable by a personal inquiry. Again and again have I discovered, by a little questioning, a well-marked history of insanity, of which no record whatever existed in the official case-book; and it is my opinion that, although statistics based upon these may be of value as showing the *relative* importance of the different factors, they are practically valueless as an indication of the precise extent to which these factors occur.

It was the recognition of the incomplete and unsatisfactory details in the case-books, including some of those which have formed the basis for previous generalizations on this matter, which decided me to conduct an independent and personal inquiry into the causation of amentia. Unfortunately, the taking of a reliable family history involves much time and trouble. It is essential to gain the confidence of the relatives, and it is often necessary to interview several members of the family before all the requisite details can be elicited. Moreover, family histories can rarely be considered satisfactory unless they include particulars of three generations. For these reasons a personal inquiry of this kind can only be based upon a comparatively small number of cases; but what is lost in quantity is more than compensated for by accuracy and wealth of detail. As a matter of fact, although I have had access to several thousands of cases, in only a little over 200 were the details sufficiently complete to be of use.

With regard to this morbid neuropathic heredity, the following additional facts may be cited: of 124 patients with neuropathic heredity, it was present in the direct line only in 58; in the collaterals only in 26; and in *both* direct and collaterals in 40 cases. It was present on the paternal side only in 61 ; on the maternal only in 39 ; and on *both* sides in 24 cases.

It is seen from these latter figures that paternal is more common than maternal inheritance. Voisin found the reverse to be the case. It is therefore probable that a sufficiently large series of cases would show that there was little difference in this respect. In my cases the transmission occurred equally to the same and to the opposite sex.

2. Alcoholism.

This is the hereditary factor next in importance, and in my own series of cases a pronounced history of family alcoholism occurred in no less than 46·5 per cent. It is to be remarked, however, that in five-sixths of these definite neuropathic heredity was present in addition ; whilst in most of the remainder there were other morbid influences.

The results obtained by other inquirers are somewhat divergent. Beach and Shuttleworth found a history of alcoholism in but 16·38 per cent. of their cases ; Kerlin (Philadelphia) in 38 per cent. ; and Bourneville (Paris) in 62 per cent. Howe (America) found that in nearly 50 per cent. of idiots the parents were habitual drunkards. On the other hand, Looft (Norway) found it present in but 3·7 per cent., and Kind (Hanover) in only 11 per cent.

There can be little doubt that long-continued, excessive indulgence in alcohol has a considerable effect upon the germ and sperm cells, and that it results in an impairment of the nervous system of the offspring. In fact, I believe that such psychoses as hysteria, migraine, epilepsy, etc., are often due to this cause.*
In my experience, however, alcoholism is rarely the immediate and sole cause of amentia, although where other factors exist—particularly neuropathic heredity—it is a most important contributory agent.

But there is another mode of action which has to be considered—namely, the *direct* effect of alcohol upon the embryo. This is not hereditary, but environmental ; it will, however,

* Interesting evidence on this point is furnished by a laborious research conducted by Dr. Crothers of Connecticut, U.S.A., and published in the *Quarterly Journal of Inebriety*, January, 1901.

be convenient to refer to it in this place. The ingestion of alcohol is very speedily followed by its appearance in the blood, consequently the alcohol imbibed by a pregnant woman very soon comes into close contact with the tissues of the embryo. It has been conclusively shown by numerous experiments* that alcohol exerts a most marked baneful influence upon growing protoplasm, and the systematic abuse of alcohol during gestation is liable to be followed by decidedly injurious consequences to the offspring. These consequences are often widespread, but anomalies of mental action are the most frequent, as they are certainly the most important. Occasionally actual idiocy may result, of which several instances have been recorded.

Some authors have endowed one particular moment—that of conception—with quite phenomenal possibilities; and Langdon Down, Sabatier, Quatrefages, Lucon, Morel, Bourneville, and several other writers, are of opinion that idiocy is a common sequence of drunkenness at this time. Accurate information on such a point is, of course, very difficult to obtain, and it is not easy to eliminate other factors. Drunkenness at such a moment is more likely to be an incident in a life of intemperance than a solitary lapse, and in many cases it is probably actually symptomatic of a neuropathic diathesis. Perhaps the influence of this factor *per se* is best judged by the instances mentioned by Ireland,† in which in some parts of Scotland whole villages of the lower classes get drunk at New Year time, or where the herring fishermen have a carouse upon their return to port. Dr. Ireland states that it has never been noticed that the resulting children are idiotic. I have histories of idiots conceived under such circumstances, but so I have of normal children; and my

---

* It was shown by Féré of Paris that the effect of the vapour of alcohol upon incubating eggs was to produce 63 per cent. of normal births, 16 per cent. of incompletely developed embryos, and 21 per cent. of monstrosities and chickens of "idiotic and imbecile grade." If the experiments were made with alcoholic solutions of absinthe, the effects were still more marked, there being but 25 per cent. of normal births, 31 per cent. of incompletely developed, and 44 per cent. of abnormal and defective chicks. ("Comptes Rendus, Société de Biol.," Paris, vol. lii.)

For further particulars as to the effect of alcohol, see Horsley and Sturge, "Alcohol and the Human Body," 1907; also a very interesting paper on "The Problem of Heredity," by W. L. Andriezen, *Journal of Mental Science*, January, 1905.

† W. W. Ireland, "Mental Affections of Children," 1898.

opinion is that, whilst this may be a cause in some cases, the number of such is—in this country, at any rate—exceedingly small.

3. TUBERCULOSIS.

I believe that this factor is but rarely the direct and sole cause of amentia; but my observations show that, like alcoholism, it has a very important indirect and contributory influence. Its indirect effect is seen in its undoubted potency to produce the milder forms of nervous instability in the offspring, such as migraine, hysteria, and mild epilepsy; whilst its importance as a contributory agent is shown by the large proportion of aments who come of a tuberculous stock. I found that in the families of 34 per cent. of aments there was a pronounced tendency to tubercular lesions. Beach and Shuttleworth found the same in close on 30 per cent. of their cases; Langdon Down in 22·5 per cent., Kerlin in 56 per cent. In four-fifths of my cases, however, this tuberculous diathesis was associated with a neuropathic inheritance, and in the remaining fifth other conditions—usually alcoholism—were also present. Some additional evidence as to the prevalence of a tubercular diathesis in the mentally defective is afforded by the large number of these persons who succumb to this disease. Ireland estimates the proportion as fully two-thirds of all cases, and although in many, or most of them, the general deficiency in mental and bodily vigour may increase their susceptibility to the action of the specific bacillus, I think the large death-rate from this cause warrants us in saying that there must be an inherited predisposition beyond the ordinary.

I regard these three morbid ancestral conditions—namely, disease of the nervous system, alcoholism, and consumption—as being far and away the most frequent causes of mental defect. The two latter appear to me to be rather remote than immediate in their action, their effect being to initiate the neuropathic diathesis, which (if unchecked) eventually culminates in amentia. It is comparatively rarely that they give rise to actual mental deficiency in the immediately succeeding generation, although they may do so in some cases. In my own series there were 7·5 per cent. in whom no other cause was discoverable. In four-fifths of these the ancestry was literally saturated with both alcohol and consumption, in the remainder with alcohol alone. Most of these patients suffered from a mild degree of imbecility accompanied by epilepsy.

On the other hand, where a neuropathic inheritance exists on one side, the presence of either of these factors appears to exert a most potent contributory influence. As showing the extent to which they occurred in combination, it may be stated that, of 124 patients coming of neuropathic stock, 28 had in addition an alcoholic, and 15 a tubercular, heredity; whilst in 19 both of these contributory causes were present.

4. SYPHILIS.

Most observers are agreed that syphilis alone is not a frequent cause of amentia. Fletcher Beach found it present in but 1·17 per cent. of the 2,400 pauper aments he examined from the London area. Langdon Down and Shuttleworth found it in about 2 per cent. of cases, and in my own series it occurred in 2·5 per cent. It is probable, as stated by Mott, that "there would undoubtedly be a considerably larger proportion of defective children from this cause were it not for the very high rate of sterility, miscarriages, stillborn and short-lived offspring that it produces."

The action of syphilis in these cases may be truly hereditary—namely, by impairing the vitality of the germ or sperm cells, so that perfect development cannot take place. Fournier* has shown that this devitalization is by no means an uncommon result, but inquiries show that in cases of amentia there are generally other factors, especially neuropathic heredity, present in addition to the syphilis.

On the other hand, syphilis may be "inherited" without being hereditary in the sense in which we have been speaking, and cases of "congenital" syphilis are of this nature. The actual disease is here transmitted to the child through the maternal tissues. The condition is not truly intrinsic, but environmental; yet we may, as a matter of convenience, refer to it here. Children thus suffering from inherited syphilis present the characteristic lesions of that disease; but the proportion who are in consequence mentally defective appears to

---

* Fournier, "Les Affections Parasyphilitiques," 1894. See also Mott, "Heredity and Disease," *British Medical Journal*, October, 1905.

be small. As a result of my examination of over 1,000 idiots and imbeciles of varying grades in Darenth Asylum, I found only about 0·5 per cent. whose condition could be attributed solely to syphilis. It is also clear, from a study of the numerous cases of congenital lues which may be seen in the out-patient department of any large hospital, as well as from the number of adults marked with the characteristic signs, that a normal mental development is quite compatible with the existence of this disease. Where amentia does result, it is generally because other factors are present in addition.

It has been suggested by Dr. Sutherland that syphilis is a frequent cause of that variety of defect known as "Mongolism." My experience, resulting from the careful investigation of many family histories and patients of this type, does not confirm this view.

Alcohol, tubercle, and syphilis are probably by no means the only poisons which have a devitalizing effect upon the germ and sperm cells, and which therefore contribute to arrest and anomalies of development. They are, however, the most prevalent, and on that account the most important. As an example of the action of other poisons, reference may be made to *lead*, some striking figures regarding which are furnished by Constantin Paul.* This observer relates that out of thirty-two pregnancies in which the father suffered from lead-poisoning, the mother being free from that condition, there were twelve stillborn and seventeen deaths under the age of three years, another one dying later in childhood; whilst only two were found to be alive, aged twenty years and twenty-one months respectively.

5. CONSANGUINITY.

The statement has been frequently made that the marriage of near blood relations is attended with disastrous results to the physical and mental condition of the offspring, and this factor used to be alleged, and is now considered by many persons, as a prevalent cause of idiocy. Certainly in some such marriages the consequences upon the offspring are appalling, as has been well shown by numerous writers. On the other hand, there are instances where repeated intermarriage has taken place for many

* Constantin Paul, Plumbism and the Fœtus," Paris, 1861.

generations without the slightest untoward result. Thus, Voisin, who investigated the offspring of forty-six consanguineous marriages in the commune of Batz, where intermarrying had been the rule for several generations, says that " insanity, idiocy, and deaf-mutism are unknown "; and the same author could not find consanguinity the cause of mental deficiency in a single case at the Bicêtre and Salpêtrière. Huth* also is of opinion that this practice is not attended with harm if the family is healthy, and instances the inhabitants of Pitcairn and Iceland in support of his statement. George Darwin† arrived at a similar conclusion. The crux of the whole question is the presence of morbid heredity, not of consanguinity, and I believe the result to be entirely dependent upon the presence or absence of a constitutional taint. Should such be present, it will, of course, tend to be accentuated, and the effect upon the offspring may be disastrous. In its absence, however, I doubt whether any untoward result is likely to follow, and I certainly do not think that amentia will arise. As a matter of fact, a considerable amount of intermarrying still takes place in certain localities of our own country, such, for instance, as inaccessible islands in the North of Scotland and out-of-the-way rural districts; but I know of no statistics showing that in these cases it has been responsible *per se* for the occurrence of mental deficiency. At the same time there are many physiological reasons against the practice, and it is not one to be advocated.

In my opinion, therefore, the statement that consanguinity is, in itself, an important cause of amentia is one not supported by facts. In my own series of cases I found that only 5 per cent. of defectives were the offspring of blood relations, and in all of these a pronounced neuropathic heredity was present. A similarly small percentage is revealed by several other inquirers. Thus, Beach and Shuttleworth found consanguinity in 4·2 per cent., Down in 7 per cent., Kerlin in 7 per cent., and, in fact, the result of careful research is decidedly to discount this factor as a cause of amentia. Langdon Down, indeed, says: " I am by no means sure that by a *judicious* selection of cousins the race might not be improved."

* Alfred Huth, " Marriage of Near Kin," London, 1875.
† G. Darwin, *Journal of the Statistical Society*, June, 1875.

6. AGE OF PARENTS.

There are reasons for thinking that the age of the parents at conception is not without influence upon the vitality of the child. Thus Korosi,* as a result of the investigation of 24,000 unselected individuals, came to the conclusion that the children of fathers below twenty and above forty years are weaker than when the fathers are between these ages ; also that the children of mothers over forty years of age are weaker than those born when the mother is below this age. Matthews Duncan† was of opinion that premature and late marriage were influential in the production of idiocy, and Langdon Down‡ found that in 23 per cent. of idiots there was a disparity of more than ten years in the ages of the parents. Amongst my own patients a similar disparity existed in 4 per cent. of cases, in all of them the father being the elder. In one case the difference in age was as much as thirty-two years. In all these families, however, a well-marked neuropathic diathesis was present, and as I have knowledge of several cases in which a similar difference existed without morbid heredity, where the offspring is perfectly healthy, I am of opinion that the influence of such a condition is, in itself, really infinitesimal.

(B) Causes Extrinsic to the Germinal Plasm—Environment.

The abnormal factors of the environment may most conveniently be referred to under the three headings—*Before, During,* and *After Birth.*

Those acting *before birth* are mostly referable to some unhealthy mental or physical condition of the mother during pregnancy, although an actual injury to the fœtus may also occur during this time. *During birth* they chiefly relate to the various abnormalities attending labour, and in this place reference will also be made to primogeniture and premature birth. *After birth* the factors are either traumatic, toxic, convulsive, or some disturbance profoundly influencing nutrition.

There is no doubt that a history of one or other of these factors

---

* Korosi, Transactions of the International Congress of Hygiene, London, 1891, vol. x.
† Matthews Duncan, *Lancet*, January and March, 1883.
‡ Langdon Down, "Notes of One Thousand Cases of Idiocy."

can be elicited in a considerable number of cases of amentia. In my own series of cases they were present in no less than 65 per cent. There is, however, much difference of opinion as to their importance as a cause of this condition.

1. BEFORE BIRTH.

1. *Abnormal Conditions of the Mother during Pregnancy.*—The unhealthy state of the mother may be either *mental* or *physical*. The former embraces *worry*, sudden *shock or fright*, and the much-debated question of *maternal impressions ;* whilst the latter may be due to the presence of actual *disease*, or to a *general state of imperfect health* independent of any specific illness. Perhaps in some instances these physical conditions may operate upon the germ cells before conception, but it is convenient to refer to them under the heading of environment.

I found one or other of these abnormal conditions to be present in about one-fifth of the cases I examined, but in most of them there was, in addition, a pronounced morbid heredity, generally insanity or epilepsy. As a consequence I have come to the conclusion that, although these conditions may have an important contributory influence, it is with extreme rarity that they can be considered to be the sole cause of mental defect.

I am of opinion that the bodily, rather than the mental, state of the mother is of most importance to the developing embryo, and a condition of general physical prostration or malnutrition is more commonly present in cases of amentia than is actual disease. In poorer people especially this malnutrition can often be directly traced to an insufficiency of food during this period, due to the fact of the bread-winner of the family being out of work, although it is probable that frequently recurring pregnancies may so lower the mother's vitality as to produce a similar result.

I have already stated that the presence of alcoholism, tuberculosis, and syphilis in the mother constitute an adverse environment, and may in that way decidedly interfere with the normal development of the offspring. Other poisons may so act, and one of the chief of these is *lead*. Rennert[*] states that many of the women employed in the pottery factories of Germany suffer

---

[*] Rennert, *American Journal of Obstetrics*, October, 1882.

from a form of plumbism, which gives rise to frequent abortions, deaf-mutes, and macrocephalics. It is possible that ecbolics may have a similar effect, and it is even stated that in America the use of these drugs is responsible for a considerable number of cases of feeble-mindedness. Moreover, the influence of a toxic environment upon the offspring has been experimentally demonstrated by Féré in the interesting series of investigations upon eggs already referred to. It must, however, be emphasized that cases of amentia resulting from these causes are relatively rare, and that in the large majority of defectives an abnormal condition of the mother during pregnancy has a contributory or determining influence only.

But in cases in which hereditary neuropathic predisposition is but slight, contributory influences of this kind may become of considerable importance, and may make all the difference between a development of the nervous system compatible with the needs of everyday life and one of mental deficiency. As will presently be seen these and similar contributory factors explain why it happens that an idiot may be born into a family of which the other members of the same generation show no obvious mental or physical deterioration.

Illegitimacy has been credited with the causation of amentia. It is no doubt responsible for a very high proportion of infantile deaths,* and statistics show that this is on account of the adverse environment in such cases, but I do not think it is ever in itself a direct cause of mental defect.

With regard to the much-debated question of *maternal impressions*, without entering into this subject in any detail, it can be said that both these and the sudden frights and shocks which are often alleged to be the cause of the patient's condition really have very little influence. So far I have been unable to discover a single case of this nature in which hereditary influences commonly insanity) were not forthcoming upon a careful inquiry into the antecedents, so that, whilst being unable to deny the possibility of amentia resulting from such conditions, it can certainly be positively affirmed that such instances are exceedingly rare.

An instance which is sometimes quoted in support of the influ-

* See Dr. Lankester's report, quoted in Newsholme's " Vital Statistics."

ence of maternal impressions is the siege of Paris. Legrand du Saulle says : " Out of 92 children born in Paris during the great siege of 1870–71, 64 had mental and physical anomalies, and the remaining 28 were weakly ; 21 were imbecile or idiotic, and 8 showed moral or emotional insanity." But may it not be that these effects were the result of the *physical* condition of the mothers attending this dreadful time—of the *environmen* rather than of any *mental* impression ?

As showing what little real effect the mother's *mental* state has upon the child, I may here refer to the case of children born whilst, or shortly after, the mother was insane. This is by no means an uncommon event ; in fact, a certain number of children are born every year within lunatic asylums, and I have traced the subsequent history of thirty-eight of these up to periods at which any mental abnormality would have been evident. In fourteen of these women the insanity was of a temporary nature, due solely to nervous breakdown at a trying period, and morbid heredity was absent. Out of the fourteen children, *ten were alive and well* in body and mind at ages varying from three to fifteen years, whilst *four were dead*. On the other hand, in twenty-four women, the attack of insanity was accompanied by a pronounced morbid inheritance. Out of these children only *three were alive and well*, whilst *twenty-one had succumbed*, all, with one exception, a few months after birth. Owing to the great difficulty of following up such cases, these figures are necessarily small ; but I cannot do other than regard them as additional evidence of the slight effect of the mental state during gestation, and of the important influence of morbid heredity.

2. *Injuries to the Fœtus.*—In a few cases amentia is attributed to an *injury* received during intra-uterine existence, but, as these in no way differ from those in which injury is inflicted after birth, it will be better to consider them with the latter group.

2. DURING BIRTH.

1. *Abnormal Labour.*—It is generally considered that this is a very important and frequent cause of mental deficiency. Beach and Shuttleworth attribute no less than 17·5 per cent. of their cases to such cause, of which 14·2 per cent. were due to protracted

labour causing pressure, and 3·3 per cent. to instrumental delivery. It is to be remembered, however, that these statistics were confined to institution cases, and I believe that such are hardly representative of amentia in general.

Where difficulty in parturition causes mental defect, it is because a gross lesion of the brain has been produced; such cases are generally of a severe degree, and consequently tend to gravitate to the special institutions. In corroboration of this, I found that a history of these factors was much more common among the severer grades at Darenth Asylum than amongst the patients in the London County asylums; but even in those at Darenth careful inquiries elicited that in the majority pronounced morbid heredity was also present. Out of 18 per cent. of cases in which I obtained a history of abnormal labour, precipitate labour occurred in 2 per cent., protracted labour with asphyxia in 14 per cent., and instrumental delivery in 2 per cent.; but in only one-ninth of these was there no neuropathic predisposition. All of these latter were cases of asphyxia neonatorum, and as they are confirmed epileptics, it is probably largely owing to the convulsions that the mental arrest is due.

I am therefore of opinion that the importance of abnormalities of labour as a cause of amentia has been much overrated, and that the total number of cases which are the immediate consequence of these conditions is relatively very small, being probably not more than 1 or 2 per cent. of all aments. It is true that the parents of the patients are generally quite satisfied with this explanation; they find it much more comforting to believe that the unfortunate child is the victim of some extraneous factor than the product of hereditary taint; but I am convinced that if careful inquiries are made into the family histories of these cases, pronounced hereditary tendency will be found in a very large proportion. On the other hand, there can be no doubt that where such morbid heredity exists, any difficulty during labour—and especially if attended with asphyxia—will have an important contributory effect; and it is certainly responsible for many of the gross brain lesions, with their resultant convulsions, which are so common in the feeble-minded. It is to be remarked that abnormal presentations of the foetus are probably of much greater frequency in psychopathic than in mentally sound women, as also with defective than with normal children.

Little,* in an important paper published in the year 1862, was the first in this country to draw attention to mental and physical defects resulting from abnormalities of labour. He collected a series of 63 cases presenting various defects of this kind, the most common cause being asphyxia due to protracted delivery; but he himself says : " It is obvious that the great majority of stillborn infants whose lives are saved by the attendant accoucheur recover unharmed from that condition "—a statement which has since been fully endorsed by many eminent obstetricians, and which is confirmed by everyday experience. It is indisputable that in a certain small percentage of cases in which asphyxia or hæmorrhage occurs some degree of paralysis results—indeed, this condition is known as "Little's disease "—also that of the cases so affected a small number may show mental impairment. Out of the 63 cases of lesions collected by Little, however, there were only 11 in which the intellect suffered, 2 of these being actually idiotic, and the remaining 9 suffering from various degrees of feeble-mindedness. In all his cases the patients were seen at an age at which mental impairment would have been noticed had it existed, and in some of those who were physically defective the mental capacity is described as being beyond the average. Unfortunately, Little did not inquire into the family history of his cases, but his paper affords no evidence that amentia is at all a common result of abnormality of labour. In this connexion it may be remarked that it is recorded of Samuel Johnson that " he was born almost dead, and did not cry for some time."

With regard to instrumental delivery, we have only to consider the number of children who are delivered by forceps every day, and the fact that the head of the child is even normally subjected to great pressure in the parturient canal, to arrive at the conclusion that the proper use of the forceps can play no practical part in the production of amentia. It may further be remarked that artificial compression of the child's head after birth has been long practised by several races of people, and is still in use in the Toulouse district of France, without

*, Transactions of the London Obstetrical Society, 1862.

any apparent evil effects, and certainly without producing idiocy. Dr. Delisle* says that, although in France the practice is slowly dying out, it still persists to a surprising extent. He finds, however, that it shows no tendency to become hereditarily impressed upon the race nor is there any sufficient evidence to support the belief that it causes either any arrest of physical or mental development, or any unusual tendency to insanity. Lastly, Spiegelberg† says that "the indentations and depressions which result in the cranial bones from pressure have a comparatively unimportant influence on the children."

2. *Primogeniture.*—It is said that first-born children are more liable to be mentally defective than are those born subsequently, and this is attributed partly to a supposed increased mental instability of the mother during a first pregnancy, and partly to the undoubted fact that labour is more protracted in primiparæ. But it has already been seen that neither the mother's mental state nor protracted labour really have very much influence upon the intellectual status of the child in the absence of neuropathic predisposition, so that the question of primogeniture as a cause of amentia need hardly be seriously discussed. As a matter of fact, I believe the statement that an undue proportion of idiots are first-born children is decidedly open to question, and my own experience is to the effect that it is more common for the later-born, and not the first-born, to be affected. In those families in which there is a pronounced tendency to mental and physical degeneracy, the effects usually appear to be more and more marked upon each successive child, and often enough the idiot is actually the last born. I have notes of not a few families in which the first one or two children presented no great departure from the normal; these were followed by one or two others who succumbed to ordinary children's ailments, from which healthy children would probably have recovered; then came the idiot, in some cases to be succeeded by a number of still-births.

3. *Premature Birth.*—Where hereditary predisposition exists, it is probable that the child who is prematurely born will have

* Delisle, "Artificial Deformity of the Skull," *Bull. Soc. d'Anth. de Paris*, 1902, fas. 2.
† Spiegelberg, "Text-Book of Midwifery."

less chance of attaining complete mental development than will the one who goes to full term ; but in the absence of other factors I do not believe that premature birth has any effect upon the resulting mental condition.

3. AFTER BIRTH.

The factors acting after birth which are capable of producing, or assisting in the production of, amentia may be considered under the following headings :

    1. Traumatic.
    2. Toxic.
    3. Epileptic and teething convulsions.
    4. Defects of nutrition.

It may be said at the outset that, although most of these conditions *may* give rise to amentia unaided, the number of cases solely and simply due to them is relatively small, and for the most part their influence is contributory or exciting only.

1. *Traumatic.* — An injury to the child's head in the early months of life, or whilst it is still within the uterus, is a frequently alleged cause of mental defect ; but in most cases careful inquiry will serve to show the extremely trivial nature of the injury received, and will make it abundantly clear that it could have no connexion with the patient's deficiency. In other cases, however, the history—particularly of unconsciousness—leaves no room for doubt that a severe trauma has been inflicted, and I believe that in a small number of cases this is the direct cause of amentia. In such cases it is probable that rupture of vessels has taken place, leading to the destruction of a localized area of brain tissue, and in most of these patients the amentia is accompanied by epilepsy or paralysis.

2. *Toxic.*—In a certain proportion of cases of acute infectious disease occurring in infancy, such as scarlet fever, enteric, whooping-cough, diphtheria, and measles, as well as in otitis and rhinitis and acute polio-encephalitis, there are objective signs that a cerebral lesion has been produced. Perhaps in some of these affections (particularly pertussis) the change may be in the vessels of the brain or its meninges ; but in most the symptoms rather point to a direct poisoning of the brain cells ;

accordingly I have grouped them together as "toxic." The majority of children so affected die ; others make a complete recovery ; whilst in a few others death does not take place, but a permanent legacy remains in the form of paralysis, epilepsy, or amentia. I shall refer to these cases again in considering the question of pathology, but here it may be stated that, although toxic processes of this kind may undoubtedly produce amentia, the number of such cases is relatively small. In exceptional instances the amentia may be caused indirectly through "sense deprivation."

It is probable that the variety of amentia known as " infantile cerebral degeneration " or " amaurotic family idiocy " is really due to some form of toxin, although the pathogenesis of this disease is as yet very obscure.

Sunstroke is an uncommon cause of mental defect, but I have seen three cases in which the closest inquiries failed to reveal any other cause, so that I am disposed to think that the exposure of a young infant to a very hot sun may occasionally produce a cerebral lesion and lead to an arrest of development. In two of the cases the exposure occurred in India ; in the third, in this country during a very hot summer, and all of them were attended with unconsciousness.

The above are the chief etiological factors responsible for the gross cerebral lesions which sometimes lead to amentia. In addition, cerebral new growths may occasionally so act.

3. *Epileptic and Infantile Convulsions.*—Convulsions of some kind or other are amongst the most frequently alleged causes of amentia ; but it is easy to mistake effect for cause, and careful inquiries show the number of aments so produced to be relatively small.

Severe and frequent *epilepsy* in the adult often leads to degeneration and dementia, and in infancy, whilst the brain is still rapidly growing, it may cause imperfect development and consequent amentia. But such cases are comparatively infrequent, and in all probability do not comprise more than about 3 or 4 per cent. of all aments.

Infantile convulsions, particularly those occurring during dentition, are often assumed to be entirely distinct from epilepsy, but in reality there is no clear line of division between the two.

Causation

In many, perhaps most, cases of infantile convulsions the history will show the presence of an hereditary predisposition, and in many patients they recur in later life as ordinary idiopathic epilepsy. Sir William Gowers states that "a considerable number of cases of epilepsy date from infantile convulsions." In the presence of morbid heredity, it is often exceedingly difficult to say whether convulsions are the cause of the mental deficiency, or merely symptomatic of it, but my own experience is that true "eclampsic" amentia is a comparatively rare condition. Some further remarks on the relationship existing between convulsions and amentia will be given in subsequent chapters.

4. *Malnutrition.*—There can be no doubt that the general environment, and especially the quantity and quality of the food, the amount of fresh air, light, warmth, and the care bestowed upon the growing child, have an important influence upon his bodily development. This is well shown by a comparison of the physique of town and country children. But the same does not seem to hold good with regard to mental development. Here sensory stimulations seem to be almost as important as food, and the intellect of the gamin of the slums is often vastly superior to that of the lusty country clodhopper.

In some instances, as will be seen in treating of mentally defective children, an adverse environment gives rise to delayed mental development, and the same result may follow serious ill-health or disease ; but on the whole it may be said that these factors have comparatively little influence in producing amentia in the absence of hereditary predisposition. Rickets is sometimes the accompaniment of mental deficiency, but I doubt whether it is ever its cause. One variety of defect, however— namely, *cretinism*—is undoubtedly due to the deprivation of a specific nutritive material.

General Considerations.

Having seen what are the chief *intrinsic* and *extrinsic* factors associated with amentia, as well as the extent to which they occur, we may now consider the manner in which they act.

With regard to these two groups, it is clear from the account already given that a history of one or other factor of the environment (extrinsic) is found in a very considerable proportion of cases (65 per cent.); and, bearing in mind that evidence of this kind is much easier to elicit than is a history of morbid heredity, it is not surprising that many writers have attributed great importance to these external factors. At first sight I was inclined to do so myself, and it was only when I found how often pronounced morbid heredity lay behind that I came to a different conclusion. I am far from denying that the environment, even when morbid heredity is present, has no effect. Whether the fertilized ovum be inherently defective or not, it is evident that its development may be interfered with by injury or disease; also that it must be to a considerable extent dependent upon the quantity and quality of the nourishment it receives, either whilst within or without the uterus. Consequently, a condition of actual disease, ill-health, or starvation of the mother cannot but be injurious to the growing embryo; and the same may be said of the improper food, impure air, deficient light, and inadequate sleep, which are so often the lot of young children in our city slums. What I wish to point out, however, is that, as far as my experience goes, injurious external factors of themselves but rarely give rise to mental defect, and when they do so it is usually because they have produced a gross lesion of the brain.

The result of my inquiries has been to convince me of the immense importance of morbid heredity in the production of amentia. It would, of course, be desirable that these statistics should be compared with similar ones regarding the mentally normal population. As far as I am aware, none such exist, but for several years past I have been gathering details from hospital and private patients, and I am fully satisfied that the amount of morbid heredity is absolutely insignificant in the mentally normal as compared with the defective population. Instances of an ancestor dying of consumption, or being addicted to drink, or even being epileptic or insane, are not uncommon; but it is decidedly exceptional to find definite and pronounced neuropathic heredity in an individual of normal bodily and mental development. Conversely, the number of cases of pronounced mental defect (in which a tolerably complete family history is forthcoming) which can be solely attributed to extrinsic or environmental causes is probably not more than 20 per cent. at the very outside.

So much, then, for the relative importance of the two classes of factors. Let us now consider the *modus operandi* of each in bringing about arrest of cerebral development.

1. Intrinsic or Hereditary Influences.

It would obviously be out of place to enter into any detailed account of the various theories regarding heredity, but there are some points which have such an important bearing upon the causation of amentia that they must be alluded to. Now, it is contended by Weismann* that the environment has practically no effect upon the germinal plasm, but that this latter is handed down unaltered through all the ages, and simply transmits qualities or possibilities of development which have existed *ab initio*. Upon this assumption disease and unhealthy surroundings, however much they may affect the individual, are powerless to influence posterity, and " degeneracy " is an utter myth. I am decidedly of opinion, however, that this theory is contradicted by the facts of everyday life, and I believe that the germinal plasm *is* capable of modification by the environment, and that the alteration so produced may very materially affect subsequent generations.

Weismann's doctrine apparently receives a good deal of support from the statement that " acquired properties are not transmitted," and there is no doubt that of certain acquirements this statement is true. The examples generally adduced are such mutilations as the docking of dogs' tails, the nose-slitting of savages, systematic compression of the cranium, and, above all, the practice of circumcision. It is true that mutilations of this kind have been performed systematically upon generation after generation, and yet they show no tendency to be transmitted to the offspring or to impress themselves upon posterity. Acquired local properties of this kind, therefore, are certainly not transmitted.

But there is another kind of modification which stands on quite a different footing, inasmuch as it is not local, but general

* Weismann, " The Germ Plasm," and other works.

and universal in its extent. I refer to the effect of certain diseases. In some diseases the pathological change is almost as localized as are the mutilations just referred to; but in others there is abundant evidence that the whole organism is affected. For instance, in such conditions as extensive pulmonary tuberculosis, chronic alcoholism, acute rheumatism, syphilis, diabetes, pyæmia, anæmia, and possibly also in some cases of cancer and other wasting diseases, it is clear from both clinical and pathological experience that not a local, but a general, change has been produced. Can we imagine that, amid all this disturbance of metabolism, the germ and sperm cells remain unaffected, that they lead a charmed life, utterly indifferent alike to the effect of poison or the quantity and quality of their food? Assuredly not. The germinal plasm, endowed as it is with functions of the utmost importance, is yet in its origin but a highly specialized somatic tissue. Like other tissues, it is dependent for its growth and development upon the blood-supply, and, also like them, it is susceptible to the action of poison. Under certain abnormal conditions its maturation may be delayed, and there are many facts, some of which have been cited in previous pages, which conclusively demonstrate that it may be injured by certain bodily diseases.

It is on this point that the experience of the physician is diametrically opposed to the doctrine of Weismann. One observes in medical practice so much difference between the mental and bodily vigour of those children who are the offspring of pronounced alcoholic or phthisical fathers, as compared with children of healthy parentage, that it is impossible to avoid the conclusion that a serious deterioration of the germinal plasm has taken place. Not only the subject of mental deficiency, but everyday experience supplies ample evidence of the importance of morbid heredity upon offspring, and, however much the theorist may ignore its influence the physician is unable to do so.

I think, therefore, that it cannot be questioned that the germinal plasm shares in those alterations of the bodily protoplasm hich result from disease and environment. According as this is vourable or unfavourable, the modification will be progressive · retrogressive; consequently, each individual is a potent influence for good or ill in the development of the race. The environment of to-day will become the heredity of to-morrow, and the statement that the sins of the fathers are visited upon the children unto the third and fourth generation is an undoubted and important physiological truth.

With regard to the causation of amentia, I believe that there are certain diseases which bring about a deterioration of the germ plasm. The chief of these are alcoholism and consumption, although it is probable that other poisons, sexual excesses, and many factors of modern life, may, by lowering the general vitality, produce a similar effect. In consequence, there results a pathological change in that part of the offspring which is at once the most elaborate, the most vulnerable, and of most recent development—namely, the cerebral cortex. This change consists in a diminished control of the higher, and increased excitability of the lower, centres, and is manifested clinically as neurasthenia, hysteria, migraine, and the milder forms of epilepsy. We may say that a neuropath has been created. Should the adverse environment continue, or should such a person marry one similarly tainted, then the nervous instability becomes accentuated in the following generation, and insanity, the graver forms of epilepsy, and early dementia, make their appearance. If the process is further continued, the third generation will be characterized by a tendency to imperfection of anatomical development, and there will be a strong probability of one or more children suffering from amentia; should the morbid heredity be accompanied by any injurious factor of the environment (such as those we have described), this probability will become a tolerable certainty. Degeneracy is here well established, and the well-known " stigmata " are usually abundant. Finally, complete sterility appears, and the family becomes extinct. For this form of amentia due to hereditary influences I have proposed the term PRIMARY.

It is not suggested, of course, that the three grades of mental disease above described are necessarily restricted to three successive generations. All the degrees may exist, and frequently do, amongst members of one and the same generation. Neither do I wish to infer that the neuropathic heritage always culminates in amentia in the third generation. It may be so modified by the admixture of fresh blood that this end may be much longer delayed; it may, indeed, even be eradicated in some instances. On the other hand, it occasionally happens that idiocy of the grossest type results from the presence of alcoholism and consumption in the immediate ancestors without any intermediate abnormality of the nervous system having been produced. This, however, is exceptional, and I believe that the outline given above is, on the whole, a tolerably accurate picture of the successive steps in the production of amentia. In many of the families of whom I have histories it is actually possible to trace this downward march, and further evidence to the same effect is afforded by statistics regarding the etiology of the other mental affections. For instance, in persons suffering from migraine, neurasthenia, and hysteria, it is uncommon to find marked ancestral nervous or psychic disturbance, but a history of alcoholism and phthisis, as well as of modes of living attended with severe nervous stress and strain, is frequent. In the milder forms of epilepsy morbid neuropathic heredity becomes more marked, and in the severer forms of this affection it is present, according to Sir William Gowers, in about 35 per cent. of cases. In persons suffering from insanity the morbid heredity rises to 50 or 60 per cent.,* whilst in amentia, as we have seen, it is present in 80 per cent. of cases.

These figures well show the gradual accumulation of morbid heredity which lies behind the different grades of mental disability, as well as the potency of the hereditary factor in the causation of amentia. We may, indeed, say of this latter affection that it is the final manifestation of a progressive psychopathic diathesis.

As throwing some further light upon amentia from this aspect, it may not be out of place to refer to the contemporaries of these persons. Whilst inquiring into the causes of amentia, I took the trouble to ascertain the number and condition of all the brothers and sisters of 150 patients. I divided these into two classes, which were designated "satisfactory" and "unsatisfactory." The *satisfactory* group comprised all those who were said to be healthy in mind and body, and were able to support themselves.

* J. S. Bolton, "Amentia and Dementia," Mott's "Archives of Neurology," vol. ii.

Causation

The *unsatisfactory* consisted, in addition to those prematurely dead, of those who were either mentally affected, or were suffering from marked and permanent ill-health, or were leading a life of vagabondage or crime. Such details were, of course, difficult to get, and as the valuation was generally that of the parents, the figures are almost certainly more favourable to the class than the real facts. These figures are shown in the following table:

TABLE VI.

SHOWING THE CONDITION OF 150 AMENTS WITH THEIR BROTHERS AND SISTERS.

(*In the* 150 *families there were* 1,269 *children born.*)

Unsatisfactory.		Satisfactory.	
(a) Born dead	170	Said by parents to be mentally and bodily healthy	456
(b) Since died :			
Under 1 year .. 138			
„ 3 years.. 107			
„ 10 „ .. 37	315		
„ 20 „ .. 8			
Over 20 „ .. 25			
(c) Mentally affected ..	245		
(d) Diseased, paupers, or criminals	83		
Total	813	Total	456
		1,269	

Some points in this table are worthy of note. *Firstly*, the large number of children born. According to the Fortieth Annual Report of the Registrar-General (1876), the average number of births to a marriage in England and Wales is 4·63. The number of children in 150 normal families would therefore be 694 ; whereas in the families we are now considering the number born alive is 1,099, or an average of 7·3 per family. *Secondly*, the large number of still-births. No precise data exist with regard to the number of these in the normal population, as they are unregistered, but Farr and Newsholme estimate them at about 4 per cent. of the total births. If these families were normal, we should therefore expect to have 44 children stillborn, whereas we find 170. *Thirdly*, the mortality of these children is even more remarkable. According to the life table of the Registrar-General, based upon the years 1881-1890 (Supplement to Fifty-fifth Annual Report, 1895),

Had the 1,099 Children belonged to the "Average" Class, there would have been surviving—		Whereas there were surviving—
At end of 1 year	937	961
,, ,, 3 years	864	854
,, ,, 10 ,,	823	817
,, ,, 20 ,,	800	809

In other words, the mortality is practically identical with the normal.

I do not wish to press the point unduly, because the number dealt with is but small. Statistics of this kind are exceedingly difficult to obtain, and I know of no others at present existing; but if further observations should confirm these here given, it would follow that, although the progeny of neuropaths are greatly in excess of those born of the average population, there is, as a whole, no corresponding excess of mortality; and this in spite of the fact that, as we shall presently see, the expectation of life of those who are actually mentally deficient is subnormal. Even assuming that the 456 brothers and sisters of these aments are really sound in body and mind, as stated by their parents (which, however, I greatly doubt), it is to be remembered that they come of a pronounced morbid stock, and are not only capable of, but exceedingly likely to, transmit the taint to a subsequent generation. In fact, it is in regard to these rather than the actual aments, that the greatest danger of propagation lies.

The following family history charts afford graphic illustrations of many of the points referred to.

In them amentia, insanity, or epilepsy, is shown as ●; alcoholism, tuberculosis, general ill-health, neuroses, and premature death, as ●; whilst persons presumably healthy, dying from natural causes, or of whom no information is obtainable, are shown as O.

Causation

CHART I.

SHOWING GOOD HEREDITY CONTAMINATED BY SLIGHT ALCOHOLIC HEREDITY AND TOWN LIFE.

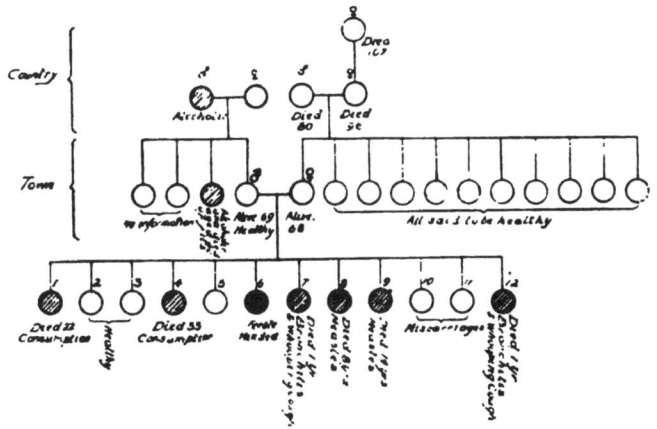

Case No. 131, W. J. G.

CHART II.

SHOWING GOOD HEREDITY CONTAMINATED BY MORBID HEREDITY.

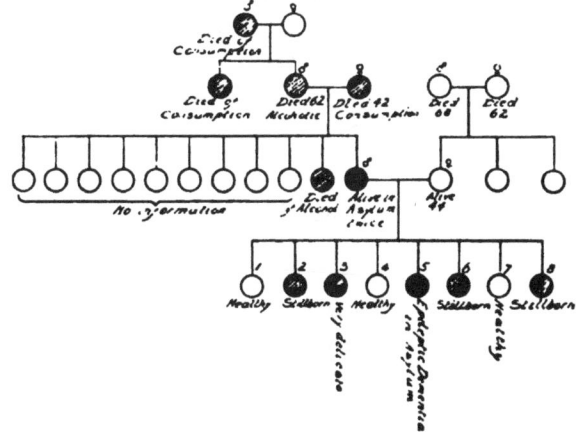

Case No. 10, A. C.

CHART III.

SHOWING GOOD HEREDITY CONTAMINATED BY INSANE HEREDITY.

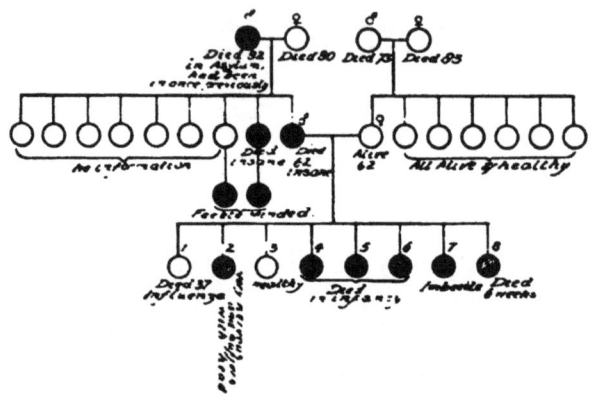

Case No. 5. J. W. J.

CHART IV.

SHOWING THE EFFECT OF INSANE + PHTHISICAL HEREDITY.

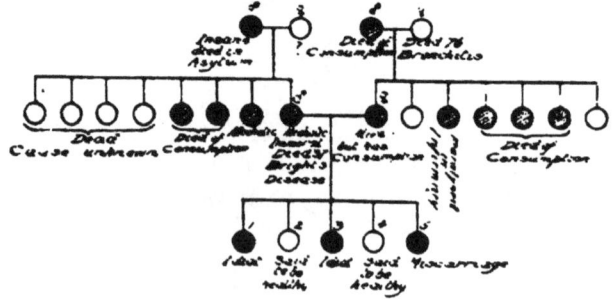

Case No. 99. F. W.

CHART V.

SHOWING EFFECT OF ALCOHOLIC AND INSANE INHERITANCE + PHTHISICAL INHERITANCE.

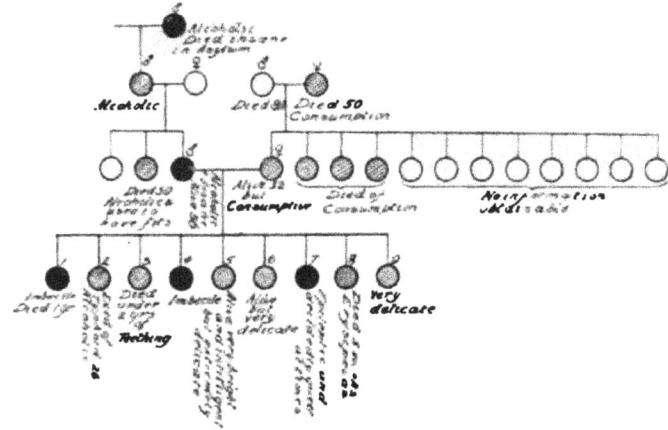

Case No. 174, C. B.

CHART VI.

SHOWING THE EFFECT OF DOUBLE MORBID HEREDITY.

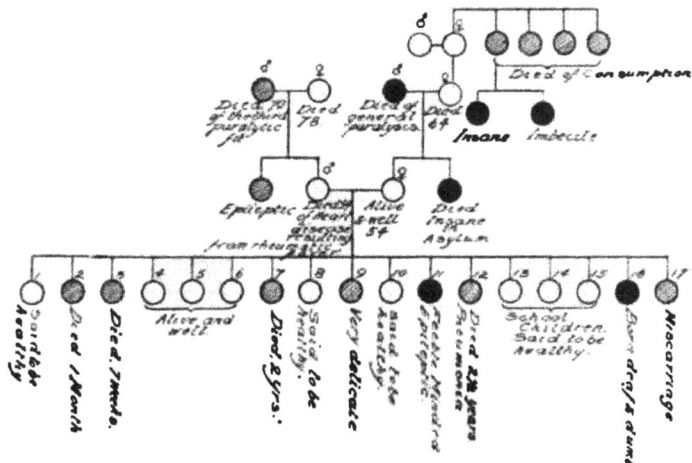

Case No. 9, S. V.

CHART VII.

SHOWING THE EFFECT OF DOUBLE MORBID HEREDITY.

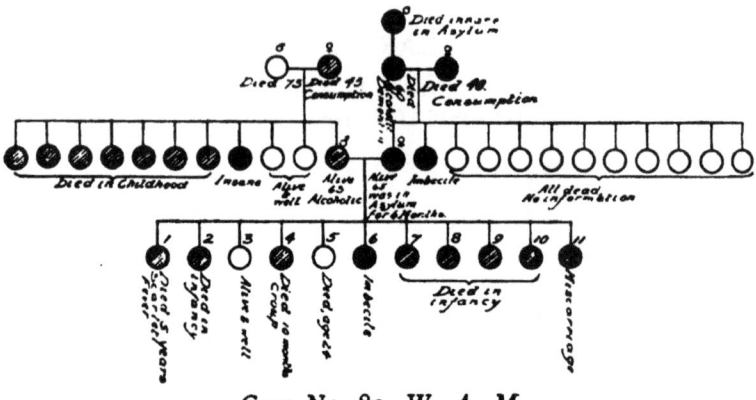

Case No. 83, W. A. M.

CHART VIII.

SHOWING THE EFFECT OF A DOUBLE INSANE INHERITANCE + SYPHILIS.

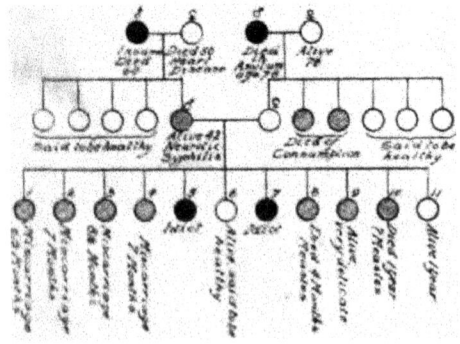

Case No. 97, P. W.

Causation 45

CHART IX.

SHOWING THE EFFECT OF CONSANGUINITY WITH A TENDENCY TO VASCULAR LESIONS OF THE BRAIN.

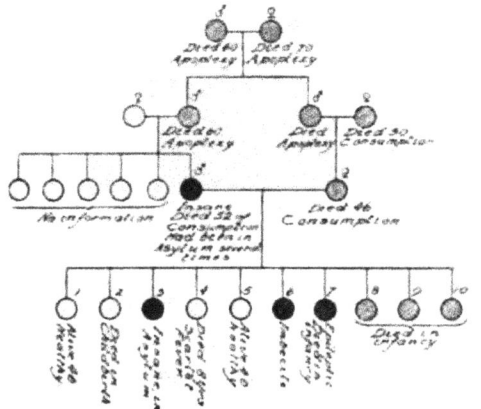

Case No. 70, F. E. V.

We must now refer to another type of case which at first sight appears to be quite distinct from the one just described, inasmuch as the patient may be the only one of the family showing any sign of deterioration, his brothers and sisters being well developed in body and mind. Similar hereditary influences exist here also, though not in such marked degree, and it is in these cases that they are mostly present on one side only. Evidently in these instances, however, the condition cannot be attributed entirely to defects in the germinal plasm, as in that case other members of the family would also show signs of defective development; the question therefore arises as to why one alone should be affected.

It is under these circumstances that I believe the condition of the mother during gestation to be of most vital importance to the child; obviously it is a difficult matter always to obtain precise and accurate information on this point, but I have been much struck by the fact that it is just in these—what one might call sporadic—cases of idiocy that nearly all the instances of abnormal condition of the mother during pregnancy have occurred. These conditions have already been discussed, and it will be sufficient to note here that the one most frequently associated with the birth of an ament is a state of general ill-health and exhaustion, in the poorer classes often accompanied by a deficiency of proper food. In several cases it has happened that during this time the father was out of work.

Apparently, under these less-pronounced conditions of hereditary predisposition, the germ plasm, although to a certain extent vitiated, is still capable of proceeding to the perfect structural development of the embryo, provided no untoward circumstances intervene to further embarrass its growth ; but should there happen at this time any deterioration in the health of the mother, whereby the blood supplying the rapidly growing ovum is considerably modified in its nutritive qualities, then incomplete development is very likely to happen. As far as my experience goes, the physical condition of the mother is of far more importance than her mental state, except in the cases in which this may modify the physical condition.

In other instances the same result is attained by a somewhat different contributing or, as it may be termed, exciting factor. One fairly common such is premature birth ; if by any unfortunate chance this should happen where there are already present p edisposing factors, even if slight, the child is extremely likely to show some mental deterioration as compared with his brothers and sisters. In other cases prolonged labour, attended with more or less asphyxia, may act in the same manner ; the temporary obstruction of the cerebral circulation need not be enough to give rise to any actual lesion, or in a healthy child to produce any damage whatever, but in the present instance it is all that is required to interfere with the perfect development of the nerve cells, and some degree of weakmindedness is the result.

In the same way act some of the factors occurring after birth, such as trauma, convulsions, rickets, infectious fevers, meningitis, etc. It has already been seen that in the larger proportion of these cases ancestral defects are present, and the exciting factor probably acts by causing a derangement of the cerebral circulation or metabolism from which the nerve cells are unable to recover.

It is necessary to bear in mind that in the majority of cases of amentia factors such as the above are only accessory, and that the real origin of the condition lies in the defect of the germinal plasm, the result of morbid heredity.

The term *developmental* was applied to such cases by Langdon Down, but in view of their inherent defect it might be preferable to refer to them as instances of *delayed primary amentia*.

2. Extrinsic or Environmental Causes.

It has been seen that, although adverse conditions of the environment are present in a considerable number of cases of amentia, the proportion in which they are the direct and sole cause is relatively small—probably at the most not more than 15 to 20 per cent. To this extent, however, the environment does seem capable of producing amentia, although in many instances this is but the incidental phase of a process which is really degenerative and of which the end is dementia. As such cases are entirely independent of morbid heredity and of any inherent defects of the germinal plasm, I have proposed to call this variety SECONDARY *amentia*. I have already enumerated these factors, and since many of them are pathological processes which result in a gross lesion of the brain, it will be more convenient to describe the manner of their action together with their clinical characteristics. A few, however, give rise to a general arrest of development without any naked-eye lesion, and these may briefly be referred to in this place.

Under normal conditions the brain of the child grows with extreme rapidity during the first few years of life. This is in consequence of its inherent capacity for growth plus the stimulation of sensory impressions and the presence of an adequate quantity and quality of blood. This inherent capacity may be normal, but the necessary stimulation or food so deficient that the gradual unfolding of the mental faculties does not take place, or takes place so tardily that some degree of backwardness is the result. Cases of this kind, in which development is delayed, are extremely common, and it usually happens that upon the removal of the cause mental expansion rapidly ensues. Should the adverse conditions continue sufficiently long, however, the brain cells seem in some cases unable to recover ; the mind never makes up the lost ground, and some degree of mental deficiency is the result. In my experience actual idiocy is never caused in this way, and the resulting defect is of comparatively mild degree only ; it is nevertheless a true amentia. I do not think that cases of this kind are very common, but they form a certain percentage of the adult feeble-minded and of mentally defective school-children, particularly in the large towns. The cause seems usually to be that combination of factors—drink, dirt, and depravity—which go to make up slum life in its worst form.

With regard to the influence of slum life and all its associated conditions in producing amentia, it is necessary to sound a note of warning. It does happen sometimes that the real mental defectives of our large towns hail from the slums, although I do not think such is disproportionately the case. Still, a sufficient number of defective children come from such areas to make the superficial inquirer, content with that which is apparent, jump to the conclusion that the pernicious environment is therefore the cause of their defect. My own inquiries have convinced me that in the great majority of these slum cases there is pronounced morbid heredity, and that their environment is not the cause, but the *result*, of that heredity. The neuropath is one who is at an economic disadvantage in the struggle for existence. He frequently finds it difficult to hold his place, and he is often possessed of careless, improvident, and intemperate propensities, which cause him to fritter away the money he does earn. He is on the down grade. No wonder, then, that he drifts to the slums.

Factors of Causation in Regard to Local Variations of Incidence.

Before concluding this account of causation, it is necessary to refer to the connexion existing between certain etiological factors and local variations in the prevalence of amentia.

We have already seen (Chapter II.) that the incidence of amentia is not uniform throughout the country, but that in some localities it is relatively much higher, and in others much lower, than the mean average. Into the cause of this inequality I do not propose to enter, for it is but part of a similar variation in the incidence of mental disease in general, and is therefore beyond the scope of our subject. But there are certain variations in the incidence of amentia relative to other forms of mental disease, and in the incidence of the degrees of amentia relative to one another, which are so closely connected with the question of causation that they must be referred to.

The Incidence of Amentia relative to Insanity.—The statistics of the Royal Commission show that, broadly speaking, insanity is more characteristic of the urban and industrial, and amentia of the rural, populations of this country. We have already seen that the causes of these two conditions are identical in kind—namely, morbid neuropathic heredity—but that they differ in degree, inasmuch as the heredity is usually more pronounced in amentia than in insanity. Now, the towns have been built up and are being steadily increased by the immigration of persons from the country, and it is justifiable to conclude that the persons so migrating will possess the qualities of initiative, enterprise, and mental vigour in a higher degree than those who are content to remain upon the land—that, in short, a comparatively smaller proportion of them will come of a pronounced neuropathic stock. This process inevitably tends to the accumulation in the rural districts of those most saturated with morbid heredity—a state of affairs which is often accentuated by intermarrying, and so the conditions in these areas become more and more favourable to the production of actual mental defect. On the other hand, in our towns and densely packed industrial centres competition is keen, the stresses and strains of life are severe, alcoholism is rife, consumption is very prevalent, narrow streets are densely packed with overcrowded houses, women advanced in pregnancy continue to work in the mills and factories, infants who should be at the breast are reared artificially, and, in short, all the conditions are present to produce an instability of the higher parts of the nervous system—the precursor of insanity. This, in subsequent generations, leads to actual defect of structure and consequent amentia, but the constant immigration drags fresh blood into the vortex, and tends to make insanity rather than amentia the prevailing type of mental abnormality.

The Relative Incidence of the Different Degrees of Amentia.—As has been shown in Chapter II., not only is amentia absolutely more prevalent in rural than in urban districts, but the grosser degrees of defect are relatively in excess also ; whilst in the towns mentally defective children are relatively and absolutely more prevalent than in the country. I am of opinion that there are three chief factors of town life which tend to bring about this result—namely (1) a lessened production, (2) an increased destruction of the more severe grades of defect, and (3) the presence in the towns of cases of delayed development which simulate mental defect, and so cause an apparent increase of mild deficiency.

(1) Lessened Production of Severe Defect : This is due to the same causes which bring about a diminished incidence of amentia generally—namely, a lessened neuropathic heredity in the town dwellers. (2) Increased Destruction of Severe Defect : I am unable to give any statistical proof of this, but I think it is possible that the relatively higher infantile mortality of the towns may be not without effect in causing a diminution of the worst grades of defect in these situations, since the mortality of aments would seem to be directly proportionate to the degree of defect. (3) It has already been remarked that a small proportion of cases of secondary amentia are the result of a faulty environment, and this I believe to be more prevalent in town than country. As we shall see, however, in considering mentally defective children, there is a condition of delayed development which is very much more common in densely congested areas, and which simulates real amentia very closely. I believe this is responsible in no slight degree for the apparent increase of the juvenile feeble-minded in towns. In corroboration of this is the fact that in the towns there is no relative increase of the adult feeble-minded, even when it is remembered that a small proportion of those actually born in the towns are gradually squeezed further afield in the struggle for existence.

CHAPTER IV

PATHOLOGY

BEFORE discussing the pathology of amentia, it will be an advantage to allude to the salient features in the development of the cells of the cerebral cortex.

Development of the Normal Brain.

The first indication of the brain is seen very shortly after fertilization of the germ cell, and consists in an expansion of the anterior end of the rudimentary spinal cord to form four primary cerebral vesicles. It is by a series of elaborate infoldings of these vesicles, and by the multiplication around them of the cells composing their walls, that cerebral development takes place. By the time the embryo is six months old the brain has assumed the general shape of the adult, although there is as yet a complete absence of all those secondary fissures and convolutions which are such a characteristic feature of the fully developed organ.

At birth many of these convolutions are present, and the brain weighs* from 280 to 330 grammes. During the first six months of life growth is exceedingly rapid, the weight of the brain at the end of this time being more than double what it was at birth—namely, from 600 to 680 grammes. By the end of the first year the weight has reached about 750 grammes, and from this onward it still continues to grow until the age of twelve or fourteen years, when its average weight is 1,150 grammes in the female and 1,300 grammes in the male. A further slight increase takes place during the next seven years,

* According to R. Boyd, Phil. Trans., 1860.

and at the age of twenty-one the brain has attained the weight of 1,244 grammes in the female and 1,374 grammes in the male. From this period growth is very slow, until, according to Broca and Peacock, the maximum average weight of 1,269 grammes (45 ounces) in the female and 1,421 grammes (50 ounces) in the male is attained between twenty-five and thirty-five years of age.

The progressive increase in size and weight is due, firstly, to the rapid multiplication, and secondly, to the individual, development, of the nerve cells. These arise from the cells lining the floor of the primitive cerebral vesicles, and at first they are of one uniform indifferent type. Subsequently, however, differentiation occurs, and features appear which are characteristic, and which persist throughout life. It is as a result of this differentiation that the brain cortex acquires its peculiar laminated appearance. Coincident with lamination delicate protoplasmic processes arise from these nerve cells, and, pursuing definite directions throughout the cerebral mass, constitute the association and projection systems of fibres. The former serve to link together in the most complicated manner all parts of the brain ; they also compose the great association centres of Flechsig ; the latter are the pathways by which the brain is connected with the various parts of the body.

Development does not proceed simultaneously in all parts of the brain. The nerve cells of certain areas reach maturity much earlier than do those elsewhere, and the frontal and parietal regions, which there is good reason for thinking are those most concerned with the highest intellectual functions, are the last to acquire their mature characteristics. In the frontal lobes of the seven-months embryo lamination has not yet appeared, and the cells are of a uniform undifferentiated type (neuroblasts). These are small round cells with a close and readily stainable reticulum, but quite devoid of processes, and they lie embedded in a matrix which, in the hardened and stained section, somewhat resembles the grain of marble. In the eight-months embryo the neuroblasts are somewhat larger, the reticulum is less close and has less affinity for stain, but there are as yet no definite processes. At this age it is possible to make out the beginning of lamination in this region of the cortex. In the child two weeks old (extra-uterine) the cells have made a considerable advance, and they are now readily recognizable as nerve cells. A cell body is present, although the protoplasm of this differs greatly from the mature cell, being very vacuolated, and liable to break away from the nucleus. At this age also the cells of the pyramidal layer possess an apical process, and occasionally other processes are present; but the apical one is always the best developed, and appears to be the first formed. Finally, a few years after birth the cell has assumed its mature character, and possesses axons, dendrons, and gemmules. In other regions of the brain development takes place earlier, and in the motor area of the eight-months embryo medium-sized pyramidal and also Betz' cells are readily recognizable.

The processes of the fully developed nerve cells communicate with one another (physiologically, if not anatomically) in an exceedingly complicated network, forming the bands and systems of association fibres already mentioned. It is by means of them that nervous impulses travel to and from all parts of the cerebro-spinal system, and it has even been suggested that the nerve cell is of secondary importance, and only serves the purposes of nutrition. However this may be, there is a definite relation between the appearance of the cell as seen under the microscope and the state of the fibre, and the condition of the cells forms a convenient and reliable index of the presence of disease.

There can be no doubt that the number and complexity of the cell processes, particularly those forming the association systems, are intimately connected with the degree and complexity of cerebral activity, and it is highly probable that the intellectual expansion which takes place after puberty is due to their numerical increase and the elaboration of their connexions. It has, indeed, been shown by Kaes[*] that a progressive increase in these fibres can be demonstrated up to the middle period of life, after which he states that growth ceases and a gradual diminution takes place.

Finally, to complete this brief résumé, it may be said that the nerve cells and fibres are imbedded in a network of supporting tissue (neuroglia cells and their processes), encased in a series of delicate connective-tissue membranes—the meninges—and

[*] Kaes, *Monatsschrift für Psychiatrie und Neurolgie*, 1897.

the whole organ permeated by a dense ramification of blood-vessels.

Whatever may be the relation of mind to brain, it is now fully recognized that the manifestation of mental activity is indissolubly connected with the cells of the cerebral cortex. Mind develops *pari passu* with their growth, and fails with their decay. Dementia is coincident with their degeneration and death, and, as will presently be shown, amentia is associated with their incomplete development.

It is apparent from this outline of cerebral development that the period of greatest growth is that between the first appearance of the primitive brain and the end of the sixth month of extra uterine life; consequently, it is during this period that the demands upon the environment are greatest, and that any adverse factor will be most severely felt. This entirely accords with the general experience that, where secondary amentia occurs, it is the result of an adverse environment during the early months of life. The mental development which takes place after puberty appears to be the result of the elaboration of association systems, and although, theoretically, developmental arrest might occur at this time, such would but rarely be likely to result in any pronounced deficiency. On the other hand, in cases of primary amentia, the condition is rather one of a general *inability to develop* than of an *arrest* of development, and the cause is in existence anterior to the very beginning of embryonic existence.

THE PATHOLOGY OF AMENTIA.

Many mistaken notions still exist with regard to the pathology of amentia. As we shall presently see, in a very considerable number of these patients, particularly the lower grades, there exist gross abnormalities of brain structure, or severe and extensive morbid conditions, which are visible to the naked eye. Accordingly, it was not unnatural that the earlier observers, examining isolated cases in the days when much less was known about the structure of the nervous system than is the case at present, should conclude that in these various anomalies they saw the *fons et origo* of the mental defect. As a consequence, amentia was variously attributed to the presence of porencephaly, hemiatrophy, microgyria, and the like. These views cannot be held to-day. In the first place, it has been abundantly shown that such conditions may exist without any mental defect or deterioration whatever; whilst, secondly, an increased knowledge of the structure of the nervous system, and particularly of the nerve cell, together with a greatly improved technique, has clearly demonstrated the existence of important *cellular* changes in amentia.

In support of the statement that these gross conditions cannot really be the cause of mental defect, the following observations may be cited: About thirty cases have been recorded of absence or deficiency of the corpus callosum, most of them in idiots, yet Nobiling-Jolly, Eichler, and Klob have each recorded a similar case in which there was no mental peculiarity. Likewise with another frequent accompaniment of amentia—porencephaly. Several cases have been described in which a large cavity existed in one hemisphere, and yet there was little or no appreciable mental change. Schroeder van der Kolk* mentions a number of instances tending to show that a large proportion of one hemisphere may be diseased, and yet the patient show no mental impairment. Finally, with regard to another condition—hydrocephalus—Freud† states it to be an undoubted fact that severe hydrocephalus may exist without any paralytic symptoms; whilst Ziegler‡ states that such malformations, or even still greater defects, may exist in the brain, though during life there was nothing whatever to indicate their presence.

We cannot but conclude, therefore, that although these gross changes are frequently associated with amentia, they are not essential to that condition, and in discussing the question of pathogenesis we must be careful clearly to distinguish between what is essential and what is only accidental.

At the same time it is undeniable that gross malformations and coarse lesions are much commoner in the epileptic and mentally defective than in normal persons, and it is easy to understand, from the description which has been given of the causation and hereditary predisposition of these persons, that

* Schroeder van der Kolk, Sydenham Society Transactions, 1861.
† Freud, " Infantile Cerebral Lähmung," Wien, 1897.
‡ Ziegler, " Text-Book of Special Pathology," 1896.

such should be the case. On the other hand, there is no doubt that certain morbid processes may, even in the previously healthy brain, produce such an arrest of neuronic development as to bring about amentia.

The essential basis of amentia is an imperfect or arrested development of the cerebral neurones, a fact which is now established beyond doubt by careful microscopical examinations conducted by numerous competent observers. This morbid state of the neurones is brought about by the causes which have already been described in Chapter II. Accordingly, I shall first of all describe these histological changes, relegating the various gross anomalies and diseased conditions to a second place.

The Histology of Primary Amentia.

Nerve Cells of the Brain Cortex.—As compared with the nerve cells of the healthy brain, those of the ament are characterized by the following conditions : (1) Numerical deficiency ; (2) irregular arrangement ; (3) imperfect development of individual cells ; and on the whole it may be stated that the amount of change discoverable by the microscope is directly proportionate to the degree of mental deficiency present during life.

1. *Numerical Deficiency.*—Although an actual enumeration of the nerve cells present in these cases cannot be made, I am convinced, from the careful examination of a large number of sections, that the cells composing the grey matter of the cerebral cortex are decidedly fewer than in the normal brain. In many cases this paucity of cells produces a decrease in the thickness of the cortical grey matter which is obvious to the naked eye (see Fig. 9, p. 63. Further, although the cells of all the layers are fewer than normal, it is the small and medium-sized pyramids which are most diminished in number. Hammarberg, as the result of a most elaborate and careful series of observations, arrived at a similar conclusion.

2. *Irregular Arrangement.*—Hammarberg[*] states that the arrangement of the cortical cells in amentia does not differ from the normal ; but my own experience, as also that of several other

---

[*] Hammarberg, "Studien über Klinik und Pathologie der Idiotie," Upsala, 1895.

observers, is to tne effect that an irregular and haphazard arrangement is very characteristic of this condition. The pyramidal cells show the most change, although this, of course, may be simply due to the fact that the form of these cells renders any irregularity more apparent. Throughout the brain there are in this layer numbers of cells lying horizontally, obliquely, or completely upside down, even where there is no accompanying sclerosis, and where sclerosis is present the irregularity is often extreme.

3. *Imperfect Development.*—As early as 1879 Bevan Lewis[*] drew attention to the presence, in certain forms of amentia, of incompletely developed nerve cells, and similar cells were present in cases which I examined. When stained by Nissl's method they have the following characteristics: The nucleus is large and ovoid in shape; the nuclear membrane and intra-nuclear network are very distinct. The nucleolus is often eccentric, so that in some sections it cannot be seen. The cell outline is distinct, but, instead of being pyramidal, it is globular or pyriform in shape, and angles are completely wanting. The processes of the cell are exceedingly few, and in many instances one only can be seen (see Plate I., Fig. 4). This paucity of dendrons and also of gemmules is still more evident in sections stained by the silver method.

I think it cannot be doubted that the conditions here described are due to incomplete development. I have never seen such cells in any human brain other than that of an ament; it is, however, interesting to note that, according to Bevan Lewis, similar cells exist normally in the second and third layers of the cerebral cortex of the ape. Bevan Lewis was only able to discover these immature cells in cases of amentia complicated by epilepsy, and he thought they did not occur in pure amentia; but I have seen them in cases in which epilepsy was absent.

In addition to the above, the cerebral cortex of the pronounced ament nearly always contains a large number of other cells whose development is even less complete, and which closely resemble the undifferentiated neuroblasts already described as composing the normal frontal cortex up to the eighth month of embryonic

[*] Bevan Lewis, "Text-Book of Mental Diseases," 1899; also *Brain*, October, 1879.

existence. In these there is practically no cell body, or at most a few irregular protoplasmic strands ; the nucleus is large and globular, the intra-nuclear network very distinct, and often disposed as several fine lines which divide the nucleus into compartments. In fact, they are undifferentiated and undeveloped neuroblasts, and in areas of localized agenesis—such, for instance, as are seen in microgyria—there is often no other kind of cell to be seen (see Plate I., Fig. 1).

There is another condition of the cortical cells which is exceedingly common in these cases—namely, pigmentation. This does not occur in the immature cells above described, and is chiefly seen in the deeper pyramidal layer, in which it is often a very marked feature. The pigment is generally situated at one angle of the cell, away from the nucleus, but at times it is so abundant as almost completely to fill the cell (see Plate I., Fig. 7). It is yellow in colour in Nissl or polychrome sections, but appears dark brown or almost black in those stained with Marchi's fluid, and hence gives to these sections a most striking appearance. In several of my cases it was particularly pronounced in the cells of the hippocampus (see Plate I., Fig. 8). The exact nature and significance of this pigment is unknown, though the reaction with Marchi's fluid would suggest that it was of a fatty nature. A similar pigmentation, but to nothing like the same extent, is frequently found in the central nervous system of patients who have suffered from chronic nervous disease (*e.g.*, disseminated sclerosis, amyotrophic lateral sclerosis, progressive muscular atrophy, chronic insanity, etc.). Its occurrence in these conditions as well as in aments would suggest that it is an indication of defective metabolism, in which the anabolic processes cannot keep pace with the katabolic. The pigment is nearly always associated with a diminution in the number and size of the Nissl bodies.

Nerve Fibres of the Brain Cortex.—The bands of tangentially coursing fibres comprising the association systems show a very definite diminution in cases of severe amentia, so great, indeed, as often to be apparent to the naked eye. Generally speaking, the most marked alteration occurs in the fibres composing the outer line of Baillarger, next in the super- and inter-radial bundles, whilst the superficial tangential fibres are somewhat less affected (see Fig. 9, p. 63). The regions of the brain most involved are the frontal and parietal lobes; in the motor areas the change is comparatively slight, and in the occipital lobes there is often little observable diminution.

The Neuroglia.—*Sclerosis*, or overgrowth of neuroglia, occurs in some form or other in a considerable proportion of cases. Dr. Wilmarth[*] found it in no less than one quarter of the hundred brains he examined. The cause of this condition cannot always be determined; in some cases it would appear to be a developmental anomaly, and to take place in consequence of the diminished multiplication and development of the higher elements—the nerve cells. In such cases it is probably of a *diffuse* nature. In a brain of this kind which I examined from an idiot dying at the age of twenty years, the whole organ was small, 896 grammes in weight, and exceedingly firm—in fact, almost cartilaginous in texture throughout. There were no localized patches, but microscopical examination showed the presence of a dense overgrowth of neuroglia diffused throughout all parts of the brain, including the basal ganglia and cerebellum. This involved the white as well as the grey matter, and was accompanied by a marked numerical diminution as well as irregular and incomplete development of the nerve cells and their processes. There were no signs of recent degeneration, but the piâ-arachnoid membrane was somewhat thickened in places. The patient had always been helpless and unable to do anything for herself, but no definite paralysis was noticeable. She was subject to constant choreiform movements, but there were no convulsions.

In the majority of cases, however, the overgrowth of neuroglia occurs in the form of *localized* patches. These are found in three chief situations, although all may be involved in a single case. The commonest site is the grey matter of the cerebral cortex, which may be occupied by a large number of sharply circumscribed sclerotic areas varying in size from a pinhead to a hazel-nut, or even larger. As generally seen, these are pale firm masses which project above the level of the affected hemisphere, they are often marked by a central umbilication, and the investing piâ membrane strips from them with unusual

[*] A. W. Wilmarth, " Report on the Examination of One Hundred Brains of Feeble-Minded Children," *Alienist and Neurologist*, October, 1890.

readiness and without causing decortication. This condition was first described by Bourneville,* but many examples have since been recorded under the name of *hypertrophic, nodular, or tuberous sclerosis, or gliosis.* The majority of the patients have been markedly mentally deficient and have suffered from epileptic convulsions. The patches consist of a dense interlacement of neuroglia fibres with a varying proportion of cells (probably dependent upon their age), and the lamination of the adjoining grey matter is often considerably distorted. The next most common site is the floor of the lateral ventricles, which may be studded with a number of protuberances the size of small peas. Microscopical examination shows these to consist of almost pure glia tissue, the fibres of which are usually arranged in whorls around the centre of the nodule. Finally, a dense band of fibrous neuroglia is occasionally seen immediately under the pia upon the surface of the hemisphere, closely applied to the cortex like a cap.

When neuroglial overgrowth is present to any considerable extent, it produces a marked increase in the weight and consistence, and often in the size, of the brain. With the lapse of time it tends to contract, and the relative age of the cortical protuberances may be gauged by the size and depth of their central umbilication. It is probably an early stage of extensive neurogliosis which gives rise to the cranial enlargement in the hypertrophic form of amentia, and this condition is not infrequently called "hypertrophy of the brain." The hypertrophy, however, concerns the supporting, and not the true nervous tissue.

Regarding the manner of production of localized sclerosis there is much diversity of opinion, although the lesions suggest some kind of vascular causation. Jendrassik and Marie point out that the first histological change always takes place around the small cortical arteries, and in a case of Freud's a sclerotic patch was considered to be undoubtedly the result of an embolus of a branch of the middle cerebral artery. Strümpell sees in it a possible after-effect of his polio-encephalitis acuta infantum. Moreover,

* Bourneville. Recherches sur l'Idiotie," etc. Paris 1895 ; see also Joseph Sachs "Hypertrophic Nodular Gliosis," Journal of Nervous and Mental Disease, Vol. 19, 1892, in which an account is given of previously recorded cases; also Freud, "Infantile Cerebral Lähmung," p. 136.

the view of vascular origin derives considerable support from the fact that in some cases the lesions are strictly confined to one hemisphere. It is therefore not improbable that a considerable number, at all events, of these cases of tuberous sclerosis have their origin in one or other of the vascular cerebral lesions occurring before birth or in early infancy, in some cases being caused by occlusions, in others by the dissemination of a poison. But such a result is by no means invariable in these cases, and as to why the result should in some be sclerosis, in others softening with cystic formation, or in others chronic meningo-encephalitis with neither, we at present know nothing. The nerve cells are in many cases entirely absent from these patches ; it is by some observers contended that they have been strangled by the neuroglia. It may be, however, that the neurogliosis is but a consequence, and not a cause, of their death. Where nerve cells occur they are rarely healthy, some being in a state of imperfect development, whilst others are atrophied and distorted (see Plate I., Fig. 5). The contiguous portion of the cortex is usually very irregular. The nerve fibres rarely show any acute degeneration, although the tangential and association pathways of the brain and the efferent tracts of the cord are often considerably diminished in size. The endothelial cells of the capillaries frequently contain black fatty granules, and in some of the sclerotic areas indications of old hæmorrhage exist in the presence of hæmatoidin crystals.

Bloodvessels.—As a rule the bloodvessels of the brain show little or no departure from the normal. Occasionally hyaline degeneration is present ; or there is a collection of pigment, similar to that in the nerve cells, disposed around the nuclei of the capillary endothelium. These conditions are not constant, and I do not think they have any causal relationship to the amentia.

Situation of the Cellular Changes.—With regard to the layers in which these imperfections are most evident, it was stated by Bevan Lewis that embryonic cells were particularly numerous in the second and third cortical layers (the small and medium pyramids), and my own observations are entirely in agreement with this. Incompletely developed cells occur, it is true, in all the cortical layers, and in extreme cases of idiocy they may even be seen in the spinal cord ; but it is in the small and middle pyramidal cells that the greatest change is evident. In view of the fact that these cells are normally amongst the last to attain their full development, also that they are the earliest and most affected in dementia resulting from epilepsy and chronic insanity, this fact is of considerable interest.

In cases of pronounced amentia these incompletely developed pyramidal cells are found in all regions of the cerebral cortex. There are, however, two situations in which they are most frequent, namely, the prefrontal and, to somewhat less extent, the parietal lobes. It would therefore appear that it is these regions which are chiefly concerned in the highest mental processes, for it is these same regions which show the greatest amount of degeneration in dementia. On this point the observations of J. S. Bolton,[*] whose work on the morbid histology of the cortex cerebri is probably unsurpassed for painstaking care and completeness, are of great importance. Bolton concludes that " the cellular elements throughout the cortex cerebri which are specially concerned in the performance of associational functions are those of the pyramidal layer of nerve cells ; the great anterior centre of association of Flechsig in the prefrontal region is under-developed on the one hand in all grades of primary mental deficiency, and on the other hand undergoes primary atrophy *pari passu* with the development of dementia. This region of the cerebrum is therefore concerned with the performance of the highest co-ordinating and associational processes of mind."

It is not improbable that the anatomical basis of psychic epilepsy and insanity will ultimately be proved to consist in an inherited instability, defective metabolism, or tendency to premature degeneration of these cells, the actual exciting cause of the disease being supplied by any of the numerous forms of stress and strain incident to modern life.

In concluding this account of the histological changes in primary amentia, it is necessary to remark that embryonic cells similar to those described (neuroblasts), are present in the normal adult brain, also that cells which appear to be of perfect

[*] J. S. Bolton, "Amentia and Dementia," *Journal of Mental Science* April, 1905, *et seq.*

PLATE II.

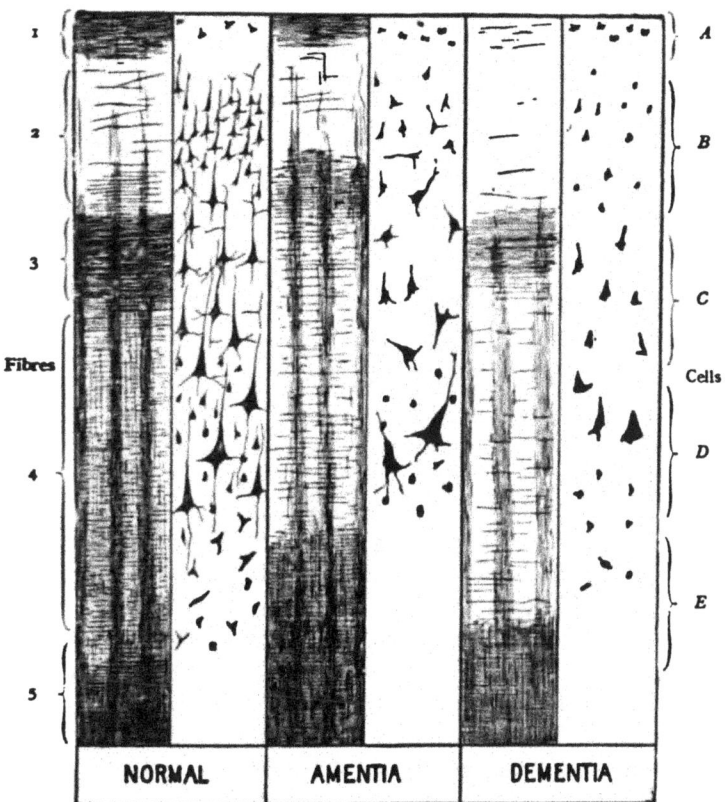

FIG. 9.—MICROSCOPICAL SECTIONS OF THE FRONTAL CORTEX IN DEMENTIA, AMENTIA, AND THE NORMAL CONDITIONS (SEMI-DIAGRAMMATIC, DRAWN BY A. F. TREDGOLD).

On the left of each are shown the *fibres* as they appear in sections stained by the Marchi-Pal method, on the right the *cells* as they appear in Nissl sections. The various layers are as follows:

FIBRES.—(1) *Tangential*, chiefly formed by the ramifications of the collateral processes from cells at A, B, C, and D, also the terminals of some of the fibres forming the medullary rays. This line is normally well defined; in amentia it is somewhat diminished, in dementia markedly so. (2) *Super-radial.* A few horizontally-coursing fibres are situated here, but this region is chiefly occupied by cells (B). (3) *Outer line of Baillarger* (line of Vicq d'Azyr), horizontally-coursing fibres composed of collaterals from cells at B, C, and D, a well-marked line normally, much diminished in amentia and dementia. (4) *Inter-radial*, a less definite bundle, probably of similar constitution to (3), diminished in amentia and dementia. (5) *White matter of centrum ovale.* The vertical bundles are composed of axones from B, C, and D, and of medullated fibres from other regions of the brain.

CELLS.—(A) *Neuroglia and small irregular nerve-cells*. (B) *Small* and (C) *Medium pyramids.* In amentia there are comparatively few cells in these layers, and those present are irregular in arrangement and of incomplete development; in dementia many of these cells are in an advanced state of degeneration. (D) *Large pyramids*, similar changes to those in the preceding layers, but not so extensive. (E) *Polymorphous cells.* It will be noticed that in amentia the whole cortex is much thinner than in the normal condition. This is principally due to the defective development of the cells at B, C, and D, but especially to those at B.

development may be seen in the brain of the idiot, even of the most pronounced type ; but whereas in the normal the number of neuroblasts is comparatively small, and the great majority of the cells have attained complete development, in the latter the reverse is the case, the bulk of the cel's being in an immature condition, and many of them also showing further indications of defective function in the presence of considerable deposits of pigment. Moreover, the proportion of such immature cells appears to be directly related to the degree of mental deficiency, and in the milder degrees the microscopical condition is rather one of paucity of cells and irregular arrangement than of pronounced imperfection of the individual cells.

The Histology of Secondary Amentia.

As has already been stated, the difference between primary and secondary amentia is that, whereas in the former the full development of the neuroblasts cannot take place by reason of an intrinsic vital deficiency, in the latter their development is arrested by some external cause. This cause may operate generally, as in cretinism, or its effect may be local, as in acute polio-encephalitis or the vascular changes occurring in birth injuries. In many of these cases the nerve cells present similar histological features to those in the primary form, although it may be possible to infer that the condition is secondary from the localized nature of the agenesis and the presence of softening, sclerosis, chronic inflammation, or other signs of disease in an otherwise well-developed brain.

In a considerable number of these secondary cases, however, degeneration of nerve cells subsequently takes place, this being often accompanied by more or less dementia. Where this happens, the detection of incompletely developed cells may be exceedingly difficult, just as the original amentia may be unrecognizable in the midst of the dementia. Such degeneration is a slow and chronic process, there being rarely any acute change discoverable by Marchi's method of staining. It begins as a chromatolysis, with accumulation of brownish-yellow granular pigment ; this is followed by a gradual atrophy of the axon and 'endrons, and then by a shrinkage of the cell body. Later disintegration of the nucleus and nucleolus occur, and this is often followed by sclerosis.

The cerebral vessels sometimes show indication of this chronic degeneration in a thickening of their walls ; whilst the endothelial cells of the capillaries and the adventitia of the smaller arteries frequently contain a considerable deposit of brownish-yellow pigment (staining black with Marchi's fluid) similar to that met with in the nerve cells.

Morbid Anatomy.

Gross Developmental Anomalies and Pathological Lesions.—Although the essential pathological condition underlying amentia is one of imperfect or arrested development of the cortical cells, yet in a considerable proportion of cases anomalies of structure occur which are sufficiently gross to be recognizable by the naked eye. These fall under two headings, viz. : (1) Faults of development, and (2) Lesions resulting from disease. The former occur in cases of primary amentia only, and they are obviously a more gross manifestation of that same germinal blight which has produced the cellular imperfection. The latter are the after-effects of pathological processes which on the one hand produce secondary amentia, and on the other may complicate primary amentia. The following are the chief of these developmental anomalies and lesions :

The brain of many mild aments, in its size, weight, and general appearance, may not be markedly different from the normal, but in the more pronounced degrees of mental deficiency differences are usually obvious. I have never yet seen the brain of an idiot, a low or even medium grade imbecile, which could be regarded as normal upon careful naked-eye examination. Sometimes it is too large, when sections will show that it contains an excess of glia tissue. More often, however, it is too small, and the average weight of the encephalon of the ament, even excluding cases of microcephaly, is several hundred grammes less than the average of the ordinary population. In many instances the texture is either abnormally soft or unusually dense. In many cases, also, there is either a decided peculiarity in the whole configuration, or the convolutions are irregular and of markedly diminished complexity. In addition there are often gross malformations of development. In cases of secondary amentia these changes may be little marked, but they are generally replaced by some obvious sign of disease.

Malformations of the central nervous system vary from a trifling peculiarity of configuration or anatomical arrangement to a complete suppression of important structures, such as is seen in anencephalia, non-development of the medulla, or even absence of the spinal cord. Such severe conditions as these are, of course, incompatible with life, and even if the children were born alive, they could only survive a few hours. The malformations ordinarily seen in post-mortem examinations of aments are much less severe, and are in most instances situate in the cerebral hemispheres or the cerebellum. This is doubtless owing, as Ziegler says, to the fact that these parts " in their development from the primary cerebral vesicles undergo the greatest amount of growth and the most important transformations."

Most of these anomalies are forms of localized hypoplasia, which in some instances may be the result of disease or vascular occlusion; in others, however, they are due to defects in the formative material of the brain. In the cerebral hemispheres the secondary, or even the primary, fissures may be imperfectly formed, there may be agenesis of a lobule or a whole group of convolutions, or there may be a general undergrowth of the whole of one hemisphere. This latter condition is called *cerebral hemiatrophy*, and the affected hemisphere may be from 200 to 300 grammes weight less than the opposite one. In a considerable proportion of cases a condition of *microgyria* is seen, in which up of contiguous convolutions are represented by thin ous folds, almost devoid of nervous tissue, and somewhat the conduplication seen in the unexpanded petals of *Porencephaly** is another not uncommon patho-, and is due to a non-development of the central around the inferior extremity of the Sylvian nsequence, a deep funnel-shaped cleft is pro- ends down to, and communicates with, the l ventricle. This cleft is lined by the piâ and

Die Porencephalie," Graz, 1882 ; also Audry, " Les rue de Médecine, June, 1888.

Pathology

bridged over by the arachnoid membrane, the contained space being filled with cerebro-spinal fluid. A somewhat similar depression may arise as the result of disease of the brain matter external to the lateral ventricle, which in many instances is brought about by a lesion of the Sylvian artery. This condition, as well as other circumscribed and cystic depressions of the brain surface, or even severe hemiatrophy, are often described as *pseudo-porencephaly*.

Other more uncommon developmental anomalies of the encephalon consist of malformations of the basal ganglia, deficiency or absence of the corpus callosum, fornix, optic thalami, corpora quadrigemina, and corpora mammillaria. Arndt and Sklarek, in a post-mortem examination on an imbecile girl aged sixteen years who died in the Dalldorf Asylum, found that, in addition to deficiency of the corpus callosum, there were abnormalities of the pillars and commissure of the fornix, of the gyrus fornicatus and fibres of the anterior commissure, as well as absence of the psalterium and septum pellucidum. They quote twenty-nine recorded cases of deficiency of the corpus callosum, most of them accompanied by other defects of brain structure, and the majority of the patients being idiots.

Anomalies of the cerebellum consist chiefly of a general hypoplasia, which occurs with considerable frequency in the Mongolian type of amentia, as well as of various forms of localized agenesis similar to those met with in the cerebrum.

It is to be remarked that such lesions, whether due to faults of development or to disease, are very likely to interfere with the growth, or to cause degeneration, of other portions of the nervous system with which the affected areas are functionally related. Thus, in lesions of the motor cortex there is sclerosis of the corresponding efferent tract throughout the pons, medulla, and cord, and corresponding to this there is often a numerical diminution of the anterior horn cells of the cervical and lumbar enlargements. Lesions of the basal ganglia may give rise to secondary changes in the cerebellum and its superior peduncle of the opposite side, also in the fillet and interolivary layer of the pons and medulla of the same side. Lesions of the motor cortex may even interfere with the development of the great association centres. In examining anomalies of the nervous system, it is thus not always easy to disentangle those lesions which are primary from those which are in this way secondarily produced.

Hydrocephalus is a not uncommon accompaniment of both the primary and secondary forms of amentia; it occurs in two varieties. In one variety the excess of cerebro-spinal fluid occurs within the ventricles, and is then known as "internal hydrocephalus." In the other it is situated external to the surface of the brain, and is then known as "meningeal hydrocephalus" or "hydrocephalus *ex vacuo*."

The cause of *Internal Hydrocephalus* is often obscure. Some cases date from early embryonic life; in others the condition first appears in early childhood. Both syphilitic and tubercular lesions have been found, and in other cases chronic thickenings of the choroid plexuses are seen. It is probable that the affection in many instances depends on closure of the communications between the cavities of the ventricles and the subarachnoid spaces in the transverse fissure; but as to the causes bringing about this closure we know very little. On the other hand, there is no doubt that in some instances internal hydrocephalus may be secondary and compensatory to non-development of the brain tissue. This is probably so in those cases where it is confined to one ventricle, the substance of the corresponding hemisphere being thin and undeveloped; also in those cases in which it accompanies a general hypoplasia of the cerebrum, such as occurs in microcephaly. Distension of the ventricles, even to a considerable extent, is a not very uncommon finding in microcephalic amentia.

External Hydrocephalus is always compensatory to disease or non-development of the cerebral tissue. The excess of fluid is situate in the subarachnoid space, and always occurs in the vicinity of the local defects. In cases of general atrophy of the convolutions due to dementia, the dilated sulci are filled with pale, clear cerebro-spinal fluid. In conditions of localized disease, or agenesis, on the other hand, the fluid is confined to form a cyst. This is particularly well seen in some cases of pseudo-porencephaly. It may happen for internal and external hydrocephalus to be present in the same brain.

Encephalitis and Meningo-Encephalitis.—These conditions are always indicative of a previous disease of the brain. They are therefore commoner in, but not restricted to, the secondary form of amentia. The cause is one or other of the toxic or vascular lesions which have already been described in the chapter on Causation; but they have no constant relationship to any particular one of them. Encephalitis may result alike from cortical hæmorrhages, thrombosis of the meningeal veins due to asphyxia, or a poisoning of the cortical cells. Sachs* considers chronic meningo-encephalitis to be a common result of the meningeal hæmorrhages occurring during birth, but Freud is of opinion that these cases do not commonly terminate in a chronic inflammatory process between the membrane and underlying brain surface.

There can be no doubt that in the majority of cases of amentia which are due to, or accompanied by, " birth paralysis " (Little's disease), meningeal hæmorrhage is present, although in occasional instances the hæmorrhage may be within the brain cortex. Where the bleeding is from the membrane, the clot is usually between the piâ and the brain surface, and it may be situated over the vertex or at the base. Holt† says that the posterior part of the base is much the more frequent site, and that a diffuse hæmorrhage is commoner than is a single circumscribed clot. He further states that, whilst the quantity of blood extravasated varies from one drachm to four ounces, it is usually about one ounce.

However produced, inflammation of the cerebral cortex usually leads to marked histological changes. In most cases there is considerable distortion of all the affected tissue, so that the lamination is exceedingly confused and irregular. In many cases the normal layers are almost indistinguishable, and the cortex consists of a haphazard collection of various-sized cells. Associated with this there may be a clear, pale layer devoid of cells at a little distance below the brain surface. In some cases areas of sclerosis are found, or there is a more diffuse proliferation of the neuroglia; in other cases there are small localized softenings. The vessels are often numerous and the

* Sachs, "A Treatise on the Nervous Diseases of Children," New York. 1895.
† R. Holt, " Diseases of Infancy."

perivascular spaces dilated; whilst if the lesion occurs in the motor region, there is usually a chronic degeneration of the efferent tract, which may be traced through the medulla and cord. The term "agenesis corticalis" has been applied by Sachs to this condition where of intra-uterine origin.

In meningo-encephalitis the piâ-arachnoid is found to be considerably thickened, opaque, unduly vascular, and firmly adherent to the underlying brain tissue, from which it cannot be detached without causing decortication. In some cases the softening and disintegration of the brain substance is definitely circumscribed; the space thus formed is filled with cerebro-spinal fluid, and bridged over by the investing membrane, forming a so-called arachnoid cyst.

In a certain number of cases of amentia, even where there are none of these gross lesions, dementia supervenes. There is then usually found more or less atrophy of the convolutions, with considerable excess of fluid in the widened sulci, and in these cases the membranes are also thickened and opaque; but the piâ-arachnoid strips with unusual readiness, unlike the adhesion in chronic meningo encephalitis. The dura-mater is sometimes firmly attached to the bone, and very occasionally osseous plates and subdural false membranes have been found. Apart from these conditions of disease or dementia, the membranes in persons suffering from amentia rarely show any pathological change.

The Skull. In most cases of primary amentia the skull is thicker and denser than normal, the diploë often being non-existent. In some instances the sutures are found firmly and prematurely united, from which arose the erroneous notion that premature synostosis was a cause of idiocy. Where extensive cerebral hemiatrophy exists, whether from disease or congenital anomaly of development, there may be considerable asymmetry of the cranium as seen from the outside; but it often enough happens that no external malformation is noticeable in this condition, the deficiency being associated with a considerable enlargement of the inner table of the skull only. In some of these cases there is no bony overgrowth at all, the space being merely filled with an excess of cerebro-spinal fluid. The various anomalies of external configuration will be described in subsequent chapters.

CHAPTER V

CLASSIFICATION

WE have seen that there are two fundamentally different *forms* of amentia ; there are also innumerable *degrees*; and it is convenient to describe certain distinctive clinical *types*. Unfortunately, the neglect of some authors to make these distinctions clear has had the effect of unnecessarily complicating the classification of mental deficiency, which is in any case a task of sufficient difficulty.

The Forms of Amentia.

The great majority of aments (probably about 90 per cent.) are the result of inherent defects of the germinal plasm—*morbid heredity*. In consequence of this blight, neuronic development is irregular and faulty, and a condition of *primary* amentia ensues.

In about 10 per cent. of cases there is no morbid heredity and no inherent inability to develop, but the growth of some portion, or the whole, of the brain is interfered with, or arrested by, disease or other adverse *environment*. This condition may be called *secondary* amentia.

At first sight these terms may appear to be synonymous with the older ones—" congenital " and " acquired." They are not so, however, for so-called " congenital " amentia may in reality be secondary and due to a factor of the environment operating *in utero*; whilst what would be called " acquired " amentia may really be the result of a primary imperfection which has been made manifest through the contributory influence of some external factor. I think, therefore, that the terms " primary " and " secondary " are not only more accurate, but materially assist our conception of the real nature of the condition present. As will presently be seen, these two forms are not only essentially different in their etiology, but they often present totally distinct pathological, psychological, and physiognomical features.

But whilst the majority of cases of amentia are readily referable to one or other of these two chief forms, there are a few which seem to be intermediate between them. In these morbid heredity is present, but the brothers and sisters of the patient are seemingly healthy, and the patient himself has seemed to be well in body and mind until the advent of some illness, " fright," or " fall," etc., in the early months or years of life. These cases have been called *developmental*, and the term is in some respects very convenient. But inquiries usually show that the exciting factor is of a comparatively trivial nature, quite disproportionate to the mental disability which follows, and such as would be incapable of damaging the nervous system of a healthy child. There can be no doubt, therefore, that in such cases the inherited condition of the nervous system is a factor of the utmost moment, and perhaps the term *delayed primary amentia* would best define the class.

The Clinical Varieties of Amentia.

In addition to the fundamentally different forms just described, persons suffering from amentia present minor differences which are exceedingly useful as a means of dividing them into clinical varieties. It is here, however, that much confusion exists, for authors are by no means agreed as to the particular characteristics which should be used. Some would attempt to divide aments according to the particular cause at work; but though this is practicable in the case of the secondary form, it is not so with regard to the primary. All these latter are the result of a germinal blight, and the effect is the same whether that blight is caused by alcohol, tubercle, or any other condition. Even with regard to the secondary group, the pathological condition would in many cases appear to afford a better means of classification than would the cause.

The classification suggested by Ireland* is decidedly the best hitherto devised, but, as that distinguished author is the first

* W. W. Ireland, " Mental Affections of Children," 1898.

to acknowledge, it is by no means perfect, and is, in reality, little more than an enumeration of the chief clinical varieties. Whilst still making use of most of Dr. Ireland's clinical groups, I believe that the investigations which have been made in recent years enable us now to arrange these groups in a much more systematic manner, and this I attempted to do in a table published several years ago. This table, in an improved form, is given on p. 77.

THE CLINICAL VARIETIES OF PRIMARY AMENTIA.

The majority of persons suffering from primary amentia present no special distinguishing features other than the anatomical and physiological anomalies common to aments in general; they may therefore be termed *simple* aments, and they correspond to the " genetous "* group of Ireland. In others, however, the imperfection of development, for some reason or other, has taken a particular form, and thereby produced marked cranial or physiognomical peculiarities; since these are often associated with special mental characteristics, we are justified in alluding to them as separate varieties. The most important of these are the *Microcephalics* and the *Mongolians*.†

In a not inconsiderable number of primary aments (particularly of the simple variety) there exist severe gross lesions. In many cases these are only revealed after death, but it occasionally happens that they are so pronounced during life as to justify the use of them as a further means of classification. Accordingly, we may describe *sclerotic*, *porencephalic*, and (occasionally) *hydrocephalic* subvarieties of primary amentia. Epilepsy and paralysis are such common complications of all these cases that their presence can hardly be said to constitute separate varieties.

THE CLINICAL VARIETIES OF SECONDARY AMENTIA.

Cases of secondary amentia are divisible into two main classes, according as to whether the deficiency (1) is brought about by a

* This term is open to the objection that *all* primary aments may in reality be called " genetous."

† Negroid, Grecian, Egyptian, and American Indian types have also been described; but as these are rare, and their characteristics by no means definite, they will not be alluded to further.

general or localized disease of the brain cells, or (2) is due to some external factor influencing their nutrition.

Class 1. *Amentia due to Cerebral Disease.*—Diseases of the brain may, for our present purpose, be divided into two groups—*first*, epilepsy, *secondly*, gross lesions. These latter may arise from many different causes which have already been specified, and the lesions themselves present different anatomical features. As a consequence there are produced more or less well-marked clinical varieties. These varieties may be classified as follows:

1. *Epileptic and eclampsic amentia.*
2. *Vascular, toxic, and inflammatory amentia*, including certain special clinical types—*i.e.,*

     Porencephalic.
     Sclerotic.
     Hydrocephalic.

3. *Syphilitic amentia.*
4. *Infantile cerebral degeneration.*

Class 2. *Amentia due to Defective Cerebral Nutrition.*—The nutrition of the brain may suffer (1) in consequence of qualitative or quantitative anomalies of the blood-supply, or (2) as a result of the deprivation of nervous stimuli from without. Cretinism is the best-known and most important example of the former, although possibly other abnormal states of the blood may so act. The absence of the necessary nervous stimuli to development produces amentia from isolation or sense deprivation. The clinical varieties of this class are therefore enumerated as—

1. *Cretinism.*
2. *Amentia due to defects of nutrition.*
3. *Amentia due to isolation or sense deprivation.*

The Degrees of Amentia.

Amentia varies greatly in its degree, irrespective of form or clinical variety. In some cases the defect is but slight; in others it is so severe that mind can hardly be said to be present at all. Between these two extremes there is every gradation and since the differences are of quantity rather than quality, of degree and not kind, any classification must be an arbitrary one.

Esquirol suggested the faculty of speech as a dividing line ; but this is unsatisfactory, as there are quite mild aments who cannot speak. Sollier* proposed the faculty of attention ; but this is also far from being a reliable criterion as to the amount of defect. In fact, there is no one faculty or function upon the presence or absence of which we can rely as a means of defining the degree of amentia.

Nevertheless, it is essential, both for purposes of description and administration, that a division should be made, and this, on the whole, is best done by means of three terms which have long been in use—namely, *Feeble-mindedness*, *Imbecility*, and *Idiocy*. To one or other of these degrees we may relegate all aments, although it is to be remembered that the boundary lines are by no means distinct, and that the one gradually merges into the other. We may, indeed, if necessary, further subdivide each of them into three others, and thus describe high-, medium-, and low-grade idiocy, imbecility, and feeble-mindedness respectively.

A concise definition of these three terms is impossible, for the reason that they are used with reference to the amount of general intellectual capacity present ; but the chief characteristics of each are summarized in the following descriptions. A definition of amentia has already been given on p. 2.

Feeble-Mindedness (High-Grade Amentia).—This is the mildest degree of mental defect, and the feeble-minded person is " *one who is capable of earning a living under favourable circumstances, but is incapable, from mental defect existing from birth, or from an early age, (a) of competing on equal terms with his normal fellows ; or (b) of managing himself and his affairs with ordinary prudence.*"†

Feeble-minded persons under the age of sixteen years come within the jurisdiction of the education authority by reason of a special Act of Parliament (Defective and Epileptic Children Act, 1899). On account of this Act they are commonly designated *mentally defective children*, and they are defined as " *those children who, not being imbecile, and not being merely dull and*

---

* P. Sollier, " Psychologie de l'Idiot et de l'Imbécile," Paris, 1891.

† This and the following definitions were suggested by the Royal College of Physicians of London, and adopted by the Royal Commission on the Feeble-Minded as the basis of classification in their inquiries.

backward, are, by reason of mental defect, incapable of receiving proper benefit from the instruction in the ordinary public elementary schools, but are not incapable by reason of such defect of receiving benefit in such special classes or schools as are in this Act mentioned."

It should be remarked that in America the term "feeble-mindedness" is not thus used specifically of the mildest degree of amentia. In that country it is applied generically to the whole order of amentia, thus being synonymous with the English term "mental deficiency." There has been an attempt in this country also to include all grades of defect in this euphemistic description, and to call the mildest degree of all (the feeble-minded) "mental defectives." The attempt has not met with much success, however, and since "feeble-mindedness" is in itself a more specific term than is "mental defect," I think it is decidedly better to restrict its use to the mildest degree.

Imbecility (Medium-Grade Amentia).—The imbecile is defined as "*one who, by reason of mental defect existing from birth, or from an early age, is incapable of earning his own living, but is capable of guarding himself against common physical dangers.*"*

Idiocy (Low-Grade Amentia).—The idiot is defined as "*a person so deeply defective in mind from birth, or from an early age, that he is unable to guard himself against common physical dangers.*"*

It may be remarked that these three terms are occasionally used of varying degrees of *dementia*, particularly the dotage of old age, just as "mental deficiency" is sometimes used generally for that condition. The practice, however, is to be deprecated as likely to lead to considerable confusion.

In addition to the above, it may perhaps be well in this place to define the **moral imbecile** as "*a person who displays from an early age, and in spite of careful upbringing, strong vicious or criminal propensities, on which punishment has little or no deterrent effect.*"

* See note p. 75.

AMENTIA

	Etiology.		Pathology.	Clinical Varieties.*	Clinical Sub-Varieties.†
PRIMARY AMENTIA	**MORBID HEREDITY**	Insanity, Epilepsy, Alcoholism, Tuberculosis, Etc.	A numerical deficiency, irregular arrangement and imperfect development of cortical neurones.	1. SIMPLE.	
				2. MICROCEPHALIC.	PORENCEPHALIC. SCLEROTIC. HYDROCEPHALIC.
				3. MONGOLIAN.	
SECONDARY AMENTIA	**ENVIRONMENT**	I. DISEASE OF BRAIN. { I. EPILEPSY. II. VASCULAR AND TOXIC: Trauma, asphyxia neonatorum, pertussis, scarlet fever, measles, small-pox, enteric, otitis, rhinitis, meningitis, primary polio-encephalitis, sunstroke, tuberculosis, syphilis, etc.	An arrested development of cortical neurones corresponding to site of lesion. Final results are: Localized atrophy, softening, cysts, sclerosis, pseudoporencephaly, and hemiatrophy.	4. EPILEPTIC.	
				5. VASCULAR, TOXIC, OR INFLAMMATORY.	PORENCEPHALIC. SCLEROTIC. HYDROCEPHALIC.
				6. SYPHILITIC.	
				7. INFANTILE CEREBRAL DEGENERATION.	
	II. DEFECTIVE NUTRITION OF BRAIN.	I. *Viá* BLOOD: Qualitative and quantitative anomalies.	General arrest of neuronic development.	8. CRETINISM.	
				9. AMENTIA due to Nutritional Defect.	
		II. *Viá* NEURONES: Defective stimuli from without.	Localized arrest of neuronic development.	10. AMENTIA due to Isolation or Sense Deprivation.	

* These may be of any of the three degrees—*i.e.*, Idiocy, Imbecility, and feeble-mindedness.
† Dependent upon presence of gross developmental anomalies, or special pathological conditions.

CHAPTER VI

THE PHYSICAL CHARACTERISTICS OF AMENTIA

WE have seen that, in an overwhelming proportion of persons suffering from amentia, the condition is the result of a blighted germinal plasm. The effect of this upon development will naturally be greatest in the case of the organ of most delicate and complicated structure—namely, the nervous system. In mild cases this alone may be involved, and it may even happen that the injurious effect is limited to the least organically fixed structures of this system—that is, to the neurones subserving the highest mental processes.

But such cases are relatively few. The majority of aments are the product of a markedly abnormal germinal plasm, and, as a consequence, not only the brain, but the whole body is marred by defects of anatomical development and physiological function. Such defects are known as *stigmata of degeneracy*.

Stigmata of Degeneracy.

In recent years much has been said and written about degeneracy, and the most elaborate tables of its "stigmata" have been compiled. These have been divided into social, psychological, physiological, anatomical, and other groups, and some writers would seem to look upon any departure from their conception of what is or should be the normal social, psychological, physiological, anatomical, or other condition, as a "stigma" of degeneracy. I do not think this view is justifiable. In the first place, there are so many variations within healthy limits that the "normal" becomes exceedingly difficult to define. Moreover, it by no means follows that a condition which is uncommon, or even "abnormal," is on that account a mark of degeneracy, or that it is even pathological at all. We have not yet reached finality, and manners, morals, mind, physiological function, even anatomical structure, are, we trust, still in process of evolution ; so that it is possible for some of these anomalies described as "stigmata" to be not retrogressive, but actually progressive.

But even where they are undoubtedly pathological or indicative of a diseased condition, it does not follow that on that account they are stigmata of degeneracy. As has already been shown, there are some diseases and toxic states of intra- or early extra-uterine life which are occasionally capable of producing secondary amentia, and in these cases, although the germinal plasm is healthy, there may nevertheless be produced physiological and anatomical anomalies. There are also other diseases, such as rickets and syphilis, which rarely produce mental deficiency, and yet which commonly result in bodily abnormalities. Even in cases of undoubted degeneracy, such as primary amentia, some of the bodily conditions which are commonly called "stigmata" seem to me to be not a concomitant effect of the germinal imperfection, but the result of the imperfect nervous action. Lastly, the examination of perfectly healthy children in public elementary schools, as well as of ordinary healthy members of the general population, will often reveal the presence of so-called "stigmata." In fact, if we are to class as degenerates all persons coming within the territory defined by some writers on this subject, there are few of us who will escape.

I am far from denying the existence of degeneracy and its stigmata. In fact, I consider primary amentia itself to be a true degeneration, and many of the anomalies of bodily condition present in these persons may rightly be described as "stigmata" of degeneracy. But I think we should be careful to restrict this term to such anomalies as are really manifestations of this state—that is, to peculiarities which are due to inherent defects of the germinal plasm. In the present state of our knowledge this differentiation cannot always be made. Some—indeed, many—of the physical characteristics of amentia to be described are certainly the result of degeneracy, and it is not surprising that such should be numerous and severe in this condition, in the lower degrees of which degeneracy reaches its culminating manifestation. But some of these characteristics are not really degenerative. I shall therefore prefer to describe them all under the heading of "Anomalies of Anatomical Development and of Physiological Function."

It has been remarked that similar anomalies occur in persons who are not otherwise abnormal. Nevertheless, it is abundantly clear that they are far more numerous in neuropaths and in aments than in the general population. Further, that the number and severity is, on the whole, directly proportionate to the degree of defect. Whilst, therefore, the presence of a single anomaly has little or no diagnostic importance, the presence of two, three, or more is of considerable significance as an indication of mental defect.

The table on pp. 82-83 shows the various anomalies which have been noted in amentia; the chief of these may now briefly be described.

Anomalies of Anatomical Development.

A. **Nervous System.**—These have already been described in the chapter dealing with pathology.

B. **Special Sense Organs.**—*Ear.*—It is probable that, owing to important alterations which have taken, and are taking place in the sense of hearing, the external ear is at present in a state of considerable evolutionary instability. It is, therefore, not surprising to find that anomalies of this structure occur in normal persons, amongst whom, as a matter of fact, they are extremely common. This being the case, it is evident that, as an indication of degeneracy, such anomalies are in themselves of little value, and I must dissent from the dogmatic utterances of some writers that a certain type of ear can be labelled "criminal," another "insane," and so on. At the same time, there is no doubt that, frequent as are such departures from the normal in the ordinary population, they are still very much more frequent in degenerates; and when they occur in combination with two other classes of defects—namely, of the cranium and palate—I believe that they have considerable diagnostic value.

With regard to the frequency of auricular defects, the following figures ascertained by Gradenigo,* although they do not relate

* Gradenigo (*Arch. de Psychiatria*, 1890 and 1892), quoted by Talbot in "Degeneracy."

specifically to amentia, are of considerable interest. As the result of his examination of several thousands of persons of both sexes, this observer found that the external ears were regular and normal—

> In 56 per cent. of males and 66 per cent. of females of the *ordinary* population.
> In 36 per cent. of males and 46 per cent. of females of the *insane* population.
> In 28 per cent. of males and 54 per cent. of females of the *criminal* population.

Also that in the insane and criminal classes, not only were ear anomalies more frequent, but they were of greater gravity. As tending to show that some ear anomalies may be progressive rather than retrogressive, it may be stated that Talbot found certain varieties were more frequent in ordinary persons than in degenerates.

The varieties of malformation of this structure which are met with in persons suffering from amentia are so numerous that a detailed account of them all is impossible. There is no portion of the external ear which may not be affected, but the following are the chief conditions met with: Defects of the lobule are decidedly the most frequent; it is often unusually large and fleshy; it may, however, be smaller than usual, and at times even absent; it is occasionally adherent to the face. Another very common deformity is that in which the whole ear is excessively large, prominent, and outstanding, with a marked convexity as seen from behind. Another common type is the reverse of this, the entire pinna being small, thin, and circular, strongly recalling the ear of the chimpanzee. With or without any of these gross changes there may be numerous minor malformations of the helix and antihelix, the tragus and antitragus. Supernumerary auricles are occasionally present, but I do not think that anomalies of the Darwinian tubercle are more frequent in aments than in the normal population. It occasionally happens that the auditory apparatus is so imperfectly developed that total or severe deafness results. This, however, is uncommon, and deafness, when present, is usually the result of disease, especially suppuration of the middle ear.

TABLE VIII.
ANOMALIES ASSOCIATED WITH AMENTIA.

System.	Organ.	Anatomical.	Physiological.
(a) Nervous	Brain	General hypoplasia { Anencephaly, Microcephaly }; Partial hypoplasia of cortex, ganglia, and internal structures	Insanity and epilepsy; various psychoses and neuroses; defects of speech; Various abnormal nerve signs
	Spinal cord	Hyperplasia (sclerosis); Micromyelia; syringomyelia; local hypoplasias; spina bifida	Various forms of paralysis; Defects of posture, walking, and general balance
(b) Special senses	Ear	Anomalies of form and size of pinna and component parts	Defects of hearing (but more often due to disease than to developmental anomalies)
	Eye	Epicanthus; obliquity of fissures; coloboma; heterophthalmos; persistence of pupillary membrane; opacity of media; strabismus; astigmatism; errors of refraction	Visual defects; conjunctivitis; keratitis; blepharitis
	Nose	Anomalies of form and size	
	Lips	Anomalies of form and size (hare-lip uncommon)	Defects of articulation
	Tongue	Anomalies of size; sfures; hypertrophied papillae	Slavering
(c) Osseous	Cranium	Abnormalities of size and shape; asymmetry; bosses	
	Palate	Saddle- and V-shaped	

The Physical Characteristics of Amentia 83

	Jaws	Small and receding, or ally protruding	
	Teeth	Irregularities of position, number, form, size, and condition	Primary and secondary dentition often delayed
	Limbs	Gigantism, dwarfism; talipes; deformities of fingers and toes; polydactylism, syndactylism; arms disproportionately long; legs short and bowed	
(d) Muscular and cutaneous	Skeletal muscles	Numerous anomalies	
	Skin	Moles, nævi; supernumerary mammæ; an unusual development of hair upon parts generally hairless, and an absence or deficiency on those usually covered (*e.g.*, beard); adenoma sebaceum	Excessive and unpleasant secretion
(e) Circulatory and respiratory	Heart	Subnormal size. Fœtal malformations	Feeble circulation; cyanosis; chilblains; subnormal temperature. Hæmophilia
	Bloodvessels	Various aberrations	
(f) Alimentary	—	Numerous anomalies of stomach, alimentary canal, and glands	Bulimia; coprophagia
(g) Urinary and generative	Kidneys and bladder	Lobulated, horseshoe; extroversion of the bladder	
	Male genitals	Epi- and hypo-spadias; cryptorchism; infantilism; cloacal opening	Late puberty; sterility
	Female genitals	Small uterus; fibrous ovaries; labial anomalies; cloacal opening; infantilism	Abnormal presentations; abortions; sterility

6—2

Eye.—Anomalies of the eye and its appendages are exceedingly common in aments, those most frequently seen being the following : Epicanthus, a ridge of skin continued from the upper eyelid around the inner canthus, and apparently due to an unusual redundancy of skin in this region ; it may be unilateral, but usually affects both eyes, and is a tolerably frequent anomaly in aments, although not unknown in normal children. Palpebral fissures, which are small and obliquely placed, so that the inner is lower than the outer end, are a characteristic feature of the Mongolian variety of amentia. Differently coloured and speckled irides are very common, as also are strabismus, astigmatism, hypermetropia, and less frequently myopia. Corneal opacities are frequent, but colour-blindness does not appear to be more prevalent than in the ordinary population.

Nose.—A clear-cut, well-formed nose is not often seen in aments, and this organ is usually either considerably flattened or depressed, or is large and prominent, with wide fleshy nostrils which look forwards rather than downwards. Deviation of the septum and nasal bones may also occur.

The *Lips* are often thick, coarse, prominent, and unequal in size. The mouth is heavy and flabby-looking, generally open, and devoid of either refinement or firmness. Hare-lip is not common.

The *Tongue* is often abnormally large, fissured, and its papillæ hypertrophied, particularly in the Mongolian variety.

C. **Osseous System.**—Abnormal conditions of the skeleton occur with extreme frequency in amentia, and the number of these persons who do not present one or more well-marked bony anomalies is small. The cranium, palate, jaws, and teeth, are the parts most frequently affected.

Cranium.—Anomalies of the cranial vault may be revealed by inspection, palpation, and mensuration ; also by tracings from pliable metal bands which have been moulded to the skull. Provided this latter method is carefully performed, it yields very accurate results, and Dr. Lapage[*] has recorded a most interesting series of observations taken in this way. The process, however, is somewhat too tedious for general work, and I think that for practical purposes mensuration is the most suitable. The following are the measurements I have been in the habit of taking

[*] C. P. Lapage, " Feeble-Mindedness in Children," *Medical Chronicle*, 1905.

for several years; they have the advantage of being easily carried out and recorded.

The measurements are taken from the upper point of attachment of the auricular pinna to the lateral aspect of the skull. This point was suggested to me many years ago by Dr. J. S. Bolton as being readily ascertainable in every case, and subject to little individual variation; it is designated " X." From the fixed point " X " of one side a *steel* tape-measure is passed in various directions to the corresponding point on the opposite side—namely, (A) over the glabella, (B) over the greatest frontal prominence, (C) vertically upwards, (D) over the greatest parietal prominence, (E) over the external occipital protuberance. An additional sagittal measurement is taken from the glabella over the cranial vault to the external occipital protuberance, and, if desired, a further measurement can be taken with the calipers between the two points " X."

These measurements are conveniently recorded by means of a diagram like the following, which can be rapidly drawn as occasion requires, or printed in one corner of the case-sheet:

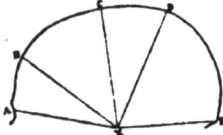

FIG. 10.

It will be observed that the measurement XAX plus XEX gives the cranial circumference, XCX its vertical perimeter, and XBX and XDX the greatest frontal and parietal perimeters respectively. If the circumference be multiplied by XBX and XDX, a figure is obtained which is a convenient index of the total cerebral capacity.

The general conclusion at which I have arrived, as the result of an extensive series of measurements of the crania of normal, insane, epileptic, and defective persons, is that, in the majority of aments there are marked departures from the normal; but that there is no particular type of skull which is characteristic of that condition. The chief anomalies are the following:

Circumference: The average normal circumference of the male adult is 22 inches, and of the female 21¾ inches. Occasionally the skull of the ament exceeds these figures, but as a rule it is decidedly less, and in cases of microcephaly it is often as little as 15 inches. There is often a diminution of the frontal and parietal perimeters, whilst a subnormal development of the occipital portion of the skull is exceedingly common. *Symmetry :* The two halves of the normal skull not infrequently differ slightly in size, but this condition is much commoner and far more marked in aments. Where paralysis has existed from an early age, this condition is very frequent, the lessened measurement corresponding to the area of brain destroyed or arrested in its development, but asymmetry of the cranium is often observed in the absence of any paralytic signs. Usually the left half is the smaller. Lapage found that lateral asymmetry occurred in 158 cases out of a total of 198, the left half being the smaller in 122, and the right in 36. *Cranial bosses* are frequently present, probably as a result of rickets, the most common situations being the ossific centres of the frontal and parietal bones. In a few cases an interfrontal ridge is seen. Finally, the whole conformation of the skull may be abnormal, as is seen in the oxycephalic type.

Palate.—The association of abnormalities of the palate with mental deficiency has long been recognized, and there is no doubt that it is one of the commonest malformations occurring in this condition. Many years ago Langdon Down* drew attention to the subject, and more recently Clouston† has recorded a large number of observations which show conclusively that, although deformed palates occur in the normal, they are far and away more frequent in neuropaths and the mentally defective. He states that deformed palates are present in 19 per cent. of the ordinary population, 33 per cent. of the insane, 55 per cent. of criminals, but in no less than 61 per cent. of idiots. Petersen,‡ who has made a most exhaustive study of this question, and has compiled an elaborate classification of the various anomalies, found palatal deformities present in no less than 82 per cent. of idiots.

Without going into ultra-refinements, it may be stated that the majority of the anomalies met with may be arranged under two headings as follows :

* J. Langdon Down, Transactions of the Odontological Society of Great Britain, 1871.
† T. S. Clouston, " Neuroses of Development," 1891.
‡ Petersen and Church, " Nervous and Mental Diseases," 1904.

1. *Saddle- or Keel-shaped Palates.*—In this, the commonest type, there is a contraction of the alveolar arch between the bicuspid and molar teeth, the palate at the same time extending upwards to a considerable distance, at the expense of the nasal cavity. In consequence an appearance like the inside of a saddle or boat's keel is produced. It is sometimes marked by a narrow central antero-posterior furrow, but the front teeth do not usually protrude in this type of palate.

2. *V-shaped Palates.*—These are not so frequent as the former, and are produced by a gradual narrowing of the dental arch from the first molars to the central incisors, the point of the V being thus directed forwards. Palates of this type may also be higher than normal, and the narrowing of the fore-part of the arch usually causes considerable overcrowding and protrusion of the front teeth.

A great deal of discussion has raged round the cause and manner of production of these anomalies.* It has been contended by E. S. Talbot that they only appear during the second dentition, between the sixth and twelfth years; but this is denied by Clouston, John Thomson, and other physicians of great experience, and I have certainly seen numerous instances before this period. I think there can be little doubt that most of them are real stigmata, and a further indication of those formative defects which play such a prominent part in the production of amentia. At the same time it is to be remembered that the palate, like the external ear, is probably undergoing considerable evolutionary changes, and many of the slighter anomalies may be due to this cause.

Cleft palate appears to be on quite a different footing, and it is doubtful if this condition and its common associate, hare-lip, can be regarded as real stigmata of degeneracy. It is but rarely met with in amentia, Langdon Down finding it only in 0·5 per cent., and Ireland in 1 per cent., of idiots; whilst Talbot† examined 1,977 feeble-minded children without meeting a single instance. These proportions do not differ materially from the normal, for Grenzer (quoted by Talbot) found 9 cases on examining 14,466 presumably normal children.

---

* See the chapter on " Genetous Idiocy " in Ireland's book.
† Talbot, " Degeneracy."

Jaws.—Many aments have a receding, others a protruding, mandible, the former being very common in microcephalics. Asymmetry of the upper or lower jaw is not uncommon.

Teeth.—Considering the frequent occurrence of deformities of the palate, it is not surprising to find that anomalies of the teeth are very common, and a good set of teeth is exceedingly rare in the mentally defective. They are usually late to appear, malformed, and unhealthy when present, and prone to early decay and disappearance. Where a V-shaped palate is present, the upper incisors and canines are generally huddled together and protruding, at times to such an extent as to be left uncovered by the lip. The remaining teeth may be very irregular in arrangement, and there are often large gaps between them. The wisdom teeth are seldom seen. It often happens that the teeth erupt at different planes of the alveolus, and I have occasionally seen a complete double row of incisors. In addition, the teeth are individually ill-formed, often honeycombed or marked by transverse striæ, very unhealthy, and surrounded by a foul mass of exudation.

Other defects of the osseous system are seen in the presence of talipes, polydactylism, syndactylism, and other deformities of fingers and toes. The arms are often disproportionately long. Very exceptionally a condition of gigantism is present. As a rule, however, the stature is diminished, and the average height of aments is several inches less than that of the ordinary population.

D. Muscular and Cutaneous Systems.—Various anomalies of the skeletal muscles have been found upon dissection, but they are hardly of sufficient importance to merit further description. Abnormalities of the skin are frequent, and consist of coarseness of the integument, excessive and unpleasant secretion, webbing of the fingers, moles, and nævi. There is often an excessive development of hair upon parts usually hairless, and a lack or deficiency upon those which are generally covered, particularly the face and chin in males.

Adenoma Sebaceum.—In this place reference may be made to this peculiar condition of the skin sometimes seen in aments, and with extreme rarity in normal individuals. Adenoma sebaceum is a papular new growth which is confined to the face, and is chiefly seen on the side of the nose, but occasionally on the fore head or chin. It is usually, but not always, symmetrical, and the lesions are often numerous. They are either firmly imbedded in, or project from, the skin, and they vary in size from a pin-head to a small pea. They are of a whitish or yellowish colour, but sometimes bright red owing to numerous telangiectases. The papules are made up of an overgrowth of sebaceous glands and capillary vessels, often surmounted by a thickened corium. In many cases they are present at birth, but in others they do not appear until late in childhood or puberty. As a rule, they persist throughout life, but occasionally undergo spontaneous involution with scarring.*

E. **Circulatory and Respiratory Systems.** — The most important anomalies are stenosis of the pulmonary artery and defects of the auricular and ventricular septa. The heart also is usually smaller than that of a normal person of corresponding weight.

F. **Alimentary System.**—Numerous anomalies of the various organs of this system have been observed upon dissection. Meckel's diverticulum is not very rare, and Talbot states that the appendix is best developed in degenerates.

G. **Urinary and Generative Systems.** — Lobulation of the kidneys is not uncommon, and anomalies of the genital organs are of considerable frequency. These consist, in the male, of epi- and hypospadias, infantile condition of the penis, and cryptorchism ; in the female, an infantile condition of the uterus is generally present, and the ovaries are often fibrous. Cloacal openings have been observed in both sexes. Supernumerary mammæ are common.

Anomalies of Physiological Function.

It is, of course, to be expected that organs which are the site of grave defects of structure or anomalies of anatomical development should also be imperfect in their physiological function. Thus, the condition of the heart leads to an enfeebled circulation, so that cyanosis and coldness of the extremities, chilblains, and sores are exceedingly common. Defects of the organs of special sense are a factor in producing a diminished perceptivity. Non-development of cortical areas or the internal structures of

* See Pringle, *British Journal of Dermatology,* 1890, vol. ii., and Crocker, " Diseases of the Skin," 1893.

the encephalon cause various degrees of paralysis, with their accompanying deformities. Indeed, the mental deficiency itself may be considered as an imperfection of physiological function due to neuronic changes, whilst the various neuroses and psychoses, such as insanity, epilepsy, hysteria, and one-sided genius, as well as the moral perversions, seen in prostitution, inebriety, and other anti-social and criminal tendencies, are of the same order.

With regard to the functions of the generative organs, there is no doubt that many of these persons can propagate their kind, and there are, unfortunately, numerous examples where this has taken place. The milder aments, indeed, appear to be unusually prolific. At the same time, in the male sex, the advent of puberty is often considerably delayed, and may not appear until late in the teens. In the male this subject has been very fully investigated by Bourneville and Sollier,* who drew attention to a considerable retardation of puberty, as well as to the presence of frequent anatomical anomalies like those referred to. In the female, on the other hand, a similar retardation does not appear to be the case, and it is stated by Jules Voisin,† who has studied the subject closely, that the development of puberty takes place at a normal age, and that menstruation recurs at regular periods. Doubtless of many, or even most, female aments this is true, and amenorrhœa and dysmenorrhœa do not appear to be commoner in them than in those of normal intelligence : indeed, the latter seems to be less so. It is, however, to be remembered that in some of the pronounced idiots menstruation never appears at all.

A similar retardation of physiological activity is seen with regard to dentition, speech, and walking. Inquiries show that a large proportion of aments do not cut their first or second teeth until some considerable time after the ordinary period. Many of them do not attempt to stand until their third year, and walking is correspondingly late. In many cases the child is four or five years old before it says a word.

But in addition to these functional defects of particular organs, many aments are characterized by a physiological inadequacy which is general and widespread. Their temperature-regulating

* Bourneville and Sollier. " Anomalies des Organes Genitaux chez les Idiots et les Imbéciles." *Progrès Médical.* 1888.
† Jules Voisin. " L'Idiotie."

mechanism is so imperfect that colds and chills are exceedingly common. Their metabolism is so defective that, in spite of abundance of wholesome food, most of them remain small, stunted, and ill-nourished. They have an increased predisposition to illness, and readily contract disease, and their physiological margin and power of resistance are so diminished that disease quickly proves fatal. In fact, the history of a very large proportion of these patients may be expressed in two words—*defective vitality*—and the supervision of the physician is often as necessary for their bodily as for their mental ailments. Langdon Down remarked the fact that " many cases of imbecility, particularly those of the Mongolian variety, lose a large amount of intellectual energy in the winter—go through, in fact, a process of hybernation, their mental power being always directly as the external temperature."

Mortality.

The physical welfare of the ament of to-day is the subject of far more care and attention than was the case a few generations back. Then many perished who, under present conditions, would have survived ; and there can be no doubt that modern medical and surgical practice, together with advances in preventive medicine, have diminished the mortality rate, not only of the fit, but of the unfit also.

Nevertheless, the virility of aments as a class is decidedly inferior to, and their expectation of life still less than, that of the ordinary population. Even amid the well-ordered surroundings of an institution the number of these persons of at all advanced age is relatively small, and in the world outside the proportion is still less. I am disposed to think that the mortality has, generally speaking, a direct relation to the degree of deficiency.

This diminished expectation of life is well shown by some figures collected by Dr. Shuttleworth* with regard to Earlswood and the Royal Albert Asylums. These are shown in the following table, together with the mortality at corresponding age periods of the whole population, as given by the Registrar-General. The difference between the mortality of aments and the general population is very striking.

* Quoted by Ireland.

TABLE IX.

Relative Mortality of Aments and Non-Aments.

Age Periods	Death-Rate per 1,000.	
	Aments (Dr. Shuttleworth).	Whole Population (Registrar-General).
5 to 10 years	50·1	6·10
10 ,, 15 ,,	33·9	3·35
15 ,, 20 ,,	45·1	4·75

With regard to age periods, through the kindness of Dr. C. Caldecott, Medical Superintendent, and Dr. F. H. Pearce, Assistant Medical Officer, Earlswood Asylum, I have been supplied with particulars of 1,000 consecutive deaths in that institution. Owing to the impracticability of ascertaining the number of persons alive at corresponding ages, these figures cannot, of course, be compared with the mortality tables relating to the general population. They are, nevertheless, of considerable interest, and are shown in the following table:

TABLE X.

Showing Age Periods of 1,000 Consecutive Deaths in Earlswood Asylum, dating back from October, 1907.*

Age	Males.	Females.
Under 5 years	2	1
5 to 9 ,,	70	40
10 ,, 14 ,,	162	71
15 ,, 19 ,,	180	101
20 ,, 24 ,,	88	42
25 ,, 34 ,,	66	38
35 ,, 44 ,,	37	28
45 ,, 54 ,,	22	12
55 ,, 64 ,,	20	9
65 ,, 74 ,,	6	4
75 ,, 84 ,,	—	1
Total	653	347
	1,000	

* Patients under the age of six are not eligible for the institution, excepting those that come in on payment scales.

The Physical Characteristics of Amentia

The following table, also kindly supplied by Dr. Caldecott, is of interest as showing the percentage of deaths to the number of patients in residence at Earlswood Asylum over a period of seventeen years. It is impossible by means of these figures to institute an accurate comparison between the mortality of aments and of the general population, for the reason already mentioned; nevertheless, they afford clear evidence of the excessive mortality rate in aments. The crude annual death-rate per 1,000 persons living, of all ages and both sexes, in England and Wales varies with different decennia, but is well under 20, whereas we see that even in a well-equipped and excellently managed institution like Earlswood the average mortality is over 30 per 1,000, and this relates to a selected age class, there

TABLE XI.

SHOWING THE PERCENTAGE OF DEATHS TO THE NUMBER OF PATIENTS IN RESIDENCE AT EARLSWOOD ASYLUM OVER A PERIOD OF SEVENTEEN YEARS, FROM DECEMBER 31, 1890, TO DECEMBER 31, 1906.

Year.	Average Number Resident.			Died.			Percentage of Deaths to Average Number Resident.		
	Males.	Females.	Total.	Males.	Females.	Total.	Males.	Females.	Total.
1890	418	191	609	8	7	15	1·91	3·66	2·46
1891	443	192	635	7	9	16	1·58	4·68	2·56
1892	426	186	612	13	6	19	3·05	3·22	3·10
1893	395	191	586	18	8	26	4·55	4·18	4·42
1894	385	187	572	14	12	26	3·63	6·88	4·37
1895	391	185	576	5	5	10	2·04	3·24	2·40
1896	388	188	576	12	8	20	3·09	4·25	3·40
1897	381	191	572	10	7	17	2·88	3·66	3·14
1898	366	188	554	13	7	20	3·50	3·72	3·61
1899	366	180	546	10	7	17	2·73	3·80	3·11
1900	346	183	529	11	4	15	3·17	2·18	2·83
1901	332	178	510	8	7	15	2·40	3·93	2·93
1902	336	179	515	6	7	13	1·78	3·91	2·52
1903	339	174	513	9	12	21	2·65	6·89	4·09
1904	330	155	485	20	9	29	6·00	5·80	5·99
1905	314	142	456	11	6	17	3·50	4·20	3·70
1906	311	142	453	7	10	17	2·25	7·04	3·75

TABLE XII.

SHOWING THE CAUSE OF DEATH IN 1,000 CONSECUTIVE DEATHS IN EARLSWOOD ASYLUM.

Cause of Death.	Males.	Females.	Totals. Number.	Totals. Percentage.
I. ZYMOTIC DISEASES:			83	8·3
Measles	10	14		
Scarlet fever	11	8		
Diphtheria	10	6		
Enteric	6	3		
Erysipelas	5	1		
Pertussis	3	0		
Influenza	1	1		
Septicæmia	2	0		
Pyæmia	1	0		
II. CONSTITUTIONAL DISEASES:			413	41·3
Tuberculosis	261	135		
Rheumatic fever	2	0		
Purpura	1	0		
Scorbutus	0	1		
Cancer and sarcoma	6	6		
Goitre	0	1		
III. DEVELOPMENTAL DISEASES:			30	3·0
Marasmus and debility	9	4		
Premature senility	11	3		
Senile decay	1	2		

The Physical Characteristics of Amentia 95

IV. ACCIDENTAL:					
Burns and scalds	..	2	2 ⎫		
Phosphorus-poisoning	..	1	0 ⎪		
Fractured jaw	..	1	0 ⎬	8	0·8
Drowned	..	1	0 ⎪		
Accumulation of hair in stomach		1	0 ⎭		
V. LOCAL DISEASES:					
(a) *Nervous System*:					
Meningitis, encephalitis, and other diseases of brain		32	21 ⎫		
Convulsions, status epilepticus, and exhaustion due to epilepsy		115	62 ⎬	236	23·6
Systemic diseases of spinal cord	..	3	3 ⎭		
(b) *Circulatory System*:					
Morbus cordis, pericarditis, syncope		26	16 ⎱	49	4·9
Dropsy, gangrene, embolism	..	5	2 ⎰		
(c) *Respiratory System*:					
Pneumonia	..	76	28 ⎫		
Bronchitis	..	6	8 ⎪	126	12·6
Pleurisy	..	5	2 ⎬		
Empyema	..	0	1 ⎭		
(d) *Digestive System*:					
Stomach (haematemesis, gastritis)	..	2	0 ⎫		
Intestine (enteritis, colitis, peritonitis, perforation, volvulus)	..	27	9 ⎬	43	4·3
Liver (hepatitis, impacted gall-stone)	..	3	1 ⎪		
Spleen (rupture)	..	1	0 ⎭		
(e) *Urinary System*:					
Nephritis	..	7	4	11	1·1
(f) *Osseous* (necrosis, mastoid abscess)	..	1	1	2	0·2

being a disproportionately small number of persons over middle age and practically none under six years, so that the two most vulnerable life periods are excluded.

Causes of Death.

I am greatly indebted to Dr. Caldecott and Dr. F. H. Pearce for supplying me with the particulars of the cause of death in 1,000 consecutive deaths at Earlswood Asylum which are shown in Table XII. These figures are not, of course, to be confounded with the mortality rates of these diseases. Nevertheless, they are exceedingly valuable as showing the relative incidence of various fatal diseases in aments.

It is seen from this table that by far the commonest cause of death is tuberculosis, which accounts for 39·6 per cent., or nearly two-fifths, of those dying. The fatal varieties of this disease are as follows :

	Males.	Females.	Total.
Pulmonary Tuberculosis	199	106	305
General ,,	37	17	54
Meningeal ,,	10	1	11
Abdominal ,,	9	8	17
Osseous ,,	6	3	9
	261	135	396

The next most common cause of death is epileptic convulsions, which claims 17·7 per cent. of the total ; whilst pneumonia is a very good third, being responsible for 10·4 per cent. of total deaths. It is interesting to note that, excluding tubercle, the nervous system is the part most frequently involved by fatal disease, being followed in order by the respiratory, circulatory, alimentary, and urinary systems. Not that diseases of the nervous system are the cause of the mental deficiency, but because the imperfection of development and imperfect function of the nervous system render it peculiarly prone to disease.

I do not profess to institute an accurate comparison between the frequency of the various causes of death in these aments and in the general population. Such is impossible, for many reasons which will at once be obvious to the student of vital statistics. It may be stated, however, that according to various Reports of the Registrar-General, it appears that of the total deaths throughout England and Wales *approximately* 12 per cent. are due to diseases of the nervous system ; 8 per cent. of the circulatory system ; 18 per cent. of the respiratory system ; 5 per cent. of the digestive system ; and 2 per cent. of the urinary system ; whilst from 10 to 12 per cent. are due to pulmonary and other forms of tuberculosis. In these aments, on the other hand, 23·6 per cent. of the total deaths are from diseases of the nervous ; 4·9 per cent. of the circulatory; 12·6 per cent. of the respiratory ; 4·3 per cent. of the digestive ; and 1·1 per cent. of the urinary systems ; whilst 39·6 per cent. are due to some form of tuberculosis.

CHAPTER VII

NERVOUS AND MENTAL CHARACTERISTICS OF AMENTIA

In addition to their general deficiency of intellect, many aments present certain other particular and important psychological anomalies, as well as irregularities and defects of sensory and motor function. These will be described in the present chapter ; in so doing, it will be convenient to consider them under the three headings, Sensory, Mental, and Motor Processes.

Sensory Processes.

The brain of the new-born child consists of a gelatinoid substance in which are imbedded myriads of embryonic nerve cells. These cells, or neuroblasts, however, are so immature that the child may be said to be mindless. Mental development proceeds by slow and orderly steps, and one of the most important means by which it is brought about is the stimulation of these cells by impressions entering through the sensory channels. Should one of the senses be diseased or defective, a corresponding area of the brain will remain permanently undeveloped, and this may lead indirectly to the non-development of other portions which are functionally correlated. Should communication with the outer world be closed viâ several sensory pathways, the growth of the brain may be so much interfered with as to produce a condition almost amounting to idiocy, and known as " amentia by sense deprivation." As instances of this, the celebrated cases of Kaspar Hauser and Laura Bridgman may be referred to. Considered, therefore, merely from the point of view of their stimulating effect upon the brain cells, sensory impressions are as necessary to mental development as are the rays of the sun to the growth and maturation of plant life.

This, however, is not their only effect. Sensations are the basis of ideas, and a comparison of ideas constitutes reasoning ; so that although the ability to receive impressions and the ability to examine, combine, compare, and work up these impressions are two totally distinct functions, yet the wealth of sensations is a factor which cannot be ignored in considering the quantity, if not the quality, of mental activity. In somewhat crude language, we may say that sensations are the materials of which " mind " is built, and, in their absence, the brain cells are probably incapable of producing a single idea. Sensation may be present without reason, but reason cannot exist without sensation.

Although it is convenient to divide the total cerebral activity into three groups of processes—viz., sensory, mental, and motor —these are all interdependent. If the more purely psychological functions are defective, not only will outgoing currents be altered, but the accuracy and extent of sensations may be greatly interfered with. Attention in particular has a most important influence upon sensation, and many of the sensory defects of aments are due, not merely to defects of the sensory mechanism proper, but to imperfections of the higher neuronic activities of the brain.

There are three elements concerned in sensation : a peripheral sense organ, a transmitting nerve, and a central receptive ganglionic area. With regard to the nerve, beyond diminished size, I know of no structural differences between aments and normal persons. The peripheral sense organ is not infrequently the seat of disease or anomalies of development which may either completely cut off, or seriously interfere with, a particular order of impressions ; but the chief cause of sensory imperfections in these persons lies in a defective condition of the central receptive ganglion cells or of the still higher perceptive mechanism.

Sensation varies very much in aments, and on the whole is directly proportionate to the degree of mental deficiency. In the feeble-minded sensory defects are but slight, and consist chiefly of a diminished range and acuteness. In imbeciles more or less actual obtuseness of the senses is seen ; whilst in idiots this often reaches such an extreme degree that one or more of the senses seem to be actually wanting.

Generally, apart from the presence of disease or congenital anomaly of a particular sense organ, the defect is uniformly incident upon all the senses ; but to this there are some remarkable exceptions, as will be seen in a subsequent chapter.

Vision.—The chief peripheral defects have already been described ; they are strabismus, corneal ulcers and opacities, cataract, astigmatism, hypermetropia, and, less frequently, myopia. A few low-grade aments are congenitally blind, but colour-blindness does not appear to be commoner than in normal persons. These conditions, and, indeed, all anomalies of the end organs of special sense, are more frequent in the severer grades of mental deficiency.

In the milder degrees of amentia visual defects consist chiefly in an inability to discriminate between the slighter differences of form, size, or colour. An octagonal will be confused with a hexagonal figure ; no difference will be noticed between the size of a florin and half-crown ; and, although these patients may differentiate between the primary colours, they are often unable to detect differences of shade. As we proceed down the scale of amentia, these defects become more marked, until in the severe forms of idiocy they exist to a very pronounced extent. The colour perception of the low-grade imbecile and idiot often seems limited to the recognition of red, and it is interesting to note that this is the colour which is usually most attractive to, and first recognized by, the normal child. The appreciation of form and size by idiots is very imperfect, and although they will distinguish between a child and a grown-up person, and between a man and a woman, many of them are incapable of any more delicate differentiation. Voisin states that in most imbeciles the perception of relief is wanting.

Hearing.—Developmental anomalies of the external ear are very numerous, but it is very rarely that such interfere with hearing. Where there is a peripheral cause for deficiency of this sense, it is nearly always of inflammatory origin and situate in the middle ear. Otorrhœa occurs with considerable frequency in aments of all grades.

Apart from cases of amentia due to sense deprivation, complete deafness is not common in the mentally defective. Some idiots and imbeciles will pay not the slightest regard to questions, to the sound of a whistle, or noises of many kinds, and they are on that account often thought to be deaf. That this is due to want of interest and attention, however, and not to deafness, is often shown by the fact that they will at once turn upon the rattle of a spoon and plate. Itard's wild boy of Aveyron was unresponsive to many sounds, and yet he showed a marvellous aptitude for hearing those in which he was interested. In the feeble-minded grade of amentia there is not usually any marked deficiency of this sense, although hearing, as a rule, is neither so acute nor are the finer differences of tone so well detected as by the normal person.

Taste.—In the milder aments there is not usually any marked impairment of this sense, although I doubt whether they have the delicacy of taste of an ordinary person. They have their likes and dislikes with regard to food, and they appreciate sweets and object to nasty medicines. In the more severe grades there is often an extreme defect of taste, whilst in many cases there is marked perversion of this sense. Thus, some idiots will munch sugar, quinine, or even soap, quite indifferently, and without the slightest indication that they distinguish one from the other. Others will eat and drink anything which comes within their reach, including wood, leather, grass, earth, stones, even urine and fæcal matter or offal of the most putrid description.

One of the chief characteristics of the Mongolian variety is a large fissured tongue, with hypertrophied papillæ, but this does not appear to be accompanied by any particular anomaly of taste.

Smell.—This sense is closely related to the preceding. In the milder aments ability to perceive odours is present, but is lacking in delicacy. In the more severe grades there often seems to be a complete absence of the sense. Many idiots will smell the most filthy compounds without the slightest sign of repugnance, and some will sniff strong ammonia without any reflex movement. In these latter a defective condition of the olfactory mucous membrane would appear to be present.

Cutaneous and Muscle Sensibility.—The milder defectives can differentiate by the sense of *touch* between bodies which are hard or soft, rough or smooth, but they cannot appreciate the finer gradations of these qualities so well as the normal child. The same remark applies to the sensation of *pressure*, as tested by weights or small pill-boxes filled with a varying number of coins or shot, and placed on the palm of the hand. In the imbeciles this sense of discrimination is still less acute ; but this may be apparent only, and due to the difficulty of examination. In the idiots such a test is practically impossible.

Alterations of *temperature* are certainly appreciated by the mild aments, but in many of the idiots this capacity seems to be wanting. They will sit in front of the hottest fire, under the most blazing sun, or exposed to the coldest wintry blast, without showing any concern. *Pain* is experienced by feeble-minded children ; they will complain of headache, toothache, or stomach-ache, but such sensations are often not so acute as in normal children, and many of the feeble-minded will suffer the extraction of teeth and other operations of minor surgery with relatively little concern. In the pronounced imbeciles, and more particularly in idiots, inability to feel pain is often a very marked characteristic. There are many idiots who will knock themselves against floor or walls, poke their fingers into their eyes, pull out their hair, teeth, or toe-nails, and injure themselves severely in many ways, without showing the slightest indication that the process is painful. I knew a boy some years ago who had such an incurable habit of sucking his fingers that the bone had been completely denuded of flesh, yet the practice seemed to afford him extreme pleasure rather than discomfort. It is practically impossible to make any experimental inquiries as to the condition of *muscle, tendon*, and *joint sensations* in these persons ; but, judging from their general clumsiness of manipulation, bodily balance, and movement, one is justified in assuming that such cannot be of a very high order.

Organic Sensations.—The sexual instinct is by no means absent in the feeble-minded, also in many imbeciles, and even in some idiots ; indeed, in some of the milder degrees it is often inordinately developed. In the profound idiots such primitive organic sensations as those of hunger and thirst are wanting, and such persons would die of starvation if not fed. On the other hand, many of the partial idiots are extraordinarily gluttonous and voracious. In the lower types the painful sensations which accompany organic disease are often not appreciated, and these persons will be acutely ill, with pneumonia, gangrene of the lung, or tuberculosis, without making any complaint. In such cases there will be no subjective symptoms to guide the physician, and his diagnosis will have to depend entirely upon objective signs.

Mental Processes.

The essence of amentia is a defective development of the neurones which are the physical basis of the internal and more purely psychological functions; these we have now to consider. In many cases disorders of sensation or motion are present as well; but in the mildest examples these mental processes alone may suffer. In some instances we can even point to a special default of some one particular function, such as that of attention, imagination, memory, etc.; but the mind cannot be thus divided into watertight compartments, and no particular defect can exist without disturbing the harmonious working or potentiality of the mind as a whole.

Attention.—The act of attention consists in the focussing of consciousness upon an idea or the mental image of an object, to the exclusion of other ideas. It may be *spontaneous and involuntary* or *active and voluntary*, and it is necessary to consider these separately.

Spontaneous attention occurs when a sensation or idea is so sudden, so intense, or so unusual, that it holds consciousness reflexly and without any mental effort. Of this nature is the flash of lightning, the peal of thunder, or any sight or other sensation to which the beholder is utterly unaccustomed. This form of attention is characteristic of children and the lower animals, and although, of course, dependent upon the nature of the stimulus, variations in it are more influenced by the condition of the cerebral cells with regard to their inherent excitability. It may be compared to the violent shock inflicted upon the cerebral mass of the child of a few weeks old by any sudden noise, and which results in a general start of the whole body; with the development of consciousness this general bodily change is often still seen when attention is involuntarily aroused.

In the lowest type of idiocy feeling is very rudimentary, and hence even this spontaneous form of attention is defective.

But even where perception is present the cerebral excitability may be so diminished as to bring about a considerable deficiency of spontaneous attention, and this is the case with many idiots and imbeciles as well as with a few feeble-minded. Such persons are dull and lethargic ; they seem to be utterly unconcerned by anything happening around them, and they have no curiosity or initiative. If in school, they sit at their desks gazing vacantly in front of them ; if in the playground, they stand aloof in a corner, without the slightest desire to take part in the games of their companions. They respond tardily, or not at all, when addressed, are stolidly indifferent when interfered with, and are, in fact, so generally inert as to give rise to the impression that they are deaf. But there is no real sensory defect, and the condition is simply one of general brain inertia. By appropriate methods of training, the excitability of the brain cells may often be increased and the child aroused out of his lethargy.

Active or voluntary attention takes place when the idea or sensation attended to has no compelling power of its own. Attention to it may, indeed, be distasteful, and the focussing of consciousness upon it, so that other ideas and impressions are for the time being shut out, demands a very considerable voluntary effort. It is plain that attention of this kind is indispensable to the acquirement of knowledge and the conduct of human affairs, and the person in whom it is greatly lacking will cut but a sorry figure in life.

This is the case with a large number of aments. They are quite incapable of concentrating their thoughts upon a particular subject, and they consequently have no power for sustained work. It follows that their education and training is exceedingly difficult. Persons of this type differ from those lacking in spontaneous attention in several noteworthy points. Instead of being heavy and lethargic, they are often active and restless, and attracted, but distracted, by every sight and sound around them. The condition is thus the exact opposite of the former type, and at first sight would appear to result from an excessive, instead of diminished, nervous excitability. This, however, is by no means necessarily the case, and very often the fault seems to lie rather in a defective power of co-ordination and control. It is often associated with the presence of tricks and habits. As Maudsley says, " The person who is unable to control his own muscles is incapable of attention."

This condition of imperfect muscular control and defective attention is, of course, characteristic of normal infancy ; but whereas it is but a phase in the development of the healthy child, it is a much more persistent, and often permanent, condition in the mentally defective. It is undoubtedly responsible for much of the faulty perception and discrimination of these persons, and, since our stock of ideas is dependent upon the multiplicity and accuracy of sensations from the outer world, some would see in this defective power of attention the psychological *fons et origo* of mental deficiency. But, whilst admitting to this faculty a most important share in the quantity and quality of the intellectual processes, its lack in these persons is not sufficient to account for their imperfect reason and want of common sense. Moreover, there are many aments in whom attention is not lacking. We must therefore consider the defective attention of aments, not as the prime cause, but as only one factor of that general imperfection of mental faculty which constitutes amentia.

Association and Memory.—If a healthy, intelligent child of between three and four years be asked to describe, from memory, some common object—such, for instance, as a cat, a chair, or table—and if a little direction be given to his thoughts by not too leading questions, a very good estimate will be formed as to his capacity of memory and association. To those unacquainted with the mind of an intelligent child of this age the result is often surprising, and contrasts in an extremely marked manner with a similar examination of the mentally defective child of much greater age. I have often found the mental images in a defective child of twelve or even fourteen years to be far simpler, and to have only a fraction of the associations which are present in the former case. In the lower aments the deficiency is still more marked, although such an examination in their case is extremely difficult. We may therefore say that aments generally are decidedly inferior in the power of association and recall.

No doubt much of this is due to a faulty perception, which in its turn may be the result of a defective attention and incapacity for mental effort ; and although, as we have seen in speaking of pathology, one of the distinguishing features of the ament's brain is a paucity of association fibres, it is a moot point whether this is a primary deficiency or a secondary result of their faulty perception.

But although there is a diminished complexity of association, the connexions which do exist seem to cling together with a very considerable, and at times even extraordinary, tenacity. This is shown in the remarkable powers of some aments for repeating poetry, remembering dates and names, and other similar feats of memory. Such instances are, of course, exceptional; but in many aments the general tenacity of memory for striking events and certain isolated occurrences which have appealed to them does not seem to be markedly inferior to that of the normal person. In their general power of recall, however, and in their ability to remember ordinary things and the little occurrences of everyday life, there is, as a rule, a decided defect.

Imagination.—Fantasy, reverie, and day-dreaming occur in some of the milder aments, although in a much simpler form than in the normal person. Moreover, many of those of unstable type have delusions without either mental exaltation or depression. A few are even capable of a certain amount of constructive imagination, as is shown by their skill in drawing and mechanical invention, as well as by the cunning with which they commit thefts and the ingenuity with which they invent plausible lies to screen themselves and incriminate their companions. On the whole, however, there seems to be a decided defect in the faculty of imagination in aments. The higher types may copy a drawing or design; they may produce faithful models of flowers or fruit; they may, indeed, have a very high degree of manipulative skill; but their work is generally a slavish imitation, and they hardly ever originate. And when they do, the result is not usually creditable to their imagination. If mentally defective schoolchildren be watched drawing, brick-building, or pattern-making, it will generally be found that they follow the same stereotyped plan, and that they do not evince a fraction of the originality shown by the normal child. In the imbeciles and idiots the deficiency is much more pronounced.

Ideation.—In view of their defects of attention, perception, and memory, it necessarily follows that the capacity of aments for forming ideas is limited, and conversation readily reveals the general crudity and childishness of their thoughts. One may, indeed, say that the intellectual life of these persons consists almost entirely of perceptions, and not conceptions—that is, of simple ideas relating to objects which are immediately present to their senses. I cannot agree, however, with the statement so often made, that the ament is utterly wanting in the capacity for forming abstract ideas. It is true that the concrete is much more readily grasped than the abstract, and it is interesting to note that many feeble-minded school-children find it much easier to express their ideas by means of a drawing than by a word ; but there is no doubt that many of the milder grade are quite capable of conceiving such universals as mankind and womankind, goodness and badness, and the like. Of abstracting in the logical sense, however, most of them are probably quite incapable.

Judgment and Reasoning.—To reason is to think, but thinking is not reasoning. Most of our thinking consists simply of a review of mental images which successively rise into consciousness in accordance with the laws governing association. The thought which is past has suggested that now present, and this in its turn suggests that to come, the series depending upon previous experience (perceptions) and the type of our mental constitution. Thinking is thus to a great extent a form of reverie, although thoughts may be directed and confined to a certain channel by an effort of will.

Reasoning, on the other hand, is not only a definite and deliberate effort of volition, but it also involves other processes which are not concerned in mere thinking. Without attempting to discuss what these are, or the manner of their working, it may be said, briefly, that reasoning consists in, firstly, the deliberate contemplation of certain ideas ; the abstraction from these of their essential attributes ; the comparison of these abstractions ; and, finally, the construction of an idea or judgment which is new to our mental experience.

Reasoning thus involves activities of a higher order than any hitherto considered, and the chief characteristic of amentia is a defect of these functions. This defect reaches its maximum in the most pronounced degree of amentia, and in the majority of idiots the ability to reason may be said to be completely absent. The absolute idiots would even die of starvation, in the midst of food, if they were not fed. The feeble-minded, on the other hand, are by no means destitute of this faculty; for instance, if a mentally defective child, who is ignorant of money values, be offered the choice of a shilling or half-crown, he may choose the latter "*because it is bigger.*"

Upon asking a feeble-minded adult, whose daily work consisted in cleaning the type in the printing-room, what he was cleaning it with, he said, "Turps." Upon then asking him what he washed his hands with, he replied, "Soap and water." But he was for a time quite nonplussed when asked why "turps" wouldn't do for his hands, or "soap and water" for the type. At length, however, after much floundering, I got out of him that soap and water wouldn't get the ink off the type, and that turpentine would make his hands sore. Nevertheless, although these persons possess some power of reasoning, it is so limited that they are quite unable to steer a course upon life's sea, or even to keep their heads above water, without support.

The imbeciles, as a class, are intermediate between these two extremes. I sent a feeble-minded and an imbecile youth respectively to fetch an article out of a room, the door of which had been locked and the key hung up in a conspicuous place above the handle. The feeble-minded one went to the door, tried the handle, found it locked, seemed nonplussed for a moment, then saw and took down the key, opened the door, and performed his task. The imbecile tried the door, gazed vacantly at the key, turned round, and said, "Locked." Upon being asked where the key was, he pointed, and said, "There," but when again told what to fetch he made no effort to use the key. Upon my placing the key in the lock, he turned it, opened the door, and got the desired article. A somewhat similar test was tried between two other children. It was a pouring wet day, and I placed an umbrella near the door, and told them to fetch a certain flower out of the garden. The feeble-minded child opened the door, saw the rain coming down in torrents, and, after a pause, picked up and opened the umbrella. The imbecile would have got wet through had he not been called back, but, when given the umbrella, had enough sense to open it before going out.

Temperament.—Temperament is dependent upon physiological peculiarities of nerve action, and the mentally defective person is just as subject to differences in this respect as is the normal.

Since the days of Aristotle it has been customary to describe four temperaments—namely:

Choleric, where the *excitability* is great and *after-effect* great.
Sanguine, where the *excitability* is great and *after-effect* small.
Phlegmatic, where the *excitability* is small and *after-effect* small.
Melancholic, where the *excitability* is small and *after-effect* great.

I cannot recall an ament who could rightly be described as choleric; most are of the phlegmatic type, some are sanguine, and a few—chiefly of the mildest grade—are melancholic.

Although most aments will display a childish, and at times keen, interest in spectacular displays, they are not, as a rule, aroused thereby to the same pitch of enthusiasm as a normal child. Moreover, the impression quickly fades, and they soon cease to talk about it. Although by no means insensible to praise or blame, pleasure or punishment, they are not, as a rule, greatly affected thereby, and the sensation is but fleeting. Some of the milder grades, it is true, evince a considerable amount of mental perturbation on first leaving their friends for the care of strangers; but they are seldom really home-sick, as is the ordinary child, and they rapidly settle down to their new surroundings with hardly a thought of the old. Of most of them it may be said that their general attitude is one of placid indifference, and that they are decidedly less affected by the happenings of life than are ordinary people.

A few may be described as sanguine. They are quick, lively, and readily attracted by anything happening around them, and easily moved to laughter or tears, passionate anger, or cloudy sullenness. But this state is very fleeting, and leads to little result. Though seemingly full of interest in everything, they settle down to nothing.

Another small proportion belong to the melancholic type. In these, although censure, punishment, or neglect seem to make little impression at the time, the child or adult becomes morose, and begins to brood over his real or fancied wrongs. Sometimes a state of true melancholia results, and I have known several persons of this type who have attempted suicide.

Emotion and Sentiment.—The emotions most commonly seen in aments are the simple ones of pleasure, grief, affection, anger, fear, and surprise. The more complex states of shame, awe, contempt, disgust, indignation, hate, and jealousy, are comparatively rare and of little intensity. On the whole, the capacity for experiencing emotion seems to be directly proportionate to the amount of general intelligence present, although much depends upon the particular variety of nervous temperament. In the absolute idiots emotion is lacking altogether.

Moral Sense is lacking in the lowest grade of amentia, and in the imbeciles and feeble-minded it rarely reaches a high degree of development. Most of these persons act upon the impulse of the moment, quite unaffected by any altruistic feelings. They may develop the habit of refraining from lying or pilfering because they realize that such lead to punishment; but the majority do not understand that any obligation is morally due from them, or that they should be virtuous for virtue's sake. On the other hand, a few do acquire rudimentary notions of unselfishness and good behaviour, and some, even, are capable of hazy anthropomorphic ideas of a Superior Being, thus showing the germs of a **religious sense**. They may be taught, and in a simple way understand, the Bible stories; they may tell one that after death the good people go to heaven and the bad ones to hell, and this belief may be not without effect upon their daily behaviour; but of theological dogma or doctrine beyond this the majority have little conception.

Finally, as a connecting link between mental and the more obvious motor phenomena to be next described, we may refer to the subject of **Will**. Volition, although frequently leading to action, is not to be confounded therewith; in fact, in its highest form it is probably more often associated with the inhibition rather than the initiation of movement. Consequently the restless activity and the sudden impulsive acts of feeble-minded children are by no means an indication of will power, but rather the reverse. Will is always accompanied by mental effort, and of this, to any great extent, the mentally deficient are often incapable. Their inability to keep an ideal or course of action steadfastly in front of them leads to the absence of fixity of purpose or capacity to offer serious resistance to the will of others. Consequently many of them readily fall in with suggestions which are made to them, and easily become the prey and tools of designing and evil-disposed persons.

Motor Processes.

Mind is manifested as motion, and mental and motor activities run on parallel lines. The motor functions of the body, as seen in movement and speech, are generally similar in quantity and quality to the more purely psychological processes just described, and, since they are capable of more ready investigation, they often afford valuable indications as to the nature and working of the mind. This relationship has been ably pointed out by Dr. Francis Warner,* and to this author we are indebted for much valuable information regarding anomalies of motor function, or, as he terms them, "abnormal nerve signs," in the mentally defective.

Movement.—The simplest form of movement is, in all probability, the result of explosions within the motor ganglion cells taking place in consequence of their own inherent instability. Such movement is *spontaneous*, and is seen in the spreading of the fingers and toes of the young infant (the "microkinesis" of Warner), later in the inarticulate babblings which denote the first activity of the motor cells concerned in speech. Presently, as a result of the laying down of pathways within the cerebral mass, the motor cells require two connexions. One of these brings them into relation with the sensory areas of the brain, the other with the higher levels concerned in ideation and volition. As a result of the former of these connexions, the simple spontaneous movements become so modified and controlled by the quantity and quality of the incoming sensations as to be perfectly adapted to them. We then have a *co-ordinated* movement, in which an optimum result takes place with a minimum expenditure. When this result has been attained, and

* Francis Warner, "Anatomy of Movement," "Mental Faculty," and numerous other writings.

a well-worn pathway established between sensory and motor areas, the appropriate movement is readily called forth upon the presentment of its customary stimulus, producing a *reflex co-ordinated* action.

The new-born child comes into the world with some of these channels already laid down, so that it is capable of so-called *instinctive* or hereditary movements, such as sucking and crying. Many of the ordinary reflex movements are the result of spinal rather than cerebral action.

The second connexion, which links up the motor cells with those portions of the brain concerned with the intellectual processes, brings the motor functions under the influence of the will, and so makes *volitional* action possible. Such action is always preceded by an *idea* of the motion to be performed (motor idea). The nature of this volitional action, however, will be different according as other intellectual associations act as a drag or not upon immediate response. In the simplest and lowest type of mind an immediate response follows the presentment of the idea, and the action is *impulsive.* Such may take place almost with the rapidity of a reflex act ; indeed, by constant repetition the motor idea to an action of this kind may be subconscious, and the action truly reflex. On the other hand, the motor idea may call up other associates, so that deliberation intervenes to delay or inhibit the natural tendency to immediate action. After a longer or shorter period of deliberation, in which the pros and cons are carefully passed in review, a choice is made, and finally the highest type of action—a *deliberate, purposeful* manifestation of will—results.

We thus see that in aments various anomalies of movement may occur as a result of their imperfection of development. The metabolism or excitability of the motor ganglion cells may be abnormal, and the *quantity* of movement defective or excessive. Sensations may be imperfect or distorted, or the connexions between sensory and motor areas faulty, leading to defects in the *quality* of movement or inco-ordination. The connexions between sensory and motor centres which are normally laid down at birth may be lacking, producing a diminution or absence of the instinctive movements—a condition which is by no means infrequent in idiocy. On the volitional side response may occur immediately upon presentment of the idea, and impulsive action of this kind is very characteristic of many aments. On the other hand, response may be tardy, not because of the intervention of deliberation, but because the cerebral cells generally are lethargic and unexcitable, and the connexion between volitional and motor centres a comparatively untrodden pathway; and this kind of slothful action is characteristic of another type of aments. Finally, anomalies of movement may occur in consequence of gross lesions or disease of the cerebro-spinal axis. We may now consider the chief of these anomalies of the motor functions somewhat more in detail.

Deficient Movement.—In a considerable number of aments movement is deficient in quantity, and this is the result of a generally diminished excitability of the nerve cells. The condition is most common in the severest grade, but it is also seen in the imbeciles and feeble-minded. In the most pronounced cases it is obvious from birth, and the child never cries, sucks, or looks about him like an ordinary child; in the milder forms these instinctive movements are present, but the child is backward in his first attempts at sitting up, standing, and walking, whilst speech is very much delayed. The appearance of such children is usually characteristic; the face wears a dull, heavy, vacuous expression, and there are many indications of want of muscular tone. In the temporal and masseter muscles this often shows itself by dropping of the lower jaw and a persistently open mouth. The general balance of the body is feeble, and when the child walks, he does so with a slothful clumsiness. If told to follow an object with his eyes, he either makes no response or turns his whole head round in a slow and laboured manner. His arms are listlessly extended to command, but the fingers and hands hang flabbily down, and the whole arm very soon drops to the side. His whole appearance and behaviour are indicative of cerebral and spinal inertia.

Excessive Movement.—In another type of aments all movement is in excess, and the condition is one of chattering, ceaseless activity. This also is noticeable soon after birth, and the remark is often made by the parents that the child "never sleeps." This, of course, is not really the case; for although these children do not have regular long periods of sleep like ordinary children, or even ordinary idiots, there is no doubt that they do have brief but frequent snatches. There is equally no doubt, however, that their sleep is very light and readily disturbed. This condition is the antithesis of the one just described, and is due to hyper-excitability of nervous tissue. For some time after birth it is manifested as an excess of spontaneous movement, but, as the motor cells acquire connexions with sensory and ideational areas, this type of movement alters, being replaced by actions of a higher order. Of these there are three chief forms—namely, ideo-motor repetitive actions of subconscious type ; ideo-motor repetitive actions of conscious type ; and impulsive volitional actions. It is to be remarked that, although these varieties of excessive movement are very common in amentia, they are not characteristic of that condition, but may occur in a merely neurotic child. Most of these forms of excessive movement are accompanied by a diminished capacity for sustained attention, and this is well seen in the restless ament whose attention is so distracted by every sight, sound, or feeling reaching his sensorium that steady continuous work becomes an impossibility.

In a considerable number of aments excessive action is chiefly pronounced in certain groups of muscles, and, by being constantly repeated, the movements acquire an automatic and subconscious character. They are then popularly known as *tricks* or *habits*. The most frequent of these are spasmodic frowning and knitting of the eyebrows (which may be symmetrical or unilateral), grinning, smiling, and grimacing ; nodding and shaking of the head ; shrugging of one or both shoulders ; opening and shutting of the hands, and swaying of the body ; biting the nails, sucking the thumb, and many others of like character. The characteristic of these movements is that, at first irregular, they subsequently tend to be repeated at more or less regular intervals, and are particularly marked when the child is in the presence of strangers and conscious that he is being observed ; further, unlike the irregular, purposeless movements of chorea, they are definite co-ordinated acts. Originally it is probable that many of them had a purpose ; for instance, I have sometimes traced the repeated shaking of the head, which is very commonly seen in neurotic children, to the presence of long, straggling hair hanging in front of the eyes. The frequent repetition of the act produces in time a kind of obsession, and this leads to its automatic unconscious performance when the original cause has been removed. In aments it often lasts throughout life.

Closely related to these automatic actions are others of a somewhat higher character, inasmuch as they are always voluntarily performed. Dr. John Thomson* enumerates the chief of these as pica, or dirt-eating, sucking the tongue, thumb, etc., biting the nails, head-rolling, head-banging, rocking and swaying movements of the body, and masturbation. Dr. Thomson says that " the normal act causes little pleasure to the healthy child, whilst its morbid counterpart has an extraordinary fascination for the children who practise it. . . . The essential character which serves at once to distinguish these habits from certain motor neuroses (*e.g.*, spasmus nutans and habit spasm), which some of them superficially resemble, is their *deliberateness*. The child's will is implicated; and what he does is done intentionally—at first, at least—because he likes doing it. They have a strong tendency to occur when the patient is feeling dull and not being interested by his surroundings. They are almost always stopped when the child's attention is taken up with anything that interests him."

Finally, another type of excessive movement is seen in the impulsive volitional actions which are of such frequent occurrence in certain mental defectives. With these persons, an idea is no sooner presented than it is acted upon, quite regardless of right or wrong or possible consequences. Many of them belong to the milder degrees of amentia, and some are by no means unintelligent; but their whole life is actuated, not by intelligence, but by impulse. The essential basis seems to be an undue motor excitability, and the defective deliberation and control allow this to have free play. They comprise the " unstable " type of aments, of whom more will be said in subsequent chapters.

Inco-ordinate Movement.—Co-ordination, in the wide meaning of the term, requires a series of motor explosions which are regular in time, degree, and sequence, as well as their harmonious

* John Thomson, "On Certain So-called 'Bad Habits' in Children," *Archives of Pediatrics*, April, 1907.

adaptation to the various sensory stimuli concerned in the movement performed, particularly those coming from the muscles. It is therefore dependent upon perfectly working sensory, commissural, and motor mechanisms; but even where these exist, as in the normal child, perfect co-ordination is only attained by constant practice.

In persons suffering from even the mildest degree of amentia, co-ordination is often acquired with difficulty, and remains imperfect; and although many of them may learn to use their hands with a considerable amount of dexterity, the balance and movement of the body often continue clumsy and ungainly. It is frequently years before the mentally defective child manages to lace his boots, button his clothes, or manipulate his spoon at table. Even the best of them (with a few remarkable exceptions) rarely attain to the precision and neatness of movement of which an ordinary well-trained child is capable.

In the lower degrees the defect is still more marked, and many imbeciles experience the greatest difficulty in picking up a pin or a coin, and are incapable of any but the coarsest movements. Ireland remarks that considerably more imbeciles than normal people are ambidextrous; but I think it is not that both hands are used equally well, but rather equally badly, and I should prefer to say that they were adextrous. Many of their defects of speech are due to imperfect muscular co-ordination.

An extremely delicate test of the degree of control over muscular action is afforded by the "transfer" and "imitation" movements of Dr. Warner. In performing imitation movements, the child stands a little distance in front of the observer, who performs a series of extensions, flexions, and other movements with his own arm, forearm, hand, and finally individual digits, each of which the child must imitate as it is performed. In the transfer movements the child stands with closed eyes and extended hands. The observer then performs passive movements upon the digits, etc., of one limb of the child, who is required to make corresponding movements with the other. Dr. Warner tells me that he considers these tests to be extremely delicate, and that even in a healthy person slight imperfections may be observed as the result of fatigue.

Finally, it may be remarked that anomalies of movement

Nervous and Mental Characteristics of Amentia 117

due to localized or general disease of the brain are not uncommon in aments. The chief of these are nystagmus, athetosis, epileptiform and epileptic convulsions, and chorea ; but they do not differ from similar affections in the mentally sound.

Speech.

The speech of aments is a matter of considerable interest and importance, for several reasons. In the first place, defects of speech are very frequent, and their examination affords a means by which certain sensory, associative, and motor functions may be conveniently tested and recorded. Further, quite apart from its mere mechanism, the language of these persons is one of the most valuable means we have of gauging their stock of ideas and the general capacity and nature of their intellects ; whilst in the milder degrees the training of speech, if conducted upon scientific principles, and after a careful study of the needs of the individual, is a very important means of improving sensory and motor functions, and regulating mental action generally.

True speech is not merely the ability to utter articulate sounds : it is the faculty of using words to express thoughts ; and before this can take place certain conditions must be fulfilled. These are, firstly, the power to hear sounds ; secondly, a conscious recognition of the object or idea for which the sound heard is the symbol ; thirdly, an ability to reproduce the sound as the expression of the same object or idea. It is thus seen that the faculty of speech is composed of an *afferent* pathway (normally auditory, although exceptionally other sensory channels may serve instead, as in lip reading), with its prolongation to a higher conscious station ; of a connexion between this conscious station and the motor speech centre ; and thence an *efferent* pathway to the muscles concerned in phonation and articulation. In addition, there is good reason for thinking that a more direct and subconscious connexion exists between the sensory and motor centres. The nervous mechanism concerned in speech may therefore be represented by the capital letter **A**, in which the side-limbs denote the afferent and efferent paths respectively to and from consciousness, and the cross-piece the shorter subconscious connexion between the sensory and motor stations.

In the normal child sounds are differentiated in the early months of life, but it is not until he is nearly a year old that he begins to associate words with objects and ideas, and to understand what is said to him. At this age he has still little command over the motor speech centre, the first evidence of activity in which consists of cooing and babbling interjections of spontaneous origin similar to the incessant small movements of fingers and toes. Presently, however, owing to the faculty of imitation, these irregular sounds become co-ordinated into copies of those he hears, and very soon after this the child acquires the power of expressing his simple thoughts and wants by articulate speech. After this progress is usually rapid, and during the third year the child may possess a vocabulary of several hundred words.

In the ament defects of speech are exceedingly common, probably being present to some extent in fully three-quarters of all cases. In these persons the advent of speech is nearly always delayed, the first indication of spontaneity in the motor cells, which normally appears during the third or fourth month, not being noticed until much later. It may be five, six, or even more years before the mentally deficient child gives utterance to a definite word as the expression of an idea. In the severest grades of mental defect the faculty is never developed, and the majority of idiots are incapable of articulating a single word. Others of this degree can say a few monosyllables, such as " man," " cat," but none of them are capable of forming sentences. In the imbecile speech is usually present, and he is able to understand and speak short sentences ; but his vocabulary is small, and his utterance often almost unintelligible. In the feeble-minded degree, imperfections of utterance tend to be somewhat less, and the vocabulary considerably more extensive ; but these persons are usually neither capable of forming nor understanding a sentence at all complicated in its construction.

It is thus seen that on the whole there is a tolerably close relationship between the capacity for speech and the degree of mental defect, and this led Esquirol to suggest the use of this faculty as a means of classification. But to this there are many exceptions : some quite low-grade imbeciles are possessed of exceedingly good articulation and fluent speech, whilst a small number of the feeble-minded are limited in their utterance to a few words, and even these may be almost unintelligible. The remarkable genius of Earlswood Asylum, of whom a description will be given in a subsequent chapter, is an excellent example of this latter class. It is true that those imbeciles whose speech is so fluent often have little or even no idea of the meaning of the poetry or sentences they so glibly repeat, and it is quite open to question whether their articulatory capacity properly comes within the strict meaning of the term "speech." But, even apart from this, I am of opinion that there is no such constant relationship between wealth of ideas and capacity of expressing them as would justify us in accepting speech as a means of differentiation; and the physician must be upon his guard against judging of the degree of mental deficiency by the amount of speech.

In cases where there is no deafness, and speech is markedly deficient, it is highly probable that *some* degree of defect is present, and delayed speech is often one of the first signs to attract the parents' attention, and causes professional advice to be sought; but, as an indication of the *amount* of defect, expression and general behaviour may be of far more importance than speech.

Defects of speech may be due to anomalies of the sensory, motor, or intellectual (association) pathways; but in most cases it is the two latter which are chiefly at fault. *Sensory* defects may be auditory, causing an imperfect perception of sounds; or they may concern the tactile and muscular sensations coming from the tongue and lips during the act of articulation. It has already been remarked that the range and delicacy of the sensorium of the ament is often diminished, and in a few more or less actual deafness is present. I do not think, however, that imperfections of hearing play a very important part in the defective speech of these persons.

Anomalies of the *motor* mechanism are much more frequent, and these comprise imperfections of the cortical speech centre, or of the end organs concerned in the production of voice and speech. With regard to central defects, pure motor aphasia is rare; but one boy, who was under my care for several years, was a perfect example of this condition. In this case there was at times considerable inattention; but the boy had no loss of hearing, and could understand and obey commands perfectly well. He could also make grunting and other inarticulate noises, but the only approach to a word which we could get him to say after years of training was "Cuckoo." This case, however, was one of secondary and not primary amentia, and resulted from an attack of encephalitis in the early months of life. Another and much more common cortical anomaly is the want of co-ordination which results in stuttering and stammering. Peripheral deficiencies are exceedingly numerous, and the whole character of the voice and speech may be profoundly altered by deformities of the tongue, lips, teeth, and palate, as well as by enlarged tonsils and adenoids. I doubt, however, whether shortness of the frænum linguæ ("tongue-tied") can ever be considered a cause of delayed or even imperfect utterance.

Defects of pronunciation are exceedingly common in even the mildest grades of amentia, and are generally attributable to imperfect co-ordination. It is not usual to find any marked impairment of the vowel sounds, the chief imperfections being noticed in the consonants ("lalling"). The physiological alphabet of Wyllie* forms the basis upon which many interesting observations have been made in recent years, amongst which those of Dr. Henry Ashby† and Dr. Lapage‡ deserve particular mention. To this latter inquirer we are indebted for a most careful research into the consonantal defects of the feeble-minded child, and the following table is to a great extent compiled from his work. In this table the consonants are placed in the order in which Dr. Lapage found them most frequently defective, the sounds commonly substituted being also shown (see Table XIII.).

It is of interest to compare this defective power of pronunciation, which is so common in aments, with the marked aptitudes in this respect of some of the lowest savages. Darwin, in his "Voyage of the *Beagle*," relates that the Fuegians "could repeat with perfect correctness each word in any sentence we addressed to them, and they remembered such words for some time. . . . All savages appear to possess, to an uncommon degree, this power of mimicry. I was told of the same ludicrous habit among the Caffres; the Australians, likewise, have long

* Wyllie, "Disorders of Speech," 1904.
† Ashby, "Speech Defects in Mentally Deficient Children," *Medical Ξicle*, October, 1903.
‡ Lapage, *op. cit.*

Nervous and Mental Characteristics of Amentia 121

been notorious for being able to imitate and describe the gait of any man, so that he may be recognized." As will be seen in speaking of idiots savants, such extraordinary powers are occasionally present in aments; but they are the exception, and not the rule.

The disorders of speech which are chiefly due to *commissural* and *intellectual* defects include the misapplication of words and the inability to recall appropriate words; whilst it is only to be expected that where ideas are few the vocabulary will not be

TABLE XIII.
Consonantal Defects.

	Consonant.	Commonly replaced by	As in
Most frequently defective	1. Th	F or T	Fumb, tee*f*, mou*f*, *t*ank.
	2. R	Y or L	Yabbit or *l*abbit, pa*ll*ot.
	3. Y	R or L	*L*ellow.
	4. S	T or Ts	Tissors, *t*soap.
	5. G	D	Dun, do*d*, su*d*ar.
	6. Ng	D	Strin*d*.
	7. Sh	Tsh or T	Tsheep, Tshu*d*ar, *T*irt.
	8. K	T	Tat, *t*oat, bla*t*.
	9. V	B	Belvet.
	10. L	Y	Yeg, *y*ad.
Less frequently defective	11. F	T	To*tt*ee.
	12. Z	Dse	No*dse*.
	13. W	M (or omitted)	Mindow.
	14. P	T or D	Dader.
	15. N	D	Tose, Ped, Ped*d*y.
	16. D	T	Toor, la*t*.
	17. T	D	Dee*f*.
	18. M	B	Jab.
	19. B	P	Pag.

extensive. The enunciation of the grown-up ament often retains much of the character of childhood, whilst a general brain inertia (sometimes, however, a timidity under examination) causes speech to be slurred, hesitating, indistinct, and at times almost unintelligible. As Max Müller remarks, correct and distinct speech requires a definite mental effort, and of this many aments are incapable.

In some aments the condition known as *coprolalia*, or "filthy speech," exists. This is a more or less sudden outburst of language of the most vile and disgusting character, and it is remarkable that it often occurs in persons brought up amid every refinement. It is usually accompanied by a general state of mental excitement, for which, however, no cause may be discoverable, and it has considerable analogy to the motor convulsions of the epileptic. It is also common in the insane.

Finally, mention must be made of that curious speech disturbance known as *echolalia*. In this condition, although the child can, and often does, use words to express his ideas, any question put to him is followed, not by a reply, but by its repetition. Sometimes, after repeating the question once or twice, the child will answer it; but in other cases he is merely repetitive, and often copies the tone and manner of the questioner with remarkable exactitude. I recently saw a mentally defective child with this peculiarity, whose parents assured me he could speak quite sensibly, and yet to my questions the only words I could get out of him were, " What is your name ? " " Who is this ? " (pointing to his mother), " Shut the door," and similar repetitions of every question or command. This condition is not very common, and is somewhat difficult to explain. I am disposed to think that it may be due to the child's consciousness being so swamped or occupied (by emotions of fright or anxiety in some cases at the presence of a stranger or unaccustomed surroundings) that auditory sounds only reach a subconscious motor idea centre, and are thence immediately translated into speech. There is, in fact, a short-circuiting of the nerve current. This condition, as far as I am aware, does not occur in persons of normal mental development, although it is, of course, by no means uncommon for a person to speak who is totally unconscious of his surroundings. Many normal children, whilst busily engaged in some occupation, will repeat words which are pronounced near them, without seemingly understanding the words or being at all aware of the fact that they have copied them. It is presumably by a similar subconscious mechanism that echolalia occurs.

It has already been mentioned that some aments have an extraordinary faculty for repeating sounds with extreme accuracy. This ranges from the humming of a tune to the repetition of poetry or sentences in an entirely unknown tongue. The subject will be again alluded to under Idiots Savants, but it is worthy of passing mention in this place.

CHAPTER VIII

FEEBLE-MINDEDNESS IN CHILDREN
(MENTALLY DEFECTIVE CHILDREN)

THE term *feeble-mindedness* is applied to the mildest of the three degrees of amentia. In the extent of their deficiency there is no difference between the feeble-minded child and adult; but as the former are subject to the provisions of a special Act of Parliament, which brings them within the jurisdiction of the education authority, it is necessary to consider them separately. In this chapter, therefore, we shall consider feeble-minded persons below the age of sixteen years, or, as they are designated in the Act, mentally defective children; those over this age will be described as " feeble-minded adults " subsequently.

After the passing of the Education Act of 1876, making attendance at public elementary or other schools compulsory, attention began to be directed to the educational needs of the mentally deficient. It became apparent that a group of children existed who were so far defective that they could not be satisfactorily taught in the ordinary public schools, but who were not sufficiently defective to be certified as imbeciles or idiots under the Idiots Act of 1886. Many particulars regarding this class were brought to light through the inquiries of medical men and scientific and philanthropic societies, amongst whom special mention must be made of Dr. Francis Warner, Dr. Fletcher Beach, Dr. Hack Tuke, and Dr. Shuttleworth; the British Association, the British Medical Association, and the Charity Organization Society. The researches of Dr. Francis Warner in particular were of the most painstaking nature, and were based upon the examination of 100,000 school-children.* As a result of these inquiries,

* See " Report on the Scientific Study of the Mental and Physical Conditions of Childhood," Parkes Museum, 1895; also " Report on the Feeble-Minded," etc., C.O.S., 1892.

a Departmental Committee of the Board of Education was appointed in 1896 to consider and report upon the question.

This Committee presented its report in 1898.* It recognized that a number of children existed in public elementary schools who, in their mental capacity, were intermediate between the ordinary " dullards " and certifiable imbeciles, and it estimated the proportion of this class as approximately 1 per cent. of the elementary school population. Its inquiries showed that these children were incapable of receiving proper benefit from the ordinary instruction in these schools, but that they were capable of receiving considerable benefit from the individual attention and instruction given in special classes—that, in fact, under such conditions there was a fair prospect of many of them being enabled to take their place in the world. It considered that these defective children would suffer by association with imbeciles, and should not, therefore, be educated with them; and it recommended that special classes and schools should be established to meet their requirements. This report led to the passing in the following year of the Defective and Epileptic Children (Education) Act.

This Act (62 and 63 Vict., ch. 32, 1899) was the first legal recognition in this country of the mildest or feeble-minded grade of amentia. It defines the class as those children who, "*not being imbecile, and not being merely dull and backward, are defective—that is to say, by reason of mental (or physical) defect are incapable of receiving proper benefit from the instruction in the ordinary public elementary schools, but are not incapable by reason of such defect of receiving benefit from instruction in such special classes and schools as are in this Act mentioned.*"

This Act, therefore, clearly differentiates between the mildest degree of amentia and the more pronounced affection of imbecility, and although it does not apply the term " feeble-minded " to this class, the condition it defines is clearly identical with that to which this term has for long been specifically applied in this country. Mentally defective children are, in fact, the juvenile feeble-minded. The Act permits the local education authorities to establish special classes and schools for the mental defectives

* " Report of the Departmental Committee on Defective and Epileptic Children." 1898.

within their district, and where such are established attendance is compulsory up to the age of sixteen years, instead of fourteen, as in the ordinary schools. Unfortunately, owing to its permissive and not obligatory nature, the Act still remains a dead letter in many parts of the country ; but since it has been adopted by the whole of London, as well as by over twenty of the largest towns of England, the education of mentally defective children may now be said to have become an integral and important part of the educational system of the nation.

The investigations instituted by the Royal Commission of 1904 throw further light upon the number and condition of this class ; but, whilst agreeing in several respects with the conclusions previously arrived at, they differ on two important points.

Firstly, as will be seen immediately, the 1 per. cent estimate is found to be somewhat too high ; secondly, a more extended experience of these children shows that the views which were formerly held as to the amount of amelioration under training, and their possibility of becoming self-supporting citizens, are too optimistic.

Numerical Incidence.

As the result of a careful analysis of the reports of the Royal Commission, I estimate that the mean average incidence of mentally defective children throughout England and Wales is 0·73 per cent. of the children on the registers of public elementary schools. This number is somewhat lower than previous estimates, but as these inquiries, in addition to being more recent, were obtained under more favourable methods of examination, and also embrace a larger variety of districts, I am inclined to give preference to them. These figures, however, do not include defective children who, for various reasons, are not attending elementary schools, and if these be included the total number of mental defectives is raised to 0·83 per cent. of the school population. I calculate that in the whole of England and Wales the approximate total of these children is 50,665.

But, as will be seen from the accompanying Table XIV., showing the percentages in the respective districts investigated, this is the mean average of two widely divergent extremes. In Durham, for instance, the percentage is only 0·24, whilst in Dublin it is as high as 1·85, and it becomes necessary to consider the cause of these extreme variations.

Much of the difference is clearly due to the fact that the incidence of mental abnormality in general (insanity and amentia) is not uniform throughout the country, but is subject to very considerable variations from causes which at present are not fully understood. This we shall not consider. But there are smaller variations which appear to be decidedly dependent upon

TABLE XIV.

SHOWING THE PERCENTAGE OF MENTALLY DEFECTIVE CHILDREN TO THE PUBLIC ELEMENTARY SCHOOL POPULATION IN CERTAIN DISTRICTS INVESTIGATED BY THE ROYAL COMMISSION OF 1904.

	District.	Percentage.
Urban	Manchester	1·20
	Birmingham	1·03
	Hull	0·30
	Glasgow	0·74
	Dublin	1·85
	Belfast	0·50
Industrial	Stoke-on-Trent	0·59
	Durham	0·24
	Cork	0·35
Mixed industrial and agricultural	Nottinghamshire	0·66
	Carmarthenshire	0·76
Agricultural	Somersetshire	0·61
	Wiltshire	0·55
	Lincolnshire	0·96
	Carnarvonshire	0·47
	Galway	1·33

sociological and other influences, and since these relate, not to mental abnormality in general, but to the particular class with which we are now dealing, they must be referred to.

Relative Incidence in Town and Country.—It has been shown that although amentia as a whole is more prevalent in rural, and insanity in urban, districts, and the number of idiots and imbeciles in the country far exceeds that in the towns, nevertheless the incidence of mentally defective children is decidedly greater in the towns than in the country. In view of the fact that these children differ only in degree, and not in kind, from the idiots and imbeciles, this is in itself singular ; but it becomes even more so when it is found that the feeble-

Feeble-Mindedness in Children 127

minded adult, who is simply the mentally defective child grown up, is not more prevalent in town than in country, but is actually less so.

What, then, is the cause of this excess of mentally defective children in a town as compared with a country environment ?

The answer which at once suggests itself is that the many adverse factors of the environment of our towns, the improper feeding, the faulty ventilation, the overcrowding, and, in fact, slum life generally, are responsible for the excess ; and since a history of morbid heredity is often very difficult to obtain in these cases, the (perhaps not unnatural) conclusion has followed that environment plays a very important part in the production of this mild degree of amentia. That feeble-mindedness may occasionally so result I do not deny, but I believe that the increased incidence of mental defectives in towns is to a great extent apparent only, and is due to the inclusion of a number of children who are not aments at all.

In examining school-children in both town and country, I have often been struck by the fact that the ill-washed, ill-clad, and ill-fed—in short, the victims of faulty environment—were not as a rule the mental defectives. In fact, such children were often alert and quick-witted beyond the average, although probably by no means keen on book-learning. This fact led me somewhat to discount environment as being a frequent cause of amentia. Next, in examining certified mental defectives in special schools, I discovered a proportion of cases which I had no hesitation in saying were not aments at all, but merely suffering from backwardness, and this caused me to make some inquiries as to the number of such children who *recovered*.

Now, the essence of mental defect is that it is incurable, and by no " special " education, however elaborate, can a case of amentia be raised to the normal standard. Some defect must always remain, and upon this fact all authorities are agreed. When, therefore, it is found that a proportion of the urban defectives attending special schools are returned as cured to the ordinary schools, it is clear that an error of diagnosis has been made, and that they were not defectives. The proportion so returned varies very much in different towns, and in many the special classes have not been established sufficiently long to form a reliable test. The following is the percentage (of the admissions) of " mentally defective " children who have so far been returned *cured* to ordinary schools in some towns in which I made inquiries: Birkenhead, 6 per cent.; Bradford, 15 per cent.; Bristol, 3 per cent.; Derby, 5 per cent.; Leeds, 2 per cent.; Leicester, 20 per cent.; Liverpool, 4 per cent.; London, 10 per cent.; Nottingham, 10 per cent.; Plymouth, 8 per cent.; Sheffield, 4 per cent. I think these figures show conclusively that a varying, and in some cases considerable, proportion of the town defectives are not aments at all. On this point I may quote the opinions of two physicians who have had large experience of these children. Dr. Evan Powell, of Nottingham, writes: " I agree with you that a large number of so-called defectives are in reality not so, but are merely suffering from temporary arrest." And Dr. Ralph Crowley, of Bradford, writes: " I have no hesitation in saying that, where many go back, the reason is to be found in the fact that the children in the first place belonged to the ' merely dull and backward group.' "

I shall have occasion again to refer to these cases of delayed development, which simulate mental defect, in speaking of diagnosis; but I have thought it well to allude to them here for the reason that the neglect to distinguish them may cause totally erroneous views as to the increased prevalence of mental deficiency in towns, as well as of its cause and its possibility of cure. It seems to me probable that the real incidence of defect in town is not much, if any, greater than in country districts.

With regard to the **social status** of these children there is little to be said. The labouring classes have no monopoly of morbid heredity, and, although I am unable to give any actual figures, my general impression is that mental defect is just as prevalent amongst the upper as the lower classes of this country.

With regard to **sex**, there is a considerable preponderance of males, the relative proportion of boys to girls being practically as three to two.

Description.

Mentally defective or feeble-minded children differ greatly in the degree of their deficiency. The lower members of the class closely approximate to, and cannot be distinctly separated from,

PLATE III.

MENTALLY DEFECTIVE SCHOOL-CHILDREN.

FIG. 11.

FIG. 12.

FIG. 13.

FIG. 14.

FIG. 15.

FIG. 16.

[*To face page 108.*]

the imbeciles. The higher members, on the other hand, are but little removed from the merely dull and backward of the normal population. It is therefore clear that no general description can be given which would be applicable to every mentally defective child ; but the following are the chief characteristics of the class. Illustrations of the milder degrees are shown in Plate III.

Physical Condition.—A small proportion of children suffering from mental defect would pass muster as normal if their diagnosis rested upon inspection only ; but such cases are exceptional, and the majority present unmistakable anomalies of bodily structure or function, as well as of mental development.

Anatomical anomalies, or so-called stigmata of degeneracy, are usually neither so plentiful nor pronounced in the feeble-minded child as in the imbecile or idiot ; nevertheless Dr. Lapage, as a result of his examination of 200 children, found such to occur in no less than 90·5 per cent. of the total number examined. The defects were usually in combination, and in 23·73 per cent. were triple. In my experience the cranium is the most common site of defects, and I believe it to be abnormal either in shape or size, asymmetrical, bossed, or ridged, in fully half of these children. When the child first comes to school, and between the ages of seven and ten or twelve years, the maximum circumference is usually about half an inch less than that of a normal child of corresponding age and sex ; but this discrepancy becomes more and more marked, and by the fourteenth or sixteenth year the difference may be as much as an inch, or even more. Next in frequency to the cranium, anomalies of the palate are found ; whilst malformations of the external ear and of the eye and its appendages occur a little less often.

Inquiries will nearly always show that in these children dentition, standing, walking, and speaking have been abnormally delayed. It may be four, five, or even six years before the child says a word. This retardation continues with advance in years, so that at every period of its school-life the mentally defective child compares unfavourably in its bodily growth and acquirements with the one of normal intellect. Moreover, the bodily functions are often imperfectly performed : the circulation is feeble, so that chilblains and sores are frequent in cold weather; assimilation is defective, consequently the child remains thin and ill-nourished; the vitality generally is diminished, and catarrhs and ill-health are exceedingly common. It was ascertained by Dr. Ashby that the children in special schools at Manchester averaged 2 to 4 inches less in height and 3 to 12 pounds less in weight than the normal. To some extent this may be due to the nature of the environment in these cases. As already stated, the home conditions of the feeble-minded are often very faulty, and I have usually found that the defectives in the country are sturdier and of better physique than are those in the towns; but this is not the full explanation, for the same applies to normal children, and, whatever their situation, mentally defective children compare unfavourably with their mentally sound fellows.

Abnormalities of Nerve Action are very frequent. In some children there is a general diminution of activity, and such are heavy, stolid, tardy in response, and laboured in all their movements. In others the reverse is the case, and all movement is in excess. Such children cannot sit or stand still; they are distracted from their task by every little thing around them, and they are often full of " tricks " and " habits." Co-ordination of movement is slowly and laboriously acquired. The making of pothooks and hangers presents difficulties unknown to the ordinary child, and paper-folding, card pricking, and the simple kindergarten occupations are in the first instance performed with a laborious clumsiness. Many of the milder defectives, as a result of special training, do learn to use their hands extremely well, but even these rarely acquire the degree of dexterity attainable by an ordinary child who has been similarly trained. In some instances speech is accompanied by " spreading " action, as seen in corrugation of the forehead, grinning, and at times twitching of the whole body.

The net result of these anomalies of nerve action is a peculiarity of balance and movement and of physiognomical expression which is exceedingly characteristic of the class, and which frequently enables the expert to detect mental deficiency at a glance. The expression varies from a look of heavy, immobile stupidity and vacuity, which is chiefly seen in those lacking in action, to a general restlessness and inattention to the subject hand, often accompanied by spasmodic twitches, tricks, and bits, which is characteristic of those in whom action is excessive. *Speech*, as well as being late in making its appearance, is defective in fully one-third of these children. It is very rarely lacking entirely, although the speech of some children, before training, is so imperfect as to be quite unintelligible to a stranger. The chief defects consist of a thickness and indistinctness of utterance, an imperfect articulation of consonants, and (rarely) stammering and stuttering. The former of these conditions is partly attributable to abnormal configuration of the palate, lips, jaws, or pharynx, and partly to a general brain inertia and inability or unwillingness to make the effort necessary for distinct enunciation. The consonantal defects are due to similar causes plus a want of co-ordination. It may be remarked that inability to pronounce, not one in particular, but *many* consonants very commonly indicative of mental deficiency.

Mental Condition.—*Sensation.*—In a small proportion of these children sensation is imperfect by reason of disease or anomalies of the peripheral or central organs; but on the whole serious sensory defects are not a prominent feature of the feeble-minded degree of amentia. Defects of hearing (which are generally due to disease of the middle ear) are present in about per cent., and defects of vision in about 15 per cent., of cases. Colour-blindness, although in many cases seemingly present, is not in reality any more common than in ordinary children.

But there is a great difference in the educability of the perceptive faculties of feeble-minded children. The ordinary healthy child possesses an initiative and enterprise which brings him into daily contact with sights, sounds, and impressions of every description. His faculties of attention and curiosity cause him to observe, smell, and handle everything he meets, and in consequence the range and delicacy of his sensorium soon becomes very considerable. The feeble-minded child is defective in many of these qualities; consequently the development of his sensorium has to be aided and encouraged by special means, and until this has been done his power of sensory discrimination is decidedly inferior to that of the normal child of similar age. I have frequently observed that, upon their admission to a special school, the sensory capacity of defective children is comparatively obtuse, and that they have little ability to discriminate between sensory impressions of the same order, but of slightly differing intensity. Under suitable training much of this is remedied, and the sensory functions of many of the milder types who have been thus trained does not seem to be much inferior to the normal. But the lower types are lacking in this power to develop, and in them the most persistent special training fails to bring the sensorium up to the normal level. In this latter class the organic sensations of pain, cold, hunger, and discomfort are also somewhat obtuse, but these do not appear to be so much affected as do the special senses.

Attention.—In the lethargic, inert type of feeble-mindedness there is a defect of spontaneous attention ; but this is never so marked in this degree as in the more serious grades of amentia. The general stir and excitement aroused by a visitor is much more pronounced in the special school than in the imbecile ward. On the other hand, active or voluntary attention is commonly in defect, both with regard to its intensity and its duration. The most trifling thing serves to distract these children from their occupation, so that even where the attention is readily gained, it is with difficulty held. Many of them become capable of pursuing a congenial task with a certain amount of patience, but the majority have neither power of concentration nor will sufficient to be capable of sustained mental effort against inclination or interposed obstacles. They must go with, for they cannot fight against, the stream ; and this lack of will-power and driving force is one of the most distinguishing characteristics of aments at all ages.

School-teachers often complain of the lack of *memory* of these children, and if this faculty is to be judged by their inability to remember items of scholastic knowledge, there would certainly appear to be a decided deficiency. Some of them have very great difficulty in connecting a word with a thing, or in recognizing a printed character or numeral as the symbol of a concrete object or number of objects. It is the same with colours : many can match colours perfectly well, thus proving that their colour-sense is not defective, and yet they may constantly confuse the *names* of colours. It is probably this which has given rise to the impression that colour-blindness is common amongst them.

It is not to be expected that such a child would remember historical or geographical data, but the defect seems to be rather one of association and comprehension of the abstract than of memory proper. In the tenacity of their memory for things which are really understood, I have been unable to satisfy myself that feeble-minded are at all inferior to normal children, and many of them retain items of knowledge which have been demonstrated by concrete examples, as in object-lessons, remarkably well.

As a class, mentally defective children are imitators rather than originators. They may faithfully reproduce, but they rarely create, and their faculty for evolving new ideas—*imagination*—is decidedly lacking. But some of them evince considerable cunning in the commission of misdeeds, as well as no little ingenuity in the invention of lies to escape the consequences; and in many there is abundant evidence of the existence of the day-dreams and flights of fancy which figure so largely in the mental life of the normal child. I have often seen them look forward with delight to the approaching Christmas-tree, and several of my little patients have taken me into their confidence in recounting their ambition to be a judge, a soldier, sailor, policeman, or engine-driver. Nevertheless, the fact remains that in constructive imagination and inventiveness there is usually a considerable defect.

Control is very feebly developed in these children, and action is always along the line of least resistance. Volition is by no means absent, but their behaviour is more often the result of sudden desires and impulses than of deliberate purpose. They are capable of such simple feelings as pleasure, pain, fear, astonishment, anger, surprise, and the like; but their emotions, like their sensations, are usually weak and evanescent. They are rarely stirred by hate, indignation, anguish, awe, or a consciousness of the sublime. They are readily amused by anything ridiculous and touched by anything pathetic; but they have little real sense of humour.

All of them are lacking in the logical, and most of them in the æsthetic, sense. In a small proportion there is, in addition, a marked deficiency or perversion of the moral sense, and such will lie, pilfer, and generally misconduct themselves, without the slightest compunction. Some of this type are exceedingly cunning, and a few are guilty of acts of marked cruelty to other children or to dumb animals. They will also make utterly unfounded accusations with a considerable amount of detail and appearance of truth. On the other hand, there are many who are contented, obedient, well-behaved, and affectionate, and they may even possess a tolerable conception of their moral and religious obligations. Some are capable of understanding and being influenced by simple theological doctrines, but on the whole the religious sentiment in these children is of a decidedly poor order.

Scholastic Acquirements.

All these children are greatly improved by suitable training, but their developmental capacity and response to education vary enormously. On this account it is convenient to divide them into three grades.

The **first grade** is composed of children who make tolerable progress in elementary school knowledge. They are capable of writing a simple letter, they can read children's books, and they can perform simple arithmetical exercises mentally, as well as the first four rules on paper. They have a knowledge of money values, and they can be trusted with simple commissions. Their handiwork is often extremely good, and they do little drawings, brush-work, cutting-out, basket and wicker work, rug-making, and the like, with a dexterity which is often surprising. They have some common sense, but they lack resource and judgment, and often initiative.

The **second grade** fall considerably behind the former in purely scholastic attainments, and also, although not to the same extent, in handicraft. They are rarely capable of mental, and seldom of paper, arithmetic, and their reading and writing ability extends no further than simple words of one syllable. Some are even unable to do this.

They can perform the same kind of manual work, but the result is not nearly so good, and they require more constant stimulation as well as much closer supervision. They have decidedly less general intelligence.

The **third grade** form a connecting link with the imbeciles, from whom, indeed, they are but little removed. The improvement effected by the special school is limited to the development of some capacity for manual work under supervision, and to the formation of habits of obedience, tidiness, and regularity. Their scholastic acquirements are practically nil.

As a concrete example of the difference between mentally defective and normal school-children, I may give the following brief account of the pupils attending a typical " special " school under the London County Council.

This school* contains over sixty defective boys and girls, who are divided into three separate classes, each under a mistress. In the *lowest class* the average age of the children is from eight to nine years, the youngest being seven and the oldest about twelve years. In age, therefore, they correspond approximately to normal Standard II., in which the school-work consists of— *Reading* equivalent to Æsop's " Fables." *Writing:* transcription and dictation equal to the same. *Arithmetic:* tables up to 12 × 12 ; pence table ; compound addition, subtraction, multiplication, and division ; four simple rules and problems introducing two or more rules at one time. *Drawing:* simple freehand ; use of ruler and set-square. *Geography. History. Object-lessons* in animal and vegetable life and simple science.

The work actually done by the defective children in this class consists of recognition of letters of the alphabet and reading words of three or four letters ; transcription of the same from a blackboard copy ; recognition of simple numerals, and writing the same from dictation ; simple addition up to ten and simple subtraction of single figures. None are capable of writing from dictation, and all sums are done in the concrete by means of beads or tablets. In addition, the children are taught the use of the ruler ; they learn simple paper folding and cutting, brush-work, and rough clay modelling. They also engage in musical drill and games.

The average defective child takes two years before he or she becomes proficient enough to be passed out of this class. Some never do attain to this proficiency, although they may be moved up on account of their size. A few are sufficiently

* Goodrich Road Special School, East Dulwich, S.E., in the charge of Miss N. Mumbray.

advanced to be transferred after six months, but I am of opinion that the majority of these are not really defective, but merely dull and backward.

In the *middle class* the average age is from ten to eleven, the youngest being eight and the oldest sixteen years. It thus corresponds to normal Standard IV., in which the work consists of—*Reading* from Geographical, Historical, and Literary Readers. *Writing*, the same, with short essays and letter-writing. *Arithmetic:* simple exercises in money, time, weights and measures; simple vulgar and decimal fractions. *Geography, History, Grammar, Object-lessons,* and *Drawing,* all more advanced.

The work actually done in this class is reading simple words of one and two syllables from Infant Reader I.; transcription and dictation in simple words of one and two syllables; addition, in the abstract, of simple numbers up to 100; subtraction of tens and units; simple multiplication and, rarely, simple division by one figure. The occupations consist of rather more advanced brush-work, paper-folding and threading, cutting paper in the form of leaves for flower-making, and clay-modelling. The average time spent in this class is about two years.

In the *highest class* the average age is twelve years, the youngest being ten and the oldest nearly sixteen. One-fourth of the pupils are over thirteen. They thus correspond in age with Standards VI. and VII., in which the school-work consists of—*Reading* from more advanced Literary, Geographical, and Historical Readers. *Writing*, the same, with short original essays on geographical and historical topics. *Arithmetic:* simple and compound practice; problems in greatest common measure and least common multiple; the first four rules in vulgar and decimal fractions. *Grammar*, with analysis and parsing. More advanced *History* and *Geography*. *Geometry* and *Model-drawing*. Elementary lessons in *Physics* and *Chemistry*.

The work done by this class consists of reading and writing equivalent to normal Standard II.; compound addition and subtraction up to 1,000, and simple multiplication and division. Excluding a few children—who, in my opinion, are not really defective—it may be said that the scholastic acquirements of none of these children come up to normal Standard II. In occupations and manual work they are decidedly better, and a considerable proportion of the children in this class can cut out and make simple artificial flowers, knit rugs and weave baskets, with a really very creditable amount of dexterity, which redounds in no slight measure to the patient, persevering, and systematic care of their teacher.

With the object of testing their capacity for attention, memory, and general comprehension, Miss Mumbray was good enough to place for me a collection of twelve small articles, such as a pencil, tape, bottle, scissors, etc., on a board, and let the children look at them for two minutes. The board was then removed, and the children given ten minutes in which to write down, either in words or graphically, the things they had seen. Out of eighteen competitors, all but one found it easier to draw than to write the names of the objects; five children remembered the whole twelve articles, four remembered eleven, four ten, one nine, one eight, two seven, and one only five. In the majority of the children the drawings were sufficiently good to enable me to readily recognize the several objects for which they were intended, whilst some were really excellent.

Such are the chief abilities and disabilities of mentally defective children. They differ, however, not only in the degree of their deficiency, but also in their temperament, disposition, and general behaviour. In fact, they possess individuality just as do normal children, although this is not, as a rule, a pronounced and dominating feature until after puberty. Moreover, there are certain readily recognizable clinical types of these children, just as there are of aments in general, whilst superadded complications are not uncommon. The great majority suffer from primary amentia, and although most of these are of the simple variety, between 5 and 10 per cent. are microcephalics, about 2 or 3 per cent. macrocephalics, and about the same number are of the Mongolian variety. In probably about 10 to 15 per cent. of these children the amentia is of the secondary form, most of them being of the vascular or post-febrile varieties. In a small proportion of these some degree of paresis or paralysis is present, although this is neither so prevalent nor so severe as in the imbeciles and idiots. Another small proportion are cretins, and in a still smaller number there is evidence of syphilis. Indications of rickets are not uncommon, whilst in about 10 per cent. of cases the feeble-mindedness is accompanied by epilepsy.

But whatever the particular features may be, there is one quality which characterizes all the varieties and grades of these children, and that is their inability to swim against the stream, or even to keep their heads above water, without the assistance of some kindly hand. Whilst the ordinary child of fourteen or sixteen years has not only a considerable knowledge of common things and events, but has in addition acquired notions of qualities and conceptions of the abstract ; whilst he has developed the faculty of comparing, relating and judging between these conceptions, and of tracing a connexion between cause and effect ; whilst his mind now enables him to take an intelligent interest in his daily work, and allows him to shape plans for his future ; whilst, in short, he has learned to put away childish things and has become capable of standing alone—the mentally defective one of similar age is still happy with his toys, and his whole behaviour and conversation still indicate the infantile and imperfect character of his mind. Bodily and mentally he is always in arrears, and with each advancing year his intellect is left farther and farther behind that of his more fortunate fellow. His special training has done much for him, in so far as it has inculcated habits of regularity and conformity to the will of others ; further, and more important, because it has converted him from a useless, and often dangerous, member of society into ⟨one⟩ capable of some amount of useful work. But this latter can ⟨only⟩ be accomplished under supervision, and the future of the ⟨feeble⟩-minded child, as he passes out of the door of the school ⟨for the⟩ last time into the great world beyond, will entirely depend ⟨on h⟩ow thorough and careful this supervision is.

Diagnosis.

⟨O⟩wing to the Defective Children (Education Act) of 1899, the ⟨diagn⟩osis of this condition has become a matter of considerable ⟨impor⟩tance, and merits our special attention. It may be ⟨remar⟩ked that parents sometimes resent a diagnosis of mental ⟨defect⟩, and the examiner may be called upon to convince a ⟨magist⟩rate of its accuracy, in order to enforce attendance at a special school. The points to be considered are : (1) The family history ; (2) the personal history ; and (3) the present state of the child. All these are of importance.

With regard to the family history, we have seen that morbid heredity occurs in a very large proportion of cases ; consequently its presence or absence in any given child is an indication of value. In secondary amentia, however, it is absent ; and even where existing in primary cases, it must be remembered that its ascertainment may be a matter of very great difficulty. In a large number of these children it is impossible to elicit more than the most fragmentary family history.

In investigating the personal history, inquiry must first be made as to whether the child's mental condition is of recent or long standing. In most cases of real amentia of the primary form, it will be found that some dullness or peculiarity has been noticed from infancy, and that there has been a general retardation of physiological development (see table of normal developmental data, p. 364). Thus, the child has usually been backward in cutting his teeth, in sitting up, in attempting to stand, to walk, and to talk. Delay in any one of these particulars is of little importance, for the range of normal variation is very considerable ; but delay in several particulars, provided there is an absence of bodily disease, such as rickets, etc., must be regarded as very suspicious, particularly if accompanied by a neuropathic family history. Exceptions to this occur in cases of *delayed* primary or *developmental* amentia, in which, although morbid heredity may be present, the bodily and mental condition of the child are often normal prior to the advent of some infantile illness or other determining factor.

Most cases of secondary amentia are the result of epilepsy, or of some serious toxic or vascular lesion of the brain, of which there will usually be a clear history. Prior to this the child's condition has been normal.

Lastly, the child himself must be carefully examined. In doing this it is necessary to remember that many children, whether defective or sound, are nervous and ill-at-ease under examination, and I think that a large number of mistakes in diagnosis arise from the inspector's failure to gain the child's confidence. This should be the first concern, and the whole examination must be quiet and deliberate, but kindly and free from the slightest appearance of harshness. The child must, of course, be compared with his compeers in age and social position.

The first point to be attended to is the physical condition, paying particular attention to the presence or otherwise of illness or disease, anatomical and physiological anomalies or stigmata of degeneracy, and abnormal nerve signs. The state of nutrition and the general physiognomy must also be carefully considered. By this examination indications of great value will be forthcoming.

Finally, an examination must be made of the child's mental condition. This is done by conversation, careful consideration of his manner, behaviour, general conduct, and scholastic and manual ability. It is impossible to lay down any precise rules, and skill in diagnosis can only be gained by a constant association with the class and familiarity with their characteristics as described in the preceding pages. There is no single psychological test ; but, as we have seen, the chief mental peculiarities of these children consist in a lessened range and acuteness of perception, defect of voluntary attention, crudity and childishness of ideas, feeble reasoning power and will, and, above all, deficient " common sense." In their general mental development and capacity, especially in their scholastic attainments, these children are markedly behind normal ones of similar age; although, as will presently be seen, inability to progress in school is by no means diagnostic of mental deficiency.

Dr. Warner says : " The trained observer can read off the physiognomy of the individual features and their parts, the facial condition and eye movements, the balance of the head and body, etc., as quickly as a printed line." To this I would add that the expert who has meanwhile been chatting with the child, by the time he has proceeded thus far, will also have arrived at a tolerably accurate estimate of the degree of mental capacity. A few simple tests as to the condition of the special senses, the extent of memory, the power of reasoning, and the scholastic and manual attainments, supplemented by particulars from the teacher or parent as to the child's habits and special propensities, will usually provide him with all the data necessary for diagnosis.

The Act of 1899 requires the mentally defective child to be differentiated from the " merely dull and backward " and the imbecile. It may therefore be useful to refer to the chief features of these, as well as some other not uncommon conditions of childhood, which may more or less closely simulate mental defect.

Dull and Backward Children.—The " dull and backward " children are the least intellectually gifted members of the *normal* population. They are a numerous group, but their proportion varies considerably in different localities. In some parts of Somersetshire I found them to the extent of 5 per cent., in others from 15 to 20 per cent., of the school population. On the whole, I think they are commoner in country than in urban districts. These children fall into two classes, according to whether the backwardness is confined to an inability to acquire school learning only, or affects the whole mental faculties. The former class are, as a rule, readily distinguished; but in the latter diagnosis may be a matter of much difficulty.

As an example of the dullards or dunces, I may mention the case of two brothers, aged ten and twelve respectively, who, during my examination of a large country school, were produced by their teacher as being very bad cases of defect. They were both in Standard II., and my examination showed that they were certainly unequal to the work. But I soon found that they had a very good knowledge of many details of country and farm life—of the cows, the corn, and the bird-nesting, and that they were by no means backward in the playground. In fact, I had little difficulty in demonstrating to the teacher that, although these boys could hardly do the simplest sum, and could only read and write words of one syllable, yet they had plenty of common sense, and were by no means mentally deficient. I have frequently found this failing to run in families, and in a conversation on this subject with an intelligent old dominie of a country school, I was shown an excellent example in three members of one family who were present in school at that time, and who were such hopeless dunces that their attendance seemed a complete waste of time. My informant told me that the father of these children, and *his* brothers and sisters, had all been through his hands in their turn, and they were just the same; but although the father could only just manage to scrawl his name, and could not read the newspaper, he nevertheless worked a small farm with complete success. Children of this kind occur in the towns also, and although they cannot or will not (I think it is a little of both) make any headway with their lessons, they are as sharp as needles on the playground and in the streets.

It is possible that some observers would consider this condition to be one of mild, but none the less real, mental defect. I do not think, however, that they should be so classed. Their family history is generally good; they are sturdy, well grown, free from stigmata of degeneracy, and fully up to the average in every faculty except ability to acquire book-learning. It seems to me that they are perfectly normal, and not diseased specimens of mankind, and that their condition is simply one of a somewhat tardy evolution of certain faculties, the result of the manner of life of generations of ancestors. However this may be, I am sure that inability to progress at school is not necessarily indicative of mental defect, and this fact the medical examiner must keep in mind, and not be led into a too hasty diagnosis from the school report only.

But in a certain number of children the backwardness is not confined to school-work; it is general. These children are not only dunces at learning, but they are dull at games and in outdoor and home life; in fact, their whole demeanour and behaviour are characterized by a more or less dull stolidity. Here, again, I do not think the condition is necessarily one of mental defect; it is physiological, and not pathological, although undoubtedly it is the normal in its lowest mental form. It is these cases which cause no little perplexity to the medical examiner, and an accurate diagnosis will need all his skill and experience. Perhaps the following points will help: The family history is decidedly useful, because if morbid heredity is at all pronounced it is highly probable that the case is one of real defect. I do not think that information as to the previous personal history is of value, for most of these generally dull and backward children resemble the real defectives in having been in arrears all along. Careful examination of the child is of the greatest importance. In a considerable number of defectives there are stigmata of and apparently suffering from undoubted mental deficiency, astonishes everybody by suddenly waking up.

I have already referred to these cases, and have shown that they form a variable, but often considerable, proportion of the pupils of " special " schools. There is, of course, no objection to their admission to these schools—in fact, the individual attention and special training thereby afforded are the very best things for them. It is, however, extremely desirable that the condition should not be confounded with real defect, as this leads to entirely fallacious ideas as to the prevalence, causation, and curability of amentia. It must be admitted that the diagnosis is often extremely difficult, and may be impossible until the touchstone—special training—has been applied. I think, however, that if the examination reveals an entire absence of morbid inheritance, if there are no stigmata of degeneracy nor signs of irregular nerve action, and if the state of nutrition is poor and the environment is known to be bad, that then there are grounds for suspecting that the case is one, not of arrested, but of retarded, development, and the diagnosis must be provisional accordingly.

Dullness due to Disease.—Children suffering from defects of vision, hearing, speech, or from serious constitutional disease, often appear to be dull and stupid, and might possibly be thought to be mentally defective. I do not think that the physician would be very likely to fall into this error, but it is necessary to bear the fact in mind, as such a mistake is often made by school-teachers. I have had boys and girls produced as cases of serious defect who merely wanted the attention of the oculist or nose and throat specialist, and I have examined a child returned as defective who was mentally sound, but suffering from severe pulmonary tuberculosis. Ordinary care should suffice to prevent these mistakes, although the presence of illness or disease does not, of course, negative mental defect.

Another condition, more often seen in the consulting-room than the school, which may give rise to a suspicion of amentia is that of nervous exhaustion. The child is dull, listless, and inattentive. He cannot be got to answer questions, and if given a simple sum he does it wrong. His co-ordination is imperfect, his memory is faulty, there is often tremor, his head may be small and asymmetrical, and his lower eyelids are baggy and relaxed.

The history will generally show that the mental hebetude is of recent origin, and that previously the child has been of ordinary, sometimes unusual brightness; but as against this the inquirer may elicit a neuropathic family history. The condition here is probably one of neurasthenia in a child with but a small reserve of nerve force. It is often accompanied by severe headache, and is usually the result of overpressure. These children form the class from which a considerable proportion of the insane population is drawn, and although most cases recover under suitable treatment, the dullness of mind occasionally persists until the child becomes a complete mental wreck. In older children this state may owe its origin to masturbation.

Epilepsy.—It is necessary to remember that, although the mentally defective child may be subject to fits, epilepsy may give rise to a transitory mental dullness which is not amentia. In most of these cases there will be a history of fits, but they may be nocturnal only, and unknown to the parents. The physician will then have to be guided by the loss of memory and alternating brightness and stupidity, which have little in common with the fixed mental state of the real defective. In many of these cases, however, amentia, and subsequent dementia, may be induced.

Insanity might possibly be confused with mental defect, but the relative rarity of this condition, and the usually evident fact that the child is suffering from a disorder, and not an arrest of mind, ought to prevent such a mistake.

Imbecility.—Having ascertained that the mental condition of the child under examination is not due to disease or ill-health, is not merely dullness and backwardness, but is really one of deficiency, the physician who is examining for the purpose of certification to a special school will be required to exclude imbecility. In pronounced cases of this latter there will be no difficulty, but in the milder degrees a differential diagnosis will be far from easy. The following points may be found of assistance:

As a rule, the mentally defective school child knows the names of common objects, and can give some account of their use, whilst the imbecile of corresponding age is generally lacking in this knowledge. Neither child may know his letters, but the mentally defective will usually recognize and name various articles shown to him in pictures. Speech is often a valuable indication, although it is to be remembered that many merely feeble-minded children speak exceedingly badly. It is rather the matter than the manner of speech which must be attended to, as showing the degree of general intelligence. Some imbeciles will repeat questions; others obviously fail to understand what is said to them; others ramble on in an utterly nonsensical manner, and are quite incapable of carrying on the simplest conversation. The inability to execute some simple command or the manner of doing so often affords most useful information. Above all, however, the imbecile is markedly deficient in common sense. He can rarely be depended upon to perform any simple errand or task unless watched the whole time, and he often will sit outside in the rain and get wet through without making the slightest effort to shelter.

If there should be any doubt in the examiner's mind, then I think it is kinder to give the child the benefit of it. It may seem a small matter, but it is to be remembered that for children of the working classes, who cannot afford to pay considerable fees, the only alternative to the special school is often the workhouse or county asylum. Excellent special idiot asylums exist, it is true, but in the absence of means admission into these is often a tedious process. I should certainly hesitate to commit a possibly improvable case to an institution which does not profess to have training facilities, until he had been tried, and found wanting, in a special school.

CHAPTER IX

FEEBLE-MINDEDNESS IN ADULTS

Definition.—The term *feeble-minded person* is applied to an individual suffering from the mildest degree of amentia, who is over the age of sixteen years, those under this age being known as " mentally defective children."

The feeble-minded person is defined as " *one who is capable of earning a living under favourable circumstances, but is incapable, from mental defect existing from birth or from an early age, (a) of competing on equal terms with his normal fellows, or (b) of managing himself and his affairs with ordinary prudence.*"

Number.—The inquiries of the Royal Commission show that about 40 per cent. of all aments in this country are feeble-minded persons, and I calculate that in England and Wales on January 1, 1906, their approximate total was 54,114. This number is rather less than half the total insane on the same date, and corresponds to 1·57 feeble-minded persons in every 1,000 population. But the incidence is not uniform throughout the country; it varies directly with the prevalence of mental abnormality in general (which is subject to a very considerable range of variation); it also differs according to the environment. The prevalence in the respective areas investigated has been shown in Tables I. and IV., pp. 6 and 10, from which it is seen that the feeble-minded adult, both absolutely and relatively, tends to be commoner in agricultural than in urban districts.

The cause of this is not at first sight clear, for these persons are but grown-up defective children, and this latter class is apparently much more numerous in the towns than in the country. As I have shown, however, there is good reason for thinking that a large proportion of the so-called mentally defective children of our towns are not defective at all, but simply suffering from delayed development ; so that the real incidence of mentally defective children is probably not appreciably greater in urban than in rural areas. In addition, the increased competition of town life is decidedly unfavourable to the feeble-minded adult, and there is evidence to show that as a consequence a certain number of those born in towns are gradually squeezed out into the country.

Sex.—On the whole, males and females occur to about an equal extent, and the investigations of the Royal Commission show that, of a total of 4,291 feeble-minded persons, 2,179 were males and 2,112 were females.

Description.

Physical and Mental Characteristics.—The child is father to the man,' and in the main the physical and mental characteristics of the feeble-minded adult are similar to those of the mentally defective child ; but a few points of difference must be noticed.

With regard to their *physical condition*, the anatomical stigmata of degeneracy of course persist, whilst defects of stature and general development tend to become even more noticeable as the years advance, in comparison with the normal adult. On the other hand, a certain amount of improvement of function has taken place, so that the bodily nutrition is better, and the proneness to ailments not nearly so marked. Nevertheless, the expectation of life in the feeble-minded is decidedly less than in the ordinary population. Improvement is also usually een in nerve action, and although the diminution or excess of vement which characterized the child is still a feature of the lt, and the balance and carriage of the body are often clumsy and ungainly, the adult has, with the practice resultom years of experience, gradually acquired a certain amount cular control. As a consequence, the tricks, habits, and narked inco-ordination of the child are less frequently the adult.

rly with the *mental condition*. A certain amount of ive is acquired by experience, and mental action generally e been considerably improved by special training. But ity of these persons only extends to the things with which they are familiar, and they cannot rise to any work or circumstances outside their daily routine. They still show the same lack of observation and reasoning power, they have little ability to generalize or to apply their limited knowledge to new conditions, and their ideas still retain much of the crudity of childhood. It results from this that, although the feeble-minded adult may be, and often is, capable of useful employment of a routine nature under supervision, he is as a rule incapable of steering his own course, or even of providing for himself without some assistance. And when contrasted with a normal individual of similar age, his lack of mental capacity is even more prominent than in the case of the defective child.

On the whole, I think that the foregoing description is applicable to the bulk of the feeble-minded; but it must be remembered that there are many degrees, and that no account can be given which would fit every member of the class. This description is probably too flattering to some of the more pronounced defectives; on the other hand, to the highest types of all such an account may be somewhat unfair, for many of these are tolerably well grown and developed, and show little indication of their weakness if they are not scrutinized too carefully. Those of this mild grade belonging to the upper and wealthier classes—for poverty has no monopoly of feeble-mindedness—do not usually find the daily round of society beyond their capacity; they even marry or are given in marriage, and it is only when a situation arises which calls for management and judgment that their defect becomes patent. So long as they are under supervision they pass muster, but once let them take the reins and chaotic disaster speedily results.

It is, however, rather in the matter of *character* that the greatest difference exists between the grown-up and juvenile feeble-minded. Ordinary persons approximate to one common type much more in childhood than in adult life, and although individual differences are observable from the first few weeks of life, they become much more pronounced about the age of puberty. So it is with the feeble-minded. The advent of puberty often sees the evolution of habits and propensities which have the greatest effect upon the future life, and which have hitherto been latent. Possibly to a considerable extent these may be dependent upon the early environment and training, or absence of training; but heredity often plays an important part, as in the ordinary child. Whatever their origin, the mental defect and lessened power of control of these persons tend to bring these habits and propensities into extreme prominence.

These propensities are many and varied, and from the point of view of administration they demand the closest attention. Indeed, I would go so far as to say that, in dealing with the feeble-minded, there could be no greater administrative blunder than to treat mental defect in the abstract, and pay no regard to these peculiarities of the individual. Some feeble-minded persons are placid, well-behaved, and industrious; others are perfectly harmless, but possess pronounced wandering proclivities; others are exceedingly facile; whilst yet others have a strong predisposition to insanity or crime. On the whole, I think that all of them may be divided into two main classes, according as their mental equilibrium tends to be stable or unstable, and these we may briefly describe.

Feeble-minded of Stable Mental Equilibrium.—Many feeble-minded persons are quiet, placid, inoffensive, and good-natured individuals who go on their way comparatively unmoved by the happenings of life. They are not insensible to pleasure, and they evince a certain amount of delight, just as would a child, at a theatre, a circus, the sight of a company of soldiers, or the like. They are also conscious of, and affected by, praise, rebuke, or ill-treatment; but their joy or sorrow is neither excessive nor of long duration, and their general demeanour is that of happy placidity. The mental constitution of such persons is in striking contrast to that of the class we shall next consider, and they may be appropriately designated as of stable equilibrium. I can give no precise figures, but my impression is that this type comprises about 30 to 40 per cent. of all the feeble-minded. Owing to the present lack of organization for providing these persons with suitable employment, a considerable number of them are idle, and spend their time roaming the villages and country lanes; but most of these will cheerfully carry a parcel or do any odd [job they] may be asked to do, and those for whom continuous [employment is] found prove themselves to be steady, industrious. [Ill]ustrations of this type are shown in Plate IV.

In the country a certain number of them are employed upon the land in some simple capacity, such as helping with the hay or corn, the plough or roots, scaring the birds, or bringing up the cows ; and although they cannot be trusted to do the full work of an agricultural labourer, they often take the place of a boy to the satisfaction of their employer, and they are quite worth their keep and the shilling or two a week they receive. It is probable that most moderate-sized villages possess at least one of these " softies," " naturals," " dafties,"or " not exactlies," as they are called ; and although they are at times made fun of by the urchins of the place, they are not, as a rule, unkindly treated. In the towns, on the other hand, this type is not nearly so common. Such persons may occasionally be seen selling newspapers, distributing bills, hawking firewood, or doing odd jobs for some charitably disposed person ; but the increased competition of town life is decidedly against them, and they rapidly tend to be squeezed further afield or to gravitate into the workhouse or some charitable institution.

The life of these persons is one of conformity to habit, and not to ideals. They rarely think of, much less make plans for, the future ; and the few who have vain imaginations as to what they would like to do or become are lacking in the necessary intelligence or will to direct their actions accordingly. Indeed, one of the most pronounced features of the feeble-minded person is his utter lack of purpose. If given work and told exactly what to do, he may often be trusted to do it ; he may even acquire the habit of performing the same task day after day, year in and year out, without supervision. But the work must be strictly of a routine nature, for he would be quite unable to cope with any unforeseen occurrence. And should he lose his employment, he is incapable of any strenuous attempt to seek more. To use a homely phrase, we may say that the bread of these persons must be put into their mouths.

The following is a fairly typical illustration of this stable type of high-grade feeble-mindedness :

A. C. is a man of twenty-two years, although he looks only about seventeen. He went to an ordinary elementary school, and was in the sixth standard when he left ; but his schoolmaster tells me that he was only moved up each year on account of his size and age, and that his scholastic attainments were really only equal to Standard III. During the two years following school he had several situations, mostly as errand-boy, but he was discharged from each place in turn on account of general incompetency. Then he was taken, largely from philanthropic motives, into a printing-office, and there he has remained until the present time. His work is purely mechanical, and consists in helping a man with the machine, carrying bales of paper, and so on. He began with a wage of nine shillings weekly; this has been increased, and he now has a standing wage of eleven shillings, but he often puts in overtime, and he usually earns about thirteen shillings. He lives at home with his parents, and he gives his money to his mother, who allows him a shilling weekly as pocket-money. When clothing or boots are required, his mother buys them, and, in fact, he is treated exactly as a child. He is perfectly happy and contented with his lot, and has no ambition to be other than what he is; but it is difficult to say what is going to happen when he has no home to go to and no parents to look after him. I asked him if he had ever thought of getting married. He said: "No." I asked him if he ever kept company with anyone. He said he did for a time, and used to " walk out " with a girl every night. To my questions as to what he used to say to her, he said : " She used to ask me how I was getting on at my work. I said : ' Pretty fair.' I used to ask her how she was getting on at her work. She said : ' All right.' " There do not appear to have been many love-passages, for he admits that he never kissed her. After six months the maiden tired, and she now walks out with one of his more enterprising mates. This youth once conceived the desire to join the Volunteers, and applied to the local non-commissioned officer. The Sergeant-Major, a shrewd man and a good judge of men, rejected him, and, when I asked if he didn't come up to the physical standard, said : " His body was all right, sir ; but he had too little brain-pan." He has a few stigmata, can read and write tolerably well, and can do simple sums ; he can also copy drawing very creditably, but he has little other knowledge. After a good deal of consideration, he told me that history was " what happened before," and that geography was " about towns and rivers," but he has no historical or geographical knowledge. I asked him which was the first war that he learned about. After much cogitation he said : " It was near Trafalgar Day. It was when Nelson fought. He defeated the Spaniards." On being asked how long ago that happened, after a very long pause he said : " From then to now, do you mean ?" and, on my replying in the affirmative, said : " About seven hundred." His knowledge of geography was of the same order, and although he told me he had got a Sunday-school prize, to my query as to who God was he replied, after much thought : " The Son of man."

I am acquainted with a feeble-minded man, *John C*——, who has steadily and industriously cracked stones by the roadside for the past forty years. He lodges in the village with a labourer and his wife, and the latter wakes him in the morning, gives him his breakfast, makes his dinner into a parcel, and sends him off to work. When dinner-time comes, which he knows by seeing the labourers in the field leave off work, he eats the contents of his parcel. Sometimes John feels hungry, and eats it before. About five o'clock, which he also knows by the passing of the postman, he leaves off work and returns to his lodging. He has his tea, sits by the fireside until about eight, and then goes to bed. Occasionally John has been known to get tired of work and come home in the middle of the afternoon ; but such lapses are very rare, and on the whole he is exceedingly methodical and industrious. He knows that Sunday is a day of rest, but he must be told that it is Sunday, or he would go to work as usual. John's landlord once played him the prank of not telling him it was the Sabbath, and he went off as usual without any suspicion. But he had intelligence enough to notice the trick on passing through the village, by seeing that the shop was closed, and he came back vastly amused at what he thought was a fine mistake. He receives a few shillings each week from the Rural District Council, and this he faithfully carries to his landlady, who allows him a penny now and then when he asks for it. This, however, appeared to be seldom, for John seems to be in the happy condition of having all his wants supplied.

One might describe many cases similar to these, both in town and country ; but it is unnecessary. They illustrate very well the stable type of feeble mind, and the manner in which routine work may be performed by this class with comparatively little supervision. I have even known several who have served their time in the army. It is necessary, however, to remember that their intelligence is limited, and that these persons must not be entrusted with work beyond their capacity, or the result may be disastrous. I may mention a striking example of this which occurred in the case of a feeble-minded woman resident in a workhouse. Her daily occupation was washing in the laundry, which she did very well. But one day the charge-nurse of the maternity ward most unfortunately gave her a baby to wash. She did so in boiling water, with, it need hardly be said, a fatal result.

But although these persons are capable of useful employment, they have no capacity to lay out the money they earn or to manage their affairs. Food, clothing, and shelter must be provided for them, just as with children, and in the absence of some one to look after them they soon get into a most woeful plight.

As an instance of their general " incapacity to manage their affairs with ordinary prudence," I may mention the case of a woman I met in a small village in Somerset. She was the daughter of the village shopkeeper, and upon her parents' death had inherited sufficient cottage property to keep her in comfort for the rest of her life. Unfortunately, however, no one was appointed to look after her, and so it came about that little by little she was diddled, by relatives and acquaintances, out of every penny she possessed, and when I saw her she had been taken in out of pity by the wife of a labouring man, who received a few shillings weekly from the parish to look after her.

Throughout the country there are hundreds of feeble-minded persons, many of them gentlefolk by birth, in like case. As long as they are provided with a home, and have parents or relations to generally supervise them, things go well. They perform little household and outdoor duties, take up simple hobbies like pokerwork, stamp-collecting, and amateur cabinet-making, and enter into the ordinary social amusements of the class to which they belong. Most of their friends recognize that they are not quite "all there," but they often pass muster with casual acquaintances. But once let them get away from the parental apronstrings, and assume the responsibilities of an independent existence, and their want of mental capacity is fully revealed,

PLATE V.

FIG. 20.—A feeble-minded girl of unstable mental equilibrium—facile type.

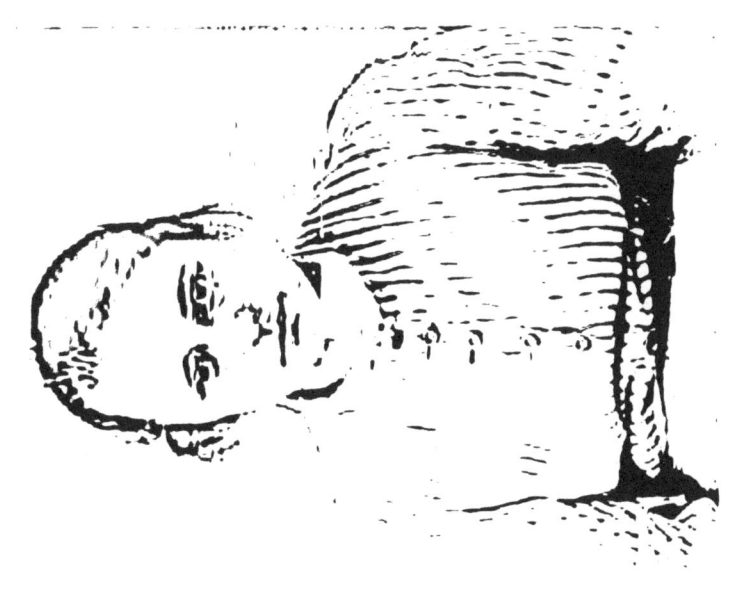

FIG. 19. A feeble-minded girl of unstable mental equilibrium; impulsive and deceitful.

[face page 154.]

and results in their complete undoing. In the case of feeble-minded girls this general inability to take care of themselves is particularly evident, and demonstrates in the most forcible manner the urgency of the need for their protection.

Lastly, it may be said that, although the religious and moral sense of these persons is rarely of a high order, most of them are conscious of the difference between right and wrong, and of the fact that they have certain obligations towards their neighbours. A goodly number, indeed, are quite capable of understanding simple theological doctrine.

Feeble-minded of Unstable Mental Equilibrium.—It is not, perhaps, surprising that the mind which is defective should also lack balance, and in a very considerable number of feeble-minded persons—indeed, I think in the majority—the mental defect is accompanied by more or less mental instability. This may not become evident until the physiological epochs of puberty or adolescence have been reached, and one meets many cases in which the whole disposition of the individual seems to undergo an alteration at these times; but often the condition can be detected in childhood, and is shown by the fits of irritability, excitement, moroseness, sulkiness, or so-called " bad temper," which are present in a considerable number of defective children.

The degree of instability varies much in different individuals, and at different times in the same individual. Some are simply giggling, emotional, and impulsive, liable to sudden fits of waywardness, but readily controllable, and on the whole capable of doing useful work. In these the attack has much of the character of an epileptic seizure. I have known one of this type, a silly, giggling, weak-minded girl, to plunge her head into a pail of water without the slightest hesitation when the suggestion was made to her. I have known another to set fire to a hay-rick, and another to dash her hand violently through a window-pane in a sudden access of temper. And yet all of them, on the whole, were good, willing workers and in fairly constant employment (see Plate V.).

In others, however, the instability is more persistent, and the person is so changeable and undependable that continuous employment is out of the question unless the closest supervision can be maintained. Many of these are girls, and the following case is a very good example of the type :

Alice S—— is a feeble-minded girl of nineteen years. She is the daughter of working people, and went to the Board-school until she was fourteen years of age ; but her schoolmistress says she could make nothing out of her, that when she left she could only just read and write, and that she was " always spiteful, untrustworthy, and a regular nuisance." Upon leaving school a situation as day-girl was found for her. She ran away on the third day, and refused to go back. Then she got another place, but only stayed a week, as her mistress " could not put up with her ways." This went on for over two years, during which time she had no fewer than twenty-two situations. She was then sent to a laundry training home, and here for the first few weeks she was much quieter, and it was hoped that she would settle down into good habits. But the hope was futile. The matron found that not the slightest dependence could be placed upon her word, that she was dirty in her person, lazy, an incurable pilferer, and up to the most cunning tricks to annoy and irritate her companions. She was therefore sent home again. Here she remained for some months, doing no work, and causing her relations endless trouble and worry. On several occasions she was brought home by the police, and finally, within a year of her return from the training home, she was admitted into the maternity ward of the workhouse. It was there that I first saw her, and although she was a strong, active girl, and quite capable of doing domestic work, she was nevertheless so erratic, impulsive, and generally irresponsible, that nothing could be made of her.

The following is a somewhat similar case :

F. H., a feeble-minded man twenty-three years of age, having the appearance of a youth of seventeen or eighteen. He is 5 feet in height, and weighs $7\frac{1}{2}$ stones, is thin and ill-nourished, and has numerous stigmata. He is extremely unstable, at times being quiet and well-behaved, at others noisy, restless, talking and laughing to himself, and interfering with those around him. In one of these fits he attacked his brother with a hammer. He has had several situations, but has been unable to keep any of them. He can read, write, and do simple sums, and although, when questioned, he seems to have a fair knowledge of many common things, he is too defective and unstable to turn his knowledge to any account. He is a ready talker when in the mood, and gives a very plausible account of himself. He says he is " what you call an orphan, and only has his brothers to be acquainted with now. Was in the sixth standard when he left school, and used to do reading, writing, arithmetic, composition, and geometry ; was never at the top of the class—master used to think him a backward boy. It was writing from memory that was his worst subject ; memory was always bad. Once got a prize for religious catechism. Was in the boys' home learning printing for nine months, but they gave him the sack because he accidentally spoilt a special job. Has had other chances, but never seemed to get on very well. If they would only give him another chance he would do his very best. Several of the other people have interfered with him, and then, of course, he has to take care of himself. One of his masters told him he would get on better if he didn't allow himself to be put on, and looked after himself more."

Lastly, in another group of these unstable feeble-minded a condition of actual insanity is present ; but as this is a complication of some importance, I shall deal with it in a subsequent chapter.

As already remarked, it is likely that a good deal of the mental instability of these persons is the result of an unsuitable environment in early life, and it is probable that careful and firm training during childhood might do much to prevent it. I am certain, however, that it is often inborn, just as is that instability of mental constitution in the " normally " developed which is so often the precursor of insanity ; indeed, I am inclined to look upon all feeble-minded persons of this type as potential lunatics.

It is easy to understand that criminal actions may be committed by such persons, and there is no doubt that they constitute the great majority of feeble-minded criminals. Also, although probably not so often the case to-day, there is little doubt that in years gone by those of the facile type were frequently made use of to further the schemes of the professional law-breaker. It is not merely that these persons are incapable of appreciating the consequences of their actions—for that might be said of most of the feeble-minded—it is rather that their defect is accompanied by such a general instability of mind that they are either peculiarly susceptible to any suggestion, or are liable to flare up for the most trivial cause. The train is already laid; it is only the spark that is needed. It is obvious that feeble-minded persons of this type are much more likely to come into contact with the authorities than are the harmless, placid individuals previously described ; and, as a matter of fact, a very large number of them are inmates of our workhouses, prisons, asylums, or charitable homes. Still, the number at large throughout the country is not inconsiderable, as is shown by the investigations of the Royal Commission.

To this account of the chief characteristics of high-grade amentia we may add that, although defect may be especially pronounced in some one particular faculty, there is no one single defect which is typical of the feeble-minded ; consequently there is no single psychological test of this condition. Deficiency of some kind or other is always present in the highest mental faculties, but the nature of this is subject to considerable variation. In many persons there is an utter inability to acquire any kind of book-learning, although they may use their hands with considerable dexterity. On the other hand, there are those who possess a remarkable aptitude for acquiring certain forms of knowledge, but who are so simple and childish as to be utterly incapable of providing for their daily wants. Others, again, as will be seen in treating of moral defectives, have a degree of cunning and intellectual quickness of a certain order which is at times astonishing ; whilst yet others are stolid, indifferent, and entirely negative. It is thus seen that mental defect cannot be looked upon as simply a lower grade of the normal, but as a distinctly pathological condition in which defective is accompanied by *irregular* development. Considered from the standpoint of practical daily life, the essential characteristic of this class is that, whereas the ordinary person, whether quick or dull witted, profits by his experience, and learns bit by bit to take care of himself and to adapt his behaviour to the exigencies of the moment, the feeble-minded person does not. The defective and irregular development of his mind have combined to bring about a lack of that quality which is so hard to define, and yet so essential to success in life—common sense. In any doubtful case, therefore, the diagnosis must rest not only upon the examination as to the present mental attainments, but also upon a careful consideration of the previous history and general conduct of the individual.

CHAPTER X

IMBECILITY

Definition.—The term "imbecility" (Latin *imbecillus*, doubtfully derived from prefix *im* for *in*, and *bacillus*, a staff—one without a stay or support, hence feeble, helpless) is applied to the medium grade of amentia; and although there are many members at the top and bottom of this grade whose condition closely approximates to the feeble-minded and the idiots respectively, nevertheless it is one which, as a whole, has tolerably well-defined features. The imbeciles stand above the idiots in the possession of an instinct and capacity for self-preservation, but below the feeble-minded in their inability to perform sufficient work to contribute appreciably towards their support. They are defined as "*those persons who, by reason of mental defect existing from birth or from an early age, are incapable of earning their own living, but are capable of guarding themselves against common physical dangers.*"

Number.—I estimate the total number of imbeciles existing in England and Wales on January 1, 1906, at approximately 25,096 persons, corresponding to 0·73 per 1,000 of the population. The class is thus nearly half as numerous as the adult feeble-minded, and about three times as numerous as the idiots. The inquiries of the Royal Commission show that imbeciles, both absolutely and relatively, are more prevalent in rural than in urban and industrial areas.

Sex.—There is a slight preponderance of the male sex, and out of 1,807 imbeciles discovered by the Royal Commission 959 were males and 848 females.

Description.

All imbeciles come within the terms of the definition just given, in that they are possessed of wit sufficient to understand and avoid the common physical dangers which threaten life, but insufficient to enable them to pursue any continuous occupation in such a manner as to provide for their sustenance. But whilst they all agree in these common characteristics, a certain proportion present such marked physiognomical, and often mental, peculiarities as to form distinct clinical varieties. These varieties will be described in subsequent chapters, the general account which will here be given of imbeciles and idiots, as also the preceding account of the feeble-minded, referring to the *simple* type (the "genetous" group of Ireland), to which the great majority of these persons belong. (See Chapter V., "Classification.")

Physical Condition.—In a small number of persons suffering from imbecility of the secondary form (in which the defect is accidental and symptomatic of some acquired disease of the brain), the features, stature, and general bodily development may not differ from those of a healthy person. But these cases are not numerous, and in the great majority of simple imbeciles of the primary form the bodily as well as the mental condition is obviously defective.

Occasionally gigantism is seen, but as a rule the stature is several inches less than that of the normal person. In addition, the body is ill-formed, its balance and carriage are ungainly, there are many oddities of walk and bearing, whilst stigmata of degeneracy are both numerous and prominent. The expression of the imbecile is usually in itself sufficiently striking to attract attention, varying from a stolid vacuity to a fatuous and childish smile or a look of sly cunning. Disturbances of physiological function are common. Various degrees of paralysis occur in a certain proportion of cases, and probably about 40 per cent. of all imbeciles suffer from epilepsy. On the whole, the bodily condition is so distinctive that even the casual observer has little difficulty in dubbing one of this class a "daftie" or "natural." (See Plates VI., VII., and VIII.)

Mental and Nervous Condition.—In some imbeciles one or more senses are markedly defective; in others there is an increased, and even extraordinary, delicacy of a particular sense; in the majority, however, sensory perception is obtuse, and a condition similar to, but decidedly more aggravated than, that in the feeble-minded is present. The tenacity of memory for isolated events does not appear to be diminished, but the range of memory

PLATE VI.

FIG. 22.—A mischievous, excitable imbecile; usually grimacing as shown.

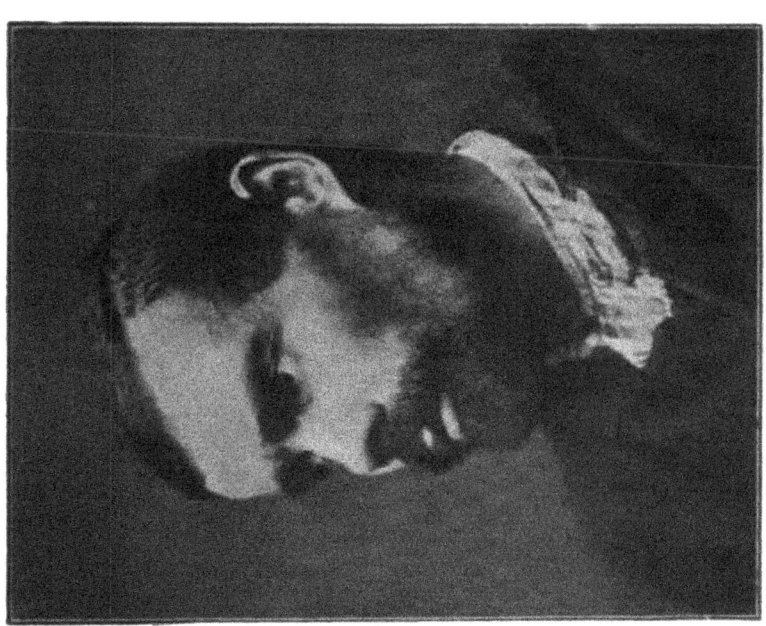

FIG. 21. A mentally unstable imbecile suffering from melancholia.

To face page 160.]

Imbecility

is decidedly inferior to that of the normal person. Probably this is largely the result of a defective power of association. Spontaneous attention is sometimes diminished. Although many of these persons can be habituated to perform routine work of a simple kind, they are quite incapable of any task necessitating a sustained effort of voluntary attention. A few of the milder types show some evidence of imagination, but the majority are lacking in this faculty. Where the feeble-minded person will invent plausible excuses to escape punishment for his misdeeds, the imbecile will simply lie without embroidery. Many have some capacity for imitation, and at times this may be educated sufficiently to enable them to perform a certain amount of useful work; but they readily tire, and in most cases the value of the work done is not worth the supervision it entails. Occasionally the imbecile is markedly defective in volition, but this is by no means always the case, for some of these persons have exceedingly strong desires, and are capable of no little strength and cunning to obtain their ends. It is often easier to lead than to drive an imbecile, and some of them are particularly amenable to suggestion. It is, however, in reasoning capacity that the most marked difference is seen between this class and the feeble-minded. The latter person, although very defective, is still capable of simple mental comparisons, and of arriving at simple judgments; but the imbecile is usually quite incapable of this.

Abnormalities of movement are of very common occurrence. In the apathetic type there is a general diminution, whilst in those of the excitable form all movement tends to be excessive. These excitable imbeciles are constantly chattering, running about, and generally interfering with everybody and everything. Some of them are violently aggressive, and a few become actually insane. Defects of co-ordination are both commoner and more pronounced than in the feeble-minded. Most imbeciles can speak, although they can only form simple sentences, and their vocabulary is a meagre one. The development of the faculty of speech is invariably late. A few are exceedingly voluble in conversation, but the matter is childish and inconsequent. Defects of pronunciation are numerous. Some imbeciles can read simple sentences, and a few learn to add and subtract upon their fingers, or by means of beads, but the scholastic acquirements of the class as a whole are of a very low order.

Like the feeble-minded, imbeciles are divisible into two chief types—the apathetic or stable and the excitable or unstable. Accordingly, they differ greatly in their disposition and general behaviour. Some are harmless, inoffensive, and well-behaved; but others are just the reverse, and require to be under constant observation. These latter are often sly and cunning to a degree, always in trouble, and possessed of pronounced immoral and anti-social tendencies. Some are clean in habits, modest, and possess a tolerable sense of decency; others are absolutely destitute of any idea of shame or modesty. Masturbation is very frequent in imbeciles of both sexes, and many of them will practise it in the most open and outrageous manner. Some imbeciles show unmistakable signs of jealousy, and a considerable number are exceedingly vain, not only of their dress and general appearance, but even of their mental attainments.

The following cases illustrate the chief features of simple imbecility:

C. H., a fat, smiling man, forty years of age, who has been in the asylum since boyhood. He has no friends living, and, beyond a note in the case-book to the effect that there is insanity on the father's side, there are no particulars. He understands and can carry on a simple conversation, but he cannot read or write, and has no conception of figures. He can, however, appreciate pictures, and will laugh immoderately at anything funny. He is good-tempered and obedient, but a perfect glutton, and will devour any scraps he comes across. He is too defective to be entrusted with any work without supervision, but is very willing and spends most of his time with the gardener in the grounds.

J. F., male, twenty years old, is the last born of a family of seven, of whom three died in early childhood (one of convulsions); two are said by the mother to be "all right," whilst another is mentally defective. The father is alive, but has been insane in an asylum twice; one of his brothers died in an asylum. The mother is alive, but in delicate health. Two of her sisters and one brother died of consumption.

James has always been "delicate": he did not stand until turned two years, and did not walk until his fourth year. He was

PLATE VII.

FIG. 24.—A mischievous, restless, and destructive imbecile of semi-Mongolian type; usually grimacing as shown.

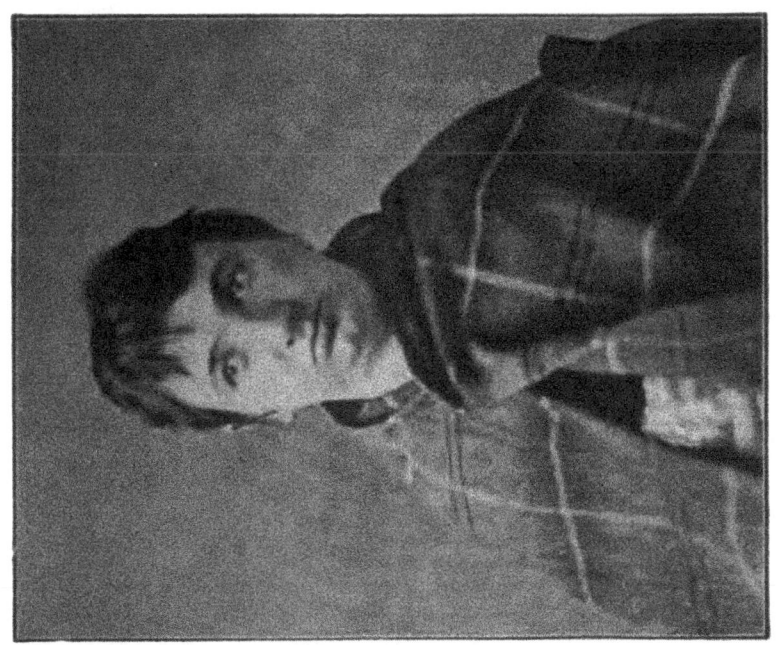

FIG. 23. A pronounced imbecile; quiet and well-behaved, but idle and untidy.

Imbecility

over five before he spoke, and even now his vocabulary is limited to about a dozen words. These he uses very sparingly, and it is rarely that he can be got to reply to questions, although he understands a good deal of what is said to him. He never attended school, as the head-mistress refused to have him. He remained at home quite unoccupied until fifteen years of age, when he became unruly and more than his mother could manage. Since then he has been in the asylum.

He is a short, stumpy, fat youth, with coarse features, large outstanding ears, and a typical imbecile expression. He has a high saddle-shaped palate and very irregular and malformed teeth; but these cannot always be demonstrated, as he usually obstinately refuses to open his mouth. Cranial circumference, $22\frac{1}{2}$ inches. There is no paresis, but he is clumsy and heavy in all his movements. There is no marked defect of the special senses, but, owing to his usually taking not the slightest notice of any question addressed to him, he has been thought to be deaf. This, however, is not the case, as I have succeeded in getting him to turn round at the sound of a whistle, and have once or twice managed to get him to execute a simple command. He seems to have little idea or care as to where he is, is apparently unconscious of the flight of time, and is, as a rule, perfectly stolid and inoffensive. But occasionally he has a noisy outbreak, and then he will rush about the ward grunting, yelling and interfering with anyone whom he meets. I saw him one day munching biscuits out of a paper bag which had been brought him by his mother. I intercepted each biscuit on its way from the bag to his mouth. He did not seem to mind, and placidly got another out of the bag. When I had succeeded in getting them all, he stood still in a vacant, perplexed sort of way, without seeming to understand or care very much, and after a time he walked away.

H. C., female, seventeen years; is the fourth of a family of eight, three of whom died in infancy; insanity and epilepsy on father's side. No others are mentally affected, but mother says they are all delicate. The patient never seemed the same as the other children from birth, and did not walk until her fourth year. She has never talked properly.

She went to school for several years, but never learned anything, and finally the mistress said she had better not come any more. She has since been at home. She understands a good deal of what is said to her, and can execute simple commands, such as to shut the door or fetch a chair. She can answer simple questions in monosyllables, but her articulation is so defective as to be unintelligible to a stranger. She has no idea of number, and everything is " two." She has no knowledge of letters, but can make strokes and ciphers on a slate. She also knows the names of the common objects of the house. On the whole, she is quiet, obedient, and good-tempered. She is not actively destructive, but will always pick a patch off her clothes if they have been mended, and her chief joy is to have a piece of cloth given her to fray out. She cannot wash or dress herself, but can feed with a spoon, and is of clean habits. Her chief peculiarity seems to be that, as soon as she takes the first mouthful of food, she invariably goes to sleep, and has to be wakened to finish her meal.

PLATE VIII.

FIG. 26.—An imbecile of the stolid, apathetic type; does a little work under supervision.

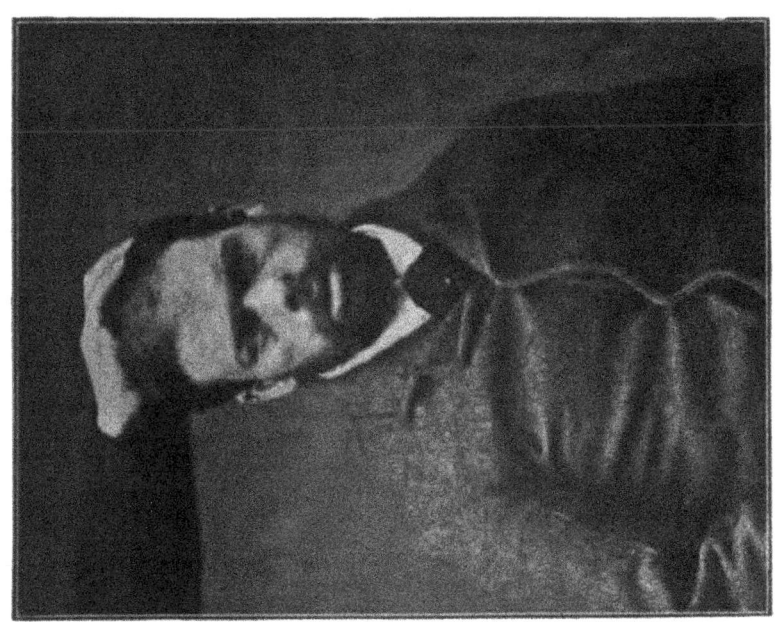

FIG. 25. A pronounced imbecile. Idle, destructive, and at times aggressive; subject to frequent epileptic fits.

To face page 164.]

CHAPTER XI
IDIOCY

Definition.—In the idiots we see the third and lowest degree of defect, and the mental deprivation in these persons is indeed such as to fully justify the term *idios* (a person " private," " apart," or " solitary ") which is applied to them.

The line between this class and the imbeciles has been variously drawn by different writers. Some would consider the presence or absence of speech as the criterion, but there are many imbeciles —and even feeble-minded—who cannot speak. Others, again, would use attention or volition, but these are not necessarily lacking in the idiot. If a line is to be drawn, and, if only for purposes of description, it is clearly a great advantage that we should have some means of differentiation, then I think that the absence of the instinct or power of self-preservation constitutes the most convenient one, and this we shall accordingly use.

The idiot is therefore defined as " *a person so deeply defective in mind from birth, or from an early age, that he is unable to guard himself against common physical dangers.*"

Accepting this as the criterion, it is at once seen that idiots are divisible into two groups. In one of these the defect is so profound as to involve the fundamental organic instincts, and even that of sucking is absent. These are termed *complete, absolute,* or *profound idiots*. In the second group the primitive instincts are present—there is even some glimmering of mind— but there is not sufficient intelligence to understand and avoid the common physical dangers which threaten existence. These may be termed the *partial* or *incomplete idiots*.

Number.—The number of idiots existing in England and Wales on January 1, 1906, was, approximately, 8,654 persons, corresponding to 0·25 per thousand of the entire population. The class is thus about one-third as numerous as the imbeciles, and comprises about 6 per cent. of all aments. As we have already seen, idiots are absolutely and relatively much more numerous in rural than in urban districts, and, taking areas with a similar incidence of total amentia, we find that there are often from four to five times as many idiots present in the former as in the latter situation. A similar variation of incidence with regard to environment has been shown to obtain with the imbeciles also, but the disproportion is much greater in the case of the idiots.

With regard to sex, the inquiries of the Royal Commission show that, of 585 idiots existing in the 16 areas of the United Kingdom which were investigated, there were 303 males and 282 females.

Description.

Partial or Incomplete Idiocy. — *Physical Condition.* — The various anatomical and physiological anomalies present in the imbeciles, and to a somewhat less extent in the feeble-minded, reach their maximum in the idiots ; and the members of this degree consequently present an appearance which is in itself distinctive. Some of them are grotesque, but the majority are such stunted, misshapen, hideous, and bestial specimens of morbid mankind that they arouse feelings of horror and repulsion rather than of levity. (See Plates IX. and X.) Paresis or paralysis is very often present, and this tends still further to aggravate their defective physical condition. In some cases this paralysis is due to a non-development of the tracts of the cord ; but in the majority it is the result of disease or severe gross lesions of the brain or nervous system superadded to the original developmental defect, such as porencephaly, hydrocephaly, microgyria, localized atrophies, and anomalies of the internal ganglia. The paralysis may be slight or severe. It may involve a hand or foot, or be a complete hemiplegia or diplegia. Many of these creatures are in consequence chair- or bed-ridden. Occasionally the condition known as " scissor-legs " is seen, in which e is paralysis of both lower limbs, with dislocation of hip-joints, so that the legs are permanently crossed like a

PLATE IX.

PRIMARY AMENTIA (IDIOCY).

FIG. 28.—A case of partial idiocy, accompanied by sclerosis.

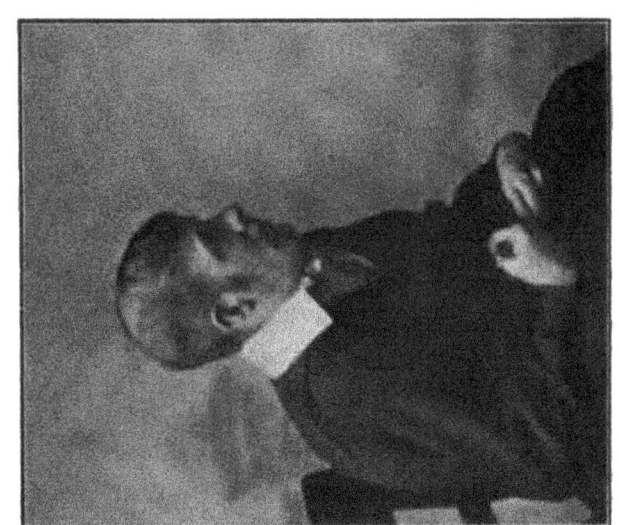

PRIMARY AMENTIA (IMBECILITY).

FIG. 27. A pronounced imbecile with right hemiplegia.

To face page 166.]

Idiocy

pair of scissors. There was a very perfect example of this at Darenth Asylum a few years ago. The feature of most of these paralyses is that they are the result of lesions occurring before or shortly after birth; consequently the limb involved is stunted in its growth and development.

Epilepsy is very frequent in simple idiots, and occurs in about 56 per cent. of cases; various forms of tremor and athetosis are also frequently seen.

Many idiots are extraordinarily voracious, and gulp down their food with such haste as to be in imminent danger of choking. It has more than once happened, where spoon diet has not been given, that tracheotomy has had to be performed for the removal of a lump of food from the larynx. In a few cases rumination is seen. Troublesome diarrhœa is a very common result of the gluttony of these persons. Ireland mentions two cases in which inordinate thirst was present, the patients drinking almost any kind of liquid in enormous quantities; neither was diabetic.

Most idiots are sterile, but this is not always the case, and in some sexual feelings are obtrusively evident. As a class they are unusually prone to disease and to early death, particularly from tuberculosis.

Mental and Nervous Condition.—Defects of sensation are very common in idiots, and although morbid conditions of the end-organs of special sense are very frequent, nevertheless the lack of perception seems to be more often due to a central than to a peripheral defect. All the senses may be affected, but it usually happens that one is most so. We thus find some idiots particularly impervious to sounds, others to sights, tastes, or odours.

It is difficult to test the memory of these persons, but on the whole I am inclined to think that it is usually in default. Imagination seems to be wanting altogether, but some of the milder types have a certain capacity for imitating the actions of those around them. Active attention is very deficient, but spontaneous attention is by no means always absent. Such thoughts as exist must be of the simplest description, and limited to objects immediately present to their senses. They have no power of reasoning, and although a few can connect simple words with the objects to which they relate, the majority cannot do this. Idiots have to be washed, dressed, and fed like little children; many of them are utterly inattentive to the calls of nature, but some can be taught habits of regularity and cleanliness in this respect. They are by no means lacking in energy and volition, and many of them apparently experience satisfaction in destroying anything they can get hold of; but their energy cannot be directed into any useful channel, nor are they even capable of intelligent play.

Tears are very rarely seen, but there is no doubt that some of milder degree are capable of the simpler emotions. They evince anger, passion, and fright, and some of them will run away with a look of alarm upon the entrance of a stranger. They seem to be absolutely lacking in any sense of right or wrong, and these ideas cannot be implanted in them.

Speech is usually absent, although a few learn to articulate such simple monosyllables as *man, cat, eat*, etc., but none of them can form sentences. Their utterances mostly consist of inarticulate grunts, screeches, and discordant yells; but there can be no doubt that these often express their feelings, just as do the cries of animals, and an observant physician or attendant is able by this means to discern whether they are satisfied or dissatisfied, contented or annoyed, sometimes even to interpret their simple wants. It is noteworthy that, although quite unable to articulate, some idiots will hum a tune which they have heard, with tolerable accuracy.

Movement is often abnormal in quantity and quality. In the apathetic type of idiots it is deficient, in the excitable excessive. In both these forms co-ordination is usually very imperfect, and they are hardly ever capable of any delicacy of manipulation. In standing, walking, or running the same defect of co-ordination is seen.

Apathetic and Excitable Idiots.—We have seen that the less-pronounced grades of defect are divisible into two classes according as they are of stable or unstable mental equilibrium; the same is true of the idiots, some of these being apathetic, and others excitable. The former are mild, placid, inoffensive creatures who give little trouble, and who even evince a certain amount of affection for those who feed and attend to them. The excitable type, on the other hand, are passionate, violent, untrustworthy, and intractable. Many of them are so exceed-

PLATE X.

FIG. 30. Partial idiocy of the excitable type.

FIG. 29. Partial idiocy of the excitable type.

[face page 168.]

Idiocy

ingly destructive that nothing is safe within their reach. They will destroy clothes, toys, picture-books, even furniture, and if left alone for a few hours, the probability is that they will either wreck the room or set fire to or seriously injure themselves in some way. I have seen several of this class in cottages where the only available means of curtailing their activities to a reasonable sphere of influence was to tether them to the table leg. Often they are exceedingly cruel to animals, and seem to experience pleasure at the cries of their unfortunate victims.

Those of this type who are chair-ridden still manage to find an outlet for their excitability in the almost ceaseless performance of automatic actions. Thus, some will spend the day turning the head from side to side or nodding up and down; others rock the body to and fro, or beat upon the chest with the hand, often keeping time to the movement with a monotonous, inarticulate chant; others unceasingly suck their fingers. These movements do not occur during sleep, and they are terminated by the advent of feeding-time or the entry of a stranger, although at times a visitor seems to stimulate them into still more violent activity. It is evident that they are attended with satisfaction, for the patients commonly resent forcible interruption, and resume the movements again the moment they are free. In a proportion of cases this condition of restless activity is not constant, but intermittent, and resembles the periodical outbreaks of maniacal excitement which occur in the milder aments. Such persons will rush about the room or dormitory uttering hideous screeches and yells. In moments of passion they will even hurl themselves violently against walls or floor, and in so doing often sustain serious injuries. But the process seems to be rather pleasurable than painful. Even in those of the apathetic type, the advent of puberty often ushers in a marked alteration of character and behaviour, and there are many idiots who, having been fairly manageable and inoffensive until this time, then become so destructive and unreliable that the restraint of an institution has to be sought.

The following are illustrative cases :

E. J., female, age thirty-two years. A pronounced history of insanity and epilepsy on the maternal, and alcoholism on the paternal, side. Has been in the asylum since seven years of age. A repulsive-looking woman with a muddy, freckled face, coarse red hair, and numerous stigmata ; cranial circumference, 21 inches. She can walk, but spends the day sitting in a chair turning her head from side to side, rocking herself to and fro, and biting her hands. She is of unclean habits and is unable to do anything for herself. She is quite deaf in the right ear, but listens attentively to the ticking of a watch held close to her left. She seems to have no knowledge of time or place, and apparently no understanding of anything said to her. But when the piano is played, she at once ceases her rhythmic movements and listens attentively. She cannot speak, but she will hum the tunes she has heard so well that they are readily recognized. As a rule she is harmless, but upon any attempt at examination she makes violent resistance and tries to bite, and she is at times spiteful and interferes with the other patients.

A. D. P., female. Has been in the institution since childhood, but the family history is not obtainable, as there are no friends living. On admission she was unable to dress or feed herself, and had no apparent understanding of anything said to her. She showed no curiosity, no imitativeness, and no power of attention. Her habits were unclean, and she was constantly dribbling from her mouth. She was a voracious eater. She was unable to speak, but addicted to violent yells, often interspersed with a peculiar sound like the braying of a donkey. She was at times exceedingly violent, kicking, biting, and scratching the nurses and other patients indiscriminately, and, in fact, was generally a source of endless trouble to the whole ward. She remained in practically the same condition until thirty-five years of age, when she had an epileptic attack. From this time until her death she was subject to occasional recurrences of the fits, and she died at the age of thirty-six, of gangrene of the lung, resulting from the aspiration of a small portion of food. The cranial circumference was 20 inches, and there were numerous stigmata of degeneracy.

On making a post-mortem examination, I found a very thick, dense skull with an absence of diploë. The brain was small, weighing 1,022 grammes, but, beyond being very simply convoluted, there were no naked-eye anomalies. Microscopical examination, however, revealed extensive imperfections of the cells of both brain and spinal cord like those already described.

Absolute, Complete, or Profound Idiocy.—In this condition we see humanity reduced to its lowest possible expression. Although these unfortunate creatures are, indeed, the veritable offspring of *Homo sapiens*, the depth of their degeneration is such that existence—for it can hardly be called life—is on a lower plane than even the beasts of the field, and in many respects may almost be described as vegetative. They come into the world without even the hereditary instinct of sucking. As they grow up they have to be fed, and would die of inanition amid abundance of food were it not put into their mouths. If they are conscious of excessive heat or cold, they are devoid of any idea of the remedy. They respire, assimilate, and excrete, but they have no sexual instinct, and cannot reproduce their degenerate species. They may be capable of inarticulate cries, but they cannot speak. They possess the power of muscular movement, but locomotion is absent. They have eyes, but they see not ; ears, but they hear not ; they have no intelligence and no consciousness of pleasure or pain ; in fact, their mental state is one entire negation. The short existence of most of these creatures is spent in bed, where they lie huddled up in an ante-natal posture. They are hideous, repulsive creatures whom Nature permits to enter, but not to linger, in the world, and in their life and death are revealed the culminating and final manifestation of the neuropathic diathesis.

Diagnosis.—The diagnosis of simple idiocy and imbecility can rarely present much difficulty by the time the child has attained to the age of five or six years. Even before that age, a careful consideration of the family history, of the general backwardness of development, and of the many indications of defective physical, nervous, and mental condition which should be apparent to the physician, although they may not be noticed by the parents, will usually suffice to make the nature of the case quite clear. The idiot or pronounced imbecile is usually either phenomenally passive or abnormally restless from the first few days after birth. In the one case he is inert, showing no tendency to suck or grasp, so that even the nipple must be held in his mouth ; no tendency to cry or to be attracted by any sight or sound ; no response to the caresses of his mother ; and, in fact, no spontaneity of any description. In the other case he is constantly crying, and refuses to be pacified ; he restlessly tosses about from side to side in his cot, and from time to time may have convulsions. In some of these cases the screaming and general restlessness are so constant that the parents will complain that the child never sleeps. With either of these conditions there are usually present various anomalies of anatomical development, and although I do not mean to say that the combination of stigmata with one or other of these unnatural states is pathognomonic of amentia, nevertheless it is extremely suggestive of that condition, and the probability is greatly increased should there be a neuropathic family history. Careful attention to these points will often enable a diagnosis to be made in the first or second year, and should prevent the physician deluding the parents with the vain hope that the child will " grow out of it." With the advance of each year the nature of the case becomes more obvious, for the progressive mental development of the normal child gradually leaves the ament farther and farther behind.

Where some added complication or particular pathological process is present, as in the special varieties of amentia to be described in subsequent pages, the clinical appearance is still more characteristic, and a diagnosis may then be possible at an even earlier age.

CHAPTER XII

THE CLINICAL VARIETIES OF PRIMARY AMENTIA

It is probable that nearly 90 per cent. of all aments belong to the primary group, and the majority of these, as already mentioned, present no special distinguishing features beyond the anatomical, physiological, and psychological anomalies common to primary aments in general. These, which may be termed the *simple* variety, have been described in the preceding pages.

A small proportion, however, present such special characteristics as to form distinct clinical types. The chief of these are the *Microcephalics* and *Mongolians*, and these will be described in the present chapter. We shall also briefly deal with some clinical subvarieties which are the result of superadded morbid complications.

The Grecian, American-Indian, Negroid, and other ethnic types which have been described by some authors do not seem to me to possess sufficiently distinguishing features to merit special notice.

MICROCEPHALIC AMENTIA.

By the term " microcephalic " is usually meant a person whose skull is less than 17 inches in its greatest circumference. But in view of the fact that other persons, with a greater cranial measurement than this, present similar mental peculiarities as well as skull configuration, I am disposed to think that the criterion should be one of shape rather than size. Most members of this variety belong to the more pronounced degrees of amentia, and, if the test of measurement be the one adopted, they probably do not comprise more than about 5 or 6 per cent. of all aments. If, however, the milder cases be included, and the criterion be that of cranial shape, this number is considerably increased, and probably reaches 10 or 12 per cent. Many of these latter are merely feeble-minded.

Causation.—The condition is one which has attracted much attention, particularly from anatomists, and two views have been put forward as to its causation. The first of these is that it is an atavistic variation ; the second, that it is a pathological condition due to premature closure of the cranial sutures.

One of the earliest advocates of the atavistic theory was Charles Vogt, of Geneva, who, in a paper published in 1867,* attempted to show that microcephaly was a reversion to a prehuman type. Many cases were examined, and most minute dissections made by accomplished anatomists on the Continent and in this country. Conclusive evidence was adduced in support of the view, and equally conclusive facts in denial of it. It was at a time when the evolutionary theory was attracting widespread attention, and it was not to be wondered at that the curious appearance of microcephalics should cause them to be looked upon as instances of a reversion to a simian type. It is unnecessary to enter into the pros and cons of the argument ; it is sufficient to state that the fact has now been established, as a result of many examinations, that microcephaly is not an atavistic variation, but a pathological condition, and that these persons, although degenerate, are still human.

The second theory, that microcephaly was due to a premature synostosis of the cranium, attracted hardly less interest. Baillarger[†] seems to have been the author of this view, and he enunciated it on the strength of some apparently very definite statements by the mothers of microcephalic children, that at birth the anterior fontanelle was closed. These statements were corroborated by Baillarger's examination of some cases in which synostosis was present. But it has since been found that many microcephalics exist in whom the sutures are not closed ; in fact, such is the exception rather than the rule, and hence this theory is now discarded. In the instances in which bony union has

---

* C. Vogt, Geneva, " Mémoires sur les Microcéphales ou Hommes Singes," 1867. On this subject see also " I Cervelli dei Microcefali," Professor Giacomini, Turin, 1890 ; also an excellent chapter in Dr. Ireland's work.

† Baillarger, *Gazette Médicale de Paris*, 1857, p. 482 ; also Cruveilhier, " Anatomie Pathologique Générale," Paris, 1876.

taken place, it is much more likely to be the effect than the cause of the arrested cerebral development.

The real truth is that microcephaly is neither atavistic nor accidental, but the result of inherited blight, just as is amentia in general. In most of the cases which I have examined morbid heredity was present; in fact, microcephalics usually come of a pronounced neuropathic stock, their brothers and sisters are often typical degenerates, and frequently one or more of them suffer from the same condition. They are simply the result of a more gross developmental arrest than that which obtains in the majority of aments.

Pathology.—The characteristic of this condition is a hypoplasia of the cerebral hemispheres, which is more particularly pronounced in the temporo-sphenoidal, parietal, and occipital regions, so that the posterior lobes of the cerebrum rarely suffice to cover the cerebellum. To this the peculiar "sugar-loaf" conformation of the skull is due. In most cases, although underdeveloped, the primary sulci may be traced; but in some instances these are very imperfect; in the majority of cases there is also a marked deficiency in the secondary gyri, so that the complexly convoluted aspect of the normal brain is entirely wanting. In addition, there is often localized agenesis of particular areas, resulting in the condition described as "microgyria," as well as gross developmental anomalies of the corpus callosum and internal ganglia. Not a few cases are complicated by some recent morbid process, of which the commonest are encephalitis and hydrocephalus. The cerebellum is smaller than the normal, but is not affected to anything like the same extent as the cerebrum. The hypoplasia nearly always involves the spinal cord, which is much thinner and shorter than normal. The parts most affected are the pyramidal tracts and columns of Goll, the anterior columns and direct cerebellar tracts somewhat less so. From the stage of development of the cerebral fissures, it is quite evident that the cause is one which has been at work before birth. Microscopical examination of these cases usually reveals a similar condition of irregular and imperfect development of the cells of the brain cortex to that already described. The anterior horn cells of the spinal cord also frequently show similar changes.

The weight of the brain varies very much in these cases. The lightest on record is the one described by Dr. Sander, as mentioned by Ireland, which only weighed 170 grammes (about 6 ounces). A case described by Dr. Fletcher Beach weighed 198·4 grammes, whilst the brain of the celebrated Helene Becker weighed 219 grammes. But these are somewhat exceptional examples, and typical microcephaly may be present with a brain weighing several hundred grammes more than these. The normal weight, it may be remembered, varies from about 1,100 to 1,400 grammes in the male (mean average, 1,374 grammes or about 48 ounces), and 1,000 to 1,300 grammes in the female (mean average, 1,244 grammes or about 43 ounces).

In view of the extreme smallness of the brain in these persons, the question naturally arises as to the influence of size of brain upon intelligence. There is, no doubt, a brain weight and cranial circumference so small as to be incompatible with anything more than a state of idiocy, and Félix Voisin places this at 13 inches circumference. It is tolerably certain that with a cranial circumference of 17 inches the mental capacity will not range above that of imbecility, and it is probable that the adult whose cranial circumference is more than 2 inches less than the normal minimum will be feeble-minded. But beyond this we cannot go, and even these statements can only be considered as of general application.

The average size of the skull in aments is decidedly less than the mean average of normal persons, although there are a few (excluding hydrocephalics) in which the normal measurements are exceeded. But even in aments, apart from extreme cases like those of microcephaly, there is no constant relationship between the amount of intelligence and the cranial capacity.

The same is true of normal persons. The range of variation in the mentally sound is as much as 700 to 800 grammes (about 26 ounces), and there have been even eminent men who have diverged from the normal to a greater extent than this. For instance, the heaviest healthy brain on record is that of Turgenieff, the Russian novelist, which weighed 71 ounces, whilst that of Gambetta weighed but 40·9 ounces. The brain of Napoleon was 53 ounces, and that of Cuvier 58·3 ounces. In fact, a whole race, the ancient Peruvians, attained to a very considerable degree of

PLATE XI.

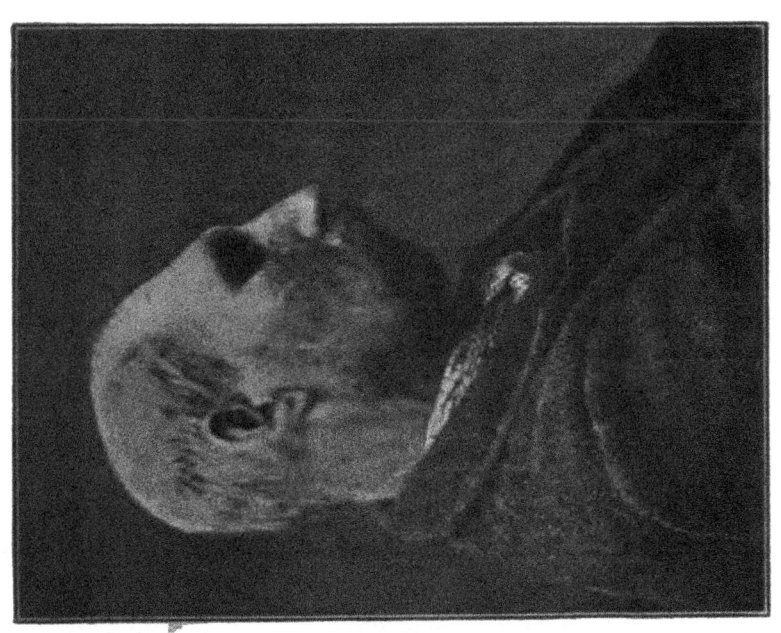

FIG. 31.—Microcephalic imbecile, also subject to epilepsy. Head circumference, 18¾ inches.

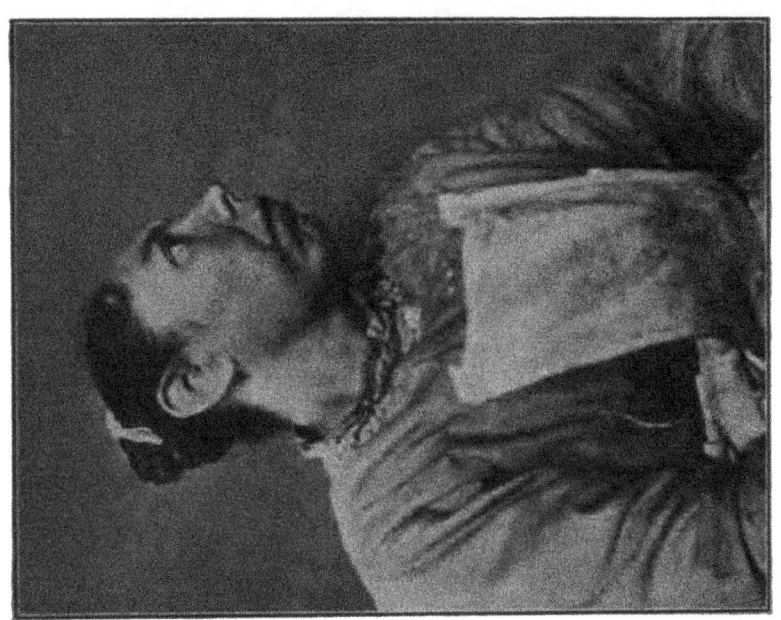

FIG. 32.—Microcephalic imbecile; a tolerably good worker in the wards. Head circumference, 17 inches.

To face page 176]

social development and excellence in the arts with a mean average brain capacity of only 40·1 ounces.

The fact is that intellect is dependent upon quality as well as quantity of brain, and although in many aments a quantitative defect is present, there is always a qualitative deficiency also. Accordingly it results that even in microcephalics there is no constant relation between size of brain and mental capacity.

Description.—*Physical Condition.*—The two chief clinical distinguishing features of this variety of amentia are the peculiar configuration of the skull and the (usually) very small stature. As a result of the cerebral hypoplasia, there is a marked deficiency in the frontal and occipital regions of the cranium, which in consequence shelves away in a curiously " sugar-loaf " or cone-like manner. This shape, by some termed *oxycephalic*, is always present in microcephaly, and, taken in conjunction with the receding chin, gives a very characteristic and bird-like appearance to these creatures. (See Plates XI., XVIII., and XIX., In consequence of the diminished surface of bone to be covered, the scalp is nearly always extraordinarily thick and redundant. In some cases it is permanently thrown into a series of deep furrows running antero-posteriorly, a condition which was first described in this country by Dr. T. W. McDowall,* and which seems to be confined to microcephales.† In addition the hair is usually extraordinarily coarse and wiry, and on more than one occasion I have known the teeth of the clipper to be broken whilst the hair was being cut.

As already remarked, the cranial circumference in these cases varies very much, and the diagnostic feature is one of shape rather than of size. There have been several cases recorded in which the greatest circumference was 15 inches or under ; on the other hand, I know several typical microcephalics with a cranial circumference of 19 inches and more, and one whose

* T. W. McDowall, " Abnormal Development of the Scalp," *Journal of Mental Science*, January, 1893.

† Dr. McDowall was good enough to place a portion of the scalp of one of these patients, who died under his care, at my disposal for examination. I found a considerable thickening of all layers, the average thickness down to the roots of the hair follicles being from 4 to 5 millimetres, and this after hardening in spirit.

skull measures as much as 21 inches. It is to be remembered that the actual brain capacity is less than a mere circumferential measurement would suggest, by reason of the deficiency being chiefly in the upper parts of the skull.

The second characteristic, that of diminished stature, is not so constant; nevertheless, as a class, microcephalics are the smallest of the varieties of amentia, and many of them may be called dwarfs. Few of them grow to more than 5 feet, although " Joe " (described by Dr. Ireland) reached 5 feet 9 inches in his boots. But this is decidedly exceptional.

In other respects microcephalics present the anomalies common to aments in general, and which have already been described. They rarely live to an advanced age (in this respect also I think " Joe " is unique, since he was sixty years old at his death), and the majority die of tuberculosis.

Mental and Nervous Condition.—The intellectual capacity of these persons varies within very considerable limits, and we thus have microcephalic aments of each of the three degrees of deficiency. A considerable number are idiots, unable to do anything for themselves, unable to understand more than a few words, and incapable of speech. Others, and the majority, belong to the imbecile class, and are capable of understanding most of what is said to them, can say a few words, and can perform simple tasks. A few are merely feeble-minded. The case of " Joe " is probably the best example of the mildest degree of defect, for Dr. Ireland says that until after forty years of age he was apparently able to earn sufficient wages to maintain himself. I know several typical microcephalics amongst mentally defective children attending special schools who can read, write, do simple sums, and who probably possess sufficient intelligence to earn their living under supervision; and one woman of this type, with a cranial circumference just under 17 inches, is one of the most industrious inmates of a county asylum.

The mental features common to most microcephalics are the absence of any sensory defect, a general vivacity, restlessness and muscular activity, a considerable capacity for imitation, and, usually, an inability for sustained effort. In their perceptive faculties these persons often compare favourably with aments of considerably higher general intelligence, and many of them not only have remarkably good hearing and sight, but extremely quick powers of observation. The restlessness is sometimes expressed by the performance of peculiar actions which have caused them to be likened to various animals. Thus, Lombroso describes a " bird man," a " rabbit man," and a " goose man." Their power of mimicry is often very marked, and this, combined with their general alertness, causes them to be amongst the drollest inmates of the imbecile ward. There was a chattering, restless ament of this type at Darenth a few years ago, who was very pat in making remarks upon anything coming under his observation, and who was a source of endless amusement to the attendants by his witticisms concerning one of them in particular. Another boy, aged eleven years, with a cranial circumference of $15\tfrac{3}{4}$ inches, was most adept in mimicking the various performers in the band.

In disposition the majority are affectionate and well-behaved. Many of them, before training, it is true, are apt to be quarrelsome and difficult to manage, but they usually soon lose these propensities and become quite amenable to the discipline of an institution.

The majority of microcephalics of the idiot degree suffer from a condition of general helplessness, which causes them to be unable to do anything for themselves, and many of the imbecile grade even experience considerable difficulty and unsteadiness in walking. This does not appear to be due to actual paralysis (although I have seen a few cases with typical spastic paralysis and increased tendon reflexes), but to an imperfect development of the tracts of the spinal cord. About half of them are subject to epileptic fits.

In conclusion we may briefly cite the chief instances of this interesting condition which have been recorded.*

Dr. Wilbur described (1857) an idiot aged twelve years, in the New York State Asylum, whose cranial circumference was only $13\tfrac{1}{4}$ inches. He was passionate, uncleanly in his habits, could distinguish a variety of forms and colours, knew the names of all objects in the schoolroom and about the house, and recognized a great number of pictures of objects. He made but little progress in speaking, and after being in the asylum five years,

* For these particulars I am largely indebted to Dr. Ireland's work.

though improved in many respects, he was found incapable of further progress, and was dismissed.

Antonia Grandoni was described by Professor Filippo Cardona of Milan (1870).* She was a typical microcephalic, with a cranial circumference of 15 inches ; her height was 49¼ inches ; and she died at the age of forty-one years. She had no sensory deficiency; in fact, her hearing was very quick and her observation very keen. She understood what was said to her, and was able to converse. She had a good memory for persons and events, was of a sociable and decidedly amorous and erotic disposition, and much addicted to dancing. Although decidedly defective, she had sufficient intelligence to do simple domestic duties and to run errands ; in fact, considering the extremely small size of her brain, her intelligence was altogether remarkable.

Helene Becker died of phthisis at the age of eight years, and a very careful and complete examination was made, and report published, by Dr. Bischoff of Munich (1873).† This girl was a low grade idiot ; she knew her own name, but was practically incapable of understanding anything beyond, although she knew when people were angry with her. Her speech was limited to one word. She was very restless, always moving her hands and arms and the upper part of her body. The brain weighed 219 grammes. Another child in the family was microcephalic.

The "*bird man*," a microcephalic with a cranial circumference of 15 inches, was described by Professor Cesare Lombroso (1873).‡ He was so named from a habit of chirping like a bird, hiding his head under his armpit, leaping on one leg, and stretching out his arms like wings. He was said to be wanting in touch, taste, and smell, was dirty in his habits, and given to coprophagy. Professor Lombroso also recorded two other microcephalics under the designation of the " rabbit man " and the " goose man," also the three brothers, *Nicolò, Serafino*, and *Giovanni Cerretti*. These were aged twenty-one years, thirteen years, and ten years, and had a skull circumference of 17¾, 16¼, and 16¼ inches respectively.

The "*Aztecs*" were a pair of microcephalic aments, boy and girl, of American-Indian origin, who were exhibited all over Europe

* *D' Una Microcefala*, Milano, 1870.
† *Anatomische Beschreibung eines mikrocephalen, 8 Jährigen Mädchens*.
‡ *Rivista Clinica di Bologna*, July and November, 1873.

and America for forty years, and who have been described at various periods by different writers, including Professor Owen. They were seen by Dr. Dalton when aged seven and five years respectively, and were described as being only able to repeat a few isolated words, but very excitable, vivacious, in almost constant motion, and full of curiosity. Their habits as regards feeding and taking care of themselves were those of children two or three years old. They were publicly married in London in 1867, but had no offspring.

Freddy, who was under the observation of Dr. Shuttleworth for twenty years at the Royal Albert Asylum, died at the age of twenty-nine years, of phthisis. At the time of his death his height was 4 feet 8 inches, the cranial circumference was 15 inches, and the weight of the fresh brain was 12¼ ounces. The cranial circumference at eight years was 14⅜ inches, and at twelve years 14½ inches. Dr. Shuttleworth describes him as manifesting good powers of observation, but only able to express himself in a few monosyllabic words. He had considerable will-power, and though it was found impossible to train him to much that was useful, he was in no sense a low-grade idiot. A very complete examination of this case was made and recorded by Professor J. D. Cunningham and Dr. T. Telford-Smith (1895).*

Joe, who was examined by Dr. Ireland in the Lancaster Workhouse at the age of forty-five years, had a cranial circumference of 17 inches, and attained the unusual height of 5 feet 9 inches (in boots). Until eighteen months previously he had earned enough wages to keep himself, and he died at the age of sixty years, of phthisis. This case also was fully described by Cunningham and Telford-Smith.

MONGOLIAN AMENTIA.

The *Mongolian* or *Kalmuc* variety of amentia was first so named by Dr. J. Langdon Down, from the resemblance of these persons in certain particulars to members of the Mongolian race. Then

---

* Transactions Royal Dublin Society, vol. v., Series 2, Part VIII. An excellent recent account of microcephaly is that by Dr. Giovanni Mingazzini (*Monatsschrift für Psychiat. und Neurologie*, Band vii., Heft 6, June, 1900). This gives most of the literature to date.

peculiar characteristics give rise to a physiognomy and clinical appearance which is exceedingly distinctive and unmistakable, but it must be admitted that not a few aments are met with who present only some of the features of this class, and who are thus intermediate between the Mongolian and the simple variety of amentia. Such are often called "semi-Mongols."

The number of Mongols is not large. If only those with well-marked characteristics be included, they probably do not form more than about 4 or 5 per cent. of all aments. One often hears it said that they are on the increase, but I know of no data in support of this statement, and impressions regarding such matters are notoriously misleading. Still, it is by no means improbable. Many of the physical features of this class are noticeable at, or shortly after, birth, and this fact, together with their retardation of development, causes them to be not infrequently seen in the consulting-room and the out-patient department of hospitals devoted to children. They bear a superficial resemblance to, and are often confounded with, cretins ; in fact, this type of amentia used formerly to be called "cretinoid" idiocy.

Causation.—Dr. G. A. Sutherland,* in one of the best accounts we have of Mongolism as seen in the early years of life, remarks that these children "resemble each other so closely that they appear to be members of the same family," and he very truly argues from this that the cause is more likely to be particular than general, such as those concerned in the production of the majority of aments. "General causes," he says, "such as parental alcoholism, nervous disease, or insanity in the family, etc., are not likely to produce such an exact type of disease as exists in Mongolism. It seems probable that one and the same cause is at work in all cases." Sutherland found that, out of his total of twenty-five cases, syphilis was definitely present in eleven patients, and from the symptoms and history it was strongly suspected in three others. He therefore suggests that, whilst further investigation is required to ascertain the exact etiological factor, the condition may turn out to be a parasyphilitic one.

It is undoubtedly true that the curious assemblage of physical

* G. A. Sutherland, "Mongolian Imbecility in Infants," based on a 'dy of twenty-five cases, *Practitioner*, December, 1899.

signs which are present in typical Mongolism do suggest a certain uniformity of causation in these cases. But it is necessary to remember that Mongolism consists in a particular *combination* of anomalies rather than in anomalies which are distinctive in themselves, and there are many ordinary aments who possess one or more of the features which go to make up the *tout ensemble* of the Mongol; in fact, I do not know of any single feature of these persons (with the possible exception of the tongue) which may not be seen in other aments. It is, therefore, the *combination* only which is distinctive. Granting, however, that this is probably due to a uniform cause, it by no means follows that this is some *single* and *particular* etiological factor. With regard to the question of syphilis, the evidence produced by Dr. Sutherland is undoubtedly very strong; but, as equally strong evidence to the contrary, it may be stated that, in over twenty cases of this variety in which I investigated the family history, I was unable to discover any preponderance of syphilis, and in some of the cases I have no hesitation in saying positively that syphilis was not to be thought of. In nearly all my cases there was a neuropathic family history, and frequently a strong tubercular taint; but over and beyond this, what I did frequently find (and what I think may possibly be the factor common to this type) was a history pointing to a condition of uterine exhaustion or ill-health of the mother during gestation. Many of the patients were the later born of a large family, often numbering as many as ten or twelve, and where this was not the case there was usually a state of severe physical prostration of the mother during the gestation period.* It is possible that many conditions, syphilis included, may bring this about, and I have on several occasions seen children produced by weakly

* Dr. Bodil Hjorth, of Copenhagen, in a paper recently published on the " Etiology of Mongolism," gives particulars regarding the antecedents of twenty-one cases. " The observed conditions assumed as possible causes are phthisis in the parents or grandparents, neuropathic heredity, and alcoholism. None of these occur so often as to show a preponderating influence. There is no record of syphilis in any of the cases. Twins presenting the specific characters are noted, these children being the eighth and ninth of a family of ten. Out of the twenty-one cases, twelve were the last children in the family " (*Journal of Mental Science*, January, 1907).

mothers, at the end of the child-bearing period, who had quite a Mongolian type of physiognomy, but who were mentally normal.

I am disposed to think, therefore, that Mongolian amentia is the result of the two factors, morbid heredity and uterine exhaustion, and that with a pronounced degree of the latter the hereditary defects may be only slight. In one of my cases there was no neuropathic heredity, but the mother had suffered from severe albuminuria and anæmia whilst carrying the child.

Pathology.—The brain of the Mongol is usually smaller and less complexly convoluted than that of the normal person. In addition, there is a diminution in the size of the pons, medulla, and cerebellum. This is not a noticeable peculiarity of ordinary aments, and it seems to be a constant characteristic of this class. Dr. A. W. Wilmarth,[*] as a result of the examination of five Mongols, found that the brains were of good size for imbecile brains, but that the pons and medulla were very small, being only about half the normal weight. He suggests that the low nutrition of these patients (and possibly other anatomical peculiarities) may be due to the imperfect development or absence of certain cell groups in this region.

I have had the opportunity of examining the central nervous system of a male Mongolian who died aged fourteen days. In this the weight of the complete encephalon was 340 grammes, which may be considered as normal. The weight of pons, medulla, and cerebellum was 19 grammes, the relationship between these structures and the cerebrum being thus 1 to 16·8. According to Huschke, the normal relationship between these and the cerebrum is as 7 to 93 (roughly, one-thirteenth) at birth. The relative and absolute weight of the cerebellum undergoes a considerable increase with age, however, and in the adult the proportion to the cerebrum is as 13 to 87 (roughly, one-seventh). It is thus seen that in this case there is a definite diminution of these basal structures. No other naked-eye changes were observed. Microscopical examination showed an immature condition of the cells and tracts of all portions of the encephalon and spinal cord ; but the degree of development did not appear

[*] A. W. Wilmarth, " Report on the Examination of One Hundred Brains of Feeble-Minded Children," *Alienist and Neurologist*, October, 1890.

PLATE XII.

PRIMARY AMENTIA (MONGOLIAN VARIETY).

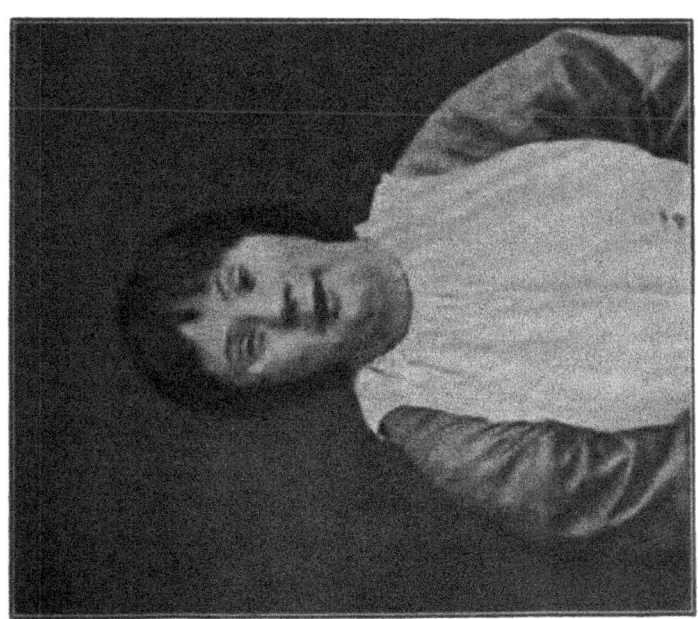

FIG. 33.—Mongolian imbecile.

FIG. 34.—Mongolian imbecile.

[To face page 184.]

to be behind that of a normal nervous system of similar age. The brain cells of the normal child at birth are in a very embryonic condition, however, and it is hardly to be expected that any microscopical differences would be discoverable at this early age.

It is very probable that the imperfect development of the basal parts of the encephalon results in a deficient expansion of the base of the skull, and Sutherland plausibly suggests that this may be a factor in causing the characteristic physiognomy of these persons.

It may be stated that, beyond the presence of congenital malformations common to all aments, dissections have hitherto failed to reveal any abnormality of glandular or other bodily structures which would account for the peculiar characteristics of this class. The amentia is in all probability idiopathic and due to hereditary defects, but these special physical characteristics may be brought about by morbid influences or malnutrition acting during the period of intra-uterine growth.

Description.—*Physical Condition.*—The three anomalies most constantly present in Mongolism, and whose combination may be said to be characteristic of this condition, are of the skull, the palpebral fissures, and the tongue. These are often so pronounced as to render a diagnosis possible at, or very shortly after, birth. In exceptional cases, however, only two may exist. In addition, there are many other peculiarities of frequent occurrence; but these are less distinctive of Mongols, many of them being by no means rare in ordinary aments. Several illustrations of this type of amentia are shown in Plates XII., XIII., and XIV.

The skull is small, rounded, and diminished in its anteroposterior measurement (brachycephalic), the face and occiput being considerably flattened. But there is no marked recession of the frontal and supra-occipital regions, so that, although Mongols are of the small-headed type of aments, the cranial conformation is markedly different to the microcephales proper. The palpebral fissures are narrow and oblique, sloping downwards and inwards. It was this peculiarity which caused Langdon Down to apply the name " Mongol " to the type; but although generally present, it is not invariably so. Dr. C. H. Fennell,* in a series of twenty-one cases, found it absent in three, whilst in one the direction was reversed. Moreover, it occurs in the mentally sound, and I know several remarkably intelligent persons possessing this peculiarity.

An exceedingly characteristic feature is the tongue, which is unusually large, marked by hypertrophied circumvallate papillæ, and scored by a series of irregular transverse fissures. Fennell regards this condition as pathognomonic, and says: "In the examination of the tongue in over 200 idiots of all other types, I met with none which at all recalled it." But a few Mongols of mature age do not present this peculiarity. Some very interesting details with regard to the tongue have been recorded by Dr. John Thomson,† of Edinburgh. He finds that, although the organ may be noticeably large at birth, the other characteristics of fissuring, swollen papillæ and sodden rawness, do not develop until considerably later. He says the enlargement of the papillæ most commonly begins between the third and ninth months, whilst the fissuring generally begins to appear in the course of the third or fourth year. It may be present in a slight form, however, during the second, and it may not be noticeable till as late as the sixth year. Dr. Thomson suggests that these changes may be partly due to an abnormal vulnerability of the mucous membrane, but that what chiefly determines the swelling and cracking is the habit of sucking the tongue which is commonly present in these children. I am of opinion that this is an exceedingly probable explanation, for it is an undoubted fact that a very marked feature of Mongolism is the tendency to chronic inflammatory conditions of skin and mucous membranes; whilst Thomson has shown that the exciting factor—tongue-sucking—occurs in at least 80 per cent. of these patients.

The ears are usually small and rounded, the nose short and squat, with triangular nostrils which often look forwards rather than downwards. Epicanthus is often seen, and strabismus and nystagmus are frequent in the first few months of life, but tend to

* C. H. Fennell, "Mongolian Imbecility." *Journal of Mental Science*, January, 1904. An excellent account of Mongolism as seen in institutions, based upon twenty-one cases.

† John Thomson. "Notes on the Peculiarities of the Tongue in Mongolism." *British Medical Journal*, May 4, 1907.

PLATE XIII.

PRIMARY AMENTIA (MONGOLIAN VARIETY).

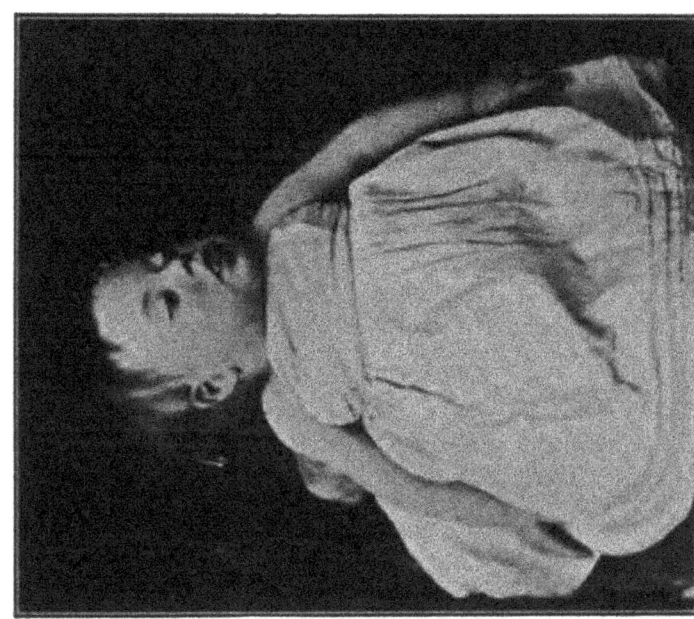

Fig. 36.—A female Mongolian. Age, 2 years.
(*From a photograph lent by Dr. J. Thomson.*)

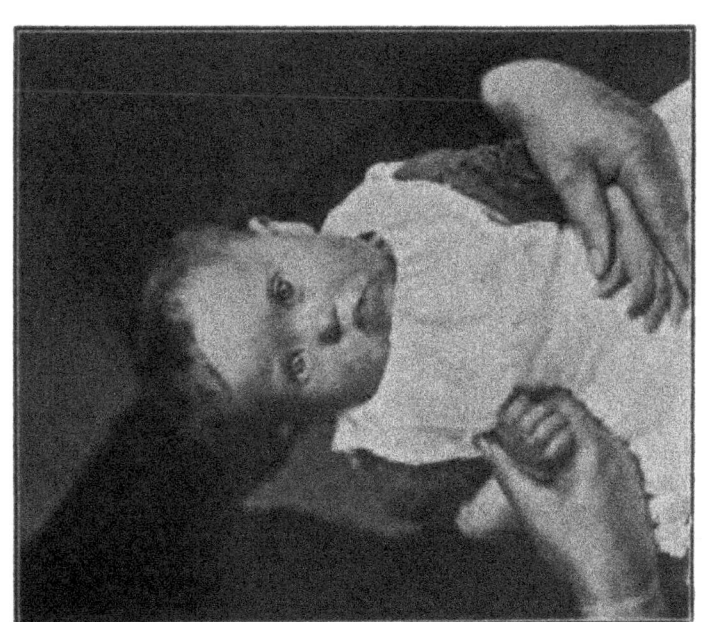

Fig. 35.—A female Mongolian. Age, 6½ months. With deep cyanosis due to congenital heart disease.
(*From a photograph lent by Dr. J. Thomson.*)

To face page 186.]

disappear as the child grows. Speckled irides are very common, a condition to which my attention was first drawn by Dr. R. Langdon Down. The same observer also considers that hypermetropic astigmatism is unusually prevalent. The hair is generally very scanty and wiry. There is frequently seen a bright red flush upon the scheek of these patients, very much like that occurring in myxœdema. The palate is often high and narrow, the mouth open, and the tongue partly protruding. Adenoids are exceedingly frequent.

The hands and feet are commonly broad, flabby, and exceedingly clumsy-looking; in fact, they may often be said to be spade-like. Dr. Telford-Smith described a curious incurving of the little fingers as very characteristic of Mongolism, but in my experience it is no more common in this type than in aments in general. What I have frequently found is that both the little fingers and thumbs are much shorter than normal, and that whereas in the ordinary person or ordinary ament the tip of the little finger usually ends opposite the last joint of the ring-finger, in Mongols it is very common to find it extend no farther than the middle of the second phalanx. In the early years of life there is usually an exceedingly lax condition of the joint ligaments, and this gives rise to a greatly increased mobility. Very often the fingers and knees can be hyperextended to a considerable degree. Knock-knee and flat-foot are common. The skin is rough and dry, and often covered with fine hairs. The subcutaneous tissues frequently have a curious boggy feeling, like that present in myxœdema, but there is no pitting on pressure. The abdomen is usually large and tumid, particularly in infancy, and umbilical hernia is occasionally seen.

In many of these persons the circulation is very defective, and blueness and coldness of the extremities, sores and chilblains, are exceedingly prevalent. This is probably due to congenital cardiac anomalies, such as imperfect closure of the foramen ovale, pulmonary stenosis, etc.; but in some instances it may be the result of intra-uterine endocarditis. Dr. A. E. Garrod* described five cases of Mongolism in which congenital cardiac lesions were found, and one-fifth of the cases examined by Dr. Sutherland presented well-marked systolic basal murmurs

* Archibald E. Garrod, *British Medical Journal*, October 22, 1898.

which were evidently congenital. One very marked peculiarity of these persons is their tendency to chronic inflammatory lesions of the respiratory and alimentary tracts. Nasal catarrh, bronchitis, and diarrhœa are exceedingly common, and the majority are constant sufferers from blepharitis, rhinitis, and cracked lips.

Such are the chief physical peculiarities of this interesting variety of amentia. It is rarely that they are all present in any one person, and there is probably no one of them which is really pathognomonic of this condition, except perhaps the tongue. This latter, with the peculiar conformation of the skull and palpebral fissures, the cheek flush, and the general tendency to mucous catarrh, seem to me to constitute the essential symptom-complex. As a rule, these peculiarities persist throughout life; but I have seen a few cases in which advance of time seemed to bring about a marked amelioration, and caused them to become much less evident. This, I think, is more common in the originally milder cases; but a short time ago Dr. Caldecott, of Earlswood Asylum, showed me an imbecile whom the casual observer would hardly have recognized as a Mongol, but who in former years had possessed very well-marked characteristics.

As a rule, Mongols die early, the chief cause of death being phthisis. They are rarely met with above the age of thirty years, although at the present time there are two at Normansfield between thirty and forty; and Dr. R. Langdon Down tells me that he had a female Mongolian under his care for many years who reached the advanced age of fifty-seven years.

Mental and Nervous Condition.—The mental characteristics of this class are not nearly so distinctive as are the physical; nevertheless, there are several peculiarities common to them. From the beginning, the Mongolian infant is placid, good-tempered, and readily amused. There is at first no apparent mental hebetude; on the contrary, he often looks bright and intelligent, has plenty of curiosity, is attracted by everything around him, and is very imitative. But one of the most common of the early signs of amentia is seen in the tardy evolution of the power of sitting up, walking, and talking. Moreover, he is full of grimaces and facial contortions, which are accompanied by wrinkling of the skin, and are foreign to the normal child. As he grows up

PLATE XIV.

PRIMARY AMENTIA (MONGOLIAN VARIETY).

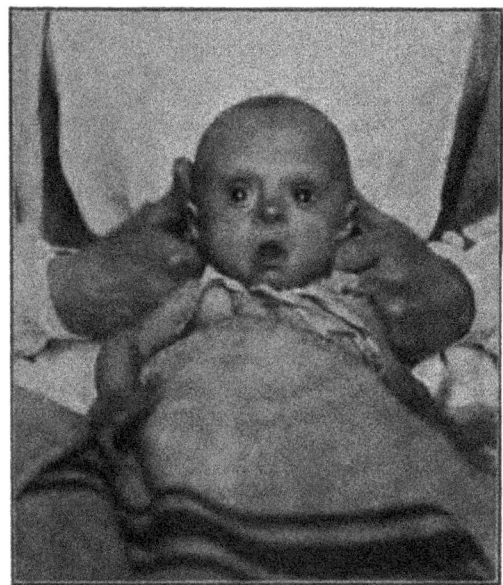

FIG. 37.—A female Mongolian. Age, 3 months.
(*From a photograph lent by Dr. J. Thomson.*)

FIG. 38.—A male Mongolian. Age, 14 months. With talipes varus and cubitus varus. Died 2 months later of general tuberculosis.
(*From a photograph lent by Dr. J. Thomson.*)

The Clinical Varieties of Primary Amentia

he want of intellect becomes more and more apparent. But he till retains his happy disposition; he is very affectionate, readily pleased, and usually a great favourite with all around him. He often has a very considerable power of mimicry, as well as a remarkable sense of rhythm and love of music, and many of these children are adepts at drill and dancing.

The degree of intellectual deficiency varies very considerably, and on the whole I am inclined to think that there is a direct relation between this and the intensity of the bodily signs. Many of them are merely feeble-minded, a few are pronounced idiots, but the majority belong to the medium grade of defect. The milder members generally learn to read, write, and perform simple duties with a fair amount of intelligence, but their power of summing is decidedly poor. Dr. Shuttleworth says that some of these, after appropriate education, even pass muster with their brothers and sisters. The imbeciles, on the other hand, rarely make much headway, and, although very imitative, it is not often that in them this faculty can be turned to any practical purpose. In the performance of useful work they are often surpassed by ordinary imbeciles of far more vacant and less prepossessing appearance. Even in the milder cases the clumsy and ill-formed condition of the hands usually precludes any kind of work requiring dexterity, and most of these persons do best in the garden or on the farm.

Cerebral complications are not common in this class, and actual paralysis and epilepsy are rare in comparison with other aments.

It will be seen that Mongolian aments have certain points in common with sporadic cretins, and in the early stages a considerable number are treated with thyroid gland, and hopes of amelioration held out to the parents, as a result of a mistaken diagnosis. The chief points of resemblance are the general backwardness of bodily development, the stumpy and spade-like hands and feet, the squat nose, and the bogginess of the subcutaneous tissues. Careful examination, however, will reveal far more points of difference. In the Mongols the head is small and rounded, instead of large; the tongue, although somewhat like that of the cretin in being large and protruding, is marked by hypertrophied papillæ, and later by numerous fissures. The slant of the eyes, the lax joints, and the chronic catarrh of the

Mongol are very distinctive; whilst his active, bright, and vivacious manner is totally unlike the dull, expressionless inertia of the cretin. Finally, the rate of bodily growth is entirely different in the two conditions. I have known thyroid gland, also thymus and pituitary extracts, given to Mongols persistently for years, but never with any appreciable amelioration of the physical or mental defects; whereas, as is well known, the effect of thyroid upon the cretin is remarkable.

THE COMPLICATIONS OF PRIMARY AMENTIA.

We have described three types—namely, *Simple*, *Microcephalic*, and *Mongolian*—as the chief clinical varieties of primary amentia. Any of these three, however, may be complicated by certain severe developmental anomalies or special pathological conditions which produce more or less distinctive clinical features, and these we shall now allude to. They are, in order of frequency:

Epilepsy.
Paralysis.
Hydrocephalus.
Porencephalus.
Sclerosis.
Deaf-mutism.

It is to be remarked that, in the cases we are now considering, these conditions merely accompany and complicate a mental deficiency which is primary; nevertheless similar lesions may, in a small number of instances, actually produce amentia. Such cases will be dealt with in a subsequent chapter.

Epileptic and Other Convulsions.—Convulsions in some form or other, but chiefly epileptic, are the most common complication of primary amentia. A special examination with regard to this condition in over 500 patients showed that in cases presenting no paralysis or other indication of gross cerebral lesions, and in whom therefore the attacks were idiopathic epilepsy, convulsions occurred in 37 per cent.; whilst in patients presenting signs of gross lesions they occurred in 70 per cent. In the great majority of the latter, however, the fits were indistinguishable from ordinary epilepsy.

The Clinical Varieties of Primary Amentia 191

With regard to the degree of amentia, it was found that convulsions occurred in 11 per cent. of the feeble-minded, 42 per cent. of imbeciles, and 56 per cent. of idiots. It is possible, however, that these figures may be somewhat too high for primary aments in general, since they largely relate to institution patients, and may therefore contain an undue proportion of the worst cases. Convulsions are most frequent in the simple and microcephalic varieties, and are relatively rare in the Mongolians.

With regard to the convulsions, as far as could be ascertained they were in the great majority of cases typically epileptic, and several of the merely feeble-minded patients have definitely affirmed the existence of a premonition or aura. In the more severe grades of defect the mental condition usually precludes any inquiry upon this point, but trained attendants can often foretell the onset of a fit by the appearance of the patient. Most of the attacks are of the major variety, although in a few cases minor seizures occur also. Their severity varies greatly, some being of the mildest possible type, others exceedingly severe and protracted. Their frequency is also subject to great variation. In some patients the first convulsion appears in the early months of life, and they thence continue almost daily during the existence of the patient. In other instances, after frequent fits during many weeks or months of early childhood, the patient remains free for years, he then has a few more, and these are again followed by years of quiescence. In yet other cases, after an initial series of fits, there is no recurrence. I have known several persons who have only experienced two or three seizures in the course of twenty years or more. It is hardly safe to reckon on the absence of epilepsy in any particular sufferer from primary amentia, although as a rule the fits make their first appearance not later than the second decade.

The effect of the convulsions is much the same as in the ordinary individual, and appears on the whole to depend upon the frequency and severity of the attacks. If severe and often recurring, the patient rapidly loses even his limited acquirements; whilst if slight and seldom, the effect may be infinitesimal.

In addition to epilepsy, the following other conditions may be mentioned as being occasionally seen in primary aments : *Chorea* is not very common, but is found in some instances. Various forms of *athetosis* are fairly frequent in the severer grades. *Intention tremor* is occasionally seen; whilst I saw at Darenth a few years ago two imbeciles (brother and sister) affected with a constant rhythmic tremor of the whole body, closely resembling paralysis agitans. The tremor was so great that articulate speech was impossible; the fingers could not pick anything up, nor could they retain their hold of any object. In each instance the tendon reflexes were greatly exaggerated, and ankle and patellar clonus were well marked, but Babinsky's sign was absent.

Paralysis.—The next most common complication is paralysis. This, like epilepsy, is least frequent in the milder, and most so in the severer, grades of amentia, and, generally speaking, the extent of the paralysis is directly proportionate to the amount of mental deficiency. In a small number of cases, particularly amongst the microcephalics, the condition is rather one of paresis and general muscular hypotonus and helplessness than of actual paralysis, and in such it is probably due to imperfect development of the efferent pathway. In other instances, it is due to the presence of a gross cerebral lesion, such as localized atrophy, porencephaly, or hydrocephaly. In these latter the paralysis is localized, and varies from a slight monoplegia to a severe hemi- or paraplegia. The affected limbs are small and ill-nourished, and often firmly contracted, and many of the worst cases are permanently chair- or bed-ridden. In a considerable number of these cases epileptic convulsions also occur.

Hydrocephalus.—Probably most cases of amentia in which hydrocephalus is at all pronounced are of the secondary form, and this condition, as well as porencephalus and sclerosis, will be more fully described in a subsequent chapter. But a few undoubted primary aments develop hydrocephalus with its characteristic symptoms, and the condition is not infrequently found post-mortem where it had not been suspected during life.

Porencephalus.—True or false porencephaly is sometimes found post-mortem when there has been little indication of its existence during life. It cannot be diagnosed with certainty, but its presence may be suspected in cases of congenital hemiplegia which are accompanied by considerable non-development of the affected limbs and marked flattening of the opposite half of the skull.

The Clinical Varieties of Primary Amentia 193

Sclerosis.—The usual indications of this complication are frequently repeated convulsions, followed by muscular tremor, weakness, or actual paralysis with contractures. In some cases there is persistent headache, the patient becomes more and more torpid, and dies after a succession of severe fits.

Deaf-mutism is seen in a small proportion of primary aments. It calls for no remark beyond the fact that such a complication naturally imposes an insuperable barrier to successful training. On the other hand, the mild mental defect which *results* from this condition is greatly ameliorated, and in many cases removed, by appropriate education.

CHAPTER XIII

SECONDARY AMENTIA AND ITS CLINICAL VARIETIES

HITHERTO we have been concerned with the primary form of amentia, in which the condition is due to an inherent incapacity for normal development on the part of the embryonic neuroblasts of the brain, the result of morbid heredity.

There is, however, a much smaller group (probably comprising not more than about 10 per cent. of all aments) in which no such intrinsic defect exists, and in which the mental deficiency is brought about by some purely extraneous factor. This form of amentia is termed *secondary*, and will now be considered.

Perhaps a connecting link between the primary and secondary forms is afforded by that variety of amentia which is due to epilepsy. In many such cases morbid heredity is present, and there may even exist some of the stigmata of degeneracy which are so characteristic of the primary form. But inasmuch as in these cases the amentia is clearly the result of the epilepsy, I have considered it better to look upon the mental defect as secondary, and we shall describe it in this place.

With this exception there is a marked difference in the clinical aspects of the primary and secondary forms. The inherent blight of the former gives rise to numerous and widespread anomalies of anatomical development which are absent in the latter. As a consequence, the sufferer from secondary amentia is often readily distinguished from the primary ament by being well developed and well grown, and by his comely and prepossessing appearance. Occasionally, however, there are deformities and abnormalities peculiar to the variety, and dependent upon the particular pathological lesion present. Further, whilst in uncomplicated cases of the primary group the general tendency is for

Secondary Amentia and its Clinical Varieties

some degree of amelioration to take place as a result of suitable training, many of those of the class we are now considering are the result of cerebral lesions which are progressive, and the tendency is rather towards degeneration and ultimate dementia.

In describing the clinical varieties of primary amentia, the classification adopted was based upon the presence of physiognomical characteristics. It is more convenient to describe cases of secondary amentia according to their particular pathogenesis.

From this standpoint cases of secondary amentia may conveniently be divided into two main classes. In the first of these the mental deficiency is brought about by a general or localized disease of the brain cells; in the second it is due to some external factor influencing their nutrition. Each of these classes contains several clinical varieties. This chapter will therefore be divided into two sections, as follows :

SECTION I.

Amentia due to Cerebral Disease.

Varieties : (1) Epileptic and eclampsic amentia.
(2) Vascular, toxic, and inflammatory amentia, including certain special types, viz. :
   (a) Porencephalic.
   (b) Sclerotic.
   (c) Hydrocephalic.
(3) Syphilitic amentia.
(4) Infantile cerebral degeneration.

SECTION II.

Amentia due to Defective Cerebral Nutrition.

Varieties : (1) Cretinism.
(2) Amentia due to nutritional defect.
(3) Amentia due to sense deprivation.

It may be well again to emphasize the fact that, although many of the etiological and pathological conditions present in secondary amentia may, and frequently do, complicate the primary form, we are only here concerned with such cases of amentia as are directly and entirely attributable to them.

Section I.

AMENTIA DUE TO CEREBRAL DISEASE.

In this class the morbid anatomy consists of a (usually) localized arrest of neuronic development, which in most instances is accompanied by lesions obvious to the naked eye. In a considerable number of cases degenerative changes supervene, in consequence of which dementia becomes added to the mental deficiency.

EPILEPTIC AND ECLAMPSIC AMENTIA.

It used to be the custom, in describing the varieties of amentia, to group together into one class all those persons who were, or had been, subject to epileptic or similar convulsions, and to label them " epileptic " or " eclampsic " aments. A close examination of this class, however, shows that it is really a most heterogeneous collection.

It is, perhaps, not unnatural that the parents should see in these convulsions the reason and cause of the mental deficiency of their child, and, as a matter of fact, there is no other single etiological factor which is so frequently advanced as the " cause." To the lay mind " fits " are both impressive and alarming. It is not surprising that even medical practitioners should frequently be satisfied with this explanation, for they are fully aware of the mental hebetude and degeneration which may supervene upon epilepsy. But I am convinced, from the examination of some hundreds of aments suffering from epilepsy, as well as from careful inquiries into their family and previous personal history, that in the great majority no such causal relationship exists as is implied by the term " epileptic."

The relationship existing between epilepsy* and amentia is of three kinds, as follows :

1. *Primary Amentia in which Epilepsy occurs as a Mere Complication.*—This has already been considered in the chapter dealing with the complications of primary amentia (p. 190).

* For convenience, the term " epilepsy " is here used to include *epileptiform* as well as *epileptic* (idiopathic) convulsions.

Secondary Amentia and its Clinical Varieties 197

2. *Idiopathic Epilepsy or Eclampsia causing Amentia.*—It is with this group that the present account deals.

3. *Gross Cerebral Lesions causing Epilepsy and Amentia.*—Here both the epilepsy and amentia are symptomatic of conditions which will be described in subsequent pages.

The following table shows the chief points of difference between these three groups in which amentia and epilepsy co-exist:

TABLE XV.
SHOWING THE RELATION OF EPILEPSY TO AMENTIA.

	GROUP 1. *Primary amentia complicated by epilepsy.*	GROUP 2. *Secondary amentia, due to idiopathic epilepsy.*	GROUP 3. *Secondary amentia and epilepsy due to gross cerebral disease.*
Morbid heredity	Pronounced	Less pronounced	Absent
Condition of patient before the fits	Some degree of amentia or general backwardness usually noticed	Normal	Normal. Onset of fits can generally be traced to some definite morbid process affecting brain
Nature of fits	Epileptic. Usually milder and less frequent than Group 2	Epileptic. Severe and frequent	Epileptic. Occasionally epileptiform; rarely constant, rhythmic tremor
Condition of patient after fits have made their appearance	Degree of amentia often much greater than would be accounted for by the severity and frequency of fits. *Paralysis* may be present also if a gross lesion co-exists	Amentia usually mild, but much dementia. No paralysis	Considerable amentia may be present with mild and infrequent fits. Paralysis often present
Stigmata of degeneracy	Marked (except in highest grades)	Slight	Absent
Prospects of improvement under special training	Dependent upon severity and frequency of fits, but on the whole better than in Groups 2 and 3	Practically none	Dependent upon time of occurrence, site, extent, and nature of lesion, and upon severity and frequency of fits. Usually intermediate between Groups 1 and 2

Epileptic Amentia.—It is common knowledge that frequently repeated severe convulsions, or even minor attacks, occurring in a person of mature cerebral development may give rise to dementia. The anatomical basis of this condition is a degeneration of the same cortical cells and fibres as are imperfectly developed in amentia.* If the development of these neurones is as yet incomplete, as in the infant, it may be irremediably arrested, and a condition of secondary mental deficiency result. For the production of amentia, then, in addition to the factors which produce dementia, the convulsions must occur during the first few years of life. This is the case in a considerable proportion of epileptics, and Sir William Gowers† states that in 12·5 per cent. of cases the convulsions make their first appearance before the age of three years. In such cases the mental development of the patient may become arrested, so that whilst his body develops his mind is no more advanced than that of an idiot, imbecile, or feeble-minded person. Savage makes the statement that epilepsy " occurring before *seven* years of age is certain to leave the patient weak-minded "; but I am inclined to think that, if by weak-mindedness is meant amentia, this is a little too sweeping. Nevertheless, some degree of amentia does certainly result in many cases of epilepsy beginning thus early. On the other hand, the proportion of aments who owe their condition to this cause, and who are truly sufferers from epileptic amentia, is a small one. In my own series of cases I find that 3·5 per cent. only of aments belong to this variety, but this number must be regarded as merely an approximate estimate. The pathology of these cases has already been described ; it is usually that of arrested neuronic development plus degeneration.

Epileptic aments differ considerably in their clinical features. In some the bodily condition is sufficiently unlike to be readily distinguishable from ordinary primary aments ; but there are others who so closely resemble that class that a diagnosis can only be made by most careful attention to the history and the capacity of the patient prior to the onset of the fits. It may be stated that, as a general rule, epileptic aments are better grown and developed, and possess fewer of the stigmata which are such a conspicuous feature of the primary group.

The degree of mental deficiency varies from a mild amount of feeble-mindedness to a state resembling idiocy ; but this latter condition is more often the result of a superadded dementia than of a pure mental arrest. In the milder cases, although the patients

* This has been recently shown in J. S. Bolton's exhaustive work, " Amentia and Dementia," *Journal of Mental Science,* 1905 *et seq.*
† Sir W. R. Gowers' article " Epilepsy," in Clifford Allbutt's " System of Medicine," vol. vii.

Secondary Amentia and its Clinical Varieties

rarely make much headway with school learning, a certain amount of manual training is possible, and many of them are able to do more or less useful work. But the persistence of the fits gradually strips these persons of any acquirements they may have possessed, and in the majority of cases dementia is but a question of time. On the whole, it may be said that the prospects of amelioration by training and the general prognosis of this class are of the most unfavourable description. There are a few cases of epileptic amentia in which the fits cease, and in these the mental condition may improve very considerably. There are other cases in which a diminution of the fits and some degree of mental improvement takes place, apparently in consequence of medicinal treatment and regimen; but these cases are decidedly exceptional, and in no instance is real mental deficiency, once produced, ever overcome.

There is one mental feature which is common to most of these cases, and that is, a general irritability and intractability. Epileptic aments are often exceedingly stubborn and difficult to manage; they are prone to sudden outbursts of temper and violence, and they are, in fact, probably the most untrustworthy of all the varieties of mental deficiency.

With regard to the fits themselves there is little to be said. They may be of either the minor or major variety, or of both. They are occasionally preceded by a definite aura, or by some recognizable alteration in the appearance of the patient, and they are usually followed by a varying period of intellectual, sensory, and, at times, motor exhaustion, transient paresis being by no means uncommon. In a certain number of cases they seem to be directly excited by indigestion, constipation, undue excitement, or some determinate cause; in others they occur independently of any ascertainable factor. The frequency of some is diminished by dieting, careful regulation of the daily life, and the administration of drugs, of which the most valuable are still the bromides. In many cases, however, the fits persist in spite of all treatment, and hopeless dementia results.

ILLUSTRATIVE CASES.

L. J., male, the fourth born of a family of eight, of whom three only are now alive; the remaining five died in infancy, and all of them were subject to convulsions. The patient's father was strongly addicted to alcohol, and died at the age of forty-seven, cause unknown ; his father's father died aged fifty-seven, and was paralyzed for six years before death. The patient's mother is alive and in tolerably good health ; she had thirteen brothers and sisters, all of whom are dead, several of consumption, and her father died aged fifty, of asthma.

The patient had fits when a month old, and they have continued on and off ever since. During infancy he used to have as many as ten daily. With the exception of the fits, he was not noticed to be different to other children until schooling began. He was then found unable to make any progress, and after a short time was discharged. He remained at home pottering about, but doing no regular work, until seventeen years of age, when he became so unmanageable that he had to be sent to an asylum. On admission he was a pale-faced, somewhat undersized youth, with slight stigmata of degeneracy. He was dull of comprehension, and slow in realizing what was said to him. Memory very defective, and in replying to questions he would constantly repeat himself. Able to draw a little, but unable to read, write, or sum, and decidedly feeble-minded. He was liable to attacks of violence before the fits, and would then attack anyone who might be near him. After the fits he remained heavy and stuporose for a day or more. He admitted that he was excited before the fits, and said it came over him "all of a sudden." He complained a good deal of headache. He remained in practically the same condition, having fits at the rate of three or four weekly, and being either too excitable or too stuporose to do any work. He is now, at the age of twenty, showing signs of dementia. (See Plate XV., Fig. 39.)

F. S., female, the eighth of a family of thirteen, three of whom are dead, the remainder living, and said to be in good health. The father has been insane in an asylum. The patient had severe fits whilst cutting her teeth, and they recurred almost daily until she was five years old. Since then they have only returned at rare intervals. She always seemed idiotic, had no idea of playing like the other children, and received no education of any kind. She remained at home until in her teens, but was a great trouble, being unable to speak or look after herself in any way. She would wander aimlessly about the house, and was

PLATE XV.

FIG. 39.—A case of epileptic amentia. Age, 20 years. Indications of dementia present.

FIG. 40.—Mild amentia with epilepsy and right hemiparesis due to cerebral lesion when one year old. Frequent fits, very passionate and impulsive at times, becoming demented. Age, 20 years.

generally very restless ; if left alone would be sure to get into trouble, and was occasionally violent and aggressive. She finally became so unmanageable that she had to be sent to an asylum.

On admission she was found to be a pronounced idiot. She had no understanding of what was said to her, and was unable to articulate. She spent the day sitting in a chair rocking herself to and fro, and occasionally screaming or making a grunting noise. She had no idea of personal cleanliness, and had to be fed with a spoon. She destroyed everything she could lay her hands on. At the present time she is twenty-seven years of age, and her condition is practically unchanged. She has had a few epileptic fits at rare intervals, the longest period of intermission being four years.

To these two examples many others might be added, but they are sufficient to illustrate the unfavourable type of amentia which may result from severe epilepsy in early life. The effect, as already remarked, is not always so serious, and I know several instances in which but a mild degree of mental deficiency has been produced, and where more or less continuous occupation is possible. But I think these latter cases are exceptional. There is no doubt that the prospect of improvement is greatest where the convulsions can be relieved by treatment, and hence the importance of careful medical supervision of these cases. Into the question of treatment I do not propose to enter, since it is that of ordinary epilepsy. It may, however, be stated that attention to the diet and the ordering of the daily life are of the utmost importance, whilst of drugs the bromides, in combination with borax, will usually be found the most efficacious.

Eclampsic Amentia.—Instability of the nerve cells of the brain is a normal characteristic of infancy, and is probably in no small measure due to the rapid growth which takes place during the early months of life. At the end of the first year the brain weighs three times as much as it did at birth. As a consequence there is no doubt that the child is much more predisposed to convulsions than is the adult ; but although convulsions are exceedingly common in infancy, I am of opinion that no ordinary excitant will produce them in a healthy child of good heredity. Where they occur, there is either some special inherited predisposition, or else the natural instability has been markedly exaggerated by a disturbance of cerebral nutrition caused by bodily ill-health. Where this special predisposition exists, such simple exciting factors as acute indigestion, constipation, dentition, or the ordinary febrile ailments of childhood, will suffice to determine convulsions. Where no predisposition is inherited, it may be acquired in consequence of anæmia, malnutrition, chronic disturbances of the alimentary tract, and, above all, rickets.

It is thus seen that, theoretically, infantile convulsions fall into two groups—those which are the result of an inherited predisposition, and those in which the tendency is acquired. The former must be considered as undoubtedly identical with idiopathic epilepsy, and they often persist throughout life ; he latter group are eclampsic only. But it is not uncommon for convulsions which have been looked upon as simply eclampsic to recur, and to persist with all the features of true epilepsy ; consequently the division between these two conditions is one which is exceedingly difficult, and at times impossible, to draw.*

The term " eclampsic amentia " should, of course, be limited to those cases of mental deficiency which are clearly the result of simple infantile convulsions due to this *acquired* predisposition. Such a result, in my opinion, seldom occurs, for in the great majority of children who thus suffer from a series of fits which do not recur, there is no permanent impairment of the mental faculties. In a few cases, however, some degree of amentia does result, but, as this is in all probability dependent upon a definite vascular or toxic lesion of the brain, it seems more desirable to include eclampsic cases under these headings.

* It is of interest to note that Dr. R. O. Moon, as a result of his examination of 200 cases of convulsions in children, says : " I have not been able to find any clear dividing-line between infantile convulsions or eclampsia on the one hand, and idiopathic epilepsy on the other. . . . On the contrary, it has seemed to me that convulsions in early life may shade off indefinitely into epilepsy or epileptiform manifestations, so that it becomes often impossible to say where the one stops and the other begins."— " Some Observations on Convulsions in Children, and their Relation to Epilepsy " (*Lancet*, September 15, 1906).

Secondary Amentia and its Clinical Varieties 203

VASCULAR, TOXIC, AND INFLAMMATORY AMENTIA.
It is by no means uncommon for symptoms indicative of a morbid state of the brain or its membranes to occur in childhood. Such cerebral symptoms may be due to injuries received during birth; they may arise during, or subsequent to, one of the specific fevers; they may follow a chronic inflammation of the nose or middle ear; or they may occur entirely apart from any other illness. It is probable that a large number of the children in whom such symptoms are at all severe, die. Others, but relatively few, appear to make a complete recovery. In yet others death does not take place, but a permanent legacy remains in the shape of a gross cerebral lesion.

The chief of these causes may be enumerated as asphyxia neonatorum and trauma (occurring before, during, or after birth); scarlet fever, measles, small-pox, enteric, whooping-cough, otitis, rhinitis, and possibly sunstroke; lastly, primary inflammation of the cortical cells (polio-encephalitis of Strümpell), a disease analogous to the acute inflammation occurring in the anterior horns of the spinal cord. This last condition is probably a toxic one, and is the one of most importance. It is probably the underlying condition of most cases of paralysis of cerebral origin occurring in infancy, as well as of many in which brain symptoms are attributed to sunstroke and other vague causes.

The lesions which result from these varied causes are, broadly speaking, divisible into two classes—*vascular* and *toxic*. The former group embraces hæmorrhage, thrombosis, and occasionally embolus, with, it may be, laceration of brain tissue. The latter group consists of cases in which there is a direct poisoning of the nerve cells. But in many instances both these conditions are present.

In course of time secondary changes take place in and around the initial lesion, so that the final product is often very different to the change in the first instance. The chief ultimate results, as seen in post-mortem examinations made many years afterwards, are localized areas of softening, atrophy, and sclerosis; cysts, meningo-encephalitis, pseudo-porencephaly or hemiatrophy, and occasionally hydrocephaly. In these later stages it is usually impossible to say whether the original lesion was vascular, toxic, or inflammatory, and as there are no characteristic clinical differences I see no object in treating of these as separate varieties ; they will therefore be considered together.

But it is not to be assumed that the child who emerges from an illness of this kind with a gross lesion of the brain will necessarily be mentally defective. The efiect of the lesion upon the patient varies very much, and in the main three phenomena may result, either singly or in combination—namely, *paralysis, epilepsy*, and *amentia*.

It is stated that if paralysis results from these lesions it is sure to be accompanied by some amount of mental deficiency. This is a complete mistake ; not only may amentia occur without paralysis, but marked paralysis may be present without amentia. I have seen quite a considerable number of cases in which there was paralysis of hand and forearm or foot and leg, or even of two limbs, without the slightest intellectual impairment ; indeed, in some of them the mental capacity was decidedly above the average. Dr. Sigmund Freud,* who has made a most careful study of the question, says : " Idiocy does not show any constant relationship to the other signs of infantile cerebral paralysis in respect of the degree of psychic arrest. There are cases of the severest paralysis with the intelligence scarcely affected, as, on the other hand, complete idiots without any signs of paralysis."

With regard to epilepsy the case is somewhat different, and where the initial pathological process is such as to produce frequently repeated convulsions, there is a strong probability that some degree of amentia will result, and that dementia will ultimately supervene. But in these cases this result is by no means invariable, and it occasionally happens even in them for intellectual development to show no sign whatever of having been adversely affected. In exceptional cases it may even happen for the mind to show no trace of defect where *both* paralysis and epilepsy are present.† Finally, in a certain number of cases

* Freud, " Infantile Cerebrallähmung." Wien, 1897.

† A good example of this was described by the writer in an article on "Amentia" in Mott's "Archives of Neurology," vol. ii. In this case there was right hemiplegia, with constant epileptic fits from birth, probably due to asphyxia neonatorum. The patient died, aged thirty-five years, from exhaustion following a series of fits, and post-mortem examination revealed

Secondary Amentia and its Clinical Varieties 205

these infantile lesions give rise to amentia, and this may be accompanied by either paralysis or epilepsy, by both, or neither. It is thus seen that these infantile cerebral lesions are attended with widely different results, and although in this place, of course, we are only concerned with those in which amentia occurs, it will not be out of place to consider the reason for such diversity.

Two possible factors influencing the result are the age of the patient when the lesion occurs and the inherited potentiality of the neuroblasts. In the new-born child cortical lamination is not yet complete, and there are a large number of neuroblasts lying among more fully developed nerve cells. I am inclined to think that a considerable number of these never attain mature development, for such immature cells may often be found in middle life. In this, as in other matters, Nature seems to act lavishly, and to provide a far greater number of cells than are developed by the stimulus of incoming sensations which comprise "education." In fact, there appears to be a potentiality of cerebral development which is never attained by the individual ; although it is probably to the gradual bringing into play of these neuroblasts that the progressive mental evolution of the race is due. With the lapse of years, doubtless, the developmental capacity of these embryonic cells becomes progressively less, and hence the older the child the more serious is likely to be the result of one of these lesions. Before cortical lamination is complete, however, I see no reason why their inherent potentiality should be inferior to others amid which they lie. Consequently it is not improbable that the destruction of nerve cells caused by a lesion occurring at or shortly after birth may be

---

chronic meningo-encephalitis of the whole of the motor region of the left hemisphere. There was also considerable non-development of this hemisphere, its weight being 105 grammes less than the right, and there was chronic interstitial sclerosis, with diminished number of nerve fibres, throughout the corresponding upper efferent tract. The motor lesion had been compensated to a great extent by a numerical increase of Betz' cells of the opposite hemisphere. And yet this patient showed no trace of amentia, and, in spite of his paralysis and epilepsy, was able to earn his living until nearly twenty years of age. He was then admitted to the workhouse in consequence of the fits, and subsequently transferred to the asylum on account of post-epileptic insanity. At the time of his death there was practically no dementia.

compensated by the development of these embryonic cells; and where the two hemispheres have a function in common, it may even be possible for such compensation to take place in the opposite side to the one affected. This view, of course, is largely hypothetical, but it finds support in a number of clinical facts which are otherwise extremely puzzling. Thus, many cases have been recorded in which the greater part of one cerebral hemisphere was practically useless by reason of porencephaly or hemiatrophy, and yet the mental and motor defect was but slight; indeed, in a large number of these cases the clinical signs (particularly of paralysis) are astonishingly insignificant when compared with the state of the encephalon.* Moreover, in the case already referred to, where practically all the large motor cells (of Betz) of the left leg area had been destroyed by a vascular lesion during birth, I was able to demonstrate a compensatory increase in the corresponding cells of the opposite hemisphere.

A diminished neuronic potentiality, due to slight morbid heredity, is the explanation of those cases of so-called "developmental" amentia which apparently result from a comparatively trifling cerebral lesion or general disturbance of health, and in all probability in the cases we are now considering the effect of these lesions upon the intellectual capacity of the patient is in no little measure influenced by his hereditary predisposition. One would also imagine that the ultimate amount of physical or psychic impairment in these cases would be considerably influenced by the amount of special training received by the patient during infancy.

* On this subject see a very interesting article on "Secondary Degeneration following Cerebral Lesions," by W. G. Spiller (*Journal of Nervous and Mental Disease,* New York, January, 1898). Dr. Spiller describes the case of a boy in whom "the motor fibres of the left cerebral hemisphere were totally destroyed, and yet the boy was able to walk without a crutch, although in an imperfect manner; he had no use of the right upper limb." Spiller says: "The conviction is forced upon one that the motor fibres to the right lower limb were transmitted through the pyramidal fibres from the right cerebral hemisphere. . . . The nervous system can adapt itself much better to altered circumstances if destruction of tissue occurs before the nerve-cells and fibres are fully formed, and it would seem that even additional fibres may develop." He quotes several similar cases which have been recorded by von Monakow, Mahaim, Déjèrine, Thomas, and Zacher.

Secondary Amentia and its Clinical Varieties 207

With regard to the kind of lesion, Freud doubts whether it is a factor of much importance. He says : " One is as likely to see a brain with diffuse lobular sclerosis, with extensive blood-cysts, porencephaly, and the like, whether the individual was idiotic or relatively well developed mentally." I cannot but think, however, that in many cases the secondary changes taking place in and around the diseased focus have contributed not a little to the patient's mental state. Some of the initial lesions tend to become localized and shut off, others to spread and cause diffuse changes, and it seems to me that such difierences, probably by bringing about alterations of intracranial pressure, cannot be without effect upon the general brain function, and therefore the mental capacity.

But undoubtedly the most important feature of these lesions is their situation and extent. If confined to the motor cortex or its downward prolongations, the result will probably be paralysis without amentia. In a considerable number of cases, however, lesions of the motor cortex also produce convulsions which may at first be Jacksonian, and ultimately become typically epileptic. It may even happen for a subcortical focus of disease to produce similar convulsions.* As a consequence amentia and dementia may be induced. A lesion in or near the motor cortex may exceptionally cause epilepsy without paralysis, and here also the convulsions may bring about subsequent mental deterioration ; in such cases paralysis may supervene later. A lesion elsewhere may give rise to epilepsy, either by acting as a source of reflex irritation, or by causing an increased intracranial pressure. Finally, a lesion of the more purely psychic areas (probably the frontal, prefrontal, and parietal lobules) may produce amentia without either paralysis or epilepsy. It is necessary to remember that not only may secondary pathological changes be induced by any of these lesions, but that an arrest of development may occur in far removed portions of the encephalon which are functionally correlated. The involvement of both hemispheres, as shown by a paraplegia, is of far more serious import than where one side only is affected.

To sum up, we may say that a severe lesion of the psychic

* Such a case was described by the author in Mott's " Archives of Neurology," vol. i.

areas will probably produce amentia without paralysis, and a lesion of the motor areas paralysis without amentia. But either of these may give rise to epilepsy, and this may also result from a lesion elsewhere. As a result of this epilepsy, amentia, and subsequent dementia, may be induced.

The clinical symptoms which usher in these cerebral complications differ somewhat according to the particular cause. In the cases due to injury during birth, well-marked asphyxia is often present, from which the child is with difficulty resuscitated. He remains torpid, respiration is apt to be slow and irregular, and the pulse is feeble. The pupils may be contracted, and the anterior fontanelle tense. He does not cry, and evinces little interest in the breast. Usually in a few days convulsions make their appearance; but in between these the muscles may still remain rigid, and opisthotonos may even be present. At a somewhat later period paralysis may be noticed. Sitting up, walking, and first attempts at speech, are all delayed, and it is gradually borne in upon the parents that the child's mind is not quite the same as that of other children. In the milder cases the initial symptoms may rapidly pass off, and it is only when the child begins his schooling that deficiency is noticed, and that he is found to be unable to make any mental effort.

Many of these children are small and delicate, and there is no doubt that a large proportion die in the early years of life, some of convulsions, others of ordinary children's ailments. But others thrive and get fat, and may live for many years; and it is these who come under notice on account of their mental defect. There is not, as a rule, any pronounced sensory disturbance, although sometimes hearing is impaired. The amentia varies from a mild degree of imbecility to gross inarticulate idiocy. If paralysis is present, it is generally a paraplegia, and the arms are rarely involved in these cases which date from birth. The affected legs are small, short, ill-nourished, and their muscles exceedingly ill-developed. They may be strongly adducted, and at times quite crossed in a sartorial posture. Contractures are often present, and the reflexes are usually much exaggerated. In some cases the paralysis is slight, and consists simply of weakness and dragging of the limbs, with some rigidity and increased reflexes. Exceptionally it is absent altogether.

Secondary Amentia and its Clinical Varieties 209

In those cases which arise during the first few years of life, either in the course of, or as a sequel to, one of the specific fevers, or as a cerebral inflammation apart from any previous illness, the symptoms are slightly different. The first indications of an affection of the brain are often malaise and vomiting, and these are followed by restless delirium or unconsciousness, fever, convulsions, and often paralysis. The fact that the onset of many of these cases is so often attended with convulsions causes them to be frequently designated "epileptic" or "eclampsic" amentia, whereas the convulsions are in reality a symptom and not a cause. They are sometimes very severe, and may recur with great frequency for several days. The temperature rarely rises to more than 102° F. Paralysis may be noticed at the onset, or it may not appear until a few days afterwards. It may even be absent entirely. When present it usually consists of monoplegia or hemiplegia ; diplegia is rare. The reflexes are increased, but there is rarely any marked disturbance of sensation. In course of time the fever abates, the convulsions cease, or continue only at rare intervals, the child recovers consciousness, and some amount of improvement takes place in the paralysis. But the psychic functions have been damaged ; in some cases an obvious impairment of the intellect is noticed immediately, in others only as the child begins to get about and mix with his companions. If he had begun to speak, he may be now speechless. The playmates and games of which he was formerly fond now cease to attract him. His whole behaviour and disposition may be so altered that the parents remark upon the change. As time passes, it is found that his capacity for learning has been interfered with, and it is soon evident that the illness has resulted in a more or less serious arrest of mental development.

In view of the widely differing ultimate effects of these cerebral lesions, it is obvious that no accurate forecast is possible. Of the children born with asphyxia, the number in whom amentia results is exceedingly small, and careful observation of the child for a few days will usually enable the physician to reassure the parents on this head. Of the cases happening during early childhood, the proportion who become aments is much larger, and this possibility can never with certainty be excluded until the lapse of some time after the illness. If paraplegia be present (which, however, is relatively rare), then it is highly probable that some degree of mental deficiency will result. Apart from this, however, the degree of paralysis affords no indication as to the amount of psychic damage. There may be extensive hemiplegia with no intellectual defect, or there may be profound amentia with but trifling or even no paralysis at all. Even were one able to exclude all involvement of the psychic areas, there would still be the possibility of recurrent epilepsy, and the consequent induction of amentia and dementia.

The mental deficiency in these cases may be slight or severe. Some patients are merely feeble-minded, and beyond a general simplicity and childishness, an inability to get on at school and to fend for themselves, they are capable of a considerable amount of useful work under supervision. Others belong to the imbecile grade, and are capable of very little ; others are idiots. In some persons the defect seems to be more particularly marked in certain faculties ; thus, we find that in some the memory is chiefly affected, in others the attention or the power of speech. In disposition and behaviour some of these aments are placid, contented, affectionate, and trustworthy, but others are very emotional and undependable. I am inclined to think that a suspicious disposition and general irritability of temper, together with a liability to be easily upset and to commit impulsive actions, are very common characteristics of patients suffering from this variety of amentia. As already remarked, there are no stigmata of degeneracy, and in the majority of these persons the bodily development and nutrition are normal. Often, indeed, as Langdon Down said, they are of winsome and comely appearance.

It is impossible to formulate more than very general rules as to the prospects of improvement in these cases. On the whole, if the case is really a secondary one, and not a case of primary amentia complicated by a gross cerebral lesion, and if convulsions are not frequent. there is a likelihood of a fair amount of improvement under proper educational methods. But such training must be begun early to be of much avail, and, unfortunately, one finds a very great tendency to postpone it until too late, under a mistaken trust that the child will " grow out of it." The extent of paralysis is no criterion as to the possibility of improvement. Some of the most hopeless cases are those in whom there is no paralysis, whilst some of those who

Secondary Amentia and its Clinical Varieties 211

suffer from a severe physical handicap may be taught to perform really useful work. Recurring convulsions are of much more unfavourable import.

Paralytic Aments.—In a large proportion of these cases paralysis is present, and such are often described as *paralytic aments*. But the association is not invariable, and it is more correct to look upon the paralysis as a symptom or complication, albeit a frequent one. The amount of paralysis varies enormously, ranging from a partial monoplegia to a hemi- or (rarely) paraplegia. In some cases the only observable defect may be a want of opposition of the thumb of one side. In others there is a severe hemiplegia, accompanied, it may be, by some weakness of the opposite foot. In the traumatic or asphyxial cases, double talipes equino-varus is not uncommon ; both legs may be completely paralyzed, and occasionally spastic paresis of the legs may be accompanied by an inability to perform certain fine movements of the hands. As a rule, the face and tongue are not involved. The muscles affected are those concerned in the performance of definite movements, and they usually become considerably atrophied ; but there is no reaction of degeneration. In course of time rigidity and shortening take place, with the development of contractures and abnormal postures. The reflexes are usually exaggerated, and Babinsky's toe sign is frequently present. In fact, the grouping and general features of the paralysis are characteristic of a lesion of the *upper* efferent pathway. In some cases, however, I am inclined to think it may descend so as to involve the lower spinal tract.

In other cases convulsions are a prominent feature, and these may occur with or without paralysis. As a rule, in their onset, course, and post-convulsive state these are indistinguishable from those of ordinary idiopathic epilepsy ; but in some cases they are of a Jacksonian character. In one of my patients both localized and general convulsions occurred, the former unattended by loss of consciousness ; but they gradually passed into the typically epileptic variety, and I think this is the tendency in most of these cases where the fits begin as Jacksonian. Sometimes paralysis may exist for years without any fits, and then epilepsy suddenly makes its appearance. Petit mal also occurs. In a few cases there is seen a constant rhythmic tremor or irregular choreiform movements without epilepsy. As already mentioned, those cases the origin of which is marked by a series of convulsions are often described as *eclampsic amentia*, whilst those in which the fits continue, and have the characters of epilepsy, are spoken of as *epileptic amentia*. In my opinion, however, this latter term should be restricted to cases of amentia due to idiopathic epilepsy without a gross lesion.

ILLUSTRATIVE CASES.

Medium-Grade Amentia, with Hemiplegia and Convulsions, the Result of a Birth Injury.—M. B., female. No family history obtainable. The patient has had fits and paralysis since a baby, supposed to be due to an injury at birth. She went to school for a few years, but could never learn. At twelve years of age was admitted into workhouse in consequence of death of parents. Was thence sent into the asylum owing to epileptic fits. She is now twenty-two years of age, and has been under my observation for two years. She is a placid, simple-looking girl of apparently seventeen years or so, rather small, but well-nourished, and devoid of stigmata of degeneracy. There is left hemiplegia involving the leg, arm, hand, and lower part of the face. The reflexes are exaggerated on both sides, and there is slight lateral nystagmus. No impairment of sensation can be made out. She is subject to convulsive attacks without loss of consciousness, the duration of which has been as long as two hours. These consist of clonic movements of the left (paralyzed) hand and arm, with twitching of the left corner of the mouth, and drawing of the head to the left side. During the attack the knee-jerks are exaggerated (particularly the left), but there is no ankle clonus, and the pupils are normal. She says that the attacks are preceded by a " feeling " under the left arm, and that whilst they last she feels pins and needles in the left face, arm, and leg. Some of these attacks are followed by a state of general rigidity, with loss of consciousness. In addition she has petit mal and convulsions which are typically epileptic. Her mental condition is that of a high-grade imbecile. She can carry on a simple conversation, but does not volunteer information, and she will agree to almost anything suggested to her. She cannot read, but can just scrawl her name. She can count up to thirty, but cannot say what two and two make. She will do what she is told, and helps in the ward-cleaning. Her memory is poor; she has no idea of time or dates, but her attention is tolerably good. She is occasionally mischievous and takes things from the other patients, but on the whole is well-behaved and gives little trouble.

Amentia with Double Talipes due to Asphyxia Neonatorum.— M. F., female. There is nothing abnormal in the family history. The patient is the fifth of a family of ten; two died in infancy, the remainder are healthy. The mother tells me that M. F. was a very large child, that the labour was very prolonged, and that she was so blue and lifeless at birth that the doctor in attendance had to make " an opening in her throat." I do not know what this could have been, and can find no evidence (at seventeen years of age) of any tracheotomy scar; but there seems little doubt that the child had severe asphyxia neonatorum. The mother says she was quite " dummy " from birth, and utterly different to the other children; that she had severe fits whilst cutting her teeth, did not walk until four and a half years, and never said a word until she was in her sixth year. She went to school, but could not learn, and she afterwards had several situations, but could not keep them, as she seemed too simple and childish. At the age of seventeen years she began to get very troublesome and spiteful; she was considered a danger to the younger children, and sent to the asylum.

Upon admission she was a fairly well-grown girl, with a decidedly childish and vacuous expression. There was no observable sensory defect. She could understand what was said to her, and was capable of replying to simple questions. She could read and write words of one syllable, and could add up to ten. On the whole she was quiet and well-behaved, and did a certain amount of work in the laundry under supervision; but she had no power of reasoning, and was obviously far too deficient to earn her living. She was of a remarkably facile disposition, and readily assented to any proposition made to her; she also had a considerable defect in the power of sustained attention. Speech was exceedingly indistinct. She had double talipes varus, with some dragging of the feet in walking, but no other signs of paresis. She is now nineteen years of age. She has had no fits since childhood, but her mental deficiency is becoming more marked. She is at times rambling and incoherent in her conversation, but is on the whole well-behaved and gives no trouble. The slight paresis of the feet is somewhat more pronounced than formerly, and the knee-jerks are exaggerated.

Amentia due to Traumatic Epilepsy.—S.V., female. The patient is the sixth of a family of ten ; two sisters died in infancy, but the remainder are well grown and quite healthy in body and mind. A complete family history was obtained, and revealed an entire absence of morbid heredity.

S. V. was born at full term without any abnormal circumstances. She cut her teeth, walked, and talked at the ordinary age, and, in fact, appeared to be a perfectly healthy child until four years of age. She then had a fall in the street, striking her head against the curb; she remained unconscious for half an hour, and then came to, but seemed dazed. Five weeks afterwards she had her first epileptic fit, and they have continued almost daily since.

I saw this girl for the first time at the age of fourteen years. She was tolerably well grown for her age, and had no stigmata of degeneracy, although quite idiotic in manner and facies. She did not understand all that was said to her, but could obey some commands by signs. She was incapable of any kind of work, and could not dress or feed without help. Constantly wet and dirty. Could say a few monosyllabic words, but most of her utterances were inarticulate grunts. She was said to be good-tempered and quite harmless. On careful examination, I found that there was slight dragging with eversion of the right foot. The right face was also less full than the left, but there were no other localizing symptoms. The fits were typically epileptic, and followed by a prolonged period of unconsciousness. I came to the conclusion that the case was probably one of combined amentia and dementia, the result of traumatic epilepsy, and although I thought it very doubtful whether anything could be done so long after the injury, I recommended operation as a justifiable and the only possible measure.

Mild Amentia, with Paralysis and Convulsions, consequent upon " Infantile Hemiplegia."—F. D. W., male. No morbid heredity.

PLATE XVI.

FIG. 42.—Mild amentia with paraplegia, due to vascular lesion at birth.

FIG. 41.—Mild amentia with paralysis and convulsions, due to infantile lesion.

To face page 214]

Secondary Amentia and its Clinical Varieties

His brothers and sisters are healthy in body and mind, and the patient appeared perfectly normal until his second year. He then had a severe illness, which left him paralyzed in the right hand and arm, and a few years later he was noticed to be more simple than other children of his age. He went to school, but could never get on, and he cannot read, write, or sum. Upon leaving school he used to help his father (who is a publican) in the bar, but he has never followed any regular employment. He was subject to occasional epileptic fits, and after one of these assaulted his father and sister, and became so unmanageable generally that he had to be sent to an asylum, where he has since remained.

He is now forty-two years of age, and is a well-developed man of medium height, with no stigmata of degeneracy. His facial expression is placid and somewhat childish. There is dropping of the right wrist, and the interossei as well as the muscles of the thenar and hypothenar eminences and forearm are very little developed. The whole of the right forearm is short and stunted, as compared with the left. He can make use of the affected arm for coarse purposes, but he cannot perform fine movements. He cannot move the toes of the right foot, and they are cold and blue, but there is no other observable paralysis of this or any other portion of the body. There is no sensory defect, and he has had no fits for several years.

His memory is only fair, and is better for remote than recent events. His power of attention is good, and he has no special sense defect. He can carry on a simple conversation, and can give a tolerably good account of his past life; but his general intelligence is poor, and he is too childish to take care of himself without supervision. He is very suspicious of strangers, and very disinclined to answer their questions. He is emotional, and readily moved to laughter or tears. He is very variable in temper, and at times surly, perverse, and very troublesome, but at others he is a not unwilling worker in the dormitories. (See Plate XVI., Fig. 41.)

Mild Amentia with Paraplegia, due to a Cerebral Lesion during Birth.—T. W., male, aged thirty-three years. Owing to the death of the patient's parents a complete history is unobtainable, but, as far as can be ascertained, there is no morbid heredity, and the condition is the result of a lesion during birth, which left the patient paralyzed in both legs and mentally defective. He has been in institutions since childhood, and although he has learned to read and write fairly well, and even to do simple sums in arithmetic, the absence of any systematic manual training, together with his general intractability, cause him to be quite unemployed.

He has an alert, and at times a decidedly cunning, look, and his features are of a low animal type, but there are no obvious stigmata of degeneracy. The skull is symmetrical and larger than usual, the circumference being 23 inches. Both lower limbs are completely paralyzed from the thighs downwards ; they are also very small and imperfectly developed, blue and cold, and covered with a plentiful growth of hair. Tactile sensation is markedly diminished in the paralyzed limbs, and the knee-jerks and plantar reflexes are absent. Walking is impossible, but the patient is very adept at propelling himself along his haunches by making use of his hands and arms as levers. There have never been any convulsions.

There is no defect of the special senses. He understands most of what is said to him, and can reply, but usually refuses to do so. His memory is good ; he is very observant, and capable of simple reasoning ; but he cannot follow an argument, and his ideas and general behaviour are characterized by a childish simplicity. The powers of attention and control are markedly defective. If asked to write his name, he takes the pencil in his hand, looks at it, and then puts it down to look at his arm. He then takes it up again and makes a start, but drops it to scratch his back. Another beginning is interrupted to look at some one coming in at the door. In fact, he is as inquisitive and curious as a monkey, and so distracted by everything happening around him that he can settle down to nothing. He is destructive and constantly tears up his clothes, and from time to time he has outbreaks of noisy violence, during which he uses disgusting language and attacks anyone who may be near him. (See Plate XVI., Fig. 42.)

Amentia with Epilepsy, due to " Sunstroke."—E. S., male. The eighth born of a family of nine, all the others being healthy. There is a tendency to alcoholism on the parental side, but no insanity, epilepsy, or consumption. The patient seemed perfectly well until three years of age. Dentition had been normal; he was able to walk well, and was making progress with his talking. When just turned three he had "what the doctor called meningitis" following exposure to a severe sun. The mother says that for nine weeks he was unconscious and repeatedly convulsed. For twelve months after this he never uttered a syllable; he then began to pick up a few words again, but made little progress, and his parents noticed a profound change in him. Usually he was dull and stupid, and seemed to have little sense, but at times he became violent and unmanageable; the fits continued at short intervals. At the age of nine he became so troublesome that he had to be sent to the asylum. On admission he was somewhat undersized for his age, and poorly nourished. His features were good, and there were no stigmata of degeneracy, but the expression was vacant. Fits occurred daily; they were very severe, preceded by cry, followed by a period of unconsciousness, and had all the characteristics of true epilepsy. He could understand what was said to him, and would occasionally reply, but as a rule he was moody and silent and resented being questioned. He was incapable of any employment. The patient steadily became worse. He was a confirmed masturbator and addicted to swallowing pebbles. He became wet and dirty, required to be fed, and needed constant attention. He took no notice of his surroundings, did not seem to understand what he was told, and if examined became very resistant and forbidding. At times he would sit in a chair flapping his arms and making hideous noises; at others he was moodily silent. He died at the age of seventeen years, of exhaustion after a series of fits.

On making a post-mortem examination, I found the skull very thick and dense, the diploë being obliterated. The brain was small, and weighed $37\frac{1}{2}$ ounces, the left hemisphere being $5\frac{1}{4}$ ounces less in weight than the right. The ventricles were dilated, and there was considerable excess of clear fluid. The membranes appeared normal. The brain was tolerably well convoluted, and presented nothing abnormal externally beyond a general diminution of size. On making careful sections, however, a localized area of softening, about the size of a filbert, was found in the left supramarginal convolution at the junction of the grey and white matters. This in all probability was of vascular origin, and the final result of the attack of encephalitis, which took place at three years of age. (See Plate XVII., Fig. 43.)

Mild Amentia with Motor Aphasia, due to an Infantile Cerebral Lesion.—The following is a case of secondary amentia consequent upon infantile convulsions (eclampsia) ; it is probable, however, that these were the result of some toxic lesion of the brain.

N. T., male, born in India, the second child of a family of six. Parents healthy, and no morbid heredity. Seemed perfectly normal until nine months old, when he had a series of convulsions lasting three days. These continued, at intervals of a few months, until he was three years of age ; they were attended with unconsciousness, and in the last attack he was given up by the doctor. He recovered, however, and has had no further fits, but from that time his parents noticed a great mental change. He failed to understand what was said to him, became restless at night, exceedingly dirty in his habits, and required constant watching during the day to prevent him destroying everything he laid his hands on. As time passed some improvement took place : he became more manageable, and able to do little things for himself. He would also help his mother in laying the dinner-table and similar household duties, but he could not be depended upon, was at times very intractable, and was quite unable to speak.

I first saw him at the age of eleven years. He was a sturdy, well-developed boy, with good features but a decidedly vacuous expression. There was no sensory defect ; he could understand simple commands and remarks ; but he was obstinate, and took little notice of anything said to him. He could whistle, but could not articulate, and he was passionate and untrustworthy. As far as could be ascertained in the absence of conversation, his general intelligence was about equal to that of a normal child of five or six years. I came to the conclusion that the case was one of mild amentia secondary to meningo-encephalitis of the frontal lobes, and involving the motor speech centre, and considered the prospect of improvement slight, but recommended special training in an institution. This has now been carried out for three years. He has improved greatly in habits and general behaviour, he is now thoroughly obedient and dependable, and evinces an affectionate disposition towards those about him. He is fond of manual work, and can perform many kindergarten occupations,

PLATE XVII.

Fig. 44.—Pronounced imbecility due to encephalitis in infancy. Mischievous, destructive, and intractable. Age, 9 years.

Fig. 43.—Amentia with epilepsy, due to encephalitis at 3 years of age. Becoming demented.

Secondary Amentia and its Clinical Varieties 219

such as plaiting and bead-threading, very well. He lays the dinner-plates with a marvellous dexterity. He has learned to make pot-hooks and hangers, knows some of his letters, and can count up to six. But he finds school work very uncongenial, and cannot settle down to it. He seems incapable of making any mental effort. He understands all that is said to him, but still remains unable to articulate, and, in spite of persistent attempts to teach him, the nearest approach to a word he can utter is a guttural "cuckoo."

In the following case there is slight morbid heredity, but mental development proceeded normally until an attack of "meningitis" in infancy. The degree of defect is mild, but it is accompanied by evidences of instability, which will probably culminate in actual insanity before adolescence is passed.

K. G., male. Was born in India, and has four brothers and sisters alive and well. His mother is an exceedingly delicate, neurotic woman, his father strongly addicted to alcohol; but there is no history of epilepsy or insanity on either side. The patient seemed all right until fifteen months old, when he was laid up for two months with some brain illness, accompanied by fits, which is described as "meningitis." From this time he became subject to fits of irritability, and showed indications of mental defect. He went to school at the age of seven, and showed a considerable taste for drawing and manual work; but he was never able to make progress in any studies, and seemed incapable of mental application. I saw him in consultation at the age of eleven; he could then read and write simple sentences, and was capable of simple addition and subtraction sums. He had a good memory, and could recount a few historical and geographical facts, but his manner was very restless and his attention very fitful; he was quite incapable of settling down to school work, and his general intelligence and power of reasoning were no greater than those of a normal child of six years. Cranial circumference, 21⅜ inches. He was affectionately disposed to those about him, but of a very undependable temper. Was addicted to hiding up trifling objects of no value, and had wandered away from home on several occasions. At times he was destructive, and would tear up clothes, toys, and picture-books indiscriminately. Occasionally he was noisy and aggressive, and had attacked those about him.

Amentia accompanied by Porencephaly or Cerebral Hemiatrophy.

As seen in the post-mortem room. these cases appear to be widely different from those just described. in which the pathological findings are cysts. localized atrophies. softening, meningo-encephalitis, and the like. Here we have to do with a condition of porencephaly or hemiatrophy of such an extent that the affected hemisphere may be 200 or 300, or even more. grammes less in weight than the opposite one, and it would seem as if such must be accompanied by special clinical features. In some instances this is so, and on that account it is desirable to refer to these conditions separately. But, on the other hand, it must be admitted that these severe conditions can often only be suspected during life, and that they are by no means rarely found after death when there had previously been nothing to suggest that more than a minor pathological disturbance was present. An interesting case of this nature has been recorded by Conolly Norman and Fraser.* It was that of a very fine female who had never been under restraint, and who presented no external evidence of extensive brain disease in the shape of atrophy, contractures, etc., and yet post-mortem there was found extreme wasting of one hemisphere, as well as of the corresponding basal ganglia. Many similar cases in which the clinical signs have been comparatively slight have been recorded by other writers— viz., Van der Kolk, Bianchi, Heschl, Spiller, Lambl, etc.

In most cases these conditions are the result of disease, and date from very early infancy, if not from uterine existence ; a few, however, seem to be due to primary anomalies of development. But the distinction can only be inferred clinically, and not always with certainty upon dissection.

During life an ament may be suspected to be the subject of porencephaly or extensive hemiatrophy if there is severe hemiplegia accompanied by contractures and marked non-development of the affected limbs, and if convulsions are also present. But, as already remarked, the hemiplegia is often astonishingly insignificant, and it rarely involves the tongue or face. The

* Conolly Norman and Alec Fraser, " A Case of Porencephaly," *Journal of Mental Science*, October, 1894.

Secondary Amentia and its Clinical Varieties 221

convulsions are of the usual epileptic type, and are fairly frequent, but cases have been recorded in which they were absent. Sometimes much headache is complained of. The diagnosis is rendered more probable if, in addition, there is marked flattening of one side of the skull, but in many of these cases the space is filled up by excess of fluid or growth of the inner table only. I know of no other distinguishing features. The amentia may be of any grade, from a mild imbecility to gross idiocy, and stigmata of degeneracy may be present or absent according as the case is one of primary amentia complicated by these lesions, or one of secondary amentia due to them. In the latter dementia often supervenes, and death frequently results from tuberculosis or follows a succession of fits. Of Kundrat's* series of eighteen cases of porencephaly, only three survived the period of infancy.

ILLUSTRATIVE CASES.

False Porencephaly with Cystic Formation.—A. E. W.,† female. Imbecile. No morbid heredity. Born paralyzed on right side. Constantly suffered from headache and epileptic fits. The paralysis involved the right arm and leg, but not the face. The affected limbs were smaller and shorter than the sound ones. There was talipes equino-varus of the right foot, but no contractures. The knee-jerks were absent. Speech indistinct, memory poor, depressed and dull mentally. She was subject to frequent fits, beginning in the affected side, and then becoming general. She gradually became more and more demented, and died at the age of twenty-two, after a succession of severe fits.

The post-mortem examination showed extensive atrophy of the lower part of the motor region on the left side, and of the corresponding efferent tract in the pons, medulla, and cord. The depression in the brain was occupied by a subarachnoid cyst. The left ventricle also was greatly dilated. The weight of the left hemisphere was 435 grammes, and of the right 585 grammes.

Cerebral Hemiatrophy with Ventricular Dilatation.—J. E., male.

* *Op cit.*
† For a fuller description of the histological appearances in this and the following case, see " Hemiatrophy of the Brain," by Mott and Tredgold, *Brain*, part xc., 1900.

Fits, paresis of right arm, and weak-mindedness from infancy. The right leg also weak, but he was able to walk, and he had been engaged as a shoeblack. He was admitted into the asylum at the age of twenty-six in consequence of frequent epileptic fits accompanied by attacks of noisy excitement. On several occasions he had attacked those about him without provocation. He gradually became demented, and died, aged thirty, of acute phthisis.

On post-mortem examination the skull was symmetrical externally, but there was marked thickening of the whole of the inner table on the left side. In some situations the thickness was more than twice that of the opposite side. The weight of the right hemisphere was 575 grammes, that of the left but 155 grammes. The left ventricle was hugely dilated, the substance of the hemisphere being reduced to a mere shell in places. The left basal ganglia, particularly the optic thalamus, were also exceedingly small and ill-developed. There was consecutive atrophy of the left crus, pyramid and fillet in the pons and medulla, with atrophy of the right half of the cerebellum and its superior peduncle. There was also sclerosis of the left direct and right crossed pyramidal tracts in the cord, of the left antero-lateral column, and marked numerical diminution of the anterior horn cells in the cervical and lumbar regions.

The following description, by Dr. Ross, of a case of *double true porencephaly* (which is exceedingly rare) is quoted by Ireland:

" The patient was a little girl who died of croup at the age of two years and five months. At the age of three months her parents first observed that she could not hold her head up, and that her hands were stiff. She never at any time suffered from convulsions. The child was small for her age, but fairly nourished. The legs were kept in a half-flexed condition, the feet extended, and the heels drawn up. The arms were held semi-flexed in a symmetrical position. The muscles of both extremities were in a state of spasmodic rigidity. Any attempt to alter by passive motion the position of the limbs caused increased spasmodic contractions. The head was kept bent forwards, the chin upon the sternum ; but she could raise her head by an effort, soon again to fall into the old posture. She ould voluntarily grasp an object with each hand, but the movements were irregular and uncertain. She could only utter a few monosyllables."

" On examination after death a deep sulcus was found in each side of the brain, about the site of the fissure of Rolando, extending from the point of bifurcation of the Sylvian fissure for about 1½ inches upwards. Each sulcus opened into the corresponding lateral ventricle by an aperture the size of the little finger. Each opening was surrounded by a ring of grey matter having all the naked eye appearances of the cortex. The ascending frontal and ascending parietal appeared to be absent, and the surrounding gyri were displaced. The crura cerebri, pons and medulla appeared quite normal to the naked eye." Microscopical examination showed that the cortex contained a number of imperfectly developed cells almost destitute of processes. The anterior pyramids of the medulla also were not more than half the size of those of a normal child of corresponding age, and the lateral columns of the cord were also diminished in size.

Bourneville* has recorded six cases of cerebral hemiatrophy, of which the following are synopses. All the patients were imbeciles or idiots, and almost all suffered from epileptic convulsions, and showed post-mortem sclerosis, atrophy, and chronic changes in the membranes and brain tissue.

1. Pseudo-porencephaly. Fifteen years old. Left hemiplegia with epilepsy. Right hemisphere, 240 grammes. Left hemisphere, 560 grammes.

2. Imbecile. Twenty-one years. Right hemiplegia and epilepsy. Right hemisphere, 465 grammes. Left hemisphere, 185 grammes.

3. Imbecile. Eleven years. Left hemiplegia and epilepsy. Left hemisphere, 570 grammes. Right hemisphere, 310 grammes, showing pachymeningitis and meningo-encephalitis.

4. Idiot. Four and a half years. Right hemisphere, 460 grammes. Left hemisphere, 200 grammes, with marked sclerosis.

5. Imbecile. Thirteen years. Right hemiplegia. Right hemisphere, 665 grammes. Left hemisphere, 455 grammes.

6. Idiot. Ten years. Right hemisphere, 477 grammes. Left hemisphere, 255 grammes.

* Bourneville, *Progrès Médical*, 1898, p. 248.

SCLEROTIC AMENTIA.

It has already been remarked that proliferation of neuroglia, resulting in sclerosis, is found post-mortem in a considerable number of cases of both the primary and secondary forms of amentia.* In many of these it is a pathological condition which has no clinical significance, and gives rise to no definite symptoms by which its presence may be diagnosed, or even suspected, during life. In a small proportion of cases, however, the neurogliosis attains such magnitude as to produce a tolerably readily recognizable type of amentia, and these we shall here describe.

Regarding the etiology of these cases our knowledge is still imperfect, and it is probable that the same result may be produced by different causes. In many—indeed, I think, in the majority of cases—inquiries into the family history reveal the presence of alcoholism, phthisis, insane and epileptic heredity, precisely the same as in ordinary cases of primary amentia; but in addition there is often a history of birth injury or other vascular or toxic lesion of early infancy which may possibly act as a determining influence. In a few cases the latter conditions alone are present. But although it seems probable that in the majority of cases sclerosis is determined by, and the after-effect of, some diseased (vascular or toxic) condition of the brain, it may in a small number of instances arise independently of such conditions in consequence of primarily imperfect neuronic development. However produced, and whether the amentia be a primary one complicated by sclerosis, or whether the sclerosis is itself the cause of the amentia, the result is pretty much the same. And since the special clinical symptoms in these cases are in the main referable to the sclerosis, and since, moreover, the cases resemble many of the pure secondary forms in their tendency to degeneration and dementia, it seems, on the whole, preferable to describe sclerotic amentia in this place.

There are two chief clinical types of this variety of amentia, dependent upon whether the sclerosis is general and *diffuse*, or occurs in *localized* patches. This division is, perhaps, not an absolute one, and cases of diffuse sclerosis have been described in

* See Chapter IV., Pathology.

Secondary Amentia and its Clinical Varieties 225

which the condition was confined to one hemisphere. Nevertheless, there are certain clinical differences in the two forms which sufficiently justify such a distinction.

In cases of *diffuse* sclerosis the dominating symptoms are general muscular weakness, often accompanied by spastic rigidity and feeble contractures, but rarely by actual paralysis. There is also marked tremor, but not often definite convulsions. In *localized*, *nodular*, or *tuberous* sclerosis, on the other hand, there are usually frequent epileptic fits without paralysis or contractures, although movements are often tottering and tremulous, and in these latter cases death often results from a succession of fits.

Extensive gliosis, in the first instance, produces an enlargement of the brain, and in this way gives rise to a clinical variety of amentia, which is known as "hypertrophic." With the lapse of time, however, the neuroglia tends to contract, and there is then produced a regular or irregular form of brain atrophy. The hypertrophic brain never tends to indefinite enlargement as does the hydrocephalic, and the effect of time in bringing about contraction of the glia tissue is well seen in the central umbilication which takes place in the tuberous areas of the localized form. This feature of the neuroglia is seen in other diseases; for instance, the spinal cord in the early stage of extensive disseminated sclerosis is greatly swollen, whilst in the later stages it becomes exceedingly small, shrivelled, and distorted.

Diffuse Sclerosis.

Cases of amentia accompanied by diffuse sclerosis fall into two groups, dependent upon whether cranial enlargement is or is not a prominent feature. We may therefore describe *atrophic* and *hypertrophic* forms. But, as already stated, it is doubtful whether there is any essential pathological difference between these two forms, and the clinical difference is probably dependent upon the extent and rapidity with which neuroglial increase takes place whilst the cranial bones are yet ununited. Where synostosis has not occurred, so that expansion of the skull may allow of cerebral enlargement, the prognosis as to life and response to training is much more favourable than where the bones offer an unyielding resistance.

(a) **Atrophic Form.**—These cases are very rare. In those hitherto recorded the mental deficiency has usually been of a pronounced grade, and although there may be some slight response to training at first, progressive dementia supervenes sooner or later. Definite convulsions are uncommon, but a condition of muscular tremor is always present. This varies from a more or less constant shaking of the head to an incessantly repeated fine tremor of the whole body. It is increased under observation or voluntary effort, and is often described as chorea; but it is more akin to the tremor of paralysis agitans. In addition there is a general muscular weakness, with spasm and incomplete contractures of the arms or legs, but there is rarely actual paralysis. The reflexes are increased. In some cases both epileptic convulsions and paralysis are present, and Bourneville* has described a case in which these were at first limited to one side of the body; but at the age of thirteen classic epilepsy appeared, and the patient died, aged twenty-one, in status epilepticus. The postmortem examination showed atrophy and sclerosis of the whole of one hemisphere.

ILLUSTRATIVE CASES.

Diffuse Sclerotic Amentia with Progressive Dementia.†—E. G., female, was admitted to Darenth Asylum at the age of twelve years. No history obtainable. Her mental status was that of an imbecile, but sight and hearing were good, and she possessed a good memory for faces. Speech was very scanty, and was slow and hesitating. Habits cleanly. She was described as a cripple, but not paralyzed. There was general muscular weakness of all the limbs, so that she was unable to wash, dress, feed, or do anything for herself. In addition there was a slight shaking movement of the head. She spent all her time sitting in a chair, but she noticed what went on round her. The cranial circumference was 19¼ inches.

After a time the shaking movements of the head increased, and eventually extended to all the limbs. There were, however,

* Bourneville, "Sclérose Cérébrale Hémisphérique," *Archives de Neurotie*, 1897, vol. iii.
† For the clinical notes of this case I am indebted to Dr. F. R. P. Taylor, merly Medical Superintendent of Darenth Asylum.

never any definite convulsions. The muscular helplessness also increased, and the arms and legs became slightly contracted at the elbows and knees respectively. She became duller mentally, less observant, and wet and dirty in her habits. Finally her temperature suddenly ran up to 104° F., and her pulse to 180, and she gradually sank and died without any signs of disease other than the cerebral sclerosis. Her age at death was twenty years.

Post-mortem examination failed to reveal disease of any organ other than the brain. The dura mater was thick and congested; the piâ thick and opaque, but non-adherent. The whole brain was small, but heavy for its size, weighing 32 ounces. Its consistence was extremely dense—in fact, almost like cartilage. Upon making a microscopical examination I found that the whole of the hemispheres, the white as well as the grey matter, were the site of a dense diffuse sclerosis; the cerebellum was similarly involved.

The following very similar case is described by Dr. O. Heubner:[*]

The patient, a boy of five years, seemed bodily and mentally sound until the age of three and a half years, except that he was late in learning to speak, and could not talk fluently. The family was said to be healthy. Apparently as the result of, or at any rate after, a fall on the back of the head, he no longer played willingly, and was often apathetic. Nine months afterwards appeared a slothfulness of all movement, and his walk became staggering. This was followed by spastic paralysis of the legs, with contractures at the hips and knees, and double equino-varus. Strong intention tremors then appeared in the arms, also followed by spastic paralysis. There was difficulty in swallowing, so that he could only take liquids, and eventually he became unable to speak. There was constant movement of the head and upper extremities, and there was slight paresis of the lower part of the right face. He became progressively weaker in mind, but able to recognize people he knew, and there was no observable alteration in general or special sensation. The knee-jerks were increased, electrical reactions normal, and there was incontinence of urine

[*] O. Heubner, " Ueber diffuse Hirnsklerose," *Charité-annalen*, 1897, xxii.

and fæces. He became much emaciated, and died of bronchopneumonia.

Post-mortem examination revealed a pale-yellow brain of unusual hardness throughout, the white and grey substances, as well as the cerebellum, being extensively involved by sclerosis.

The two following cases of brother and sister, who were kindly shown to me at Darenth Asylum by Dr. F. R. P. Taylor, are probably examples of diffuse cerebral sclerosis.

The mother of these patients is healthy, but the father is insane in an asylum. The father and mother are first cousins : the mother's father and mother were also first cousins. There have been fourteen children born in the family—five are dead and nine living : there is " something the matter with all of them," and at least one other is mentally defective.

Rose, the eldest patient, was born prematurely at the seventh month, and she has been abnormal from birth. She commenced to say a few words when about two years of age, and made attempts to walk at three ; but she never made much progress, and at the age of twelve years, on account of the mental deficiency and constant tremor, she was sent to the asylum. She proved uneducable, and the tremor steadily became worse. When I saw her at the age of twenty-one years she was a bright-looking girl, apparently quite happy and contented, but of markedly limited mental power. She understood a good deal of what was said to her, and made attempts to reply; but her articulation was quite unintelligible on account of the tremor. She spent the day sitting in a chair, and was quite unable to walk, or even stand, without support. There was spastic rigidity, with inversion and adduction of both legs and feet ; the knee-jerks and plantar reflexes were exaggerated, and ankle clonus was well marked. The head was never still in consequence of constant rhythmic up-and-down and side-to-side movements : the facial muscles were also affected, giving rise to a never-ending series of extraordinary grimaces. These movements were described as chorea, but they really had greater resemblance to paralysis agitans. They were worse under observation, but ceased during sleep.

The brother, William, was very similar, except that in his case the rhythmic movements affected the whole body—head, face, arms, hands, and legs. It was impossible for him to pick anything up, or to retain anything in his hands, but the grasp of the hands showed that tolerable muscular strength was present. He understood what was said to him, and attempted to reply, but his words were quite unintelligible. He had a moderate amount of intelligence, and obviously observed what was going on round him, and he was quite clean in his habits.

(b) **Hypertrophic Form.**—This condition is sometimes described as *hypertrophy of the brain*, but it is to be borne in mind that the hypertrophy concerns the interstitial tissue only, and not the cerebral neurones—that it is, in fact, a (probably diffuse) gliosis.

Hypertrophic amentia is relatively rare, and is characterized by an enlargement of the brain and skull and by certain bodily and mental symptoms. The largest skull of this variety I have seen had a circumference of 25 inches. Owing, however, to an increase in the density as well as the size, the brain weight is often considerably greater than would be expected even from the size of the skull. Dr. Fletcher Beach found the brain of a boy who died at the age of fifteen to weigh 62 ounces. Dr. Ireland quotes two cases described by Dr. Daniel Brunet. The brain of one, at the age of seventeen, weighed 1,632 grammes ; that of the other, dying at the age of eighteen, weighed 1,780 grammes.

Owing to the cranial enlargement, these cases are sometimes mistaken for hydrocephalus ; but, as pointed out by Dr. Fletcher Beach, there are readily recognizable differences. The skull of the hypertrophic ament tends to be square in shape instead of round, and there are sometimes well-marked frontal prominences. In hypertrophy, the greatest circumference is at the level of the superciliary ridges, whereas in hydrocephalus it is greatest over the temples. Thus, although the skull of the hypertrophic patient looks massive, it has not that " top-heavy " appearance so characteristic of the hydrocephalic. Further, in hydrocephalus there is usually bulging of the fontanelle and sutures, whilst in hypertrophy this is not generally the case ; in fact, the expansile effects and the tendency to distend the skull seem to be much greater in the former than in the latter condition. The cranium, having reached a certain limit, ceases to further expand, in consequence of the contraction of the neuroglia ; whilst hydrocephalus tends to expand the skull indefinitely.

Hypertrophic amentia is usually accompanied by headache,

which may be very severe, and by epileptic fits. In some cases the fits diminish in frequency and severity, and they may entirely cease. In others they get steadily worse, and many patients ultimately die of exhaustion following a series of fits. In a considerable number there is a general muscular weakness of all parts of the body, so that the balance is unsteady, the walk slow and tottering, and the grasp feeble. Tremor is often brought out by exertion. In consequence, manual work is performed slowly, clumsily, and with considerable difficulty. Speech is often similarly affected. Most of the cases I have seen have been somewhat undersized, heavy-looking and of good bodily nutrition, also of cheerful although somewhat simple expression.

The degree of mental defect varies very much, and seems to be dependent upon the frequency with which convulsions occur. Where these are slight, it is usually one of mild imbecility, or even merely feeble-mindedness; but if the fits are at all frequent, a condition amounting to idiocy may be present. Attacks of rage and violence have been described, but these are by no means constant, and I doubt whether they are any more common in this than in other varieties of amentia. Certainly some of these persons are harmless and thoroughly good-tempered. The severe cases, which are accompanied by frequent fits, seem to die early, and, as far as one can judge from the cases which have been recorded, few survive long after maturity. This, however, is by no means so with the milder forms, in whom fits are comparatively rare, and at the present time there is one of these patients in Earlswood Asylum who is fifty-two years of age, and seemingly in excellent health.

ILLUSTRATIVE CASES.

W. C. T., male; the only child; no morbid heredity. He seemed in every way normal until three years of age, when he had an acute illness, which the mother calls " influenza and rheumatic fever." It was accompanied by fever and very great pain in the head. He went to school at the age of seven, and left at fifteen. Was in the fourth standard, but his mother admits that he was very dull at learning, and does not think he was equal to fourth standard work. He had whooping-cough

Secondary Amentia and its Clinical Varieties

at the age of nine, which was accompanied by six fits. There were no further fits until twelve years of age, but during this time he was noticed to be very unsteady in standing and walking, and he would frequently fall down both in and out of school. In addition to being somewhat dull, he was prone to outbreaks of bad temper and irritability, and was at times spiteful. The head was first noticed to be larger than usual after the attack of whooping-cough at nine years.

I first saw him when he was fifteen years of age. He was undersized, but fat and heavy. The circumference of the skull at the level of the supra-orbital ridges was 23 inches; there was no asymmetry and no prominences; the fontanelles were closed. The upper and lower jaw-bones were also larger than usual, and as a result there were large gaps between the teeth. The teeth themselves were poorly developed, and many were decayed. The palate was broad and shallow. The nose was strikingly broad, with prominent fleshy nostrils; the lips were thick and fleshy, and the mouth large. The tongue appeared quite normal, but was always protruded markedly to the right side. There was nothing abnormal about ears or eyes. The external genitals were well developed, and there was an abundance of pubic hair. There was considerable rigidity of the hands, arms, and legs. No actual paralysis was present, but the left hand, arm, and leg were definitely weaker than the right, and he walked with a well-marked limp. The knee-jerks could not be obtained, but both plantar reflexes were exaggerated, particularly the left. Whilst under examination there were almost constant irregular jerky movements resembling chorea; these also were most marked on the left side. He was subject to tonic convulsions, averaging four or five daily. During these the right eye was firmly closed and the face drawn to the right, the left eye being open. Legs and arms were rigid and drawn up on to the trunk. No clonic movements and no loss of consciousness. There were no sensory defects, memory was good, attention rather fitful. He understood all that was said to him, and could converse quite rationally, although his speech was thick, slow, and hesitating. He used to stutter a great deal, but not now. He could read and write, but was exceedingly poor at sums. He had considerable moral and religious sense, and was obedient and well-behaved. His mental status was one of mild feeble-mindedness.

He is now twenty-one years of age, and has been under my observation for six years. At the present time the cranial circumference over the supra-orbital ridges is 23⅝ inches, over the brow 23⅞ inches. His height is 5 feet, weight 9 stones, and there is practically no alteration in his appearance. There have been no convulsions for several years, but if he gets upset or excited the hands and arms become rigid and are drawn up on to the chest. His walk is slow and somewhat tottering, and his balance is unsteady; but if he is allowed to take his time he can walk several miles. He can do odd jobs, and can clean a pair of boots, but it takes him an hour to do so. If he is hurried a general muscular tremor sets in, which makes work impossible. His hand-grasps are fairly good; the legs are spastic. He frequently complains of headache, which he refers to the parietal eminences. There is a decided improvement in his mental condition, and he can do many small jobs about the house. He can carry a parcel or a message, but his mother says that he cannot be trusted to do shopping, as he gets into a hopeless muddle with the change. His temper is irritable and perverse at times, but on the whole he is obedient and gives no trouble. I have got him into several situations, but he has been discharged from each in turn in consequence of his general incompetence.

It is worthy of note that the increased size of the jaws, with the separation of the teeth and the large and broad nostrils, give rise to a physiognomy somewhat resembling acromegaly. There are, however, no other signs of that condition, and the early onset is totally unlike it. It is quite possible, however, that the signs which are present may be due to a partial sclerosis of the pituitary gland.

I have quoted this case somewhat in detail because it seems to me to be a very typical example of that form of hypertrophic amentia in which fits have not produced serious mental degradation. At the present time there is a very similar case in Earlswood Asylum, and another patient of this type whom I have known for over ten years has managed during that time to earn his keep as a tradesman's boy. In this case, however, the

SECONDARY AMENTIA DUE TO SCLEROSIS.

Fig. 45.—A case of so-called "hypertrophy of the brain." Age, 21 years.

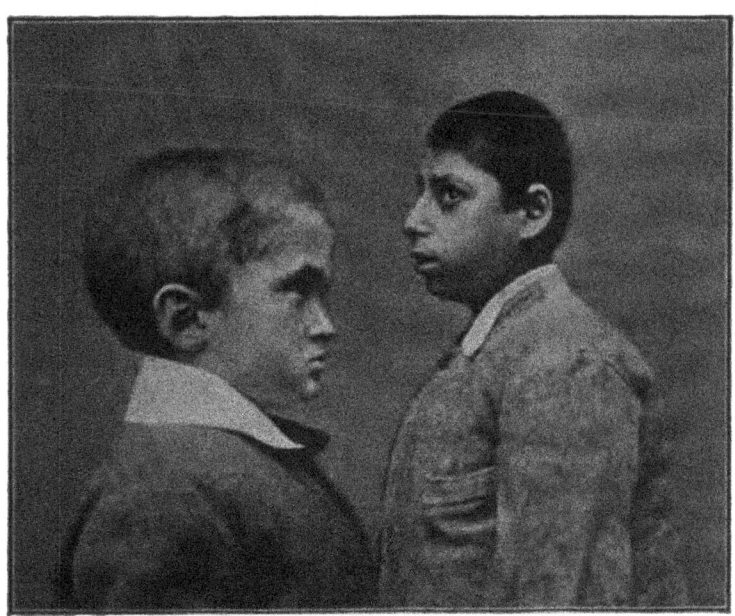

Fig. 46.—Hydrocephalic and microcephalic imbeciles.

Secondary Amentia and its Clinical Varieties 233

amentia is less marked, and his employer has treated him with considerable indulgence.

Tuberous or Nodular Sclerosis.

In this form of sclerosis convulsions are usually the first symptom to attract attention, being noticed towards the end of the first year. In a few cases, however, they are preceded by irregular muscular twitching or head-nodding. They continue during the life of the patient with tolerable frequency, in some cases occurring daily, in others at intervals of a few days. They are indistinguishable from ordinary idiopathic epilepsy, and minor attacks often occur as well. Mental impairment is noticed in the early years of life, and varies from a condition of mild imbecility permitting of some training, to a more pronounced imbecility or idiocy; usually it is of a severe grade. Headache is often present, and attacks of excitement, rage, and destructiveness are common. Muscular tremor is usually present, and the balance may be unsteady and the gait tottering; but definite rigidity and contractures, like those met with in the diffuse variety, are absent. There are no sensory disturbances. Progressive dementia supervenes, and death usually takes place in status epilepticus before the age of maturity.

ILLUSTRATIVE CASES.

W. S., male. Father insane; father's mother epileptic and insane. The patient has been subject to epileptic fits since a year old. He has always been of deficient intellect, and was unable to learn at school. He was subject to attacks of excitement and violence, and, according to his mother, would take up a knife to anyone on the slightest provocation. At the age of thirteen he became so troublesome that he had to be sent to the asylum. On admission he was found to be a pronounced imbecile, possessing numerous stigmata of degeneracy. He understood what was said to him, and was able to converse, but in a very simple and childish manner. He had a great fancy for drawing, but no ability. He was subject to frequent epileptic fits and occasional paroxysms of excitement. There was no paralysis. His memory gradually became defective and his articulation indistinct. Salivation was constant. He became more and more demented, and died at the age of nineteen from exhaustion consequent upon status epilepticus lasting seven days. During this time he had 406 convulsions.

Post-mortem examination showed a dense, thick, symmetrical skull, with a small but heavy brain, which weighed 1,445 grammes. The membranes appeared normal, and there was no excess of cerebro-spinal fluid. Both hemispheres were studded with numerous protuberances of pale sclerotic tissue, from which the piâ arachnoid stripped with unusual readiness. These nodules varied from the size of a pea to that of a small walnut ; many of them were extremely hard to the touch, and such were marked by a central umbilication, evidently due to contraction. They were strictly confined to the grey matter, the most careful examination failing to reveal them in the centrum ovale. Histologically, these nodules consisted of neuroglia cells and fibres in various stages of growth ; a few contained indications of former hæmorrhages in the presence of hæmatoidin crystals. The few nerve cells present were very irregular in arrangement, as well as being atrophied and distorted. The lamination of the adjacent cortex also was much disturbed, and there were many nerve cells in a condition of imperfect development, as well as others undergoing chronic pigmentary atrophy. Other portions of the cortex which were not occupied by nodules were surmounted by a definite band of sclerotic tissue, this being situated immediately underneath the piâ-arachnoid membrane. The corpora striata also were studded with protuberances of fine glia tissue, ranging in size from a grape-stone to a large pea ; but the ventricles were not dilated, and the ependyma was normal. Several of the leaflets of the lobus clivi of the cerebellum were markedly atrophied, and in these the number of Purkinje's cells was much diminished. There was also slight interstitial sclerosis of the pyramidal tracts and antero-lateral columns of the spinal cord. These lesions of the cerebellum and cord were probably secondary to the cortical sclerosis.

A case presenting identical histological features to the above was described by Dr. Joseph Sailer.* In this there was an

* J. Sailer, "Hypertrophic Nodular Gliosis," *American Journal of Nervous and Mental Disease*, 1898, p. 402.

Secondary Amentia and its Clinical Varieties

insane and alcoholic heredity, and spasms began at the age of ten months. The mental condition was one of low-grade idiocy. Epileptic convulsions were frequent, and the patient died, aged fifteen, of exhaustion after a succession of fits.

Another similar case was described by Dr. Margaret B. Dobson.* In this there was a marked family history of tuberculosis, alcoholism, and epilepsy, and the patient, a male epileptic idiot, died at the age of ten years from pneumonia accelerated by exhaustion from epilepsy. The post-mortem appearances were similar to those already described.

HYDROCEPHALIC AMENTIA.

Primary amentia may be complicated by hydrocephalus, and this condition is even occasionally found in making post-mortem examinations of microcephalics. The term "hydrocephalic amentia," however, is better restricted to those cases in which the mental deficiency is secondary to this lesion.

As to the cause of hydrocephalus much uncertainty exists. Some cases are the after-effect of chronic meningitis or tumours (usually syphilitic or tubercular) of the base of the brain; in others no antecedent lesion can be discovered. However produced, the essential condition consists of an accumulation of cerebro-spinal fluid, which may amount to several pints, within the ventricles of the brain. In consequence of the pressure of this fluid, the brain tissue adjacent to the ventricles is gradually thinned and destroyed. In extreme cases it may be reduced to a mere shell but a fraction of an inch in thickness, so that the hemispheres resemble a huge cyst. The parts least affected are the cerebellum and basal ganglia.

The expansile force of the fluid is usually marked upon the skull, the bones of which become widely separated; and this, with the general enlargement, produces a clinical picture which cannot well be mistaken. But in some instances hydrocephalus may exist with a small skull, owing to premature ossification of the cranial bones, and the condition will then only be revealed after death. Such are usually pronounced idiots; convulsions are frequent, and death takes place early.

* Margaret B. Dobson, "A Case of Epileptic Idiocy," etc., *Lancet*, December 8, 1906.

Occasionally hydrocephalus exists before birth, but if at all severe it is rarely possible for the child to be born alive ; and in the majority of cases met with the onset takes place in the first few months, or it may be years, of life. There can be no doubt that a great proportion of children so affected die within a few years. In other cases a spontaneous cure takes place, and it has even been affirmed by Edinger that a mild hydrocephalus occurring in childhood, and not progressing, may actually favour mental development by causing a lessened resistance to the growth of the brain. In most cases, however, there results some degree of mental deficiency.

The subsequent course differs, and in the main there are two types. In one, whilst the patient may be imbecile, or even idiotic, the mental condition is of secondary importance, in view of the active and steadily progressive nature of the disease to which it is due. Such children are acutely ill, the body is wasted, convulsions are frequent, and severe paralysis is generally present. Many of them are bedridden. They may be blind or deaf from the pressure of fluid, and optic atrophy is often seen. Although the alienist may be consulted with regard to these cases, their place is the hospital ward, and not the special institution, and death soon closes the scene. In some instances considerable amelioration of the mental symptoms takes place immediately before death.

The second type, those cases usually seen in special institutions, or which come under notice on account of amentia, are those in which the hydrocephalus is either increasing very slowly or has undergone spontaneous arrest. In these cases the mental deficiency varies from a mild degree of feeble-mindedness to pronounced imbecility, and, as a rule, a moderate amount of improvement takes place as a result of special training. Dr. Ireland quotes the case of a boy under his care who lost his hearing after being several years at Larbert, and gradually lost many of the words he had learned. " He was taught a number of figurative signs, and also to spell on his fingers ; and although he had the additional disadvantage of obscurity of sight—having dimness of the cornea, resulting from ophthalmia—his progress was as well marked as that of any pupil in the establishment."

The majority of hydrocephalic aments are quiet, confiding,

PLATE XIX.

SECONDARY AMENTIA DUE TO HYDROCEPHALUS.

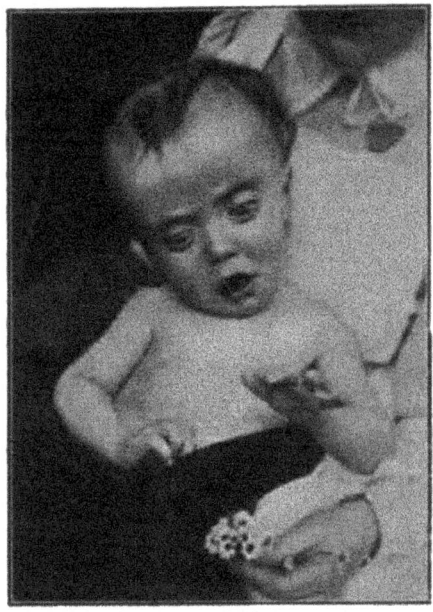

FIG. 47.—Male hydrocephalic. Age, 1½ years.
(*From a photograph lent by Dr. J. Thomson.*)

MICROCEPHALIC AMENTIA.

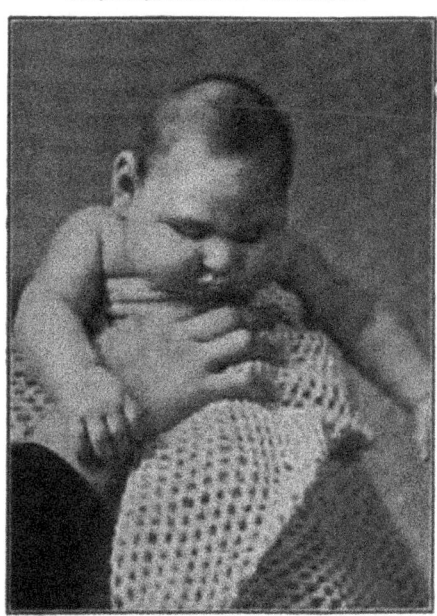

FIG. 48.—Female microcephalic. Age, 4½ months.
(*From a photograph lent by Dr. J. Thomson.*)

affectionate, and obedient, and although paresis may prevent the performance of much in the way of manual work, they are usually very willing to do what they can. Owing to their muscular weakness, movements are clumsy and badly co-ordinated, and in some cases severe paralysis may be present. The legs are more frequently and more severely involved than the arms. Impairment of sight and hearing are also common ; strabismus is frequent ; and in the more severe cases nystagmus occurs. Epileptic convulsions are usually present in the acute stage, but tend to diminish, and often disappear altogether, in the chronic cases seen in institutions. Most patients are undersized, but there are no stigmata of degeneracy. (See Plates XVIII. and XIX., Figs. 46 and 47.)

The peculiar enlargement of the skull makes diagnosis easy. The hydrocephalic skull is uniformly increased in all directions, and thus tends to assume a globular shape. The forehead is high and projecting, and there is usually a characteristic bulging at the root of the nose, but the greatest circumference is at the level of the temples. The fontanelle is tense, and the sutures often widely separated. In the arrested cases, however, these become filled in with Wormian bones, and the component parts of the cranium become firmly united. The scalp is thinned, and often marked by large and prominent veins. The excessive size of the cranium, in conjunction with the small face, causes the head, as seen from the front, to have a very characteristic conformation, resembling an inverted pyramid, thereby producing a curiously "top-heavy" appearance. The circumference varies from a little above the normal to as much as 30 inches or more. The average measurement of the chronic cases seen in institutions is about 25 or 26 inches, but there is no constant relationship between the size of the skull and the degree of mental impairment. The prognosis will depend upon whether the disease is stationary or slowly progressing. In the latter dementia is usually the ultimate result.

The two conditions which might be confounded with hydrocephalus are hypertrophic amentia and rickets. The distinction in regard to the former of these has already been given. In rickets the skull is often enlarged, but such is due to a thickening and increased density, and not a distension. Moreover, the rickety skull is usually asymmetrical, bossed, and ridged; the fontanelle, if still open, is depressed, and not elevated; there is an absence of the thin and prominently veined scalp, and other signs of rickets are present.

ILLUSTRATIVE CASES.

G. P., male, was admitted into the Littleton Home for Defective Children when six years of age. He was an orphan, and no history bearing upon his condition was obtainable. He was a delicate-looking boy of average height, with a typical hydrocephalic skull, the circumference of which was $22\frac{1}{4}$ inches. The palate was high and saddle-shaped, the teeth irregular. There was left internal strabismus, also deficient power, but no definite paralysis, of the left arm and leg. He dragged both feet in walking, and the body balance was poor. He knew his letters and numbers, and could spell a few simple words, and his mental condition generally was one of mild defect. Articulation was good, and his disposition was bright and cheerful. There was very little change for three or four months, although the boy made no headway in school. He then began to be silent and pensive, and to lose interest in his surroundings. The physical signs also increased, the legs became definitely spastic, so that walking was impossible, and all movements were performed with difficulty. By the end of six months the cranium had increased $\frac{1}{2}$ inch in circumference, and, as he was becoming physically helpless and showing signs of dementia, I was compelled to discharge him.

C. H., male. The fifth born of a family of eight, two of whom are said to be in good health, although one is a heavy drinker. A third is "very delicate," and the remainder died in infancy; one was a cripple. The father died, aged fifty-two, of bronchitis; the mother died, aged forty-seven, of general paralysis. The patient seemed all right at birth, but had a "fit" when a year old, and from that time his head was noticed to get rapidly bigger. He did not walk until late, and then very badly, and he always seemed more simple and childish than other children. He made little progress at school, and at the age of fourteen was admitted to an imbecile institution. He remained there for two years, but, becoming destructive and violent, he was transferred

Secondary Amentia and its Clinical Varieties 239

to an asylum. He was a pronounced hydrocephalic, in poor physical condition, but clean in his habits ; able to converse, and capable of helping a little in the wards. The head increased in size, and he gradually became more helpless. He is now eighteen years of age, and has been bedridden for over a year. His condition is as follows : The skull is typically hydrocephalic, and measures 25 inches in circumference. There is spastic paresis of both legs from the thighs downwards ; he can just stand, but is quite unable to walk. The arms do not appear to be affected. The knee-jerks are increased, and double ankle clonus is present ; also Babinsky's toe sign. On making movements a marked clonus of the legs appears, but there are no convulsions. He can hear and see, but is of decidedly defective understanding. As a rule, when questioned, he gazes at one in a stolid, helpless way, and makes no attempt to reply ; when he does speak, his words are unintelligible. He pulls to pieces everything which comes into his hands, but takes practically no notice of persons or things round him. It is obvious that the disease is rapidly progressing.

J. T., male. The fourth of a family of five, of whom one died in infancy ; the others are alive and well. There is insanity on the father's side, and consumption on the mother's. The patient was born with a very big head, labour being much prolonged. He did not walk until turned four years, and has always been clumsy in his movements. He was a little backward at school, but no marked mental abnormality was noticed until the age of ten, when he began to get passionate and difficult to control. He showed a remarkable memory for ages, and his mother says that he knew the age of every one of their numerous relations.

He left school aged fourteen, and was put to bootmaking ; but he never did much good, and after a short time he was taken away. He remained at home pottering about, but doing no work, until thirty-four years of age. A change then came over him ; he began to wander about at night, and sometimes stayed away from home for several days together. He would put tobacco into the teapot, and do similar foolish things. He became rambling in his conversation, and said that " Jack the Ripper " had tried to cut his throat. He refused his food, saying that it had been drugged. Finally he attacked his mother with a knife, and became so maniacal that he had to be sent to an asylum.

On admission he had a typical hydrocephalic head, convergent strabismus, and slight dragging of the left leg. He was loquacious, but of decidedly feeble intellect. The maniacal condition passed off, and he became quiet and well-behaved, and he remained in this condition for several years, subject, however, to delusions that some unknown persons put poison into his food. Then the legs became weaker, so that he was unable to get about, and now, at the age of forty-five years, he is bedridden. There is well-marked spastic paraplegia, so that he is unable to walk, or even stand, without support. The arms are unaffected. The knee-jerks are increased, and Babinsky's sign is present on the right side. Both legs and feet are blue and cold. There is no diminution in tactile sensation over any part of the body, and his power of localizing touch is remarkably good. He frequently complains of a girdle sensation round the epigastrium. There is fine tremor of the hands on extension, and of the legs on attempting movement, but no convulsions of any kind. The special senses are normal. Articulation is slightly defective, but speech is coherent and rational. Memory is very good indeed. He notices all that goes on round him, and can give a very good account of his past life, but his ideas are childish and his judgment and reasoning defective. He can read, write, and do sums remarkably well. •He has lately developed incontinence. The cranial circumference is 25½ inches.

SYPHILITIC AMENTIA.

It is a somewhat remarkable fact that, although syphilis is a frequent cause of disease in the fully developed brain, and although so-called inherited (really acquired *in utero*) syphilis is exceedingly common, yet the number of cases of amentia due to this cause is quite insignificant. They probably do not comprise at most more than 1 or 2 per cent. of all aments. One is driven to the conclusion that syphilis is a much more potent agent in producing neuronic degeneration than arrest, and this view is confirmed by the subsequent history of many aments who owe their deficiency to this cause. Further, in most of

Secondary Amentia and its Clinical Varieties 241

these cases in which syphilis is a factor there are other influences, generally neuropathic heredity, and it would seem as if the specific virus were chiefly productive of harm upon the nervous system in the presence of a neuropathic or psychopathic diathesis. In my own series of cases the number of aments whose condition was the result of syphilis *alone* (without neuropathic heredity) was but 0·5 per cent. It is interesting to note that the same applies also to degenerations of the brain and spinal cord occurring in later life. General paralysis, of which syphilis is the predominant exciting cause, has been shown to be accompanied by morbid neuropathic heredity in a large proportion of cases; and Mott has shown that the site of incidence of the poison upon the spinal cord is often determined by antecedent localized stress and strain producing a *locus minoris resistentiæ*.

There are several ways in which the poison of syphilis may conceivably determine amentia—one, by producing such a general disturbance of nutrition as to arrest neuronic growth, this I believe to be exceedingly rare; another, and in my opinion the usual *modus operandi*, by directly poisoning and so checking the growth of the developing cortical cells. It has been stated by some writers that syphilis can only produce amentia by causing gross lesions of the skull, membranes, or brain. Possibly some cases of hydrocephalic amentia are of this nature, but I do not think that this result is common. It is true that in a considerable proportion of cases the defective neurones subsequently undergo degeneration, and that considerable wasting of the brain ensues; but even this is not accompanied by the ordinary syphilitic lesions, and I think that in most cases amentia, in the first instance, results from the growth of the neurones being interfered with by a syphilitic toxæmia.

In addition to this, syphilis may, of course, produce amentia indirectly by bringing about a devitalization of the germ plasm, as we have already mentioned in treating of causation. But such cases hardly come within the category of syphilitic amentia, for this action of the poison is hereditary, and such cases are primary, not secondary amentia. The specific signs of syphilis are absent, and the condition is in reality what has been described by Fournier as " parasyphilitic."

In cases of secondary amentia directly due to, or determined by, syphilis, which are the only ones to which we shall apply the term "syphilitic amentia," the usual symptoms of inherited syphilis are present in infancy, and their characteristic lesions— —viz., keratitis, Hutchinson's teeth, scars, depressed nose, etc.— are generally found in after-life. In addition, the body is usually stunted and ill-formed, the child is backward in walking and talking (one of my cases did not speak at all until the ninth year), and some amount of mental deficiency is usually apparent in the first few years of life. As a rule, this is of a comparatively mild degree, most of the cases being merely feeble-minded or high-grade imbeciles. They go to school, but make no progress, and upon leaving they are found incapable of following any constant employment. Occasionally the mental status is that of idiocy; but up to the age of twelve to fifteen years the syphilitic ament, beyond the presence of the typical lesions, presents no special mental peculiarities which distinguish him from an ordinary ament of similar degree.

About or shortly after the usual age of puberty, however, a considerable number of these persons undergo a remarkable change. It is noticed that the patient is becoming restless and troublesome. Hallucinations and delusions often make their appearance, and in some cases there is pronounced mania or melancholia. Soon after this the balance and gait of the body become markedly unsteady, there is considerable tremor of the hands, mouth, and tongue, and the speech becomes slurred, indistinct, and hesitating. The knee-jerks are increased, and ankle clonus is often found. Sight and hearing are impaired, and if the eyes be examined the pupils will be seen to be dilated and to react sluggishly to light; at a later stage they become fixed. These changes are followed by a marked mental impairment, and the youth ceases to take any interest in his surroundings. There is no remission, and time only results in an aggravation of all these symptoms. The body begins to waste, swallowing becomes difficult, and the patient gets dirty in his habits. With the emaciation there is often considerable trophic disturbance, so that sores appear. Finally he becomes bedridden, gradually sinks into a comatose state, and dies. In males the external genitals retain their infantile condition, and in females menstruation does not appear. I have never noticed any grandiose

Secondary Amentia and its Clinical Varieties 243

ideas in these persons; but convulsive seizures are common, and these are occasionally followed by transient paralysis. The average length of time from the onset of these symptoms to the end is about five years.

It is seen that the symptoms and course of this progressive degeneration are practically identical with those of juvenile general paralysis, and this is further shown by the post-mortem appearances. In four cases which I have examined post-mortem the brain was small and simply convoluted as well as wasted, the piâ-arachnoid thickened and opaque, and the cerebro-spinal fluid in considerable excess. There were, however, no gross syphilitic lesions. Microscopical examination showed many cells in a typical condition of incomplete development, but over and beyond this there were extensive degenerative changes indistinguishable from those occurring in general paralysis.*

I do not think that this is the termination of every case of syphilitic amentia, for I have seen a few of these patients who, at over thirty years of age, showed no mental or physical alteration apart from the original deficiency. But although I have made diligent search, these latter cases are comparatively rare, and I am inclined to think that progressive deterioration, ending in paralytic dementia, is the rule in amentia due to syphilis.

The **Diagnosis** of syphilitic amentia rests upon the presence of the typical lesions, plus amentia, in the patient. In one of my cases the signs were indefinite, but the patient's mother had died of general paralysis. In another case a history was present, but no marks could be discovered upon the patient; a brother, however, presented the characteristic signs. Both these cases were considered to be probably syphilitic, and they subsequently developed general paralysis. Diagnosis at times, therefore, must be a matter of uncertainty. The remaining cases showed the characteristic lesions. It need hardly be emphasized that all subjects of congenital syphilis do not suffer from mental deficiency; on the contrary, the proportion who become aments is exceedingly small. It is probable that in most of these cases the arrest

* For one of the best accounts of the histology of juvenile general paralysis, as shown by modern methods of staining, see that by Watson in Mott's "Archives of Neurology," vol. ii., p. 621. Three, at least, of the twelve cases there recorded were aments.

of mental development is as much a consequence of morbid heredity as of the syphilitic virus, since such heredity, or some potent predisposing cause, is present in the majority of cases. Given a child with congenital syphilis, who is at the same time the offspring of a neuropathic or degenerate stock, then I think that amentia is extremely likely to result.

It has been stated by Hirsch that all individuals suffering from juvenile general paralysis have previously been of feeble intellect. With this, however, I cannot agree, as I have known several such patients whose mental condition had been quite up to the normal prior to the onset of the degenerative changes. But juvenile general paralytics who are seen in the consulting-room or asylum in the early stages of their disease are often thought to be imbeciles. Inquiries as to the previous mental status will readily distinguish between the two conditions.

Prognosis.—In view of the liability of these patients to develop general paralysis, it is obvious that a most guarded opinion must be given regarding the ultimate prospects of improvement from training, in any case of amentia which is considered to be syphilitic. Progressive dementia does not always result, but it does certainly appear to be extremely common ; and antisyphilitic treatment has been found to have not the slightest effect upon either the degeneration or the initial mental deficiency.

ILLUSTRATIVE CASES.

Syphilitic Amentia terminating in General Paralysis.—*M. D.*, female, the sixth of a family of ten. The fifth died of " water on the brain " in infancy, and the seventh and eighth were miscarriages. The remainder are said to be "all right." There is phthisis on the mother's side, but no insanity discoverable. The patient was decidedly backward at school ; afterwards she stayed at home to help her mother, as she did not seem equal to taking a place. At the age of nineteen years she began to get mischievous and destructive, and finally became so troublesome that she had to be sent to an asylum. On admission in October, 1899, she was described as being of very poor intelligence, wet and dirty in habits, noisy day and night, talking incessantly and using disgusting language without any connexion of ideas. Her condition was such that systematic

Secondary Amentia and its Clinical Varieties 245

examination was impossible. She gradually became somewhat quieter, and when seen by me, nine months after admission, her condition was as follows : A lethargic, almost stuporose, girl who spent the whole day sitting in a chair, indifferent to anything happening round her. She understood what was said to her, but was unable to carry on conversation or to answer simple questions properly. Speech slurred and tremulous. She attempted to write at my request, but her hand was so tremulous that it was impossible to do so. Knee-jerks greatly exaggerated ; extremities blue and cold. No paresis ; no seizures. Well-marked signs of rickets and congenital syphilis. I diagnosed syphilitic amentia, with beginning general paralysis, but was unable to see the patient again, and had forgotten entirely about her until going through my notes. The medical superintendent was good enough to supply me with the subsequent history, from which it appeared that unmistakable signs of general paralysis appeared towards the end of 1901 ; that phthisis was observed in February, 1902 ; and that she died on March 29 of the same year. Her age at death was twenty-three years, and the cause, as ascertained post-mortem, was general paralysis and phthisis.

Syphilitic Amentia terminating in General Paralysis. — T. C., male. Father alcoholic and insane ; his mother and all his brothers and sisters alcoholic. The patient is the second of a family of eight ; the first-born died aged two and a half months, and the mother was told by the doctor that, had it lived, " it would have been blind and an idiot." The fourth child, whom I have seen, has marks of congenital syphilis. The patient was backward in walking and talking ; his mother says he could never " get his words out properly." He went to school, but could never learn, and the schoolmaster said he was " a regular fool." He subsequently had several situations, but no one would keep him very long. At fifteen years of age he began to get very bad-tempered and strange in his manner ; he had attacks of screaming, which lasted for hours ; and ultimately, at seventeen years, was sent to an asylum with acute mania. This gradually subsided, revealing a condition of mild imbecility with beginning dementia. When asked his name and age, he would plaintively reply: " I ain't got no name " and " I ain't got no age." The dementia progressed and became extreme, and he died, aged nineteen, of exhaustion following a bout of seizures.

The post-mortem examination revealed a simply convoluted brain, weighing 1,167 grammes, and having the characteristic appearances of general paralysis. The microscope showed a condition of imperfect cellular development, plus subacute degeneration, similar to that occurring in general paralysis.

Syphilitic Amentia passing into Dementia (probably General Paralysis).—*A. A.*, male. Morbid heredity on paternal side, but no history of syphilis obtainable, although the patient has several characteristic syphilitic lesions. He was noticed to be backward from birth, and did not talk until eight years old. Went to school, but could never learn, and when he left, at the age of twelve, he was only in the second standard. He had fits between six and seven years of age, which continued occasionally until fourteen years, and then ceased. No employment. Became unmanageable, and was sent to an imbecile institution when aged seventeen. Remained there for two years, but made no progress, and was transferred to an asylum. He gradually became paretic and tremulous, with small pupils, which scarcely reacted to light. At the present time (aged twenty) he is very simple, and answers questions in a slow, monotonous, and trembling manner. He cannot do the simplest sums, and does not know how many pennies there are in sixpence. There is undoubtedly considerable mental deterioration in addition to the original defect, and it is probable that general paralysis is supervening.

Syphilitic Amentia terminating in General Paralysis.—*L. B.*, female. Was admitted into the asylum at the age of fifteen, the certificate stating : " She sits apparently dazed, taking no interest in anything that is going on. Threatened to kill herself. Tears her clothing, and at times cries and stamps her feet." The history is incomplete, but it was elicited that the patient had been dull and of defective eyesight since birth ; that her mother died, aged forty-two, of general paralysis ; and that her father was alive, and said to be in good health. Though intellectually dull, she was said to have been cheerful until the last six months, since when she had become stubborn and morose, finally helpless, dirty in her habits, and quite unable to look after herself.

On admission the pupils were dilated, the reaction to light sluggish, and her memory for time and events much impaired. She was gloomy and apathetic, and had delusions, such as that ferocious dogs were coming after her. There was left external

PLATE XX.

FIG. 50.—Syphilitic idiocy.

FIG. 49.—Syphilitic imbecility; constantly grimacing as shown.

1

strabismus, but no other observable paresis and no convulsions. The knee-jerks were exaggerated. Marks of congenital syphilis were present. Cranial circumference, 21¾ inches. She was considered to be a case of syphilitic amentia with superadded dementia. The dementia steadily increased, and the patient died at the age of eighteen years, of broncho-pneumonia.

On making a post-mortem examination, I found the brain to be of fair size (1,176 grammes), but somewhat simply convoluted. The optic nerves were exceedingly small. The brain and membranes had the characteristic naked-eye appearances of general paralysis. A microscopical examination of various regions of the cortex cerebri revealed a marked numerical deficiency of the cells; many of them were also of incomplete development and irregular arrangement. These indications of imperfect development were most pronounced in the small and medium-sized pyramidal cells of the frontal lobes. In addition, there was a considerable amount of chronic and subacute degeneration, with proliferation of neuroglia identical with that occurring in general paralysis.

Syphilitic Amentia with Progressive Dementia.—S. G., male. No relatives living, and no history or particulars ascertainable beyond the fact that he had lived in imbecile institutions since the age of nine years. In January, 1895, at the age of nineteen years, he became violent and unmanageable, attacked the attendants, and threatened to cut his throat; he was accordingly transferred to a lunatic asylum. On admission he was found to be an imbecile with aural hallucinations and mild mania. He said that voices spoke to him and told him to cut his throat. Many typical marks of congenital syphilis were present, and he had a habit of constantly keeping his mouth tightly closed in a fatuous grin, at the same time breathing noisily through his nose. (See Plate XX., Fig. 49.) He remained in practically the same condition for the next five years, at times being depressed and lachrymose, at others noisy and troublesome; he was, however, clean in habits, and was capable of doing everything for himself. In December, 1900, at the age of twenty-four years, he began to show signs of dementia, becoming stolid and indifferent to his surroundings, and frequently wet and dirty. The knee-jerks were greatly exaggerated. The dementia gradually became more marked, his gait became shuffling and unsteady, and the knee-jerks could not be obtained.

During the year 1902 he began to show marked bodily enfeeblement, the dementia still continuing to progress. In February, 1904, pulmonary tuberculosis was diagnosed; it advanced with great rapidity, and he died the following month at the age of twenty-eight years. There had never been convulsions or seizures. Post-mortem examination revealed a wasted brain presenting the usual features of chronic dementia, but none of the particular signs of general paralysis. Its weight was 1,100 grammes. There was extensive tuberculosis of both lungs.

Syphilitic Amentia passing into Dementia.*—*Family History.*—The father has had syphilis; a brother of the patient also has "tremblings"; no further details obtainable.

Clinical.—The patient was always a quiet lad, and did not seem so bright as the other children. At the age of six years he began to show definite ataxic symptoms (said to have been caused by a fright), chiefly marked in the legs. There was no actual loss of power complained of, but he was only able to stand with the feet apart, and was very unsteady and apt to fall whilst walking; the knee-jerks were absent on both sides, the pupils were widely dilated, considerable tremor of the eyelids was present, and there was occasional incontinence of urine. The patient gradually became worse, eventually becoming almost completely powerless and helpless in bed, and quite demented: he died at the age of eight years.

Upon making a *microscopical examination*, I found imperfect development and irregular arrangement of the small and medium-sized pyramidal cells of the cerebral cortex, indicating a condition of mild imbecility. In addition there was a subacute degeneration affecting a large number of these cells, and to a less extent those of the anterior horns of the spinal cord; there was also a somewhat more chronic degeneration of the cells and fibres of the pyramidal tract, and the vessel walls generally were slightly thickened. I did not see this case during life, but there are many points in both the clinical and pathological appearances which suggest that this degenerative process which was superadded to the mild amentia was analogous to, if not identical with, that of juvenile general paralysis.

* For the clinical notes and the central nervous system of this case I am indebted to Dr. F. J. Smith, Physician to the London Hospital.

Secondary Amentia and its Clinical Varieties 249

AMAUROTIC FAMILY IDIOCY, OR INFANTILE CEREBRAL DEGENERATION.

This disease is invariably fatal, and its subjects never survive sufficiently long to become candidates for a special institution for the mentally deficient ; but as it is one in which arrested cerebral development is a prominent, although incidental, feature, and as on this account it might be confounded with the more ordinary forms of amentia, it is necessary to allude to it.

The earliest account we have is that given by Mr. Waren Tay in 1881, whose description chiefly referred to the peculiar ocular conditions. In 1887 Dr. B. Sachs, of New York, described the changes in the brain in a paper entitled " Arrested Cerebral Development." Other descriptions have been given by Goldzicher, Magnus, Knapp, Wadsworth, Hirschberg, Carter, Hirsch, Petersen, and Burnet. The most complete account, however, is that of Kingdon and Risien Russell,* which appeared in 1897, and it is upon this that the description here given is chiefly based.

Infantile cerebral degeneration is a disease which usually attacks more than one child of the same family, and all the cases hitherto recorded have occurred in Jews. Male and female children are equally liable to be affected, but no particular exciting or predisposing factor has yet been discovered. There is no regularity in the order in which children of the same family are affected. It may be the earlier, later, or intermediate children, the rest remaining perfectly healthy. Kingdon and Russell describe the symptoms and progress of the disease in three stages as follows :

First Stage.—An infant, the subject of this disease, is born at the full time of gestation, and may be well formed and developed, differing in no outward respect from a healthy child, until about the completion of the third month. At this time some weakness of the muscles of the back and neck is observed, and often a suspicion that the child sees imperfectly is entertained. Should the eyes be examined with the ophthalmoscope about the fourth or

* E. C. Kingdon and J. S. Risien Russell, " Infantile Cerebral Degeneration," *Medico-Chirurgical Transactions*, vol. lxxx., 1897. This paper gives a full account of the clinical and pathological conditions, together with a bibliography of the subject.

fifth month, there will be found symmetrical changes in the macula lutea, consisting of a whitish-grey patch, somewhat oval in shape (the axis being horizontal), with softened edges slightly raised above the general surface of the retina. In the centre of this patch is seen the fovea centralis as a dark cherry-red spot. These changes in the maculæ remain unaltered, and are regarded as absolutely pathognomonic. At a somewhat later course of the disease there is definite optic atrophy and total amaurosis.

In the **Second Stage** the child is unable to sit up; its head falls backwards if unsupported; when lying on its back it is unable to turn over to either side. Objects placed in its hands are grasped but feebly, and soon dropped. It is generally apathetic, taking no notice of surrounding objects, and the face bears an expression of mental enfeeblement. Vision is reduced to perception of light, but the sense of hearing is acute, and remains so during life, any sudden sound causing the child to start. The sense of taste is also preserved.

In the **Third Stage** atrophy of the enfeebled muscles ensues, and soon those of the whole body are involved. Emaciation progresses, and becomes most marked. The deep reflexes are exaggerated, and still later in the course of the disease rigidity of the extremities and retraction of the head become prominent features; occasional spasmodic contractions cause the child to start and cry from pain. Convulsions have been noted in one or two instances during the course of the disease, but they would appear to be an accidental accompaniment, and are, at all events, not the rule. The temperature remains normal throughout the course of the disease. The heart, lungs, and abdominal viscera are also normal.

The duration of life varies from one and a half to two and a half years, but is usually less than two years. All the subjects of this disease are known to have died except two, and they were becoming worse when last seen.

The essential pathological lesion would appear to be a primary degeneration of the cortical neurones, the optic nerves, and the pyramidal tracts throughout their whole course in the pons, medulla, and spinal cord. The nature of the lesions and the general clinical course would suggest that the cause is some circulating toxine, but hitherto none such has been discovered.

SECTION II.
AMENTIA DUE TO DEFECTIVE CEREBRAL NUTRITION.

Mental growth takes place as a result of two factors. *First*, the embryonic neuroblasts must have within them a capacity for developing and acquiring certain functional connexions. *Secondly*, they must be supplied with food adequate in quantity and quality, and they must also be stimulated by impressions from without reaching them through the avenues of special sense. If either of these latter essentials to growth be absent or diminished, mental development may be so interfered with that a condition of amentia results, and this is conveniently termed " amentia due to defective cerebral nutrition." Of the type which is due to quantitative or qualitative changes in the blood, cretinism is the best, as well as most common, example. The variety due to defective stimulation is known as " amentia due to isolation or sense deprivation."

CRETINISM.

Although cretins have been recognized and remarked upon for hundreds of years (even by such ancient writers as Juvenal, Pliny, Strabo, as well as by the more modern Paracelsus), it is only comparatively recently that the cause of this condition has been at all understood. It is now established beyond doubt that cretinism is closely allied to myxœdema, and that they are both dependent upon an absence or diminished secretion of the thyroid gland.

There are two kinds of cretinism—*endemic* and *sporadic*; and although these have much in common, there are, nevertheless, important points of difference between them which make it necessary to consider them separately.

Endemic Cretinism.—Endemic cretinism is a disease of wide incidence. It is most common in Europe, particularly in the mountains and valleys of Switzerland and the adjacent countries; but it also occurs in the Himalayas of India, the Andes and Rocky Mountains of America, as well as in Burmah and Madagascar. In fact, there is hardly any quarter of the globe which is free from this affection. In England cases are occasionally seen in Derbyshire and the western portion of Yorkshire. In Somersetshire it used to be fairly common, but is not now so frequently seen. In practically all cases of the endemic form of this disease a goitre is present, but although some diversity exists in the mental and bodily condition of the patients, the effect on the whole seems to be the result of an inadequate and not excessive secretion of the thyroid gland.

As to the cause of this thyroid anomaly we know very little, but it seems to be related in some peculiar manner with the water-supply. It is probable that the future will reveal the presence of some specific microbe or virus, but hitherto none has been isolated.

In consequence of this condition of the thyroid a marked alteration takes place in the bodily and (usually) mental state of the person affected. In congenital or infantile cases the whole nutrition of the body is disturbed. The child, whilst usually remaining fat and puffy, makes very little growth, and the majority of these persons remain dwarfs. The skin is sallow or actually yellow, dry, thickened, and wrinkled, and has the appearance of being too large for the body. The head is large and the fontanelles are late in closing. The nose is broad and flat, the lips thick and swollen, and the tongue so large that it often hangs out of the open mouth. The belly is protuberant, and the lower limbs short and bowed. The whole body is unwieldy, its balance unsteady, and its gait ungainly. Puberty is often delayed, and many pronounced cretins are sterile. In fact, these children as a whole present bodily signs identical with those of the sporadic variety. In those cases in which the disease is acquired in later life, as a consequence of residence in a goitrous locality, changes analogous to those occurring in myxœdema are produced.

It has been stated that this condition of athyroidea may exist without any mental change, and although this may sometimes be true where the disease is acquired in later life, and also in very exceptional instances in the congenital form, there is usually produced some degree of mental deficiency. This ranges from a mild amount of feeble-mindedness to a state of gross idiocy, and is usually accompanied by deafness. The report of the

Royal Commission of Sardinia* divides cretins into the following three classes :

In Class I. the subjects have only vegetative faculties, are entirely destitute of reproductive and intellectual powers, and cannot speak. They are styled simply "cretins."

In Class II. they have vegetative and reproductive faculties and some rudiments of language. Their intellectual efforts go no farther than their bodily wants, corresponding only to the impression of the senses. They are called "semi-cretins."

In Class III. there is added to the faculty of the preceding one a greater amount of intellectual power without reaching the normal human capacity. They have some aptitude at learning a trade or doing different kinds of work. They are called "cretineux," or "cretinous."

Sporadic Cretinism (Cretinoid, Myxœdematous, or Pachydermic Amentia).—This condition was first described by the late Dr. Hilton Fagge in 1871, and although since then a considerable number of cases have been reported, it is nevertheless a rare disease. Cretinoid aments do not compose more than a fraction per cent. of all aments.

Although sporadic have many features in common with endemic cretins, and although in each there is a condition of athyroidea, there are several important points of difference between the two. In the first place, whilst a goitre is generally present in the endemic form, in the sporadic cases the thyroid gland is usually entirely absent. Secondly, although the sporadic cases may occur in regions in which goitre is prevalent, they often crop up quite apart from such a condition, and in families and localities in which goitre is unknown.

Etiology.—This raises the questions of the cause of sporadic cretinism and its relation to the endemic form. In a few of the cases coming under my own observation I found a marked history of morbid neuropathic heredity, just the same as in ordinary primary aments, and this led me to make further inquiries as so the prevalence of heredity in this condition. Several consulting physicians, having a considerable experience of cretins, and who

---

* For these extracts, as well as much information on the subject of endemic cretinism, I am indebted to the excellent account in Dr. Ireland's work.

were good enough to reply to my inquiries, informed me that no special neuropathic heredity had been noticed; but they added that the majority of the patients had been seen in hospital practice, and no special attention had been given to the family history. Dr. John Thomson of Edinburgh, however, had fully investigated the family history in seventeen of his patients, with the following result: In nine there was no history of nervous or mental disease or of alcoholism; of the remaining eight, in one a brother and sister were dwarfs, in four there was a family history of mental alienation, and in another of epilepsy, whilst the fathers of the remaining two patients were alcoholic.

I am greatly indebted to Dr. Thomson for his kindness in supplying me with these details, which seem to show that, although on the whole neuropathic heredity is not a marked feature of this condition, such nevertheless occurs in a proportion of cases—that it is, in fact, more prevalent in cretins than in ordinary persons. Whether in such cases the absence of the thyroid gland should be looked upon as a peculiar stigma of degeneracy complicating primary amentia, or whether it is that in these cases the athyroidea is due to the same unknown cause as in the non-hereditary cases, I am unable to say. The cause of sporadic cretinism is shrouded in so much mystery as to be at present a complete enigma, and it may be a mere chance that the neuropath as well as the non-neuropath should be affected. However this may be, it is possible that the presence of morbid heredity may be not without influence in affecting the response to thyroid treatment, which, although in many cases seemingly dependent upon the age at which it is begun, is not entirely determined thereby.

Pathology.—Whatever may be the cause of the thyroid anomaly, there is not the slightest doubt that the secretion of this gland exercises a profound influence upon the nutrition of the brain, and in most, if not all, cases of cretinism it is clearly to the absence of this secretion that the mental peculiarity is due. It is of interest in this connexion to recall the state of mental hebetude, in some cases amounting to dementia, which results in the analogous condition of myxœdema seen in adults.

The defect of this secretion does not lead to any characteristic lesion of the brain. The neurones are simply unable to develop

PLATE XXI.

FIG. 52. The same cretin, showing relative stature.

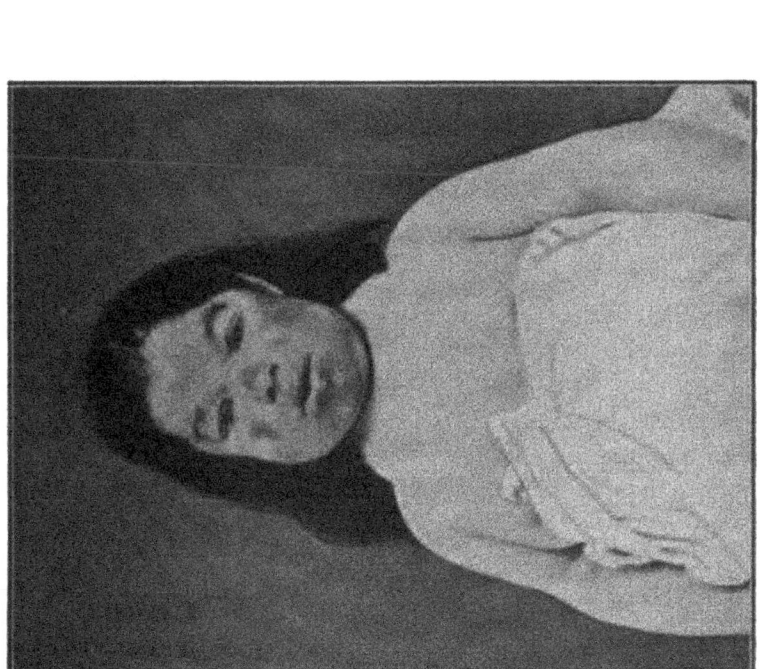

FIG. 51.—A cretin imbecile. Age, 39 years.

[To face page 254.]

Secondary Amentia and its Clinical Varieties 255

and to perform their function because an essential constituent of their nutriment is lacking. In several cases which have been examined after death, the cortical cells have been found in a condition of incomplete development, like that already described as occurring in primary amentia. Sometimes, in addition, the whole brain is found to be small and simply convoluted.

Clinical Symptoms.—The symptoms of sporadic cretinism usually make their appearance during the first year, although they are rarely noticeable until the sixth or seventh month. Exceptionally they may not occur until the second or third, or even sixth or seventh year, but such cases are rare. The parents' attention is generally first attracted by the fact that the child neither grows so rapidly nor appears as bright mentally as a normal child of corresponding age; also, in the cases with early onset, that he makes no attempt to sit up, to stand, or to talk. It is commonly said that the primary dentition is considerably delayed, but Dr. Thomson doubts this, and he has been good enough to supply me with details of ten patients regarding this point, from which it appears that, in the absence of rickets, the time of dentition does not differ markedly from that of ordinary children. The anterior fontanelle is late in closing, and has been observed open in adults. Attempts at walking may not be performed until the fifth year or later. Speech may be delayed until the seventh or eighth year, and may never appear. Usually within a few years after birth the child has assumed the characteristic cretinous appearance.

The characteristic features of the fully developed condition are as follows: The body is greatly dwarfed, and many children of fifteen or sixteen years of age do not measure more than 3 feet in height. (The accompanying illustrations (Plate XXI., Figs. 51 and 52) show a cretin, aged thirty-nine, whose height is only a little over 3 feet). The head is usually large; the legs are extremely short and bowed; the hands and feet stumpy and ill-formed. The ossification of the bones is delayed considerably beyond the normal period. The appearance of the face alone is often typical, the nose being broad and flattened, the eyes widely separated, the lips thick, the mouth partly open, and the tongue thick, coarse and protruding. In addition, the eyelids are often heavy and swollen, and the hair coarse and scanty. A very important feature is the skin, which is sallow, exceedingly dry, rough, and so redundant as to appear much too large for the stunted body. Doubtless this is the result of the under-development chiefly affecting the tissues of mesoblastic origin. The neck is usually short and thick and the belly protuberant. Umbilical hernia is common.

Puberty is usually late in appearing, and the external genitals often retain an infantile appearance until past mature age. Many of these patients are sterile. In the majority of cases the thyroid gland is completely absent, and in a considerable number of cases there are small soft swellings above the clavicles or in the axillæ. These are apparently fatty, and they disappear rapidly under thyroid treatment. The pulse and respiration are slow, and the temperature two or three degrees below the normal. As a result of his examination of the blood, Vaquez found that there was a marked diminution in the number of the red corpuscles, as well as their contained hæmoglobin, with an excessive number of nucleated corpuscles.

These children are often voracious eaters, but, although well nourished and even fat, most of them suffer from a general muscular weakness. This, together with their mental torpidity, causes the bodily balance to be unsteady, the gait slow and waddling, and all movements to be performed with a laboured clumsiness. These bodily peculiarities, associated as they are with their general slothfulness, apathy, and want of expression, produce a clinical picture which can rarely be mistaken.

Mentally these persons are characterized by a general impairment of all the faculties. There is often considerable defect in the power of hearing, but beyond an obtuseness of perception there is not any other marked abnormality of the special senses. Some of them are pronounced imbeciles, or even idiots, but in others the degree of mental deficiency is one of mild imbecility. Most of these milder cases can be taught to read and write simple words, to count, to do little sums in addition and subtraction, and to perform small tasks. Others, whilst capable of assisting in the domestic work of the institution, make absolutely no headway in book learning. Most of them can be taught to be methodical and clean in their habits. As a class they are placid, harmless, good-tempered, and affectionate; and although

Secondary Amentia and its Clinical Varieties 257

they show little trace of emotion, they are nevertheless capable of being pleased and amused in a dull, heavy sort of way. They are amongst the least troublesome of all aments.

I know of no statistics enabling the mortality of these persons to be compared with that of ordinary aments, but my impression is that they are decidedly less frail, and not so prone to early death. Phthisis does not seem to be nearly so common. The oldest cretin I know is an imbecile man aged sixty-three years. He is looked after by his sister, who keeps a small village shop, and he is apparently in good bodily health. He has never been under thyroid treatment.

Diagnosis.—In a well-marked case of sporadic cretinism the mental and bodily conditions are sufficiently characteristic to make the diagnosis easy. But all cases are not equally well marked, and there are some other diseases which, owing to certain points of resemblance, may be thought to be cretinism. The converse mistake, except, perhaps, in the case of rickets, is less likely to be made. The chief of these are rickets, hydrocephalus, achondroplasia, hypertrophic and Mongolian amentia.

1. *Rickets.*—It is not uncommon for early cases of cretinism to be called rickets, but the characteristic beading of the ribs and symmetrical enlargement of the epiphyses in this latter condition, with the absence of the typical cretinous facies, should suffice to distinguish between the two.

2. *Hydrocephalus.*—The only points in common are the large head, the muscular weakness, and the mental apathy. But the enlarged head of the hydrocephalic is totally different to that of the cretin, and the mental and bodily differences between these two conditions are much more pronounced than are the resemblances.

3. *Achondroplasia*, although very rare, is often called cretinism. It is distinguished by the facts that, although the child is dwarfed owing to imperfect development of the long bones, and although the skin is often dry and somewhat redundant, there is a complete absence of the swollen eyelids, the broad, squat nose, the enlarged tongue and mouth of the cretin. Moreover, the mental development is unaffected, and children suffering from achondroplasia are intelligent and vivacious.

4. *Hypertrophic Aments* resemble cretins in the large head and

somewhat stunted body, and the resemblance may be intensified by the tottering gait, general muscular weakness, and mental inertia. But the facies of the hypertrophic are different: the skin lacks the dryness and redundancy of the cretin, and has not the same bogginess; there is, as a rule, no delay in the development of puberty, and there is not the same subnormal temperature. Moreover, the hypertrophic ament complains of head pain, and is often subject to outbreaks of temper and excitement which are totally foreign to the lethargic, inert cretin.

5. *Mongolian Aments* are frequently thought to be cretins, and were for a long time called "cretinoids." The differential diagnosis has been given on p. 189.

Treatment and its Result.—That this condition is the result of an absent or defective secretion of the thyroid gland is fully shown by the remarkable results which follow thyroid administration. Under its influence the characteristic facies disappear, the skin becomes moist and supple, the body rapidly increases in growth, and in many cases a marked improvement takes place in the mental condition. But to obtain this favourable result the treatment must be continuous, and it must be begun at a sufficiently early age.

The effect of thyroid treatment is decidedly more uncertain and less pronounced upon the mental than the bodily development. To a great extent this appears to be dependent upon the age at which it is commenced, but there may be other factors which influence the result. Dr. G. A. Sutherland mentioned to me the case of one of his patients in whom the disease was diagnosed at the age of three months, and who after continuous treatment for six years showed no mental impairment. Dr. Robert Hutchison tells me of a case of his which has been treated from the third month, and now, at the age of fifteen years, is apparently of normal mental capacity. Dr. George Murray, of Newcastle, has also experienced such a satisfactory result. Dr. John Thomson has supplied me with particulars of a boy where treatment was begun at the age of seven and a half months, and who now, at the age of eleven and a half years, is so far improved that he reads and spells as well as the average of his age, his only noticeable weakness being in arithmetic. Another patient of Dr. Thomson's was started upon thyroid at the age of seven and a half weeks, and now, at six and a half years, is of normal appearance, somewhat above the average height, and, although not very energetic, appears to be of normal intelligence. Another case is that of a girl who has been under treatment since the age of four years eleven months. She reached the sixth standard at school, but never did much at arithmetic. She is now engaged as a compositor in a printing-office, but, owing to her slowness in lifting the type, only earns half the wage of other girls of similar age doing the same work.

It must be admitted, however, that such cases are somewhat exceptional and not the rule, and it is the general experience of those who have knowledge of these persons that the mental is rarely commensurate with the bodily development. I have in my care at the present time a patient who is an excellent illustration of this fact. He was sent to me at the age of eight years by Dr. Soltau Fenwick, with a letter to the effect that it was a case of cretinism which had been under treatment since infancy, and had improved wonderfully in all but the mental symptoms. I could detect absolutely no bodily sign of cretinism, and, instead of the torpid mental state characteristic of that condition, he was alert and active. But the boy was a pronounced imbecile, and he has made but little improvement under special training. In this case there is marked neuropathic heredity, and the mother has been insane in an asylum. Dr. Robert Hutchison tells me of a similar case which he has treated continuously since the seventh month, and yet the child is a hopeless imbecile, although not in the least like a cretin in appearance. Perhaps these instances represent the opposite extreme, for I think it is somewhat unusual for mental improvement to be so slight where treatment is begun thus early.

In many patients improvement takes place at an even later age. Dr. Caldecott, of Earlswood Asylum, has at the present time in his care a cretin who was admitted at the age of fourteen years. She could not walk, talk, nor swallow solid food, and her mental status was that of a low-grade idiot. She had never been treated with thyroid. After three years' treatment she has grown 12 inches, can walk and run about, talks fairly distinctly, and is taking her place in school.

On the whole, I think it may be laid down that, whilst in some cases *cure* may take place if treatment be initiated not later than the third month, should the first year be allowed to pass without thyroid administration, the cretin, although improving to some extent, will never make up his mental arrears.

The most convenient method of treatment is by means of tabloids of the dried extract. Usually for a child of from three to six months a dose of ½ grain once or twice daily will be found appropriate. This must be gradually increased at the rate of 1 grain per diem for each year of the child's age, with a maximum of 15 grains. Treatment must be continued after the symptoms have disappeared, or a relapse will ensue; but usually an occasional large dose is sufficient to maintain the effect.

The thyroid must be given cautiously at first, and the dose increased very gradually. In some cases it causes diarrhœa, rise of temperature, and marked acceleration of the heart, apparently as a result of the increased metabolism. It should then be discontinued for a time, and again cautiously resumed. The excessive growth of the long bones may cause them to readily bend, and in order to prevent serious curvatures movement must be carefully supervised.

In connexion with the subject of cretinism I may mention the following curious case of temporary cessation of mental and bodily development occurring in a girl at the age of puberty. I have never seen a similar case described, and the only explanation I can suggest is that for some reason or other the secretion of the thyroid gland was temporarily suspended. When I first saw the girl she was seventeen years of age, but in height, manner, and general development she had the appearance of a child of twelve or thirteen. Her mental condition was backward and corresponded to a similar age, and she had never menstruated. The mother informed me that the girl had seemed quite all right in mind and body until about four years previously, but since then she had been at a complete standstill. On examination the thyroid gland appeared to be normal, but the skin was sallow, coarse, dry, and had a curious boggy feel, the hair scanty, the mons veneris uncovered, the lips thick, and the teeth much decayed. There was also a pronounced flush over each cheek. She was extremely childish for her age, besides being unusually torpid in thought and movement. In view of these symptoms,

I decided to try the effect of thyroid treatment. The mother noticed improvement after the first week, and after three months menstruation had appeared and a great change was evident in every way. She was under treatment for about nine months, and it was then discontinued entirely. The mental and bodily improvement initiated by the thyroid steadily continued, and when I last saw her, at the age of twenty-one years, she had a normal appearance, and was regularly employed as a clerk in the Post Office.

AMENTIA DUE TO OTHER NUTRITIONAL DEFECTS.

In addition to the secretion of the thyroid gland, it is possible that there may be other internal secretions or chemical compounds which are essential to the growth of the nerve cells, and the absence of which gives rise to mental deficiency. For instance, it may be that some such special defect is responsible for the curious combination of bodily anomalies present in Mongolism. This, however, is mere conjecture. At present we know of no special nutritive agent other than the thyroid secretion, and the cases of amentia which we have now briefly to consider are those associated with a general defect of the bodily nutrition.

A state of general malnutrition may be present during intra- or extra-uterine existence, and is by no means of infrequent occurrence. In some cases the cause is obscure; in others the condition is obviously the result of insufficient or improper feeding, dirt, want of fresh air and sunlight, and general neglect. The atmosphere of ignorance, superstition, and indifference which surrounds the early infancy of a large number of the children of this country, particularly in large towns, is wellnigh incredible. In other cases the malnutrition is the result of actual disease, although this is more often than not due to preventable causes and an absolute ignorance or defiance of the laws of health.

In view of the obvious effects which such adverse environment exercises upon the physical condition of the growing child, and being aware, from our knowledge of anatomy and physiology, of the immense importance of a copious and pure blood-supply to mental activity, it is not unnatural to conclude that serious bodily malnutrition should have a deleterious effect upon the mental development of the infant. To a certain extent such a conclusion is correct. Although in many instances the ill-fed and ill-washed street gamin is far from unintelligent, experience does on the whole confirm the saying, *Mens sana in corpore sano*, and in a large proportion of such children the mental development is decidedly inferior to that of a healthy child of corresponding age. It is, however, necessary clearly to distinguish between mental development which is backward and delayed and that which is arrested. I have already referred to this subject in treating of mentally defective children, and pointed out that, whilst many of those suffering from delayed development closely simulate aments, there is in fact no real arrest, and under more favourable conditions the arrears are soon made up. It is probable that in some cases the deprivation of nourishment at a time when the cerebral neurones should be growing rapidly is so severe as to bring about permanent effects. I have, indeed, examined a few cases in which I could find no other cause. But in my opinion this is exceedingly uncommon. I have never known idiocy, or even imbecility, to result; the mental deficiency is always mild, and the proportion of aments who owe their condition to bodily malnutrition is really infinitesimal. In some cases the malnutrition may play the part of an exciting factor, and be all that is needed to produce an actual arrest in a person whose neuronic potentiality is low as a result of morbid heredity. It has already been pointed out that a large number of primary aments suffer from defective bodily nutrition as a consequence of the improper working of their nervous system. It is very necessary to bear this fact in mind in considering this question, and to avoid mistaking cause for effect.

One of the commonest disturbances of nutrition occurring in infancy is that due to rickets, and a "rachitic idiocy" has been described. I have never seen such a case. Rickets may, of course, complicate primary or secondary amentia, and there can be no doubt that the mental development of the rachitic child is often delayed and abnormal; but, so far as my experience goes, rickets alone has never produced amentia. On the contrary, I know several adults of marked intellectual ability who show clear evidence of having suffered from severe rickets in childhood.

With regard to cases of amentia due to congenital syphilis, as already stated, it seems to me more probable that these are the result of a direct toxic action than of a disturbance of nutrition.

AMENTIA DUE TO ISOLATION OR SENSE DEPRIVATION.

The growing brain cells not only require to be supplied with their own particular food, but they must also be stimulated by vibrations transmitted through the special sense pathways. The effect of these is probably similar to that produced by rays of light upon plant development, and in their absence cellular growth is as imperfect as if the brain had been starved. This is well shown by the marked agenesis of the occipital cortex which occurs as a consequence of congenital non-development of the organs of vision—a fact which has been ably utilized by J. S. Bolton to accurately map out the visual area. But not only are sensations thus necessary for growth: they are also the materials out of which thoughts and ideas are built, and the sum total of them constitutes *mind*. Should, therefore, a single sensory avenue be closed, as in blindness or deafness, the mind must for ever remain the poorer by the impressions which would have entered through this channel, and if two or more senses are defective the mind may be so impoverished as to bring about a condition of true amentia.

As we have already seen, such sensory defects are occasionally present in primary amentia, and they are then a complication which usually imposes an insuperable obstacle to successful training. In secondary amentia, however, which we are now considering, there is no intrinsic incapacity of the cortical neurones, and if other sensory channels can be so utilized as to in some degree compensate for those diseased, the mental capacity may be but little impaired. Suitable training may therefore prevent secondary amentia from these causes. That this is so is fully shown by the excellent results achieved in training establishments for the blind and deaf, as well as by some classical examples in which disease of several sensory channels had existed.

The common cause of the sensory deprivation in these cases is inflammation resulting from one or other of the infectious fevers; the lesion is usually at the periphery, and the organs most frequently affected are those of sight and hearing. Amentia can only result when such occurs during early childhood (whilst cerebral development is immature), and where special educational training has been withheld or has failed. In the absence of a neuropathic inheritance I believe failure to be exceedingly rare, and the cases of this form of amentia which are met with are nearly always in persons whose early education has been neglected. They are, in fact, as much sufferers from a deprivation of special education as of special sense. I have met several such cases in remote country districts. The child, deprived of sight or hearing in early life, is thereby excluded from the village school. The local authority provides no special form of education, and does not further concern itself with him. There may be institutions for the blind and deaf but ten miles away, but it is no particular person's business to secure him admission, and he gradually grows up without any training. He soon passes the age at which such would be of avail, and becomes an incurable ament. Although such a state of affairs still exists, it is less common than in years gone by. The necessity for, and great benefit to be derived from, training is now much more generally recognized, and in consequence cases of amentia due to sense deprivation are not nearly so prevalent as formerly. At the present time they comprise only a fraction of all cases of amentia, although the total number in existence is still considerable.

These patients are usually well grown and free from any stigmata of degeneracy. In the majority of instances the mental defect is mild, but it is not uncommon for it to be accompanied by hallucinations and delusions, and sometimes the behaviour is so erratic and untrustworthy as to necessitate committal to an asylum for the insane.

ILLUSTRATIVE CASES.

The two following are good examples of this form of amentia as commonly met with :

Mild Amentia consequent upon Early Deafness.—W. S., male, fifteen years of age. No morbid heredity. Was either born deaf or became so shortly after birth, and has never spoken. He was refused admission to the village school, and has received no education. He is well grown for his age, and has a pleasing expression. He can understand many signs, and can express many of his wants in the same way. Beyond helping his mother in the house at times, he is quite unemployed. He is by no means lacking in the faculties of imitation and imagination, and is fond of drawing on a slate or scraps of paper. It is quite evident, however, that his ideas are extremely crude and childish. In addition to his intellectual defect, he has little power of control, and is becoming more and more subject to outbreaks of passion and waywardness. On several occasions he has wandered away from home. His mother states that he is affectionate, but " cannot bear to be crossed." I am of opinion that in this case suitable training in a school for the deaf would have prevented the mild amentia now present, and would have resulted in the patient becoming a useful member of society. Even at this age I strongly urged the desirability of such training, as without it there is no doubt that he will gradually become more intractable, and will finally drift into an insane asylum.

The Earlswood case also is probably one of amentia due to deafness, but as this patient has developed a most extraordinary degree of mechanical skill, I have thought it better to describe him under the chapter on Idiots Savants.

Mild Amentia consequent upon Congenital Blindness.—E. W. C., male. Born blind. No education. Admitted into imbecile institution at the age of fifteen, but found to be intractable and violent, and transferred to lunatic asylum.

He is now twenty-nine years of age, and is a tall, well-developed and well-nourished man of pleasing expression. Cranial circumference, $22\frac{3}{4}$ inches. No stigmata of degeneracy. He is quite blind, the eyes being represented by rudimentary bulbs of white sclerotic tissue without any indication of cornea or iris. His memory is good ; he has a tolerably good knowledge of places and events, can understand all that is said to him, and can give a fair account of himself. He possesses imagination, but his ideas are simple and childish, and his power of reasoning is decidedly defective. He cannot read, write, sum, or do any kind of work, and he spends the day rocking himself to and fro in a chair and muttering to himself. After answering a question, he rambles on to himself in an incoherent way about analogies and philosophy. When asked what a philosopher is, he says: "A man who tries to make everybody else better." He then immediately goes on to talk about *Ally Sloper*, which, he says, has been read to him. He has aural hallucinations and delusions, and is very emotional and untrustworthy. In spite of his beatific appearance, he is liable to frequent outbreaks of sudden violence, and has repeatedly attacked the other patients. He is also a confirmed masturbator. (See Plate XXII., Fig. 53.)

The following well-known cases may be briefly referred to in this place, as showing the really remarkable results which may attend the systematic education of patients suffering from severe sense deprivation.

Laura Dewey Bridgman.*—An attack of scarlet fever at the age of two years caused suppuration of both eyes and both ears; taste and smell were also impaired. She was quite deaf, and sight was entirely abolished in the left eye; but she retained a slight perception of light in the right eye up to the eighth year, after which she became completely blind. She was admitted to the Perkins Institution for the Blind at Massachusetts at the age of seven years ten months, and received systematic education under Dr. Howe until she was twenty. Owing to the unremitting care and patience of Dr. Howe in training her cutaneous sensation (the only sense unimpaired), she became able to read and write in the deaf and dumb language, to express many of her feelings, to sew, knit, and perform certain household duties, and, in short, to live to a great extent the life of an ordinary person. She remained in the Perkins Institution until her death, at the age of sixty years. The general conclusion arrived at regarding her by Mr. Sangford was that "she was eccentric, not defective; she lacked certain data of thought, but not in a very marked way the power to use what data she had."

* See the "Life of Laura Bridgman," by M. S. Lamson, Boston, 1878; also an account by Dr. Howe in the Forty-Third Annual Report of the Perkins Institution and Massachusetts Asylum for the Blind. A very good abstract of this is given by Dr. Ireland in his "Mental Affections of Children."

The brain was very carefully examined by Dr. H. H. Donaldson, and described by him in the *American Journal of Psychology*, September, 1890, and December, 1891.

PLATE XXII.

FIG. 54.—The "genius" of Earlswood Asylum. Age, 73 years. Mild amentia due to deafness. (*For description see Text.*)

FIG. 53.—Mild amentia due to congenital blindness.

To face page 266.

The post-mortem examination showed that the auditory nerves, the optic nerves and tracts, and the olfactory bulbs, were very small. The grey matter of the cortex generally was thinner than usual, especially in the occipital, cuneus, and temporal lobes. In these situations there was also a deficiency in the number of nerve cells. There was a considerable non-development of the inferior frontal and temporo-sphenoidal convolutions covering the island of Reil, particularly marked on the left side. The cranial circumference was 20·8 inches.

In two other pupils of the Perkins Institution—namely, *Oliver Caswell* and *Helen Keller*—the results were almost equally remarkable. The former of these was blind and deaf from infancy, and the latter lost sight and hearing at the age of nineteen months.

Meystre, of Lausanne (Switzerland), was born deaf and dumb, and he lost his sight by an accident at the age of five years. By unremitting attention he was taught to articulate, and at the age of eighteen he was described as "a lively, intelligent, and good-humoured fellow, an excellent carpenter, a first-rate turner, and runs about the building with a certainty and confidence which none of the merely blind pupils acquire. He has a great many ideas, and an instinctive dread of death."

*Agnes Halonen** was born in Finland in 1886. At the age of eighteen months she became blind from scarlet fever, and a year afterwards became deaf. She very soon ceased to speak, and expressed her wants by means of a few simple signs, such as putting her hand to her mouth when she wanted food. She could recognize members of her family by touch. At the age of eight she was sent to the Blind School at Helsingfors. Here she was taught to sew and knit, as well as the finger alphabet. At the age of seventeen she could read books in Braille and Moon's characters, and she could also write. She had some knowledge of geography, which had been taught her by means of raised maps. She knew many of the capitals, mountains, and rivers in Europe and Asia, and she had a knowledge of the habits of plants and animals. She was able to sew, spin, crochet, plait, and make brushes, and generally was very intelligent.

* "The Blind Deaf-Mute, Agnes Halonen," by Aug. Helin, Stockholm. Abstract in *Journal of Mental Science*, April, 1904, p. 336.

Kaspar Hauser.—No account of this subject would be complete without a brief reference to this celebrated and mysterious case. It differs from the foregoing in that there was no disease of the sensory pathways, but the environment of the child for many years was such that they could not be exercised. It may fittingly be described as a case of mental arrest due to isolation.

On May 26, 1828, a youth, apparently about sixteen or seventeen years of age, was found near one of the gates of Nuremberg. He was unable to give any account of himself, and inquiries failed to discover how or whence he came or who he was. He was 4 feet 9 inches in height, very pale, with short, delicate beard on his chin and upper lip. His feet were tender and blistered, and showed no signs of having been confined in shoes. He scarcely knew how to use his fingers or hands, and his attempts at walking resembled the first efforts of a child. He could not understand what was said to him, and replied to all questions by a single phrase: " I will be a trooper, as my father was." His countenance was expressive of gross stupidity. He appeared to be hungry and thirsty, but refused everything offered to him except bread and water. He held in his hand a letter stating that the bearer had been left with the writer, who was a poor labourer with ten children, in October, 1812, and who, not knowing his parents, had brought him up in his house, without allowing him to stir out of it. This was regarded as being intended to deceive. Upon a pen being place in his hand, the youth wrote the words " *Kaspar Hauser.*"

After an official inquiry—which, however, revealed nothing—he was adopted by the town of Nuremberg, and Professor Daumer undertook his education. He was found to be extremely childlike, and to have no knowledge of the most simple facts of everyday life. He had a remarkable faculty of smell and for seeing things in the dark, however, and under the instruction of Daumer his mind expanded in a wonderful manner. In fact, probably as a consequence of its sudden awakening into activity, he became ill, and his education had to be discontinued for a time.

He was taught the use of language, and after a time was able to record his recollections. He said that he had always lived in a small, dark cell, continually seated on the ground. He had had no covering, except a shirt and trousers, and had never seen the

CHAPTER XIV
IDIOTS SAVANTS

WE have seen that amentia is often characterized by an irregular as well as a defective mental development, and in a small number of patients this is so marked as to result in special aptitudes which are quite phenomenal, not merely in comparison with aments, but often with the acquirements of ordinary persons. These persons are conveniently described as "idiots savants." The condition is exceptional and relatively uncommon; on the other hand, it is not so rare but that a considerable number of cases have been recorded.

Presumably the special aptitude is related to an increased development of certain cerebral neurones, but as to how and why this is brought about we can only conjecture. In many of the cases I have seen there has been a clearly marked predilection (which, however, has rarely been marked in the ancestors), and I can only assume that this is the result either of some primary developmental anomaly or of some fortuitous circumstance of early life which has aroused the child's interest in a particular direction, and thence led to the concentration of all his mental activities upon the one object. On the whole, I think that most of these cases are explicable on this latter view. The talent, whatever it is, and however originating, certainly owes much of its development to constant exercise.

It is to be noticed that although these persons are spoken of as "idiots," they are rarely of the lowest grade of mental defect. Most of them would more properly be classed as imbeciles or merely feeble-minded. It is remarkable, however, that they almost invariably belong to the male sex, female idiots savants being almost unknown.

Peterson is of opinion that the talents of these persons lie chiefly in the direction of imitation, and that they have no capacity for origination. He also thinks that they are frequently lost before adult life. These statements are undoubtedly true of many cases, but they are by no means invariable. I doubt whether the latter one is even the rule, and several illustrations to the contrary will be cited in the following pages.

The nature of these phenomenal acquirements varies considerably. In some persons the talent consists of an extraordinary development of one of the *special senses*. Thus, Jules Voisin describes the case of an imbecile with a wonderful delicacy of smell. She never ate or drank anything without smelling it, and if given coffee (for which she had a great fondness) in a glass which had contained wine, she would at once detect it and refuse to drink. Imbeciles have been described who were able by the sense of smell to pick out their own and their companions' clothes, and Séguin noticed many idiots even, in whom this faculty was developed to an extraordinary degree.

In other cases there is an increased development of the visual sense. Several of the drawing and mechanical geniuses have a wonderful capacity for detecting slight differences of form and size, whilst the following case, mentioned to me by Dr. R. Langdon Down, is an excellent example of this class. It is that of a boy, a patient at Normansfield, whose hobby was the collection of small bright articles of any description, and this interest had so cultivated his quickness and sharpness of sight that nothing in the shape of a pin, a minute fragment of broken glass, or any shining particle, which was invisible to the ordinary person, ever escaped him. Other patients have a phenomenal auditory capacity—as, for example, the wild boy of Aveyron described by Itard, as well as some who will presently be mentioned on account of their speech and memory. Finally, there are some cases in which the hyperdevelopment concerns the tactile sense. Dr. R. Langdon Down tells me that there used to be a boy at Normansfield whose sense of touch was so delicate and fingers so deft that he could take a page of the *Graphic* and gradually split it into two perfect sheets, as one would peel a postage stamp off an envelope.

In another group of cases it is chiefly in the motor functions that these extraordinary talents lie. Sometimes there is an almost incredible capacity for the performance of mechanical work requiring the greatest cunning and dexterity, and as an example of this the Earlswood case, which will presently be described, is probably unique. In other persons the gift takes the form of drawing, and many of the walls of Earlswood Asylum are at the present time adorned by beautifully executed crayon drawings (copies of well-known pictures) which were done by the mentally deficient brother of the patient just referred to. Occasionally the talent for drawing passes beyond mere picture-copying, as in the celebrated case of Gottfried Mind. This person, who died at Berne in 1814, was a cretin imbecile with such a marvellous faculty for drawing pictures of cats that he was known as " Der Katzen-Raphael."

Under the heading of motor we may also describe those cases possessing, if not the gift of tongues, at all events an extraordinary capacity for reproducing spoken words. Dr. Martin W. Barr* describes an epileptic idiot, aged twenty-two years, who, in spite of the most careful teaching, could learn neither to read nor to write, although he was able to perform small domestic duties. Spontaneously he hardly spoke at all, and then only short disconnected words or the simplest sentences ; but he had an extraordinary capacity for repeating fluently and with proper intonation everything said to him, whether in his mother-tongue or in such languages as Greek, Japanese, Danish, Spanish, etc. Probably those cases in which an imbecile will reel off, verbatim, cantos of poetry also belong to this category.

In a considerable proportion of these idiots savants the gift is one of *memory* in some form or other, and of this many interesting and remarkable examples have been described. At the present time there are two such in Earlswood Asylum. One of them is a man, sixty-five years of age, suffering from high-grade amentia, whose penchant is biographical history. It is only necessary to mention to him the name of any prominent personage in early or ancient history, and out there flows in a steady, unhesitating stream a full and detailed account of his birth, life, and death. His knowledge has been acquired by poring over biographical details in such books as were available, and is, of course, simply

* M. W. Barr. "Some Notes on Echolalia." *Journal of Nervous and Mental Diseases*, January, 1898.

Idiots Savants

r of memory. It is not, however, merely repetitive, for
ds cross-questioning in a manner which shows that he
ie knowledge, although not full understanding, of the
ices he is talking about. Dr. Caldecott tells me that
e last few years there has been no decline in this man's
/; latterly, however, he has begun to show signs of mental
lily old age. The other case is a somewhat younger man,
ty-six years, whose memory also relates to dates and
ices, but only such as have come under his own notice.
ι most valuable referee on matters connected with the
s life of the institution, and can repeat the year, month,
/ of coming and going, of all the medical officers during
od of residence.

.. Langdon Down showed me a similar case at Normans-
ιe patient being a high-grade imbecile thirty-eight years

In this case the phenomenal memory chiefly relates to
, but the patient also has a pronounced sense of locality.
ciality is the calendar, and if given any date during the
ι years, he states the correct day without any hesitation.
seems almost equally at home with the hymn-book, and
mptly give the number of any hymn of which he is given
t line, or *vice versa*. His home is near Maida Vale, and
g asked what streets he would have to pass through in
ome from Waterloo terminus he named each one without
htest hesitation. This patient can also give the product
two numbers under twenty with the rapidity of a reflex
ent.

'orbes Winslow* mentions the case of a man who could
)er " the day when every person had been buried in the
for thirty-five years, and could repeat with unvarying
y the name and age of the deceased, and the mourners
uneral. But he was a complete fool. Out of the line
als he had not one idea, could not give an intelligible
) a single question, nor be trusted even to feed himself."

r cases show the existence of this phenomenal memory in
olest automatic form. Thus, there are many idiots who
speak a single word, and yet can hum a tune, which they
ily heard once, with perfect accuracy. Other aments will

* Quoted by Ireland.

reel off poetry almost *ad infinitum*, yet without any understanding of the sense of what they are saying, or even the meaning of the words. Dr. Langdon Down has described the case of a boy who, having read a book, would correctly recite whole pages word for word. Dr. Maudsley mentions the case of an imbecile who could similarly repeat verbatim a newspaper he had just read, as well as another more remarkable patient who could repeat backwards what he had just read.

Most aments are fond of music, and some particularly so, but in a few instances this propensity has an extraordinary development. One of the most striking examples of this is furnished by Dr. Trélat, and this case is also interesting in being a female. Dr. Trélat* says that " they had in the Salpêtrière an imbecile born blind, affected with rickets, and crippled, who had great musical talents. Her voice was very correct, and whenever she had sung or heard some piece she knew perfectly well the words and the music. As long as she lived they came to her to correct the mistakes in singing of her companions; they asked her to repeat a passage which had gone wrong, which she always did admirably. One day, Géraldy Liszt and Meyerbeer came to the humble singing-class of our asylum to bring her their encouraging consolations." Dr. Séguin also records several cases in which a pronounced musical capacity was present.

Lastly, in marked contradiction to the general failing of aments in this respect, a few of these persons have an extraordinary capacity for arithmetic and calculations. One case described by Dr. J. Langdon Down is that of an inmate of Earlswood Asylum, an imbecile boy of twelve years, who could multiply three figures by three other figures with lightning rapidity. Dr. Howe has also recorded the case of a low-grade ament who, if told the age of anyone, would in a very short time calculate the number of minutes he had lived. Dr. Wizel† also records the case of an imbecile (apparently suffering from secondary amentia) who had a most remarkable faculty for arithmetic, particularly multiplication.

We may conclude this chapter on idiots savants with an account of the following extremely interesting case :

* Trélat, "La Folie Lucide," etc., Paris, 1861. Quoted by Ireland.
† *Archiv für Psychiat.*, Band xxxviii., Heft i.

The Genius of Earlswood Asylum.

Since the year 1850 there has been resident in Earlswood Asylum a patient who has justly earned this title, and whose skill in drawing, invention, and mechanical dexterity is certainly unequalled by an inmate of any similar institution in existence. At the present time, although seventy-three years of age, he still continues to be actively engaged in his workshop. I am greatly indebted to Dr. Caldecott for his kindness in giving me permission to examine this patient and his wonderful productions; also for freely placing at my disposal a mass of particulars and photographs regarding him which he has taken great trouble to collect.

J. H. Pullen was born in the year 1835. The family history is somewhat scanty, for the reason that the only informant now available is the patient's sister; but, as far as can be ascertained, the parents and grandparents were steady, sober, hard-working people, and there is no history of insanity, epilepsy, or any of the usual antecedents of primary amentia. The parents, however, were first cousins. Of thirteen children born in the family, six died in infancy, and of the remaining seven only three are now living. It is extremely interesting to note that another brother was deaf and dumb, and had an even greater aptitude for drawing than the patient; he died in Earlswood Asylum of cancer at the age of thirty-five years.

There are no particulars as to the age at which the patient began to walk, but he did not talk until seven years, and for a long time only uttered the word "muvver." He never went to school, as no school would take him. He showed an early taste for drawing, and used to spend the greater part of his time at this occupation or in carving ships out of bits of firewood. Such instruction as he had he received from his parents and brothers and sisters at home, and from these he learned to write and spell the names of simple objects, but this was practically the sum total of his scholastic acquirements.

Pullen was admitted to Earlswood Asylum at the age of fifteen years. On admission he was found to be active and well grown, his height being 5 feet $7\frac{1}{4}$ inches, and his weight 9 stones 11 pounds. The cranial circumference was $21\frac{5}{8}$ inches. He was described as having a good memory and power of imitation, and as being fond of drawing and examining how things were made. His senses of taste, smell, and touch were good ; he was able to wash, dress, and take care of his person, but his speech was very imperfect and he was *very deaf*.

He was put to work in the carpenter's shop, and soon became an expert craftsman. It was clear, moreover, that he possessed a capacity for initiation, imagination, resource, and attention far above the other inmates, and in consequence he was allowed considerable liberty of action and freedom to follow his own bent. The result, after sixty years, is to be seen in the fifty to sixty crayon drawings, the carvings in ivory and wood, and the wonderful models of ships and the like, which to-day adorn the walls and fill the two large workrooms placed at his disposal in Earlswood Asylum. Some idea of his skill in drawing and mechanical invention will be gathered from the accompanying photographs of his work (Plates XXIII., XXIV., XXV.), but, as Dr. Caldecott very truly says, it is difficult by this means to really appreciate their beauty, to do which the originals must be seen.

Pullen has designed and drawn a pictorial history of his life, which shows his chief occupations between the years 1841 and 1873. A reproduction of this is given in Fig. 55.

One of the most wonderful of his works, and the one of which he is the most proud, is the model of a steamship which he has named the *Great Eastern*. This, I think, he rightly regards as his *magnum opus*, and it attracted universal admiration at the Fisheries Exhibition, where it was shown in the year 1883. It took him three years and three months to complete, and every detail, including brass anchors, screw, pulley-blocks, and copper paddles, were actually *made* by the patient from careful drawings, which he prepared beforehand. The planks of this leviathan are fixed to the ribs by wooden pins to the number of nearly a million and a quarter. All of these were made by Pullen in a special instrument, which in turn he also planned and made. He also devised and executed a strong carriage on four wheels for the conveyance of the ship. The model is 10 feet long, $18\frac{5}{8}$ inches wide, and $13\frac{5}{8}$ inches in depth. It contains 5,585 copper rivets, and there are thirteen lifeboats hoisted on complete davits, each of which is a perfectly finished model. It is fitted with paddles,

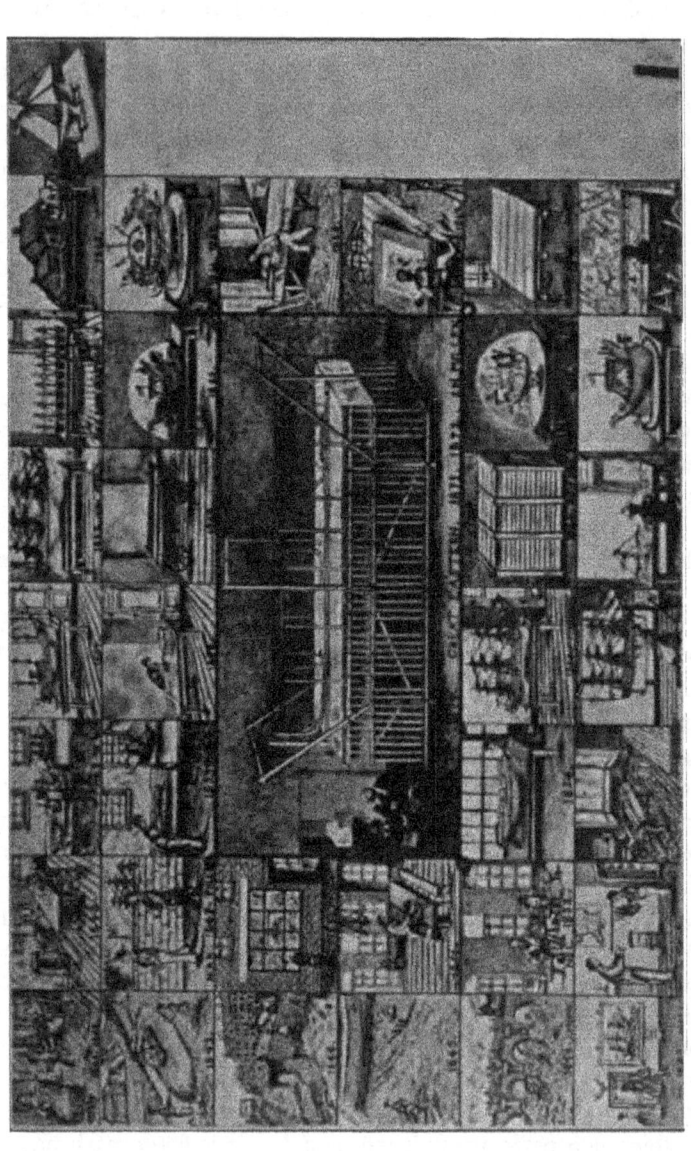

screw, and engines, and it contains state cabins, which are decorated and furnished with chairs, tables, beds, and bunks. In fact, the whole thing is complete to the most minute detail, and will bear the closest inspection. (See Fig. 59.) He has invented and attached an arrangement of pulleys by which the whole upper deck may be raised so as to show the parts below. I believe that when first put into water the huge model capsized, but that has since been remedied. It is perhaps hardly to be expected that a person with no knowledge of practical boat-building should succeed in making a vessel that would be really navigable, but as a highly finished model it is unmatched in its completeness.

Another of Pullen's productions is an immense but most beautifully finished kite in the form of a ship under full sail. Another is a fully rigged man-of-war of the old wooden type. This is copper-riveted, and contains forty-two brass cannon, all of which were made by the patient. The rigging contains 200 pulley-blocks, all capable of working. (See Fig. 57.) Another production, which testifies to his imaginative as well as mechanical faculty, consists of a fantastic barge most beautifully carved out of ivory, ebony, and various fancy woods. Upon the prow are seated four angels carved out of ivory, whilst the stern is occupied by a figure of His Satanic Majesty. There are twelve oars, beautifully jointed, and worked mechanically from one centre rod.

One of his most recent pieces of work is the representation of a monstrous human form about 13 feet high. This black-bearded, terrible-looking figure is armed with a gigantic sword, and can be made to perform a variety of movements, such as opening and shutting the mouth and eyes, protruding the tongue, rotating the head, raising the arms, etc., by means of a most elaborate internal mechanism. It is calculated to strike terror into the heart of any juvenile beholder. Of this, with the White Knight, he may truly say, " It's my own invention."

Other productions include bookcases, chairs, tables, workbenches, picture-frames, and the like ; in fact, the list of his work during the fifty-eight years he has been in the asylum would alone fill several pages of this book.

In disposition Pullen is usually quiet, well-behaved, and good-tempered, and he seems to be perfectly happy so long as he is allowed to work out his own ideas when and how he pleases

He is intolerant of supervision, inclined to be suspicious of strangers, and easily affronted by injudicious busy-bodies. At times he gets a little out of hand, and if denied requests which are quite unreasonable is apt to become sulky or passionate. On one occasion he threatened to blow up the place because a request had been refused, and it is quite likely that he would have attempted to do so had he not been mollified. On another occasion he did actually partially wreck his workshop in a fit of passion. Many years ago there was a steward of the asylum to whom Pullen took a violent dislike, and he spent many days planning his destruction. This culminated in the erection over the door of a most diabolical instrument, which was intended to guillotine the unfortunate officer, and there is not the slightest doubt that it would have done so had it not gone off a fraction of a second too late.

He once became enamoured of a female whom he had chanced to meet outside the asylum. Nothing would satisfy him but that he should have his discharge and be allowed to marry her. He moped about, utterly refused to do any work or to listen to argument or persuasion, and it became clear that the position was critical. A happy inspiration occurred to a member of the committee, and a gorgeous naval uniform, resplendent in blue and gold, was procured. Pullen was invited into the board-room and informed that his case had been carefully considered, and that it had been decided to accede to his request. At the same time it was pointed out to him that the committee would be exceedingly sorry to lose his valuable services, and that, if he would reconsider the matter, they would, as an alternative, grant him a commission as Admiral in the Navy. The uniform was then shown to him as an earnest of their intention. This was too much for Pullen; he took the uniform, and has never since alluded to the subject of marriage. This uniform he usually dons on ceremonious occasions. (See Fig. 54.)

A note in the case-book describes him as "the quintessence of self-conceit," and a consuming vanity and almost overwhelming sense of his own cleverness and importance are very marked characteristics. Whilst showing me his handiwork he frequently stopped to pat his head and say, "Very clever"; and when I produced a tape measure and asked permission to ascertain the

PRODUCTIONS OF THE "GENIUS" OF EARLSWOOD ASYLUM.

Fig. 56.—A crayon copy of the celebrated picture "Bolton Abbey."

Fig. 57.—A fully-rigged man-of-war of the old wooden type, and carriage, with the maker.

extent of his cranial capacity he was delighted, and evidently regarded me as a very sensible fellow. At the same time, in spite of his childish egotism, he is by no means deficient in some power of looking after himself, and on several occasions he has been found selling privately and for his own advantage little articles he has made. Many of his works are carried out under the real or pretended idea that he has a commission for them at a contract price, and this childish fancy, as well as his extremely limited vocabulary, is illustrated by his private memorandum-book, the photograph of a page of which is shown in Fig. 58.

What conclusion are we to come to regarding the causation and pathology, even the mental status, of this remarkable man? His powers of observation, comparison, attention, memory, will, and pertinacity, are extraordinary, as is fully shown by the foregoing account; and yet he is obviously too childish, and at the same time too emotional, unstable, and lacking in mental balance, to make any headway, or even to hold his own, in the outside world. Without some one to stage-manage him, his remarkable gifts would never suffice to supply him with the necessities of life, or even if they did, he would speedily succumb to his utter want of ordinary prudence and foresight and his defect of common sense. In spite of his delicacy of manipulation he has never learned to read or write beyond the simplest words of one syllable. He can understand a little of what is said to him by lip-reading, and more by signs, but, beyond a few words, nearly all that he says in reply is absolutely unintelligible.

My own conclusion, based upon several interviews and upon the particulars supplied me by Dr. Caldecott, is that the case is not one of *primary* amentia at all, but that it should really be classed as an example of mild *secondary* mental deficiency due to sense deprivation (deafness). Whether this deafness is the result of a congenital deficiency of the auditory mechanism or is due to disease I am unable to say, as the particulars of his early life are unfortunately very meagre; but I am inclined to think that it was owing to this deprivation that he was refused admission to school, that he was to a great extent cut off from intercourse with his fellows, and that he grew up uninstructed in, and ignorant of, ordinary scholastic attainments and the ways of the world. Left largely to himself, his amusement consisted in copying drawings and carving bits of firewood, as I have seen in other cases of early deafness. His isolated condition caused all the powers of his mind (which do not seem to me to have been intrinsically defective) to be devoted to, and concentrated upon, these occupations, with the result that he developed a power of copying drawings, of carving in wood (and later in ivory), and a general mechanical dexterity of the very highest order. The curious combination of extreme ability in these particulars, with his general childish simplicity, his egotism, suspicion of strangers, sullen or passionate outbreaks if thwarted, and, in fact, the whole of his mental characteristics, are, I think, explicable in this view. The condition is similar in kind, although differing in degree, to that frequently seen in neglected cases of congenital deafness, and it is not greatly dissimilar to that of some non-idiotic savants who, absorbed in their one particular subject, have gradually lost interest in, and severed their connexion with, the outer world.

PRODUCTIONS OF THE "GENIUS" OF EARLSWOOD ASYLUM.

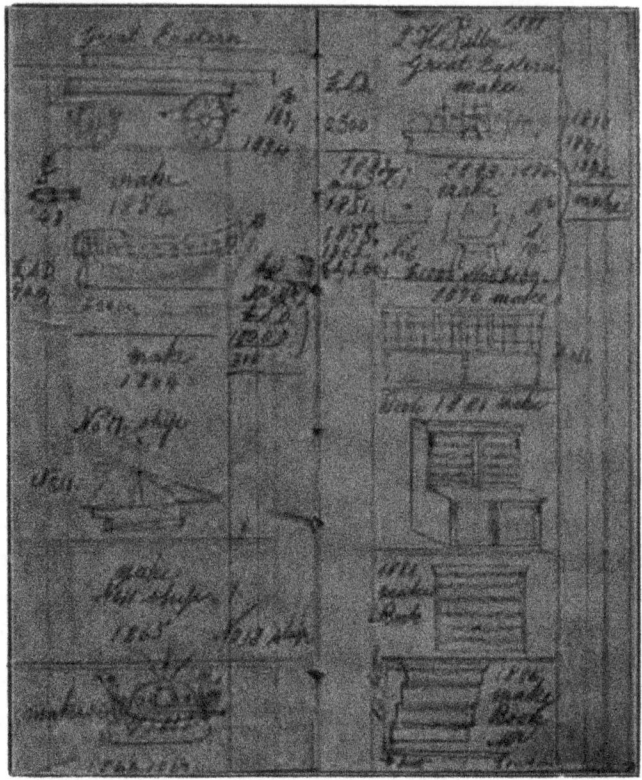

FIG. 58.—Photograph of the first page of the patient's private memorandum book.

FIG. 59.—The *Great Eastern*, with its carriage, as exhibited at the Fisheries Exhibition, 1883. (*For description see Text.*)

CHAPTER XV

THE AMENT AND SOCIETY—PAUPER AMENTS

HITHERTO we have been chiefly concerned with aments as individuals; in the next three chapters it is proposed to deal with them as members of the community, and to refer to such of their characteristics as concern their relationship to society. Until the last few years no reliable, and at the same time extensive, statistics referring to the ament as a citizen have existed. The extremely valuable ones we now possess are due in great measure to the investigations instituted by the Royal Commission of 1904.[*] Of these I shall make full use. I know of no similar inquiry or statistics concerning any other country.

Location of the Mentally Deficient.

We may first of all consider the location of these persons. This is shown by Table V. on p. 12, which relates to eleven selected areas of England and Wales, having an aggregate population of 2,321,567. The areas investigated were the three large towns of *Manchester, Birmingham,* and *Hull;* the two industrial areas of *Stoke-upon-Trent* and part of the mining county of *Durham;* two mixed industrial and agricultural areas in *Carmarthenshire* and *Nottinghamshire;* and four rural areas in *Somersetshire, Wiltshire, Lincolnshire,* and *Carnarvonshire.* The selection is thus representative of the entire country. This table is based upon the returns of the Royal Commission, to which, however, are added those aments confined in county and borough asylums, and certified under the Lunacy Act, these not being included in the Commission's inquiry.

It is seen from this table that the total number of aments

[*] See Report of the Royal Commission on the Care and Control of the Feeble-Minded, particularly vol. vi., dealing with the medical investigations.

resident in institutions or in receipt of outdoor relief—that is, wholly or partially supported by the public (Classes A and B)—is 40·5 per cent. of the whole number. A few of those in asylums are probably paying patients, but their number is so small as to be negligible. But this proportion is relative to a total which includes the juvenile feeble-minded in schools, and there can be no doubt that a large number of these, upon attaining the age of sixteen years, will go to swell the ranks of the pauper class. If these mentally defective school-children be excluded, it is found that the number partially or entirely supported by the public in each respective degree of amentia, is as follows: Feeble-minded adults, 67 per cent.; imbeciles, 52 per cent.; idiots, 54 per cent.

The proportion of aments who, to all intents and purposes, may be looked upon as paupers is thus seen to be a large one, but this is only what would be expected in view of their mental disabilities, often combined with antisocial propensities, which we have already described. It will be of interest to consider the degrees of amentia separately.

Feeble-minded.—With regard to the adult feeble-minded, it is a striking fact that nearly two-fifths of the total number discovered were found within Poor-Law institutions. From careful inquiry into the history of those in the Somersetshire area, I found that they fell into the following groups, and the same is probably true of the country generally:

(*a*) Those born in the House, nearly always illegitimate.

(*b*) Those admitted in consequence of inability to earn their living. Most of these are below middle age; they include vagrants and street loafers brought in by the police, and a small section of "ins-and-outs" driven in by stress of weather.

(*c*) Those admitted in consequence of the death of parents or relations who have hitherto looked after them.

(*d*) Women admitted into the maternity wards.

The economic disadvantage of such a large proportion of these persons being resident in workhouses is obvious when it is stated that the majority are not in the declining years of life, but are young adults, and that comparatively few of them are remuneratively employed.

The inquiries show that more than half are below forty-five years of age, whilst from one-fourth to one-third are below thirty.

It was the general experience of the investigators that more were admitted between the ages of twenty and thirty years than during any other decade. This tendency for the feeble-minded to drift into the workhouse quite early in life is even more pronounced in the large towns, and Dr. Melland found that in Manchester less than one-quarter of the total number were over fifty years of age, " in marked contrast to the normal-minded able-bodied inmates, the vast proportion of whom are above that age."

With regard to the employment of these persons, Dr. W. A. Potts, speaking of Birmingham, says : " A certain amount of employment is found for adult male defectives, who are taught boot-making, mat-making, and rope-making. Such work might be extended in this and similar institutions with advantage. It is an important proof of what can be done in workhouses." Possibly the same obtains in a few other Poor-Law establishments, but of the great majority throughout the country it must be said that there is very little attempt to employ these persons to any economic advantage, and I believe that the conditions which I found to exist in Somersetshire are very general. There I found that about half the male feeble-minded were more or less (generally less) usefully engaged in coal-carrying, wood-chopping, and the ordinary domestic work of the institution, whilst about two-thirds of the females were doing a little scrubbing, mending, and laundry work. The remainder were idle, and simply loafed about, many of them being either incorrigbly lazy or requiring so much supervision that they were more bother than they were worth.

In fact, the presence of such a large proportion of feeble-minded persons in workhouses is not due to any definite administrative attempt to provide for this class, or even to the suitability of these institutions. It is solely and simply a result of the inevitable tendency for the non-supervised ament to drift out of life's stream into the nearest backwater. I calculate that about 18 per cent. of the workhouse inmates of this country are feeble-minded.

Similarly with those in receipt of outdoor relief : most of them are young adults, and although a percentage are doing work which contributes to their support, there is no doubt that under a proper system they might be employed to much greater advantage. Less than one-fourth of those in Manchester were usefully employed ; in the country districts, however, where work of a character more suited to the capacity of these persons is available, from one-half to two-thirds manage to earn a little. The weekly allowance which these defectives receive from the parish varies very greatly in the different unions ; on the average it is probably about two shillings or half a crown, and with this and the shilling or so they earn, supplemented by an occasional gift of boots or cast-off clothes, they manage to exist tolerably well as long as they have some one to provide them with shelter, and generally take care of them. When their protectors die, the refuge of all these persons will be the workhouse.

The fact that 10 per cent. of feeble-minded persons are resident in lunatic asylums is an indication of the mental instability, as well as deficiency, of this class. For the incarceration of practically all of them is due to insanity or epilepsy.

It is apparent from these inquiries, that not only do a larger proportion of town than country defectives receive Poor-Law relief, but that both absolutely and relatively far more are relieved in the House. It is to be remembered that these remarks relate to the feeble-minded degree of defect only, a class which is defined as being " capable of earning a living under favourable circumstances." The facts are sufficient evidence as to how little favourable the actual circumstances at present are, and it may be remarked that not a few of these feeble-minded paupers have been educated at great cost in special schools. How illogical is the system which spends thousands upon the training of mentally defective children, and then turns them adrift to shift for themselves as best they can !

Idiots and Imbeciles.—Of the idiots and imbeciles about 54 per cent. are paupers, of whom about two-thirds are in institutions, and one-third in receipt of outdoor relief. Of those in institutions, nearly two-thirds are in idiot or lunatic asylums, and the remainder in the workhouse. There is no doubt, however, that a considerable number of the imbeciles at present attending elementary schools (where they learn nothing, and are often a considerable annoyance and distraction to teachers and scholars alike) will eventually become a charge upon the rates, whilst a large proportion of those not at present in receipt of relief will need provision upon the death of their parents.

With regard to the granting of relief to idiots and imbeciles, it is interesting to notice the difference of method between town and country districts respectively. The proportion actually relieved in the two situations is pretty much the same; but whereas in the towns 36 per cent. are in the workhouse and 7 per cent. outside, in the country there are but 14 per cent. in the house, as against 32 per cent. receiving outdoor relief.

Vagrancy.—We may now consider this question. Many feeble-minded persons, with a home to which they can turn, have such a propensity for wandering that they will roam the country for miles round, and sometimes be away for days together. These are often well known to all the country-side, and they frequently get a plate of food and a shakedown in the barn of some hospitable farmer; failing that, they spend the night in a dry ditch. I do not think they ever have any definite objective; they simply ramble on where the fit takes them. I remember once pursuing one of these youths, whom I particularly wanted to find, for a whole day. I got scent of him from time to time, but, although I was driving and he was on foot, it was nightfall before I overtook him, and he must have walked at least twenty miles.

On the other hand, a small number have no permanent home, but simply shift for themselves as best they may, and these, perhaps, are more properly called vagrants. As a rule, they are the least defective members of the feeble-minded, and although the bulk of them drift into the workhouse sooner or later, they do for a time, particularly in the country, manage to exist by their wits. How this is accomplished can generally only be conjectured; many of them seem to be itinerant vendors of something or other, and no doubt they often get a free meal or cast-off suit of clothes given to them, failing which they are not averse to begging. Some years ago I used constantly to meet a feeble-minded couple of this description—man and wife—who roamed the country collecting rags, bones, rabbit-skins, and such-like. But my inquiries showed that their defect gave them an unfair advantage over their normal-witted competitors, inasmuch as compassion gained for them what money had to procure for the others, and this is probably the case with most of the feeble-minded living by their wits. A few of these persons manage to earn enough to pay for bed and breakfast in a common lodging-house; these, however, are the élite, and the majority either sleep " rough " or get a bed in the casual ward. The inquiries of the Royal Commission show that on the whole about 10 per cent. of the feeble-minded come within the category of vagrants, whilst about 10 per cent. of all vagrants are feeble-minded. For the most part I think they are well-behaved and inoffensive, but some have decided insane or criminal tendencies and such are an undoubted menace to society.

I have already remarked that competition is much more adverse to the feeble-minded in the towns than in the country, and that in consequence a larger proportion of them gravitate into institutions. This is well shown by the following table which I have compiled from the Royal Commission Reports:

TABLE XVI.

SHOWING THE LOCATION OF FEEBLE-MINDED IN URBAN AND RURAL AREAS RESPECTIVELY.

	In Institutions (Paupers).	In Receipt of Outdoor Relief.	Not at Present receiving Relief.	
			Relief will probably be required upon Death of Friends.	Friends capable of making Permanent Provision.*
Urban and industrial areas	Per Cent. 76·2	Per Cent. 2·7	Per Cent. 19·2	Per Cent. 1·7
	79·0			
Rural areas..	25·7	20·7	39·8	13·6
	46·4			

Aments under Inadequate Care.

By no means one of the least important of the facts ascertained by the Royal Commission is the number of aments, in the eleven areas examined, whose care and control is inadequate, and for whom further provision is needed, either (1) in the interests of the patients themselves, or (2) for the public safety. The former group consists of persons who, in the opinion of the respective investigators, are unsuitably or unkindly cared for;

* Owing to difficulty of investigation, this class is probably understated.

The Ament and Society—Pauper Aments

the latter, of aments possessing habits and propensities which render them a source of danger to the community in which they live. It was recognized that many persons might be living under conditions which were not ideal, but these are not included, the object being to ascertain the irreducible minimum in urgent need of provision at the present time. I propose to quote these figures as affording statistical proof of the extremely unsatisfactory relationship at present existing between the ament and society.

In column 2 of the following table is shown the percentage of persons suffering from each of the three degrees of defect who were found to be inadequately cared for in the areas examined. There is no reason for thinking that these results are other than typical of the entire country; column 3 therefore shows the estimated total number of these persons in England and Wales.*

TABLE XVII.
AMENTS INADEQUATELY CARED FOR.

Degree of Defect.	Percentage inadequately cared for to Total Number in Eleven Areas investigated by Royal Commission.	Estimated Total Number inadequately cared for in England and Wales.
Idiots	40·8 per cent.	2,381
Imbeciles	46·2 ,,	7,689
Feeble-minded persons	31·8 ,,	15,793

It is of interest to note the chief locations of these persons needing further provision. In the case of the *feeble-minded*, the highest proportion of those unsatisfactorily provided for occurs in the classes at large and in charitable institutions, in which situations between 40 and 50 per cent. require further care. With regard to those at large this high proportion is not surprising, but a word of explanation is necessary in the case of the

* This estimate is calculated from the total number of aments existing in the country, as ascertained by the method described in Appendix II., p. 366. It does not include Feeble-Minded ("Mentally Deficient") Children, who, according to the Report of the Royal Commission, number 35,662, or 0·59 per cent. of the children on the school register.

charitable homes. The high proportion here is not any reflection upon these homes, but is simply due to the fact that their provision is temporary and optional only, and that most of the inmates are feeble-minded girls who have given birth to children. It is obvious that in the case of such persons detention should be permanent and compulsory. About one-fifth of the feeble-minded in workhouses, and one-fourth of those in receipt of outdoor relief, are reported to be unsatisfactorily provided for.

Of the *idiots* and *imbeciles*, the greatest proportion in need of provision occurs amongst those receiving outdoor relief. In two-thirds of these the present conditions are so unsatisfactory as to urgently call for amendment, and nearly all of these are in rural districts. Of those at large in fairly well-to-do circumstances, one-quarter require further care or control; whilst of those at large who are the offspring of the labouring class, the present provision is unsatisfactory in one-half. There can be no doubt that the presence of these persons in small and often overcrowded cottages is fraught with considerable possibilities of harm. But even apart from actual danger, want of time and want of knowledge on the part of the parents must prevent the imbecile or idiot receiving the attention he needs, and which he would obtain in an institution; whilst his presence cannot be regarded as conducive to the comfort of the home. As far as the idiots and imbeciles themselves are concerned, the accommodation provided by the workhouses is tolerably satisfactory; it is rarely, however, that any special wards exist for them, and it must be admitted that the other inmates often view the question in a somewhat different light.

Propagation by Aments.

There is no law in this country to prevent the marriage of the mentally defective, and every one knows that they do marry and have children. It is also equally well known that mentally deficient women not infrequently give birth to illegitimate children; but, as far as I am aware, until recent years there has been little definite inquiry made into this subject, and no sufficient data upon which to form any opinion as to the frequency of this evil. Some particulars ascertained by the investigations of the Royal Commission now throw a lurid glare upon the subject.

The Ament and Society—Pauper Aments

They relate entirely to feeble-minded females, and chiefly to inmates of workhouse maternity wards.

In *Manchester*, Dr. Melland found that, out of 94 women in these wards, 19 were feeble-minded, all the children except two being illegitimate. On making further inquiries of some of the younger of the other 167 feeble-minded women in the house, it was ascertained that another 13 admitted having given birth to illegitimate children, and Dr. Melland states that these inquiries were only of a partial and incomplete nature.

In *Birmingham*, Dr. Potts found that 4 out of the 34 women in the maternity wards were mentally defective, whilst at *Stoke-on-Trent* the same observer found that, of the 17 women giving birth to children during the period of inquiry, 7 were feeble-minded, all the children being illegitimate. Dr. Potts ascertained that the total progeny resulting from 16 mentally defective women was no less than 116. In the lock wards he found 5 feeble-minded women, all of whom were prostitutes.

In the rural districts the state of affairs was even worse. In *Wiltshire*, Dr. Pearse found that, of 58 feeble-minded women in the workhouse, 18 had given birth to illegitimate children. In *Nottinghamshire*, Dr. Gill ascertained that 11 out of 23 of these women had borne illegitimate children. In *Carnarvon*, Dr. Parry found that half the inmates of the maternity wards were mentally defective, nearly all the children being illegitimate; whilst in *Somersetshire* I ascertained that fully half of the women admitted into the workhouse to be confined during the previous five years had been feeble-minded; further, that out of *all* the feeble-minded women in the area (167), nearly two-fifths (61) had given birth to children, two-thirds of whom were illegitimate.

In few cases is the propagation by these women limited to a single child. More often their offspring number three or four, and one woman had given birth to six illegitimate children. All of these were by different fathers, and she was confined of each one in the workhouse. I may add that I discovered one feeble-minded woman in a workhouse who had given birth to four illegitimate children, although *she had never left the precincts of the house*.

When it is remembered that these figures only relate to a relatively small portion of the country, and that the investigations only extended over a period of about three months, it is clear that the number of children produced every year throughout England and Wales by feeble-minded women must be very great. In some cases the mothers have pronounced erotic tendencies, and many of them seem to be utterly lacking in any sense of shame, modesty, or even ordinary decency; but even the best-behaved, and those of good parentage brought up amid every refinement, are often so facile that it is utterly unsafe for them to be at large without protection.

To the above may be added a statement by Dr. Ireland, to the effect that the Scottish Lunacy Commissioners in their Report for the year 1857, "ascertained that the number of idiotic women who have borne illegitimate children, and whose mental defect is frequently manifested in their offspring, was no less than 126, and the return was not believed to be complete. Among the paupers in the parish of Kintore there was a fatuous mother with her two fatuous children. In the parish of Latheron, in Caithness, five imbecile females were named as having become mothers. The largest number of children anywhere returned to one fatuous female was five, the mother being an idiot belonging to the parish of Erskine, in Renfrewshire."

As bearing on the same question, I may cite some returns obtained by the Preventive Committee of the National Vigilance Society. As a result of special inquiries of 203 Boards of Guardians, it was found that, during the year 1889, 715 weak-minded women passed through 105 workhouses, whilst at 56 workhouses it was stated that the approximate number of such women who were leading immoral lives was 366.

With regard to the children of these mentally deficient women, it would, of course, be of the greatest interest and importance to know what becomes of them. Unfortunately, particulars of this kind are very difficult to obtain, and definite information is in consequence very scanty. I may state the following facts which were ascertained by myself: Of the 61 feeble-minded mothers whom I saw in Somersetshire, 19 were married and 42 unmarried. The 19 married have produced a total of 80 children. Of these, 16 died in infancy, 19 are imbecile or feeble-minded, 20 are either physically delicate to a pronounced degree or are mentally dull and backward, whilst 8 are too young to satis-

The Ament and Society—Pauper Aments

factorily examine. There are only 17 out of the total 80 who appear to come up to the average standard of mental and bodily health. With regard to the illegitimate children, the particulars are of necessity less complete. The 42 mothers have produced 78 children. Of these, 24 died in infancy, 5 are imbecile or feeble-minded, 2 are markedly dull and backward, 2 appear to be normal, and the remaining 45 have been completely lost sight of. It must be remembered that in practically all these cases information as to the *paternal* inheritance of these children is unobtainable.

As bearing upon the questions of propagations and the social relationship of the ament, I may cite the following cases which have recently come within my experience:

Upon the edge of a moor, in a thinly inhabited part of the West Country, stands a filthy thatched wooden hovel consisting of two rooms. Its exterior has an air of utter desolation and neglect; its interior is in a state of indescribable dirt and confusion. It is occupied by a married couple and their family. The man, aged fifty years, is of a decidedly low animal type, and has considerable moral, as well as slight mental, defect. He never refuses a drink, and picks up a living by occasional osier-stripping, and doing odd jobs on farms, but chiefly, I think, by poaching. The woman, his wife, is forty-four years of age and feeble-minded. She seems to be busy most of the day, and in her way keeps the house going; but she is utterly lacking in any capacity for management, and the filth and disorder are extreme. This woman had three children before marriage, and nine since. Of the former three, one died young of consumption, a second has entirely disappeared, and the third lives about the neighbourhood; but he quarrelled with his mother's husband, and they are not now on speaking terms. Of the nine born in wedlock, two died in infancy, three attend the village school and are mentally defective, and another also mentally defective is at home. The eldest does odd jobs with his father, and seems to be able to take care of himself. The remaining two are aged five months and three years respectively, and are too young to enable an opinion to be formed as to their mental capacity. To this it may be added that the father has had ten children by a previous wife. Of these, two are feeble-minded, one of whom is living a life of prostitution, and has already had two illegitimate children in the workhouse. The others have been entirely lost sight of.

Mary H—— is a feeble-minded married woman forty years old. She lives with her husband, a farm labourer, in a small cottage in an isolated village. She is industrious and always working, but the house is in a disgraceful muddle. At my visit there were two unwashed, partially dressed children, under three years of age, sprawling about the wet stone floor amid a litter of dirty plates and pans, potato peelings, and live poultry. Upon asking her how old she was, and how long she had been married, she replied, with a fatuous smile, that she didn't know, but her mother did. The children I saw in the house were too young to examine mentally; but two other illegitimate children whom I did see, aged sixteen and seventeen years respectively, were feeble-minded. Both of these are industrious boys, and work well under supervision, but they are quite incapable of looking after their affairs. This woman has two brothers, who are also feeble-minded; one is constantly in and out of the workhouse, but the other, aged thirty, is employed regularly with a farmer at the rate of a shilling a day. Their mother has had several attacks of insanity, but the father is dead, and no particulars were obtainable regarding him.

Rose D—— is a feeble-minded woman forty-five years of age. She is the daughter a of well-to-do farmer, but ran away from home at the age of twenty years, and since then she has been living a life of prostitution. Her usual abode is the common lodging-house, but a considerable part of her life has been spent in prison, the workhouse, and various charitable homes. She has been confined of three illegitimate children in the workhouse. The clergyman of the parish in which she lives says that he has got her into homes again and again, but she will not stay, and they cannot compel her to do so. All attempts to induce her to lead a respectable life have failed, and she is his despair and a disgrace to the civilization which permits her to be at large.

I may add that these are by no means isolated instances. Many of the particulars regarding this matter which have come under my own notice are too revolting for publication, and there is the clearest evidence that the propagation by aments is both a terrible and extensive evil.

CHAPTER XVI

MORAL DEFICIENCY AND CRIMINAL AMENTS

THE subject of moral deficiency is one of extreme interest alike to the alienist and criminologist, and although some persons would be inclined to look upon the moral or ethical sense as transcending mind altogether, it is, nevertheless, so clearly an integral part of that complex sum of processes to which we give the name *mind* that the question of moral deficiency cannot be ignored in a work dealing with amentia.

But although the moral sense is unquestionably part of the *tout ensemble* of mind, it does not follow that the person in whom it is defective is necessarily an ament. There are four chief " senses " or " sentiments " which, in varying proportions, go to make up the mind of average civilized man. These may be described as the logical or intellectual, the religious, the æsthetic, and the moral or social. The logical or intellectual sense causes us to test each new experience by the light of our previous knowledge, to criticize and carefully compare, and to accept or reject according as our judgment affirms it to be true or untrue. Such a type of mind is said to be essentially rational. The religious sense implies a conception of the relationship between God and man. It is largely made up of the emotions of awe, reverence, and adoration, and religion has been well defined as " The feeling of reverence which men entertain toward a Supreme Being, or to any order of beings conceived by them as demanding reverence from the possession of superhuman control over the destiny of man or the powers of nature."* The æsthetic sense connotes a marked appreciation of all that is beautiful in form, colour, sound, etc. Whilst, lastly, by the

* Ogilvie and Annandale, " Imperial Dictionary."

moral sense is meant the faculty of appreciating the obligations due from man to his neighbours as component units of society.

Now, these various senses are differently developed in different individuals, and this is partly a result of special hereditary tendencies, and partly due to the nature of the early environment. Some persons are full of religious and moral feeling (although the two are by no means synonymous), and yet absolutely illogical and inartistic. Others, of extreme æsthetic development, have no sense of logic; whilst yet others, of the keenest intellect and highest logical capacity, are devoid of moral consciousness. The mind of the child is usually deficient in this latter sense, and it is only by the constant force of example, the reiteration of precept, and perhaps the infliction of punishment, that it learns to think and act according to the stereotyped social and legal code of the age to which it belongs, and so conforms to moral and social law.

Although human conceptions of morality, as also of religion and art, are ever changing with social development and the progressive evolution of the mental faculties, there is every reason for thinking that some persons are so constituted that they are utterly devoid of any real moral sense, and of the *consciousness* that any obligation is morally due from them to their fellows; just as others may have no sense of religion or no conception of the beauties of form, colour, or sound. Such defect is inherent, and it may rightly be called *moral deficiency*.

Its relation to criminality, however, is another matter. It may be that, although these persons have no *feelings* of repugnance or shame at the thought of a criminal or immoral act, and although they cannot appreciate the ethics of the Decalogue, nevertheless their intelligence tells them that certain unpleasant consequences, in the shape of judicial punishment or social censure, will follow transgression, and this suffices to keep them within the prescribed legal and social code. Their moral defect is, in fact, latent.

It is the same with the æsthetic and religious senses. Many persons utterly devoid of conceptions of beauty or harmony still manage to avoid running counter to the canons of good taste by conforming to the recognized customs of society, and how many who are absolutely wanting in any real religious feeling acquire a reputation for piety and reverence as a result of their scrupulous observance of religious form and ceremony!

But although latent moral defectives of this kind are not of necessity actual criminals, they may well be described as potential criminals. They stand in the same relation to the inmates of our prisons as do the psychopaths or potential lunatics to the inmates of our asylums, or the improvident to the inmates of our workhouses, and there can be no doubt that it is from this class that one section of our criminals is drawn. Although there is no intellectual defect, and such persons fully realize the consequences of detection, yet occasionally the gain resulting from a crime or act of immorality appears so great, and the likelihood of discovery so small, that, moral sense being absent, they deliberately take the risk. Since, however, our standard of mind is an intellectual one, such persons can no more be considered as mentally deficient than can those who are lacking in the religious or æsthetic sense.

But the case is different with another class. There are some persons, likewise deficient in moral sense, who *repeatedly* commit criminal acts, and upon whom punishment has not the slightest deterrent effect whatever. These form a large proportion of the instinctive or habitual criminal class, the true *moral defectives*, and they may be defined as "those persons who display from an early age, and in spite of careful upbringing, strong vicious or criminal propensities on which punishment has little or no deterrent effect."

As to whether the members of this class are or are not intellectually deficient, opinions differ. It it contended by some that such a propensity to crime may exist without any intellectual defect, whilst others maintain that a deficiency of the intellectual faculty is also present—that, in fact, such persons are aments. The question is one which it is extremely difficult to decide. On the one hand there is no doubt that, although many of these persons commit offences in the most open manner, and from which they have nothing to gain, yet they will converse upon many subjects in an exceedingly intelligent way, whilst some are actually possessed of unusual talents. A few again, in their commission of offences and their attempts to escape detection, show a capacity, alertness, and cunning, of a very high order, and which also would seem to be incompatible with the presence of amentia. On the other hand, however, their utter inability to keep within the law and to control their evil propensities, when they know that punishment has followed, and will almost inevitably follow again, is certainly suggestive of a deficiency of intellect, or, at any rate, of a defective power of self-control.

As tending to elucidate this question, we may refer to the many characteristics which these persons possess in common with aments. During recent years numerous investigations have been carried out in England, America, Italy, France, Germany, and Russia with regard to the physical and psychological features of the habitual or instinctive criminal class, and of which many particulars are given in Havelock Ellis's most interesting book " The Criminal." To some of these we may refer.

With regard to the brain, the results do not enable one to say that a special " criminal type " exists, but nearly all the inquirers are agreed that anatomical anomalies indicative of arrested development are of much more common occurrence than in the normal population. The same is true of the face, jaws, palate, and body generally; in the habitual criminal stigmata of degeneracy abound just as they do in the ament. The Anthropometric Committee of the British Association examined over 3,000 criminals, and found them about 2 inches shorter and 17 pounds lighter than the average English population. Baer examined 4,500 Berlin criminals, and found that the average height was decidedly below the normal, and the same was observed by Hamilton Wey in America. Dr. G. Wilson, in a paper on "The Moral Imbecility of Habitual Criminals as Exemplified by Cranial Measurements,"[*] arrived at the conclusion, from measurements of the heads of 464 criminals, that habitual thieves had well-marked indications of defective cranial development associated with physical deterioration. Dr. J. Bruce Thompson,[†] in a summary of his observations upon over 5,000 prisoners, pointed out the great prevalence of mental defect, especially amongst the juvenile criminals, and also the frequency with which morbid appearances were found post-mortem. Professor Lombroso, in his book " L' Uomo Delin-

[*] A paper read before the British Association at Exeter, 1869.
[†] *Journal of Mental Science*, 1870.

PLATE XXVI.

Fig. 61.—A feeble-minded man suffering from pronounced mental instability. Has had several attacks of religious mania.

Fig. 60.—A feeble-minded youth of the criminal type. Restless, idle, untruthful, and of roving disposition.

[To face page 296.]

quente," came to the conclusion, on anthropometrical grounds, that the criminal is a manifestation of degeneracy.

Similarly with mental characteristics. Although many of the criminal class appear on casual examination to be of average intellectual calibre, there is abundant evidence to show that a large number of them present anomalies similar to those referred to in our description of the Feeble Mind. As Havelock Ellis says, " On the one hand he is stupid, inexact, lacking in forethought, astoundingly imprudent ; on the other hand he is cunning, hypocritical, delighting in falsehood, even for its own sake, abounding in ruses." And in another place, " The criminal in some of his most characteristic manifestations is a congenitally weak-minded person, whose abnormality, whilst by no means leaving the mental aptitudes absolutely unimpaired, chiefly affects the feelings and volition, so influencing conduct and rendering him an anti-social element in society." Dr. Maudsley,* speaking of instinctive criminals, says : " It is a matter of observation that the criminal class constitutes a degenerate or morbid variety of mankind marked by peculiarly low physical and mental characteristics ;" whilst Dr. Nicholson† has also pointed out the great prevalence of weak-mindedness, with instability, tendency to delusions, insensibility, and emotional nature, in the criminal class.

Finally, the close connexion between criminals and aments is further shown by the antecedents of the two classes. In inquiring into the family histories of members of the habitual criminal class, I have often been struck by the fact that, although they themselves might show little obvious indication of mental inferiority, a large number of them came of a neuropathic stock, and possessed brothers and sisters who were markedly deficient. Conversely, in examining aments, I have often found that their brothers or sisters were criminals. In dealing with the inmates of prisons it is often extremely difficult to obtain a family history, but it was ascertained that, of 233 prisoners at Auburn, New York, at least 23 per cent. were of neurotic (insane and epileptic) origin. *Rossi* found that in 71 criminals there were 5 insane parents, 6 insane brothers and sisters, and 14 cases of insanity

---

* Maudsley, " Responsibility in Mental Disease," 1872.
† Nicholson, *Journal of Mental Science*, 1873-1875.

amongst more distant relatives. *Kolk* found a morbid inheritance in 46 per cent. of criminals, and *Marro* in 77 per cent. *Sichard*, as a result of his examination of nearly 4,000 German criminals, found that there was an insane, epileptic, suicidal, or alcoholic heredity in 36·8 per cent. of incendiaries, 32 per cent. of thieves, 28·7 per cent. of sexual offenders, and 23·6 per cent. of sharpers.

Lastly, the interesting record of the Juke family, which was compiled by R. L. Dugdale,* well shows the close relationship existing between the criminal and the psychopath. This observer traced the descendants of one morbid couple through five generations to the number of 709 individuals, and found that whilst a small proportion were honest workers, the great majority were vagabonds, paupers, criminals, and prostitutes.

I think these facts (and I have only referred to a few of them) conclusively show that, although in a large number of habitual or instinctive criminals the defect may appear to be more moral than intellectual, nevertheless their persistent criminality in spite of punishment, as well as the many features they possess in common with the true aments, are a sufficient justification for our considering them as being closely related to, if not actually suffering from, a mild degree of mental deficiency.

Criminal Aments.

We may now consider a somewhat different class, namely, persons suffering from undoubted intellectual deficiency who have pronounced immoral and criminal tendencies, and who are in consequence guilty of repeated offences against law and society.

Such persons may belong to any of the three degrees of amentia. As we have seen, idiots are often extremely destructive, and they may commit homicide. Many imbeciles have pronounced thieving propensities, are guilty of incendiarism, or possess marked sexual desires, which they may forcibly seek to gratify. More commonly, however, criminal aments belong to the feeble-minded or mildest degree, and this is probably the result of their greater personal freedom from supervision, as well as their numerical preponderance—perhaps, also, partly owing to their greater knowledge.

* Putnams, New York, 1877.

Some idea of the number of mentally deficient criminals under detention in this country, and of the general policy of the Prison Commissioners regarding them, will be gathered from the reply to a question in the House of Commons on July 22, 1907. The Home Secretary said: "Both in local and convict prisons those prisoners who are not certifiably insane, but are unfit through mental deficiency for the ordinary penal discipline, form a separate class and are specially treated. In the year 1906-07 the numbers were: the local prisons 355, and in convict prisons 107. The policy of the Prison Commissioners is to place these prisoners under the special charge of the medical officers of the prisons, and to keep them continuously under the personal care of selected warders. The medical officers regulate their discipline and diet, and allow them such employment as is suited to the condition of each individual. In addition to those so classified, there are other prisoners temporarily under observation to ascertain their mental state."

The recent investigations of the Royal Commission show that about 10 per cent. of the inmates of prisons are aments. These figures must be considered rather to under-estimate than over-estimate the facts, for the uniform practice of the inquirers was to include only such cases as showed clear and undoubted signs of mental defect. On the other hand, a careful analysis of the same inquiries shows that about 10 per cent. of all feeble-minded persons have pronounced criminal and antisocial propensities.

Feeble-minded criminals, using this latter word in its widest sense, fall into three groups. On the one hand there are those who are led into the commission of offences against law and morality by reason of their extremely facile disposition, which makes them ready tools in the hands of evil-doers. The deficiency here is largely one of control or of knowledge, and they are rather sinned against than sinning. Our police-courts show that feeble-minded dupes of this kind are by no means unknown to-day, although it is likely that the number of persons profiting by this failing of the mentally defective has been considerably diminished in recent years. At the present time it is probable that prostitutes comprise the largest proportion of this type, especially in our towns and industrial centres.

Another group of feeble-minded persons are of such an excitable, explosive, and generally unstable mental constitution as to be utterly untrustworthy, and a considerable number of the offences against society are committed by this class. It may be termed "the impulsive type of criminal ament." Far from being facile, they are generally extremely obstinate and intolerant of contradiction, and they will often suddenly pass from a state of what appears to be perfect calm and indifference to one of raving, uncontrollable fury. Many of them are very suspicious, and some have definite delusions; in fact, I think that all this class have an extremely strong tendency to insanity, and that often during the commission of their offences they are actually insane. Most, but not all, are of the mildest degree of amentia. In many of their characteristics these persons resemble the epileptics, but I do not think that they commonly suffer from epilepsy. The offences most commonly committed are criminal and other assaults, acts of wanton destruction, cruelty to animals, fighting, brawling and disorderly conduct.

Feeble-minded persons in general are very intolerant of alcohol, but its effects seem to be especially marked upon the type we are now considering. I remember one youth in a country village who used to be repeatedly plied with cider by the yokels of the place in order that they might be amused by his furious excitement, pretty much in the same way as a bull is baited in the ring. The following are good examples of the type:

Thomas B——, a feeble-minded young man, twenty-five years of age, with numerous stigmata of degeneracy. He could never learn at school, and afterwards could not keep his situations. At the age of twenty-three he became insane, and was sent to the asylum for six months. Shortly after discharge he was apprehended for sleeping out, and served seven days' imprisonment. He had only been out a few weeks when he attempted rape on a small girl whom he met in the road. For this he was sentenced to two months' hard labour. On being liberated he became very violent and aggressive, and threatened to cut his mother's throat. He was again sent to the asylum, and discharged in six months. He is now living at home, and works occasionally in the factory; but his mother says that he cannot be depended upon, that some days he refuses to get out of bed, and is at times so violent that she is afraid to have him in the house.

He is a powerful fellow, who should be capable of hard work could he be controlled.

Alfred L——, a feeble-minded man of twenty-eight years. He is now occupied cracking stones, and does occasional work on farms when he can get it ; but he is very unstable, at times being noisy, excitable, quarrelsome, and absolutely refusing to do any work. He has been imprisoned at least six times for such offences as drunkenness, fighting, stealing, and setting fire to gorse, and is known and dreaded for miles round as a regular nuisance.

The third group is, I think, the most numerous of all, and consists of those feeble-minded persons who commit crimes, not under external suggestion, and not because they are passionate and excitable, but because either they cannot really appreciate the difference between right and wrong or have ineradicable and irresistible criminal propensities. In fact, they suffer, not so much from a defect of inhibition, as from a pronounced mental and moral perversion. The crimes of these persons differ from those of the two preceding groups, inasmuch as, although they may at times appear to be sudden and unpremeditated, they more often show evidence of previous deliberation and plan, and sometimes of considerable cunning to escape detection. In addition to persistent lying, thieving, indecency, acts of cruelty and wanton destruction, these individuals are often guilty of the more serious crimes of incendiarism, train-wrecking, criminal and homicidal assaults.

It is a remarkable fact that, although these persons whilst at liberty and away from supervision seem absolutely incapable of conforming to the law, they are nearly always quiet and well-behaved under the discipline of a prison. Their lives consist of an unbroken series of offences, in many cases there being literally scores of convictions, whilst in some they amount to over a hundred. They are the definitely mentally defective habitual criminals.

In most of these cases the condition is present in childhood, and is shown by habits of lying, thieving, and the like, upon which punishment has not the slightest effect. I know one boy who has not yet reached his eighth birthday, but he has already been expelled from school because nothing was safe within his reach. He has a vocabulary equal to that of any bargee, and he steals eggs, fruit, money, and anything he can lay his hands on ; he has already burnt two hayricks to the ground. In an elementary school of a provincial town I came across three children of this type belonging to one family. The two boys were only eight and five years old respectively, and the girl seven years ; but the schoolmaster told me that they had a propensity for lying, thieving, and causing trouble generally, the like of which he had never met, and that nothing seemed to deter them. They were all mentally defective, and I was informed that the father was of the same type, and more often in than out of prison. The following cases are further examples of this class :

George P——, a mentally defective child, aged thirteen and a half years, attending school in Standard I. Power of reasoning decidedly wanting, but alert and cunning, and always getting into trouble. He is said to be incorrigibly lazy at school, and a frequent truant, and the schoolmaster says that he will steal and lie without the least compunction, and that punishment seems to be without the slightest effect. He is always ready with a plausible excuse, and shows a precocious amount of cunning in covering up his misdeeds. A short time ago he stole the schoolmistress's gold watch from its accustomed place on her desk. It was not missed until the children had left, and then there was an instant hue and cry. George, finding himself pursued, secreted the watch in a tree, and then submitted himself to be searched with an air of complete innocence. Unluckily, however, for him, the manoeuvre had been seen. It is interesting to note that this boy's father is just the same (indeed, I am inclined to think that this moral perversion is generally hereditary). He is plausible and cunning, and, although he occasionally does odd jobs, I was told by the police that he never did any regular work, and that the greater part of his life had been spent in prison for such offences as stealing, poaching, and drunkenness. When I saw him he had just returned from serving a term of imprisonment for poaching.

George A——, a feeble-minded, undersized youth with a slouching walk, furtive demeanour, and physiognomy typical of mental defect. He answers questions in a simple, childish manner, and gives information regarding his past life willingly and without any appearance of shame or concern ; his memory, however, is a little defective, and his account is at times confused and incoherent. He cannot read, write, or sum, but he is quite capable of useful work under supervision, and his conduct in prison (where I saw him) is good. The youth knows nothing about his parents, and little about his early life beyond the fact that he was brought up in an industrial school, and thence put to work on a farm. He ran away because he wanted a change, and, after tramping about for a time, eventually got employment on another farm. He ran away from here because he was discovered committing acts of indecency with the cattle. He then tramped about, and was frequently in and out of workhouses. He was convicted with several others of stealing lead, and served a term of imprisonment. After this he again tramped the country, spending most of his time between the prison and the workhouse. He is now in for setting fire to a rick, for which act he is unable to give any reason.

Finally, as further examples, I may refer to the following four cases culled from the newspapers during the past few months, all of which were reported to be mentally defective.

" W. K., a ten-year-old boy, was charged at Bow Street with attempted pocket-picking in a railway-train. The boy excused himself by saying that his mother had pushed him into the train with orders to rob the lady. The police found that there was not a tittle of evidence to support the lad's statement, and an officer from the school board reported that he was mentally defective."

" H. A., a feeble-minded deaf-mute, was charged with stabbing his sister. The prosecutrix said that he had never been quite right in his mind, and that she had always treated him as a child, but that he was no trouble if he did not get into drink. The medical officer of the prison certified him as being of weak mind and likely to be easily affected by drink, but he could not certify him as insane. The charge was reduced to one of common assault, and the magistrate thought it would be good for the youth to go to prison, and committed him for two months."

" G. E. R., aged nineteen, was indicted for endangering the safety of persons being conveyed upon the London and North-Western Railway by placing a coil of disused electric wire on the line in such a position as to be in the way of any passing trains.

Prisoner was a typewriter and shorthand clerk, and no motive could be assigned for his act. He was admittedly weak-minded, but beyond that the medical officers who had had him under observation could not go. He was convicted of misdemeanour only, and sentenced to pay a fine of £50, or in default to undergo six months' imprisonment; also to find two sureties in £50 each to keep the peace for twelve months, or go to prison for six months in default."

" *T. P.*—Owing to the extraordinary series of grave outrages committed in Nottinghamshire and the immediate district during the past month, much importance was attached to a case which occupied the attention of the Mansfield Bench. The man in custody, a labourer named *T. P.*, aged twenty-three. a *deaf-mute of weak intellect*, was charged with feloniously placing a wooden gate on the Great Central line at Kirkby-in-Ashfield. *P.* has been in the habit of sleeping out, although his reputed place of abode is at Sutton-in-Ashfield, within which area there have been a number of abortive attempts at train-wrecking. In addition, the neighbouring parish churches of Kirkby and Annesley have been destroyed by fire upon successive nights, both disasters being the work of an incendiary. Prisoner was apprehended in a shed at some brickworks. He showed the police-officers a spot on the railway where he said he placed a wooden gate on the rails. Dr. Gray, who had examined prisoner, gave evidence that *P.* was a lunatic and a proper person to be taken charge of. Deputy-Chief-Constable Harrop said, as accused was certified insane, no evidence would be offered. The man was first arrested in connexion with a robbery at Ulfreton Railway-station, and the proceeds were found in his possession; other robberies on the railway had been also traced to him. Prisoner took witness and Police-Constable Fryer to Sutton-in-Ashfield, and across some fields to the Great Central Railway at Kirkby, where he pointed out the exact spot at which an obstruction had been placed on the line. He exhibited great satisfaction when a train approached, and showed where he had obtained the gate and had hidden himself until a train dashed into the obstruction. Afterwards prisoner showed exactly where two pairs of trolly wheels and a wheelbarrow attached had been placed on the line. Accused was ordered to be sent to a lunatic asylum."

Criminal Responsibility of Aments.

The law of England recognizes that persons suffering from certain forms of mental disease cannot be held accountable for their actions, and, generally speaking, this is the case with idiots and pronounced imbeciles, or any person who, in the words of Mr. Justice Tracey (1723), knows what he is doing " no more than an infant, a brute, or a wild beast." With regard to the milder degrees of defect, however, the mere presence of feeble-mindedness does not of necessity absolve a person from the consequences of his acts, and the criminal responsibility of such persons, as well as of the insane, is by no means clearly defined. There are certain precedents and rulings which are usually followed in such cases, but in any particular instance the fact of the responsibility or otherwise of the accused is a question for the jury to decide upon the evidence presented to them. Criminal offences in which this question of responsibility is raised are exceedingly common, and it is plainly the duty of the members of our profession, who alone can form a correct estimate as to the extent to which conduct is likely to be influenced by mental deficiency or disease, to formulate general principles, and to give their opinion regarding the mental condition of any particular accused person in order that the jury may arrive at this decision. These general principles, however, must be just, and whilst protecting those who are really irresponsible from undeserved punishment, they must also protect society against the escape from punishment of those who, even if mentally deficient, are rightly accountable for their actions.

The rulings of English Courts at the present time are generally based upon the replies of the fifteen Judges to the House of Lords in the middle of the last century. Briefly, it may be stated that for an accused person to be held irresponsible on the ground of insanity, it must be shown that he was of diseased mind, and that at the time he committed the act he was not conscious of right or wrong, or was under some delusion which made him regard the act as right.

This dictum, it will be observed, takes no account of the question of defective control, an omission which was pointed out in the exhaustive treatise of Sir FitzJames Stephen. According to this eminent jurist, " No act is a crime if the person who does it is, at the time when it is done, *prevented from controlling his own conduct*, unless the absence of the power of control has been produced by his own default." I do not propose to enter into any discussion regarding the diminution of the will in ordinary persons or even in insanity ; but I am quite certain that in persons suffering from amentia a diminished power of control is so commonly present, and such an essential part of their mental condition, that a grave injustice may be done if this be not taken into account. There *may* be non-defective persons who, whilst fully appreciating the nature and consequences of certain criminal acts, are yet incapable of refraining from committing them, and such cases are described as impulsive insanity. But it cannot be doubted that there *are* aments who suffer from a definite defect of control which leads them to commit criminal acts. I would therefore say that, whilst the mentally deficient person is not necessarily irresponsible for any crime he may commit, he should certainly be held unaccountable when he commits an act (1) of which he does not understand the nature or that it is contrary to law ; (2) which is the result of an impulse he was unable to control ; (3) which is the natural result of a delusion of which he is shown to be the subject.

With regard to these particular qualifying conditions a few words may be said. (1) Want of knowledge as to the nature or illegality of the act would usually be capable of ready demonstration in the case of idiots and imbeciles ; but even in the milder grades defective intelligence or education might still result in ignorance as to *how* wrong the act was or that it was forbidden by law. As was ably pointed out by Sir FitzJames Stephen : " Knowledge has its degrees like everything else, and implies something more real and more closely connected with conduct than the half knowledge retained in dreams." As an instance this author quotes the extreme case of the idiot who cut off the head of a man whom he found asleep, remarking that it would be great fun to see him look for it when he woke ; and he adds : " Nothing is more probable than that the idiot would know that people in authority would not approve of this, that it was wrong in the sense in which it is wrong in a child not to learn its lesson, and he obviously knew that it was a mischievous trick." And it cannot be doubted that the same kind of incomplete knowledge as to *how* wrong an act is exists in the case of many persons suffering from a mild degree of mental deficiency. The high grade ament at Earlswood asylum, who has been mentioned as attempting the destruction of an official who had displeased him, undoubtedly knew that in so doing he was doing what was wrong, but I do not for one moment think that he appreciated how wrong his act was, or that, had it succeeded, he could justly have been held *fully* accountable for it. Dr. Mercier,* commenting on this question in his recent philosophical treatise, says : " It is a truth on which I have insisted in season and out of season for many years, that a man may know that his act is wrong without knowing how wrong it is."

(2) Pronounced defect of control in aments is usually clearly evident from infancy, although in some cases it may not attract attention until puberty. It is one of the chief characteristics of the " facile " and " impulsive " types of amentia, and of some of the epileptics. It is also a prominent feature in many of those persons we have described as " moral defectives " or habitual criminals, who repeatedly (and often openly) commit offences absolutely undeterred by punishment. As an extreme instance of this the case related by Dr. Gray, lately physician to the Ameer of Afghanistan (mentioned in Dr. Mercier's book), is worthy of note. It is that of a man " who, after having had first his right hand, and subsequently his left hand, struck off as a punishment for theft, seized with his stumps and made off with an earthenware pot of trifling value, and of no use whatever to him. The crime was witnessed and the criminal at once arrested and taken before the Ameer, who sentenced him, as he must have expected, to be hanged ; and hanged he accordingly was." Dr. Mercier also mentions the case of a cadet at Sandhurst, who stole the boots and clothes of a comrade, although he was amply supplied by his father, and had no need of the things stolen. He stole them without any concealment, and actually wore them in the presence of their owner. He was expelled, and on his return home, although standing in awe and terror of his father, nevertheless cleared the latter's dressing-

* Charles Mercier, "Criminal Responsibility," 1905.

table of its ivory brushes and silver furniture, and sold them to a passer-by for five shillings.

Quite recently I was consulted with regard to an almost precisely similar case in the shape of a youth at a public school who, although liberally supplied from home, and having everything he needed, systematically purloined his companions' property of every description. This youth was by no means unintelligent, in fact, in several subjects he occupied a high place in his form, and his general appearance and conversation were so prepossessing that anyone not acquainted with the type would almost certainly feel that some horrible mistake had been made. His only observable peculiarities consisted of a somewhat wandering attention, a general restlessness, and several little tricks such as constantly putting his hand to his collar, etc. And yet, when I questioned him about his misdeeds, he acknowledged them without any shame or concealment, and I found that he had been expelled from two other schools for similar practices. I am inclined to think that in some of the milder cases of this kind recovery may take place under suitable treatment and some degree of moral sense be developed ; but pronounced cases like these described are practically hopeless, and although it may be extremely difficult in some of them to detect any intellectual deficiency, and to differentiate badness from madness, the fact of such senseless depredations in spite of punishment would of itself lead one to infer that an intellectual defect did, in reality, exist. On the other hand, there can be no doubt that " moral deficiency," or as it is sometimes more euphemistically described " kleptomania," is often put forward as a defence when the individual is fully accountable for his actions. Personally I should be very loth to admit defective will-power as an excuse for a criminal offence unless the accused were of one of the types which have been described, or there were evidence of the previous commission of impulsive acts.

(3) The commission of criminal acts in consequence of delusions practically only occurs in the case of aments who are also insane. These will be described in the following chapter, but here it may be stated that, although the combination of insanity and mental deficiency would raise a strong presumption as to the irresponsibility of the individual so affected, he could only justly and

logically be held unaccountable for the commission of a criminal act when it was clearly shown that his mental disease did, in fact, prevent him from knowing the nature and quality of the act at the time it was done, or from knowing that the act was wrong, or from controlling his own conduct. For as Mr. Justice Stephen said : " An act may be a crime although the mind of the person who does it is affected by disease, if such disease does not, in fact, produce upon his mind one or other of the effects above mentioned in reference to that act."

It is thus seen that, although an inquiry into the criminal responsibility of a person must, of necessity, take into account the state of that person's mind, yet the question is not in reality a medical, but a legal one. It is the duty of the physician to place before the court full and impartial evidence regarding the presence or absence of such mental disease, disorder, or deficiency as would influence conduct ; but it is the duty of the judge and jury to decide whether this defect or disease *has* so influenced conduct as to render the accused partially or wholly irresponsible for his act.

In defining the " conditions of responsibility," Dr. Mercier arrives at the conclusion that " to incur responsibility by a harmful act, the actor must *will* the act ; *intend* the harm ; *desire* primarily his own gratification. Furthermore the act must be *unprovoked*, and the actor must *know* and appreciate the circumstances in which the act is done."

With regard to **civil incapacity**, an idiot has no civil rights, but a person suffering from feeble-mindedness could only be adjudged incapable of managing his affairs by proceedings in Chancery. In such a case trustees of the estate might be appointed without depriving the person of his liberty ; in other words, he might be declared incapable of managing his affairs, but capable of managing himself.

An idiot is inadmissible as a witness, but in the case of an imbecile or feeble-minded person it is for the Judge to examine and ascertain whether he is of competent understanding to give evidence, and is aware of the nature and obligation of an oath ; if satisfied that he is, the Judge will probably allow him to be sworn and examined.

CHAPTER XVII
INSANE AMENTS

In the literal sense of the word "insanity," all aments may be looked upon, and are often described, as "congenitally insane." But nowadays there is a tendency to restrict the term to those cases in which there is a perversion of the *ego*, and it is in this sense that it is here used. Dr. Savage says a man must be considered as sane or insane *in relation to himself*, and although such a definition would render "congenital" insanity an impossibility, the variations of mental function and capacity in the mentally deficient are so great that, from the standpoint of amentia, there is much to be said in favour of using the *ego* rather than the "normal" or "mean average" as a standard of reference.

A large number of aments react to their environment in a perfectly consistent, uniform, and, as far as their mental capacity will admit, normal manner, and such may be considered sane, albeit defective. On the other hand, a certain number are characterized by lapses from their ordinary mental state of such intensity that, for the time being, they may rightly be termed insane; it is with these latter that this chapter deals.

The causes which actually *determine* insanity are many and varied, ranging from a slight alteration of the general bodily health and condition to a sudden strain or prolonged mental or nervous stress. As Mercier says, however, "a jerry-built villa is liable to be blown down by a storm of wind, but nothing short of an earthquake will destroy a well-constructed mansion." And in the great majority of cases of insanity there is a *predisposing* cause—namely, an instability of nervous tissue. This instability may be congenital or acquired, generally the former, and, in view of the defective structure which is the essential basis of amentia, it is not surprising that in many of these persons there should be a decided nervous instability and consequent proneness to insanity; this is found to be the case.

It is probable that the actual number of aments who are thus predisposed to insanity is incapable of determination, just as it is impossible to calculate the proportion of potential lunatics in the non-defective population; but an approximate estimate of the number of the feeble-minded grade of aments who are *actually* insane can be made, and a comparison of this with the number of the ordinary insane will give an idea of the relative predisposition in the two classes.

From information which has been very courteously placed at my disposal by some asylum physicians, as well as from my own observations in the asylums of the London County Council and elsewhere, I am of opinion that at least 5 per cent. of the inmates of the county and borough asylums of this country are *feeble-minded insane;* we may therefore estimate the number of feeble-minded certified lunatics as approximately 4,450, or about 8 per cent. of the total feeble-minded of the country (54,114).

The proportion of ordinary or non-defective insane to the total population is only about 0·3 per cent., from which it appears that the predisposition to insanity in the feeble-minded is twenty-six times that of the ordinary population. There are, of course, many of the non-defective insane who are not certified, but so there are of the mentally deficient insane, and I think that these figures express the relative predisposition to insanity which exists in the two classes with tolerable accuracy. On the whole I think we may say that close on 10 per cent. of the feeble-minded have a definite insane predisposition. With regard to this tendency in imbeciles and idiots, I am unable to give any figures, but my impression is that, although it is considerably less than in the merely feeble-minded, it is still much greater than in the ordinary population.

There is no doubt that a considerable number of the non-defective insane manifest signs of a diminished power of will or inhibition from a very early age, and some writers would go so far as to include these with the aments proper.* It cannot be

* See Bolton, " Amentia and Dementia," *Journal of Mental Science*, 1907.

denied that there is much to be said for such a view, for these persons often present a physiognomy, and also stigmata of degeneracy, identical with those existing in the mentally defective. I doubt, however, whether these should really be classed as aments, although they are undoubtedly on the borderland between this condition and insanity, between a brain which is the seat of an actual arrest of anatomical structure and one which is merely unstable and of defective physiological potentiality. They serve to show that, just as the three grades of amentia merge into one another, so in turn do the mildest members of the aments stand in an extremely close relationship to the insane—that idiocy is, indeed, the culmination of the neuropathic diathesis. In this place, however, I shall use the term "amentia" in the manner in which it has all along been used, and shall only refer to those persons who show definite intellectual deficiency.

In a certain number of these aments who become insane there are determining factors, just as in the ordinary lunatics; but, on the whole, these factors are much less in evidence, and as we proceed down the scale of mental deficiency they become still less and less frequent. In the imbeciles an attack of insanity may suddenly appear without any apparent determining cause whatever, and the sudden and violent storms of the idiot, which must be looked upon as of precisely the same nature as true insanity, are similarly unrelated to any obvious cause. The extreme mental instability present in these persons must be considered as of itself sufficient to determine the attack: the "jerry-built villa" topples over, not by reason of any storm of wind. but because of its own unstable equilibrium.

This instability, as I have already remarked, is usually present and recognizable from childhood. As a boy or girl the patient has been subject to fits of irritability, moroseness, or bad temper, often accompanied by acts of violence, which have been a cause not only of sorrow, but of anxiety, to friends and relations; and although these conditions can hardly be termed insanity, they are the shadows of the coming event, being evidence of that special predisposition which will almost inevitably, sooner or later, terminate in insanity. It is possible that, could the youth and adolescence of a feeble-minded person of this class be passed

PLATE XXVII.

FIG. 63.—Feeble-mindedness, with insanity and criminal tendencies.

FIG. 62.—A feeble-minded youth suffering from chronic mania and epilepsy.

To face page 312.]

in a perfectly orderly and routine manner, away from the bustle of the outside world, the attack might be long deferred, or even prevented. In the majority of cases, however, the first attack makes its appearance between the periods of puberty and adolescence, and in some cases even much earlier than this.

One of the most frequent exciting causes in the mild aments is alcohol, to the action of which the mentally defective, and, indeed, neuropaths generally, seem to be peculiarly susceptible and particularly intolerant. A severe fright may likewise precipitate an attack of insanity in one of these persons. I remember a mentally defective child who, for some breach of school discipline, was shut up by the teacher in a small dark room, little better than a cupboard. When taken out he was silent, and apparently dazed. The teacher said he was sulky, but he continued moody and depressed, and a few days afterwards passed into a state of profound melancholia which necessitated his removal to an asylum. Religious or other forms of excitement may also act as determining causes. One small boy of twelve years became acutely maniacal as a result of the popular excitement attending the relief of Mafeking. Another mentally defective youth in the employ of an Evangelical clergyman was so worried by this zealous but indiscriminate gentleman about his soul that he attempted suicide. Another feeble-minded young man became insane in consequence of the repeated theatre-going and sight-seeing provided by his relations with the idea of amusing him. In fact, almost any trifling occurrence, which would have no effect upon the mind of a healthy person, seems to be enough to upset the equilibrium of these mentally unstable defectives, and often the mere physiological changes consequent upon puberty or adolescence are sufficient.

I have already remarked that insanity is commoner in the milder than in the more severe grades of amentia, and in the latter it also tends to be of a somewhat different type to that in the feeble-minded. The insanity of the feeble-minded and high-grade imbeciles does not, on the whole, differ from that occurring in ordinary persons, and to give some idea of the relative frequency of the different clinical types, I may state that, in 62 of these cases which I had under my observation for a considerable period, *mania* was present in 32, *melancholia* in 16, *alternating mania and melancholia* in 6, *stupor* in 1, *delusional insanity* in 1, and *juvenile general paralysis* in 6. I doubt whether the relative incidence of juvenile general paralysis is really so great as would appear from these figures, in consequence of the fact that the helpless demented condition of these persons leads to the committal of an undue proportion of them to asylum care.

It will be of interest to give some particulars regarding the patients suffering from these different forms of insanity.

Mania.—Fourteen of the patients suffering from mania were males, and eighteen females. In about two-thirds of the cases definite delusions were present, chiefly relating to the identity of the patients or those about them. In twelve of the cases there were well-marked aural or visual hallucinations. All these attacks presented the usual characteristics of acute mania, the patients gesticulating, shouting, singing, and rushing about, for days together without cessation. Sometimes they were exceedingly violent, using abominable language, and smashing everything within reach, so that confinement to the padded room was necessary. One girl of fourteen years attacked her brothers and sister with a poker and table-knives; whilst another, aged sixteen, stabbed her grandmother and attempted to set fire to the house. One of these patients, who was recovering, accounted for his actions by saying that he "got some thought on his mind, which he tried to get off and couldn't; this caused the blood to rush to his head, and sent it rushing down his arms and legs." I am of opinion that a considerable proportion of feeble-minded criminals are of this type, and that their offences are often committed whilst they are actually insane.

Melancholia.—Of the sixteen cases of melancholia, seven were males, and nine females. Definite delusions or hallucinations were ascertained to be present in three-quarters of the cases. In eleven patients suicide was threatened or attempted, and in seven there was refusal of food. Both active and passive varieties of melancholia occurred, the former being a trifle more frequent. The active form was commonly preceded or accompanied by terrifying delusions or hallucinations. Thus, one young girl was frightened by seeing a fight in the street: she became timid and anxious, and in a few days developed pro-

PLATE XXVIII.

INSANE AMENTS.

FIG. 65.—A feeble-minded youth suffering from melancholia.

FIG. 64.—A feeble-minded youth of the surly, loafing type. No regular employment. Fully convinced that he has "not had fair play." Has had attacks of acute melancholia.

nounced delusions to the effect that people were trying to kill and burn her. She heard voices threatening her, thought that her food was poisoned, and refused to eat it, and, in fact, became apprehensive of harm from every imaginable quarter. She was in a restless state of tearful agitation, constantly wringing her hands, and muttering, "What are they going to do to me?" Another boy had the curious delusion that he had fallen to pieces and lost some of his parts. The passive form of melancholia of these persons seems at times to be the outcome of a morbid consciousness that they are not quite as other people. They feel neglected, or, as they sometimes say, "of no use." The rebuke or sharp word of employer or parent is keenly felt, and they acquire a habit of brooding over their fancied wrongs. It is very common to hear feeble-minded persons in this frame of mind complain that they have "not had fair play." Pronounced delusions of persecution soon follow, and these pass into a state of apathetic melancholia. If they can be got to converse at all, their remarks will often be to the effect that they are "tired of life and want to die," and, indeed, attempts at suicide are by no means uncommon. These attempts are often real and definite efforts to put an end to existence, and drowning seems to be the method which most appeals to them. Many of these patients become utterly careless of personal cleanliness, refuse to work, dress, or take food, and sometimes resist any attempt on the part of their attendants to see to these matters for them.

Stupor.—This, apparently, is not very common in the feeble-minded, but I have seen one well-marked case which, beginning as passive melancholia, with visual hallucinations and refusal of food, gradually developed into a condition of complete stupor —indeed, almost catalepsy. The patient was a mentally defective boy of fifteen years, and for weeks he sat in one place, staring vacantly in front of him, dribbling from his mouth, requiring to be fed with a spoon, and absolutely indifferent to the calls of nature. He was discharged cured from the asylum in nine months, but readmitted six months later with a precisely similar attack. This in turn slowly passed away after a few months, to be followed by a state of extreme fatuity, the youth being liable to sudden outbursts of laughter or crying without any observable cause (see Fig. 67).

Alternating Insanity.—In six of the cases the insanity took the form of alternating attacks of mania and melancholia. In these patients, however, there were no intervening periods of complete cessation, as in the *folie circulaire* of French authors. The mania, which was violent and acute, lasted for a time, and was then replaced by a state of melancholia of the ordinary variety, or *vice versa*, and so the process continued. Perhaps they should rather be classed as recurrent insanity. Two of them have now definite indications of approaching dementia.

Delusional Insanity.—I do not think that a pure delusional insanity is common in aments, but one case seems to be best placed in this category. It is that of a feeble-minded youth, aged twenty-three years, who since the age of nineteen has remained in the same condition. There is neither excitement nor depression; and he is quite happy and good-natured, telling every one that he owns a lot of money in the bank, that he teaches music at sixpence a lesson, and that he performs on the Aquarium stage. Not infrequently feeble-minded children and adults will, under the influence of delusions or hallucinations, make unfounded charges against their companions or teachers, and sometimes they will do the same from pure wickedness. It is very necessary to bear this fact in mind in any investigation, for the statements are often so circumstantial as to excite a ready credence in the unguarded.

Recurrences.—In about one-third of these cases there was no recovery from the first attack; the mania or melancholia became lessened in its intensity, but persisted as chronic insanity, to gradually terminate in dementia. In about two-thirds of the cases, however, the first attack gradually and completely subsided after a period varying from a few weeks to two or three months; but the improvement was only temporary, and, as far as my experience goes, there is scarcely any class of patient in whom a recurrence is more likely to take place. This is seldom deferred for more than a year, and in the majority of the cases it comes on within a few months of the subsidence of the original attack. The second and subsequent attacks are usually of the same clinical type as the first, and they continue to occur at periods varying from three to twelve months for many years. In the intervals the patient is fairly quiet, and

PLATE XXIX.

Fig. 67.—A feeble-minded boy. Age, 15½ years. Suffering from stupor (second attack).

Fig. 66.—Feeble-mindedness with marked mental instability. Liable to attacks of acute mania.

[To face page 316.]

may do a certain amount of useful work, although his mental deficiency and instability prevent any regular employment. With the lapse of time, however, the insane attacks tend to recur more and more frequently, and the patient gradually passes into a state of chronic insanity, which is only terminated by the development of dementia.

Dementia.—Many aments become demented in their later years, and *secondary dementia* is the natural termination of most of these cases of insanity, its advent depending chiefly upon the type and the frequency with which recurrences occur. On the other hand, *primary dementia* in young aments is of such rare occurrence that its presence, without antecedent insanity or epilepsy, is nearly always indicative of juvenile general paralysis. In the insanity accompanying epilepsy, or even in severe epilepsy without insanity in these patients, dementia is usually ushered in fairly early. In the sudden and violent storms of the emotional type, on the other hand, it is late, and I have known such patients show no sign of dementia after many years. The ordinary attacks of insanity seem to lie midway between these two extremes, and in most of my cases definite symptoms of dementia were observable within about eight years of the first attack.

It is thus seen that in the life cycle of the ament we may have an epitome of all the main varieties of mental disease. Beginning with a defective brain, he may early show signs of mental instability and imperfect function; this passes on into various types of insanity, and finally culminates in complete degeneration of all the little faculty he once possessed—dementia.

General Paralysis.—My figures are not sufficiently numerous to enable me to state definitely to what extent this occurs, but amongst rather more than 200 aments in the asylums of the London County Council I met with six instances (three males and three females). The disease may be of the adolescent or of the ordinary variety; but although a few cases of the latter have been recorded, I have not myself seen an example of it in an ament. Accepting the view that syphilis is the most common cause, one would suppose that the state of the nervous system of these persons would render them particularly liable to its action should they become infected; possibly, however, the explanation of the comparative infrequency of the ordinary variety of general paralysis in aments may be that they are not so much exposed to the chances of syphilitic infection.

In my cases the symptoms first made their appearance between the ages of fourteen and nineteen years, all the patients being well-marked aments. In three of them delusions of persecution were present, accompanied at one time by attacks of mania, at another by profound depression with attempts at suicide. In the other three cases the mental disturbance consisted of violent emotional storms. These conditions persisted with occasional exacerbations and remissions for from one to two years, when signs of dementia appeared. Several of these cases have already been described in the account of syphilitic amentia.

Epileptic Insanity.—Many feeble-minded and imbecile epileptics are excceedingly irritable and liable to outbreaks of furious passion, and a considerable number develop insanity just the same as do ordinary epileptics. There are no special features, and the tendency is usually to early dementia.

Insanity in Imbeciles and Idiots.—Insanity occurs in the severer as well as in the milder grades of amentia, and it may take the form of excitement or depression. It follows, however, from the very imperfect mental development of these persons, that the disturbance is less often of an ideational than emotional character; it is also usually of shorter duration than in the case of the mild aments. Most insane attacks in pronounced imbeciles and idiots take the form of sudden and violent maniacal attacks. During these the child or youth will rush about, making hideous noises, overturning or smashing everything in his way, animate as well as inanimate, and often dashing himself with great violence against walls, doors, and articles of furniture which he cannot displace. Such attacks are liable to recur at more or less frequent intervals.

ILLUSTRATIVE CASES.

CASE 1. *Feeble-mindedness ; Attack of Acute Mania with Delusions lasting Six Weeks ; Recovery ; Discharge.*—C. H. C., a feeble-minded youth with several well-marked stigmata of degeneracy; said to have always been very excitable; no regular employment. Admitted to the asylum, aged sixteen, with acute mania of three weeks' duration. He had suddenly become noisy and sleepless, throwing himself into strange attitudes, utterly irrational in his conversation, shouting out "God save the Queen," and asking to be allowed to fight the Boers; alternating with this he was tearful and anxious, with delusions of being constantly followed by policemen, and by boys who called "Thief!" after him. He was in a state of restless agitation, begging for the door to be kept locked. For a week after admission to the asylum he remained in this excited condition day and night, and it was quite impossible to control him. He was terrified of the other patients, thinking they were all trying to strangle him. After a week he gradually became quieter, and at the end of two months had become so quiet and well-behaved that he was able to be discharged.

CASE 2. *Feeble-mindedness; Attack of Acute Mania with Delusions and Hallucinations, subsiding in Two Months; Subsequent Recurrences for Two Years; Signs of Dementia.*—A. C., male, aged twenty-five years. Has always been backward, and never learnt to read or write. After leaving school earned a few shillings weekly by doing odd jobs, but had no regular employment. Apt to behave queerly at times from early boyhood, and on several occasions disappeared from home for two or three days. At the age of twenty-four began to attend musichalls frequently, and shortly afterwards became exceedingly strange in his manner; he refused to do any work, and spent most of his time standing at the open window talking to people he imagined he saw. Much of his conversation was about one "Flo Arnold," whom he wished to marry, for which purpose he said he had taken £2 out of the bank. He gradually became quarrelsome, and finally violent and acutely maniacal, and had to be sent to the asylum. This condition of mania, with delusions and aural hallucinations, lasted for two months, after which he became quieter. He has now been in the asylum for nearly two years. He is subject from time to time to sudden outbursts of maniacal excitement, lasting from a few hours to several days; these are probably due to delusions, although none can be ascertained. He shows indications of the onset of dementia.

CASE 3. *Feeble-mindedness ; Attack of Acute Mania, aged Sixteen, passing into a Condition of Recurrent Insanity ; no Dementia after Three Years.*—A. F., female. "Always simple from quite a child." Left school aged twelve, being only in second standard; afterwards in a training home; very bad-tempered and addicted to smashing windows; sent home after three years, as they found they could do nothing with her. At the age of sixteen she became so violent that she had to be removed to the asylum, having previously hurled a cooper's hammer at a man and thrown a heavy padlock at a woman. She remained in a condition of maniacal excitement for three months, with an occasional short interval of comparative calm. During one of these I asked her why she behaved so violently; she said something came over her and she felt she "must do it." In the next three months she became much quieter, and for the following five months she remained silent and gloomy, refusing to have anything to do with the other patients; then she relapsed into a state of restless excitement lasting for a month, followed by another period of depression. She is now nineteen years of age, having been in the asylum three years. She is at times fairly quiet and does a little ward work, but is very untrustworthy, and liable to sudden outbursts of maniacal excitement with destructiveness; she is highly emotional and unstable, bursting into fits of tears or laughter without any apparent cause. There are no indications of dementia.

CASE 4. *Feeble-mindedness ; Attack of Acute Mania, aged Sixteen ; Constant Recurrences, at Times accompanied by Delusions ; under Observation Four Years ; no Improvement.*—R. D., female. Very backward at school; left aged thirteen and went to service, but was so liable to what her mother calls "fits of temper" that she could not keep any situation more than a few months; altogether she had fourteen situations in less than three years. At the age of sixteen she became so violent that she was sent to the asylum. On admission she was in a state of acute mania, screaming, shouting, singing, and resisting all attempts to keep her in bed; she also threatened to cut her throat. This condition lasted for a few days after admission; she then became quieter, and by the end of a fortnight was doing some work in the wards. Within a month she had a relapse exactly similar to the first attack. She is now twenty years of age, and has been in the asylum four years. At times she is quiet, well-behaved, and answers questions readily and pleasantly; it is, however, quite impossible to depend upon her, and she is subject from time to time to sudden outbreaks of excitement, in which she becomes most abusive, uses the foulest language, and violently attacks anyone who may be in her way. These outbursts last for three or four days and nights; as a rule, they seem to be purely emotional storms, but in some of them delusions are present, generally to the effect that the medical officers and the nurses are trying to cut off her head or to torture her in various ways.

CASE 5. *High-grade Imbecile; Attack of Acute Mania subsiding in Three Months, followed by Frequent Recurrences; under Observation for Seven Years without any Improvement.*—E. S., female. Simple-minded from birth; did not get on at school; subsequently kept at home to help mother, " as she did not seem to have enough sense to go out to work "; was at times very troublesome, and caused much annoyance by suddenly rushing into the neighbours' houses. At the age of sixteen became so restless and excitable that they could do nothing with her, and sent her to the asylum. The medical certificate states " she exhibits undue mental excitement, talks, sings, shouts, and laughs immoderately, and behaves in an insane manner; very restless, imagines the attendants to be her former schoolteachers, and seems altogether too excited to control herself and talk sensibly." This acute condition gradually abated, and by the end of three months she had become quiet and able to do work; two months later she relapsed, again becoming excited, noisy, and destructive day and night, in which state she remained for three weeks, then becoming quiet and industrious again. She has now been in the asylum seven years, has ceased to do any work, and is subject to frequent acute outbreaks of noisy aggressiveness. In some of these attacks delusions are present; thus, a short time ago she stated that she had given birth to a child, which had been stolen from her in the night. She is very impulsive, and on one occasion, seeing a pail of water standing in the ward, she suddenly plunged her head into it. She is becoming very untidy in her dress and personal appearance, though there are as yet no other indications of dementia.

CASE 6. *Medium-grade Imbecile ; Attack of Acute Mania, aged Fourteen ; Condition practically unchanged at the End of Six Months.*—C. R., female. Never passed first standard at school ; subsequently kept at home ; could never be depended upon ; and from nine years of age has been at times very violent and addicted to using disgusting language. She had to be sent to the asylum at the age of fourteen, and on admission was in a state of mania, chattering to herself and singing or shouting the whole day. At times destructive and aggressive ; very restless at night. She has now been in the asylum for six months, and on the whole there is very little improvement. She is occasionally fairly quiet and rational, but as a rule she is raging up and down the wards singing. shouting, and swearing at the other patients. The charge-nurse says she is her most troublesome patient.

CASE 7. *Feeble-mindedness ; Attack of Melancholia with Hallucinations and Delusions, passing into a Condition of Recurrent Insanity ; Signs of Dementia in Six Years.*—C. D., male. He could never learn arithmetic at school, as the master said his " brain was too weak." Used to behave very oddly at times. After leaving school was employed in a bootshop. At the age of sixteen he was frightened by a large black dog, and shortly afterwards became much depressed, gradually passing into a condition of melancholia. On admission to asylum he was found to have aural and visual hallucinations with delusions. He thought he was surrounded and threatened by black men ; he said that he was afraid he was going to be killed in the China War, and that God told him to kill himself. For several days he was restless and anxious, afterwards becoming dull, listless, lethargic, and a confirmed masturbator ; he would occasionally waken out of this stuporose condition to become aggressive and violent. Four years after admission he had so much improved that he was discharged to his friends, only to be readmitted six weeks later, as they found it impossible to manage him. He is now twenty-two years of age, and is still in the asylum, being idle, and as a rule dull and depressed and constantly muttering to himself ; occasionally destructive and aggressive ; signs of dementia are apparent.

CASE 8. *Medium-grade Imbecile ; Attack of Melancholia with Attempted Suicide ; Recovery in Four Months ; Relapse Eigh*

Months afterwards ; now again recovering.—T. K., male. Mental deficiency noticed from early childhood ; incapable of learning at school ; no work subsequently ; never earned any money. Gave much trouble to his parents, being " very bad-tempered," and frequently wandering away from home. At sixteen years of age became much depressed, and attempted suicide by taking carbolic acid. On admission into asylum was wretched and tearful, saying that he wanted to die, and there was no reason why he should live. He gradually became brighter and even cheerful, and a month after admission was able to work out of doors; the improvement continued, and he was discharged in four months. Eight months later he was readmitted, having been found by a policeman battering his head against some iron railings. On the way to the station he said that he would kill either himself or his father, the latter stating that he had been violent and had attempted to cut his (the father's) throat. He was profoundly depressed, thought he heard voices, and that people had conspired to kill him. At the present time he has been in the asylum four months. He is still depressed and solitary, but on the whole decidedly brighter, doing a little work, and appears to have lost his delusions.

The following case of *General Paralysis in an Adult Ament* is recorded by Dr. Cappelletti :*

The patient, a female imbecile aged fifty-four years, was turned out of her home by her brother, and came to great want ; she was taken into the asylum in a maniacal condition. She had a small, asymmetrical skull, tremor of tongue, face, and extremities, hesitating and tremulous speech, wide, unequal pupils which only reacted feebly to light and accommodation. No signs of syphilis on the body. Mental condition exalted, with grandiose ideas. Death occurred after two years in consequence of apoplectiform attacks. Post-mortem examination showed thickening of the dura and piâ, with adhesions and cortical erosions. Small frontal lobes, asymmetrical hemispheres, and a narrow grey substance. The basal arteries were atheromatous.

The author refers to two other similar cases which have been described, and in a subsequent note states that the asylum register at Ferrara shows the existence of a fourth.

* *Neurolog. Centralbl.*, 1898, p. 558.

CHAPTER XVIII

DIAGNOSIS AND PROGNOSIS

THE physician who is consulted with regard to a possibly mentally deficient person will. be expected to answer three questions. *First*, Is amentia really present ? *Secondly*, To what extent can it be improved ? *Thirdly*, What is the form of treatment to be adopted ? These three matters of diagnosis, prognosis, and treatment will be dealt with in the present and succeeding chapters.

Diagnosis.

The question of diagnosis has already been considered to a great extent in previous chapters, particularly that referring to mentally defective children ; it will, however, be convenient to summarize the chief points to which attention must be paid.

In infants the symptom which usually first attracts attention, and which causes the parents to seek advice, is the presence of abnormal nerve signs. Briefly, there is either a state of torpid, listless indifference, so that the child makes no attempt to suck, does not look about him, does not cry, and, in fact, is generally lacking in spontaneity ; or the reverse of this condition is present, the child being abnormally restless, always crying and tossing about, and getting hardly any sleep. In cases of *severe* amentia, one or other of these states is generally present during the first twelve months. The latter, however, attracts most attention, for mothers are inclined to look upon the former as merely an excessive amount of " goodness," and, at first, to congratulate themselves accordingly.

But these conditions, although abnormal and indicative of brain disturbance of some kind, are not diagnostic of amentia.

They may result from inadequate or improper feeding, causing general malnutrition, or from some more serious bodily disease. The first care of the physician, therefore, must be to make a thorough physical examination of the child, and particularly to exclude such morbid states as anæmia, rickets, malnutrition, bone caries, the various forms of tuberculosis, otitis, meningitis, cerebral abscess, and reflex causes of nervous irritation.

Having done this and ascertained that there is no bodily condition responsible for the nervous abnormality, he has still to decide whether he is dealing with a child preternaturally dull and stolid, with one unduly excitable and neurotic, or with one who is really mentally deficient. Here the family history and the presence of stigmata of degeneracy or features peculiar to certain varieties of amentia will be of great value.

If with either of these abnormal nervous states there is associated a pronounced morbid heredity, there is a strong probability that the child will turn out to be mentally deficient. If stigmata of degeneracy are present in addition, this probability is greatly increased, and a diagnosis may thus be possible in the early months of life. If special features exist, such as the abnormally small skull of the microcephalic, the peculiar physiognomy of the Mongol or cretin, the changes in the fundus of infantile cerebral degeneration, or even marked paralysis, the diagnosis may be made with certainty.

But even if stigmata be absent, and the child's condition be plainly due to brain disease without neuropathic predisposition, it must still be remembered that serious disease of the brain occurring in early life may terminate in secondary amentia, if death does not previously end the scene; whilst this possibility is greatly increased in the presence of morbid heredity. The association of continuous epileptic convulsions with any of these conditions greatly adds to the unfavourable outlook as to the future mental development.

In cases seen somewhat later—say during the years of childhood—there is less difficulty in arriving at a diagnosis. Not only is there the great advantage of a longer life history, and consequently more information forthcoming as to general behaviour; but, since by the age of five or six years the normal child has made considerable intellectual advance, the arrears of the mentally deficient one at this age are by contrast much more apparent. Idiocy, imbecility, and pronounced feeble-mindedness can now hardly fail to be detected, and the chief difficulty experienced will be with regard to the mildest degrees of intellectual or moral defect. It is still necessary to remember that amentia may be simulated by bodily ill-health or disease, is well as by delayed development or dullness of intellect not amounting to defect. These conditions have already been fully referred to in treating of mentally deficient children.

At a still later age, or in the adult, it is again practically only the milder cases which give rise to any real difficulty of diagnosis. Amongst the wealthy classes, or where property is concerned, such cases may form the subject of a judicial inquiry, and the greatest care must be taken in arriving at and stating an opinion. This will be based upon a careful examination of the patient's mental capacity, as revealed by his manner, conversation, and. if necessary, the way in which he discharges some test commissions entrusted to him, as well as by a consideration of his previous general behaviour ; also by attention to the presence of stigmata of degeneracy and a neuropathic family history, as indicative of primary amentia, or the well-marked history and signs of brain disease which usually accompany secondary amentia.

The question which has to be answered is, Is this person capable of competing on equal terms with his normal fellows, or of managing himself and his affairs with ordinary prudence ? If he be not thus capable, then he is probably suffering from mental deficiency; but such a condition may also be due to insanity or early dementia, and these will require to be excluded. In most cases attention to the previous history and to the nature and motive (or absence of motive) of the acts committed or omitted, as the case may be, will settle the point. It is, however, to be remembered that, whilst delusions are common in both insanity and dementia, they may also occur in aments. In fact, insanity with delusions is a not infrequent complication of mild mental deficiency.

A person who recklessly distributes his possessions or impoverishes himself by expending large sums of money on objects for which he has not the slightest use, under the delusion that he is acting as the almoner of the Almighty or is the richest man on earth, is probably insane or demented. But if he does these things in consequence of an inability to realize the value of money, and his purchases are such as would only bring delight to a child ; if he shows a complete incapacity for business management, an undue credulity, and a lack of sense of responsibility ; if, further, he is content to be left with the barest necessities of life, whilst his patrimony is plundered by his acquaintances under his very eyes, he may justly be regarded as mentally deficient.

Perhaps the greatest difficulty of all in deciding whether amentia is present or not is experienced in certain cases presenting moral defect or perversion, and which come before the criminal courts. High-grade aments, non-defective but mentally unstable persons, and thriftless, irresponsible ne'er-do-weels and wastrels, form a very large proportion of that section of mankind which is on the down-grade. A large number of them are liable to commit offences against law and society ; indeed, it is from these classes that the great majority of our criminals and paupers are drawn. It is here that a decision as to whether mental deficiency is or is not present may be extremely difficult. It is impossible to lay down any rules, for each case must be considered on its merits ; but I think that attention to the family history, the life history and previous behaviour of the patient, together with a careful examination of his bodily and mental condition, will usually enable a decision to be made.

Prognosis.

Having ascertained that amentia is really present, the physician will next be called upon to say to what extent it may be remedied by treatment.

Until sixty years ago cases of pronounced mental deficiency were considered to be absolutely and hopelessly beyond any possibility of amelioration. But in 1846 Dr. Édouard Séguin* demonstrated to the world the capacity possessed by many of these persons for considerable improvement under patient and systematic training, and since then the pendulum has gradually

* Édouard Séguin, "Idiocy, and its Treatment by the Physiological Method," New York, 1866.

swung to the other extreme. At the present day the training of the mentally deficient occupies a more or less important place in the social system of most civilized countries, and it is even questionable if there be not a tendency to overestimate the educational possibilities, and to think the machine only needs to be sufficiently elaborate in order that the entering idiot may emerge a person of normal intelligence.

Both these views are wrong, and are to be deprecated. On the one hand, there are comparatively few cases so bad that they cannot be improved to some extent, if only in habits of cleanliness and the curtailing of destructive and dangerous propensities. On the other hand, no case of real amentia (with the exception of cretinism) ever becomes *cured*. However mild it may be, some defect will always remain, and this will render competition on an equal footing with the normal population impossible.

And here it is necessary to enter a protest against the practice adopted by some medical men, of telling the parents that the child will " grow out of it," or that he will be " all right when he is seven," or " fourteen," or " twenty-one." In some cases this is done from ignorance of what amentia really is, in others from a benevolent but mistaken idea of sparing the parents' feelings. Where the physical condition of the patient is such that death cannot be long delayed, the disquieting knowledge that idiocy is present may perhaps be withheld; but in other cases the interests of the patient demand that the parents should be told the truth, for much of the early training so necessary for improvement will be in their hands. I have known children dragged about from doctor to doctor and from quack to quack in the vain hope of seeing that change which had been confidently foretold, but which never came. I have known many pounds spent on nostrums, electrical and galvanic appliances, whilst the child was rapidly deteriorating for want of systematic training; but I have rarely met parents who were other than grateful, though sad, when the real truth was kindly told them. Few people like living in a fool's paradise, and in this case it is not a paradise, for there is often the lurking suspicion that something is really wrong, and that the practitioner does not understand the case.

To what extent, then, may the patient be improved by treatment? No absolute forecast can be given, but attention to certain considerations regarding the *form, variety,* and *degree* of amentia will enable a tolerably accurate prognosis to be given in most cases.

Prognosis of the Forms of Amentia.—As a rule, cases of primary amentia are much more capable of improvement than are those of the secondary form. In other words, contrary to what would be expected from their appearance, the stunted, misshapen, and often repulsive-looking victims of morbid heredity are more responsive to training than are the well-grown, and often well-favoured, sufferers from accidental injury or disease of the brain. This dictum was enunciated by Langdon Down many years ago, in the words that the prognosis is favourable " inversely as the child is comely, fair to look upon, and winsome," and experience has fully confirmed its general truth. The explanation of this apparent anomaly is that in the latter group we have to do with destructive lesions, whose course is often progressive, and which, by inducing a general disturbance of the whole function of the brain, make education impossible. In the former, on the other hand, although neuronic development is irregular and incomplete, there is often no actual disease.

Prognosis in Different Varieties.—The foregoing statement, however, is not rigidly exact, for the result is to some extent dependent upon the *variety* of amentia present. The prognosis of the respective varieties may be summarized as follows:

In *simple primary amentia* the result is hopeful or the reverse in direct proportion to the degree of deficiency and the presence of epilepsy or paralysis.

In *microcephalics*, with the exception of extreme instances, a considerable amount of improvement may be predicted, and the patient may eventually become capable of many simple routine tasks not requiring thought. But he will always be markedly deficient in mental capacity.

In *Mongolians* the prognosis is, generally speaking, directly proportionate to the intensity of the bodily signs. The milder cases, as a result of appropriate training, may almost come to pass muster with their brothers and sisters; but they will always require some one to manage their affairs. Many of the more pronounced cases, even, can be taught to do some useful work in the garden or on the farm.

In cases of *secondary amentia due to toxic or vascular disease of the brain*, the prognosis, as already remarked, is on the whole decidedly less favourable than in primary aments; but it differs very greatly according to the nature of the lesion. In cases in which, after the infliction of the damage, the pathological lesion ceases to progress, and serious secondary anatomical changes are not induced, the prognosis is tolerably good, always provided that appropriate training is begun sufficiently early. Many cases of birth injury and purely vascular lesions occurring in very early life are of this nature, and the improvement is probably brought about by neuronic compensation. Many of these persons who suffer from severe paralysis even may be educated to read, write, sum, and do mechanical work with surprising dexterity; but there is usually a little childishness, a want of judgment regarding the affairs of life, and an inability to make headway against competition. Dr. Shuttleworth* mentions such a case presenting right hemiplegia with athetosis attributed to injury at birth, who was admitted into the Royal Albert Asylum at the age of twelve years. "In spite of his physical drawbacks, he rapidly developed graphic abilities, and after a course of scholastic instruction in writing, drawing, reading, etc., with suitable physical and manual exercises, he was trained to woodwork in the joiner's shop, where he gradually attained such control over his irregular movements that he became an expert workman, making tables, chests of drawers, and decorative sideboards. He showed a nice taste for wood-carving, and ultimately became so skilful in it that he is now employed as instructor in this art. He is also a clever scene-painter. He is now practically ambidextrous, his right hand having been trained to be serviceable."

It is, of course, to be remembered that in many of these cases of birth paralysis the lesion concerns the motor centres of the brain only, the child subsequently appearing, but not in reality being, mentally deficient because his crippled condition has prevented his attendance at school.

On the other hand, in cases where the lesion is active or induces progressive pathological changes, the prognosis is decidedly

* G. E. Shuttleworth, "Mental Deficiency in Children," *British Journal of Children's Diseases*, March, 1904.

unfavourable, and in a considerable number dementia sooner or later supervenes. The majority of these are characterized by epileptiform or epileptic convulsions.

Amentia due to epilepsy is decidedly unfavourable, being, in fact, one of the most hopeless varieties. For epilepsy which has produced amentia will probably end by producing dementia. In other cases of mental deficiency, in which epilepsy is a complication and not the cause, it is still a highly unfavourable symptom, and imposes a considerable barrier to successful education.

In *sclerotic amentia* the most hopeful cases are those in which enlargement of the skull takes place. The majority of cases of pronounced sclerosis with crania of normal or diminished size die before, or soon after, attaining the age of puberty.

In *hydrocephalus* everything depends upon the course of the disease, which can never be foreseen. Rapidly progressing expansion of the skull is almost invariably fatal; but in cases where spontaneous arrest takes place, the resulting mental impairment may be but slight, and may be largely remedied by suitable training.

In *syphilitic amentia*, in view of the tendency to the development of general paralysis, the outlook is decidedly bad; whilst in *infantile cerebral degeneration* it is hopeless.

In *cretinism* the prognosis is, on the whole, dependent upon the age at which treatment is begun and the persistence with which it is carried out. As already mentioned, however, it is possible that other factors may influence the result—*e.g.*, the presence or absence of morbid heredity.

Amentia due to isolation or sense deprivation is curable provided special education is begun sufficiently early, and even in cases which have been neglected for years it is remarkable what results may follow patient and systematic training.

Prognosis regarding the Degree.—Finally, a few words may be said with regard to the *degree* of amentia. In the absence of contra-indication, such as epilepsy or the special pathological processes just mentioned, the amount of improvement and the final result will, of course, be dependent upon the degree of initial defect. This cannot always be gauged, but some measure of it will be afforded by a careful comparison of the physiological and psychological development of the patient with that of a normal child of corresponding age. Regarding this, reference may be made to the Table of Normal Developmental Data on p. 364.

CHAPTER XIX

TREATMENT AND TRAINING

I.—MEDICAL AND SURGICAL TREATMENT.

THERE is no drug which has the slightest direct or specific influence upon primary mental deficiency, and, we may safely assert, there never will be. Considering that this condition is the outcome of a neuropathic diathesis, due in many cases to generations of antecedent disease, we can no more hope to relieve it by medicaments than we can hope by such means to transform the worn-out tissues of age into the virile ones of youth, or to restore life to the dead.

With regard to secondary amentia, there is one form, cretinism, for which a specific exists. It may even subsequently be discovered that there are other varieties of secondary amentia due to definite qualitative anomalies of blood-supply, and for these the corresponding specific may also be found. Possibly, as already mentioned, some cases of Mongolism may be of this nature. But if such cases do exist, it may safely be stated that they are exceedingly rare, and in the great majority of instances of secondary amentia, as well as of primary, drugs have no direct influence. Pituitary and thymus, as well as other glandular extracts, have been tried without the slightest avail; and even the amentia which is directly due to syphilis shows not the slightest improvement under antisyphilitic treatment.

The same must be said of surgical treatment. When the theory was propounded that microcephalus was due to premature synostosis, it was natural that the surgeon should suggest relief by craniectomy. During the year 1890, and for a time after, a considerable number of operations were performed by eminent men, chief of whom may be mentioned Lannelongue (Paris), Victor Horsley (London), and Keen (Philadelphia). The cases operated upon were not only microcephalics, but included other varieties of amentia. The mortality was exceedingly high (about 25 per cent.), and those who survived showed no mental improvement. It is not surprising that the operation should have gradually been abandoned by reputable surgeons, and to-day it is practically unheard of. It was, indeed, founded upon a mistaken notion as to the pathology of this condition, and it may be said that to-day operations of this kind upon cases of primary amentia are absolutely unjustifiable.

The case is somewhat different with regard to certain varieties of secondary amentia. Where there is no morbid heredity, and where there is clear evidence, or even a reasonable presumption, that the deficiency is due to fracture, splintering of the inner table, or other conditions causing increased cranial pressure, then not only is operation justifiable, but it is the duty of the physician to advise it at the earliest possible moment, and before changes have been induced which may be irreparable. I must confess, however, that I know of no statistics sufficiently extensive to show the results of operation in such cases.

Nevertheless, it is not to be assumed that medicine or surgery have no place in the treatment of amentia. This is far from being the case, for *mens sana in corpore sano* is a true saying, and medicine and surgery can do much to promote the bodily well-being of these persons. I am no advocate for the systematic drenching of the ament with drugs, or for the performance upon him of operations which can contribute nothing to the improvement of his body or mind; but it cannot be doubted that conditions are often present which stand in the way of efficient training and which are amenable to treatment; and it is certain that education will be attended with most success when every means have been employed to place the body in the best possible condition.

Before systematic education is begun, therefore, it is of great importance to ascertain the existence of disease, disorder, or deformity, and to correct the same by appropriate remedies, if such be possible. It is unnecessary to describe all the diseases and ailments which may affect the mentally deficient child; their name is legion, and the chief of them have already been referred to in previous chapters. It may be stated, however, that conditions which particularly call for treatment are adenoids, enlarged tonsils, nasal polypi, cleft palate, carious teeth, errors of refraction, disease of the ear, phimosis, hernia, webbing of the fingers, etc. Troublesome contractures may often be relieved by tenotomy, and where club-foot is present, walking may be greatly improved by suitable surgical boots. Medical treatment is called for in anæmia, malnutrition, and many disorders of the circulatory, respiratory, alimentary, and cutaneous systems. Troublesome constipation is best met by attention to the diet and the administration of cascara sagrada. Diarrhœa is often caused by imperfect mastication or unsuitable food, and may need antiseptic or astringent treatment. Extract of malt, with or without cod-liver-oil, is valuable in severe malnutrition. Epilepsy is best treated by a careful control of the diet and daily life; but if this fails, the frequency and severity of the attacks are often checked by borax and the bromides. A single dose of the latter at bedtime is often useful in allaying the undue instability so common in many of the milder defectives. Enuresis, a frequent complication, is best treated by accustoming the child to evacuation at regular periods. It may be helped by withholding all fluid for at least two hours before retiring, and in many cases a few nightly doses of one of the bromides will serve to check the habit.

In addition to these indications for special treatment, the food, clothing, exercise, cleanliness, and general hygiene of these persons demand the closest attention. The dietary must be on a liberal scale, but plain, and excess of meat must carefully be avoided. Where mastication is imperfect, recourse to spoon food is often necessary, and this is always the case with the low-grade idiots. The danger of asphyxia from the impaction of food in the glottis is no fancy, and many cases of aspiration pneumonia have been recorded. Attention to the clothing is particularly called for in the Mongolian variety, as well as in other patients prone to catarrhal and circulatory disturbances. In the cold weather, the wearing of gloves may prevent troublesome chilblains. Daily exercising and bathing must always be enforced, and the greatest care must be taken that rooms are sunny, not too warm, and thoroughly well ventilated. The marked predisposition which many of these persons evince to the development of tuberculosis must be kept well in mind.

It is unnecessary to enter any further into the details of medical, surgical, and hygienic treatment, since the principles are the same in these as in ordinary children. The only point I wish to insist upon is that mental deficiency is often—indeed, usually—accompanied by bodily deficiency, disorder, and disease, and that the treatment of these latter is an essential prelude to, or accompaniment of, the training of the mind.

II.—EDUCATION.

General Principles.

Having done our best, by careful attention to the laws of hygiene—aided, where necessary, by medicine and surgery—to remove any likely impediments to training, and to bring the mentally deficient child into the best possible physical condition, the question of education must be considered. In the following pages I shall deal with the general principles upon which such should be based, particularly those which concern the physician. The actual pedagogic methods to be employed are beyond the scope of this work, and, for the most part, can only be acquired by practical experience.

Education has a threefold object. *First*, it should develop and cultivate all the latent potentialities of body and mind to their fullest extent; *secondly*, it should repress or eliminate vices and faulty modes of action; *thirdly*, it should supply, if possible, such particular instruction as will fit the individual for some useful form of work. In other words, it should aim at imparting knowledge as well as inculcating wisdom. The two former of these objects are educational in the literal sense of the word; the latter may be looked upon as technical instruction.

The development of mind takes place in consequence of two influences: *spontaneity*, or an inherent tendency of the brain cells to develop; and *stimulation* of these cells by external impressions. The brain of the healthy child has an inherent potentiality which makes it to a certain extent independent of its environment; or perhaps I should rather say that it is capable of utilizing and responding to any surroundings, within ordinary limits, in which it may be placed. A little friend of mine, aged four years, reads "Alice in Wonderland" with remarkable facility. She has never had a single formal lesson, and her knowledge was picked up solely by observing letters and asking questions. The defective mind is lacking in this power. One of its chief characteristics, if not the chief, is a want of what may be termed *mental aggressiveness;* consequently its development has to be aided and encouraged by special means. At the same time, the deficient power of control often gives full play to the lower organic feelings, resulting in vices, antisocial acts, and crimes. These tendencies have to be eliminated.

Until sixty years ago the training of the mentally deficient, where such was attempted, was conducted upon no logical method, and it is to Dr. Édouard Séguin that we owe the first clear enunciation of the principles upon which it should be based. In his words, education "consists in the adaptation of the principles of physiology, through physiological means and instruments, to the development of the dynamic, perceptive, reflective, and spontaneous functions of youth." By the painstaking and laborious application of these principles, Séguin himself demonstrated the remarkable results which may take place even in apparently hopeless idiots ; and upon his principles, extended and elaborated by the work of Froebel and Pestalozzi, most of our present methods are based.

The method of applying these principles, in brief, is to take each "function" or "faculty," each physiological system of neurones, and, by means of appropriate and carefully arranged progressive exercises, to develop them to the fullest extent of their capacity. I do not, of course, mean to suggest that we can isolate and develop separately each "function." All portions of the mental apparatus are interdependent, and education is a general process which simultaneously concerns the development of the bodily as well as the sensory, motor, intellectual, emotional, and moral functions. But it is convenient for purposes of description to make this division, and it tends to emphasize the fact, that as the child's development naturally takes place in a regular progressive order, so must the training be progressively adapted to its growing needs.

Treatment and Training

In many cases it is first of all necessary to arouse spontaneity. The child is inert, and must even be stimulated to play; until this is accomplished, and some *interest* is aroused, any further training is, of course, impossible. Having succeeded in arousing some degree of initiative by means of romping play, this is gradually replaced by more definite games, and then by orderly drill and calisthenics. In this way spontaneity becomes controlled in accordance with a definite purpose, and the child learns to acquire the habits of obedience and attention. This naturally leads up to still more regular and systematized exercises, in the shape of such kindergarten occupations as building with cubes, stick-laying, bead-threading, pricking outlines, knotting and looping, paper cutting and folding; and these, in turn, are superseded by clay-modelling, macramé work, knitting and darning, and finally by definite technical instruction in wood-carving, carpentry, basket-weaving, mat-making, needlework, laundry work, and dressmaking, etc. Coincidently, speech is cultivated, instruction is given in the three R's, and every care is taken to repress injurious propensities and to develop moral character.

The general principles of education do not differ from those in the case of the mentally normal, the difference being merely one of method and application. The whole object of the teacher is to reduce the environment of the child to a form which the deficiency of his mind is capable of assimilating, at the same time taking care that his mental pabulum is administered in an attractive shape. It may safely be said that no success will be attained unless the child's *interest* is aroused, and this must be the teacher's first care. It is by means of this interest and its progressive expansion, by gradually leading him step by step from one acquirement to another, that the capacity of the child is unfolded and that his education is accomplished. In many cases even destructive tendencies, where the child will do nothing but tear into pieces everything given to him, may be made use of as the first stepping-stone to manual work. Above all, it is necessary to remember that these children's conception of the abstract is extremely limited, that everything must be presented in the concrete, and that they will learn far more with their hands than with their heads.

It is necessary to pay particular attention to the cultivation of the sensory and motor functions. In the ordinary child these are perfected as the result of his own initiative, but in the ament special stimulation is required—not only because of the presence, in a considerable proportion of these children, of defects and irregularities of nerve action (abnormal nerve signs), which must be corrected before useful manual work can be accomplished, but because such training affords a most valuable means of developing and co-ordinating intellectual activity.

Thus, by means of suitable impressions through eye, ear, skin, muscle, nose, and mouth, the range and delicacy of the sensorium is increased, the brain rendered more receptive, the power of discrimination, as well as motor response, encouraged, and a basis supplied for future thoughts and ideas. We live, of course, in a perfect sea of sights, sounds, and vibrations of every kind, and, as already remarked, the healthy brain is so constituted that it can utilize these without any special tutorial help. I do not say that this is likely to lead to an optimum result ; in fact, I believe that the mental capacity of even the healthy child would be greatly improved by a course of sensory training on physiological lines. It is doubtful whether the mental development of anyone, even the best, comes up to the inherent possibilities. In the case of the defective mind, however, such a course of training is usually absolutely necessary, and constitutes a most important part of education.

Similarly with regard to the motor system. All mental action is expressed by movement, or inhibition of movement, of some kind or other. It may be the mere opposition of the thumb and forefinger, the play of facial expression, the complicated mechanism of speech, or the deliberate conformation of the whole being to some emotion or ideal, as seen in conduct and behaviour. Since it is by the character of his movements and actions and general behaviour that the entire relationship of the mentally deficient child to the rest of society will be determined, it is plain that the development of the motor system is of the greatest importance. We may, indeed, say that all means for the cultivation of mental faculty are of importance according as they develop, co-ordinate, and control mental manifestations—*i.e.*, movements.

Treatment and Training

Such, then, are the general principles upon which the education of the mentally deficient child must be based, and of which some further details will be given presently. It is obvious, however, that, although we must be guided by these principles, the measure of success achievable will vary enormously; and will be dependent upon the degree of initial defect—or perhaps I should rather say upon the inherent capacity for development present in any particular case. This cannot be foretold; but undoubtedly there is a limit, and a point is at last reached beyond which no further advance takes place.

In the idiots we shall get no farther than the implanting of habits of cleanliness, the development of some capacity for self-feeding and self-help, the curtailing of destructive and vicious propensities, and the expression, by signs or words, of simple wants. And we may not get even so far as this. In the imbeciles a higher stage will be attainable, and not only may they be made to be much more self-helpful and less dependent, but they may even be taught to perform a certain amount of useful routine work. Lastly, in the case of the feeble-minded the result achieved may be very considerable. A goodly number will become orderly, industrious, and well-behaved individuals, perhaps able to read and write a little, to do simple sums, and capable of performing useful work, which will at the same time keep them happily engaged and, where necessary, contribute to their support. But *cure* will never take place.

We may now refer to some points regarding the application of these principles to home and school training.

Home Training.

The training of the mentally deficient child should begin *at birth*, or as soon as the condition is diagnosed. The ament, even more than the normal child, rapidly develops bad habits, and care in the early years of life may not only do much to prevent these, but will be of the greatest assistance in paving the way for the more systematic training of after-years. This early training must of necessity be carried out at home, and, where circumstances permit, it is advisable that it should be at the hands of a trained governess; but where this is not possible it must be undertaken by the parents. In any case, the growth and well-being of the child's mind, as well as body, should be under the general supervision of the medical attendant.

I have already emphasized the necessity for telling the parents the truth regarding the condition of their child; I would here remark that it is also the physician's duty to state plainly that neglect at this time may mean the development of habits which it may take years to eradicate, whilst care, kindness, and, above all, patience, will certainly result in improvement. Suitable food, clothing, warmth, exercise, fresh air, regular bathing—in fact, attention to all concerning the general bodily health—are of the first importance, whilst the habit of cleanliness cannot be enforced too early. Its acquirement in all but the most degraded idiots is usually only a matter of patience. With regard to training, there is no need for anything elaborate; but the practice of relegating these children to out-of-the-way corners, and of depriving them of those adjuncts to development which they need far more than do ordinary children, is one which cannot be too strongly condemned. What is required at this time is a little more, and not a little less, care and patience. The child must be talked to and encouraged to play. If destructive, it must be gently but firmly repressed. If inactive, its little hands must be made to feel the contact of toys, its sight stimulated by brightly coloured balls, and its hearing by music, or even noise. Instead of depriving it of toys, let it have an abundance to see and handle, and even to break. As it gets older, encourage it to sit up, to stand, and to walk, and do all that is possible to develop and co-ordinate sensory and motor activity. If the child is to be rescued from its solitary position, the time so spent will not be wasted.

I think one of the most deplorable things in connexion with these unfortunate children is the neglect which so often attaches to their early home life. I do not think that this arises from unkindness, for I have often been struck by the manifest solicitude of parents and all those about them. It is simply a matter of sheer ignorance as to what to do and how to do it, but it often results in the development of habits which are ineradicable.

School Training.

Where the home conditions are such that adequate training cannot be obtained, or when such training no longer suffices for the needs of the child, he should be removed to a special training institution. Usually this is about the sixth or seventh year, but in certain circumstances it may be advantageous to remove the child earlier, whilst in others he may stay at home until a later age than this. The milder defectives—*i.e.*, mentally deficient children who are not imbeciles—come within the operation of the Education Act at seven years, and may then be compelled to attend special classes or schools, if such exist.

School training consists of more systematized methods, having for their object the development of the sensory, motor, intellectual, and moral faculties of the child. It is necessarily less individual than the training he has, or should have, received at home; but this defect is more than compensated for by the spirit of emulation and of companionship which results from association with other children like himself. Moreover, although children in institutions must of necessity be taught in classes, it is still possible, by carefully grading and seeing that such classes are not too large, to ensure for each child a sufficient amount of individual attention. The regulations of the Board of Education require at least one teacher to every twenty defective children, but in lower-grade aments the proportion of children must be very much reduced.

As we have seen in previous chapters, aments, with regard to the type of their nervous constitution, are divisible into two main groups. On the one hand there are those who are passive, inert, and markedly deficient in spontaneity; on the other there are those who are restless and exceedingly motile, full of " tricks," " habits," and impulsive acts, and markedly deficient in the power of sustained attention. In each of these the training is in accordance with the general physiological principles which have already been alluded to—namely, stimulation through the sensory channels—but the method is different in the two classes. The stolid group, whose main defect is one of excitability, require stimulation by means of romping games, musical drill, and vigorous impressions of all kinds. The restless and excitable class, on the other hand, require their excessive movements to be brought under the control of the will by deliberate and systematic exercises, such as are comprised in many of the kindergarten occupations. But apart from these broad differences, mentally deficient children differ enormously in their power of response as well as in the presence of particular defects or irregularities of brain function, and it is the duty of the physician in charge to make a careful examination of each child, and to advise the teacher regarding the appropriate method of training. Individual teaching must still be the keynote, and the teacher must ever be on his guard against neglecting the laggards for the sake of those of more promise.

Teaching is an art which cannot be taught. It must come by practical experience of the management of children. The following brief account simply aims at suggesting some of the chief physiological methods upon which training should proceed. The teacher with a love for his work and his pupils will have no difficulty in adapting, modifying, or extending these to suit the needs of any particular child, always bearing in mind that the chief requirements are the development of what is defective and the elimination of what is faulty.

The Training of the Senses.—The chief sensory organs through which impressions reach the brain are six in number—namely, eye, ear, nose, mouth, skin, and muscle. Probably the training of the first and last of these are of most importance.

By means of *vision*, information is gained regarding the colour, size, and form of objects, and attention should be given to each of these. It will often be found that, whilst the high-grade ament distinguishes the primary colours readily enough, he is unable to separate their shades; and that, whilst he distinguishes between the form of a triangle, a square, and a circle, he fails to see any difference between triangular or quadrangular figures of varying shape.

For teaching colour discrimination, a very convenient apparatus is a series of cardboard tables, each 1 inch square, and of a different shade. We may have six or eight shades of each of the colours blue, red, green, yellow, orange, and purple. It is unnecessary that the child should know the names, all that he is wanted to do being to separate the collection of tablets into heaps according to their shade. Subsequently he may be taught their names. Coloured beads or wools may be made use of in the same way, and as the child progresses he will find great delight in pointing out to the teachers the different colours in pictures which are shown to him. Later on the kaleidoscope may be turned to profitable account in the development of colour discrimination.

For cultivating the child's perception of form and size, it is first of all necessary to draw his attention to the coarse differences in the many objects of common use. After this we may make use of a similar series of tablets of various sizes and shapes, but of uniform colour, again getting him to divide them into heaps. "Size," "form," and "peg" boards, as well as the ordinary dissected puzzles of the toy-shops, not only afford valuable visual training, but are also of great use in developing tactile sense and in aiding muscular co-ordination.

The cultivation of the *tactile and muscle* senses is particularly called for in the case of mentally deficient children, since, in addition to its general educational value, these are functions which are absolutely essential for the proper performance of manual occupations, and the future of the ament must depend to a very great extent upon how he can use his hands.

Sensations travel to the brain from the muscles just the same as from eye, ear, nose, etc., and with a little practice they may be appreciated and compared with one another in precisely the same way. These sensations arise in two ways: *First*, when a muscle or series of muscles is moved; *secondly*, during the tension of a muscle. Generally speaking, impressions arising during muscular contraction are of use in appreciating size and distance, whilst those coming from muscular tension tell us of weight. Of course, in the actions of ordinary life we make use of several senses simultaneously, and those from muscle are aided by others from skin and eye. In training, however, it will usually be found advantageous for the pupil's eyes to be kept closed during these exercises.

In the inert, unresponsive type of aments, we may have to stimulate the sensorium by passive movements of the limbs, or by compelling the hands to grasp, to feel, and to let go objects of different texture, temperature, density, and coarseness or smoothness of surface. In the restless and abnormally motile type, control, co-ordination, and attention will be improved by blindfolding the child, and getting him to differentiate between form and size tablets by passing his fingers round their edge. Many mild imbeciles will enter with zest into the game of guessing articles in a bag by simply feeling them. Another excellent method is that recommended by Dr. Warner. It consists in accustoming the child to differentiate between varying weights of shot contained in a small chip-box held upon the extended palm. Miss Mumbray, who has had a large practical experience of the training of mentally defective children, is in the habit of directing her pupils to measure off on a sheet of paper a series of prescribed distances—say from $\frac{1}{4}$ inch to 4 or 6 inches. After a little practice at this they are required to draw lines of specified length *without* the measure. In this exercise the ocular as well as the finger movements are utilized, and the results are not only extremely good in themselves, but are of the greatest value in leading up to kindergarten occupations, Sloyd, and subsequently industrial training.

It occasionally happens that, instead of sensation being diminished, it is so much increased as to become a source of pain. The hyperæsthetic hands must then be employed in rough, coarse work until their sensibility is dulled.

Hearing is often defective in aments, but many of these children are thought to be deaf when the real deficiency is one of spontaneous attention. The best means of developing this faculty is by music. Singing, musical drill, and the concerts of the entertainment-hall, which should form part of the life of all institutions, not only develop the child's power of attention and the range and accuracy of his hearing, but are a source of the greatest happiness.

Where the senses of *taste and smell* are in need of special cultivation, this may be accomplished by placing upon the tongue such substances as sugar, quinine, salt, chlorate of potash, soda, etc., or by getting him to sniff coffee, cocoa, snuff, or various essential oils.

The Training of Movement.—It is impossible to overrate the importance of this. The mentally deficient child who has been taught to walk, to speak, and to dress and feed himself, has

Treatment and Training

obviously been materially benefited—still more so is this the case, however, when patient and systematic training has enabled him to put his hands to some useful occupation. But a higher result even has been achieved. Mental action and motor activity go hand-in-hand, and in the development of muscular co-ordination lies one of our best means of cultivating self-control and regularity of mental action.

The training of movement in the mentally deficient resolves itself into three processes : (1) the development of action, (2) its co-ordination, (3) the correction of motor anomalies in the form of tricks and habits. These two latter are accomplished by the same means. Speech is also a motor phenomenon, but it will be convenient to refer to it separately.

The Development of Movement.—As we have seen, a proportion of aments are listless, torpid, and inactive. They are quite content to sit still and do nothing, and they even evince no interest in the games of their companions. This condition is usually the result of a general sluggishness of the nervous system, but it is occasionally caused by nervous exhaustion due to ill-health. In the latter, rest, food, and fresh air are necessary ; in the former, active and vigorous stimulation is required.

The only means of stimulating the motor cells of such a child is through the sensory pathways, and these we must endeavour to excite by every possible device. The child must be talked to ;— his attention must be attracted by brightly coloured objects ; he may be bombarded with small flannel bags filled with beans, until he holds up his hands to protect himself, and eventually assumes the offensive ; he must be made to listen to and join in the romping, singing and drilling of the class ; by any means he must be made to *move*, and until this has been accomplished systematic lessons are quite out of place.

The Co-ordination of Movement.—With the development of movement, its co-ordination must be attended to. In the healthy child this takes place naturally through the constant repetition induced by its own initiative. " Practice makes perfect." In the ament the nervous discharge is irregular, and the harmonious adaptation of the motor response to the sensory stimuli, so that an optimum result follows a minimum expenditure, is slowly and laboriously acquired.

Co-ordination is more readily developed in the case of a few large muscles, such as those concerned in standing, walking, and pushing, than in the twenty odd small muscles of the hand or in the intricate muscular apparatus concerned in speech. Consequently, the first exercises must be directed towards teaching the child to maintain a proper balance of the body, to run and to walk, to push and pull, to seize, to hold, and to let go, tolerably large objects.. For this purpose such exercises as mounting a ladder placed against a wall, walking between the rungs of a ladder placed flat upon the ground, marching in, out, and over various obstacles to the accompaniment of music, and accurately covering with the feet a series of footprints chalked upon the ground, as recommended by Séguin, are of the highest service.

At a later stage finer movements of the trunk and limbs may be attended to, and here games with a ball (such as cricket, football, and rounders), free exercises, musical drill, dumb-bells, and breathing exercises, find their place. The daily occupations of dressing and feeding, particularly the management of the spoon, afford most valuable fields of instruction. In milder cases, definite " eye-drill " may be given.

Lastly, manual dexterity must be developed by the kindergarten occupations, writing, drawing, cutting-out, paper-folding, clay-modelling, and the like. The imitation and transfer movements of Warner may here be utilized in some of the mildest cases.* Dr. Warner, in fact, regards them as " far more educative than clay-modelling, drawing, and other child occupations." Theoretically this is so, but it is possible for an educational method, as for an article of food, to be so concentrated as to be inappetizing ; and these exercises have the disadvantage of being somewhat uninteresting, and of requiring an amount of attention of which the mentally defective child is often incapable. In the training of these children *interest* is everything.

The correction of irregular movements in the form of athetosis, " tricks," or " habits," is accomplished by the same methods as those used to develop co-ordination. Where the abnormality is chiefly in the hands, the kindergarten occupations, or in coarser

---

* See an interesting paper by Dr. Warner on " The Training of the Intelligence through the Hand," read at the annual meeting of the Sloyd Association, 1902.

cases the peg-board, will be found of great service. This latter is a flat rectangular board drilled with holes of varying size, into which corresponding pegs are to be fitted. Where the motor irregularity concerns the face or trunk, facial and bodily gymnastics are indicated.

The Training of the Intelligence.—No means exist, or ever will exist, by which we can *supply* intelligence to the mentally deficient. Each of these children has a certain capacity for development, which it is the object of training to educate, or "lead out," and which in the absence of appropriate training would remain undeveloped. To a very considerable extent this is accomplished, as already remarked, by systematic exercises stimulating the receptive and perceptive faculties, and developing, controlling, and correcting the motor response. In the present section I propose briefly to refer to some of the principles underlying more direct appeals to the intelligence, and here we shall also consider reading, writing, and speech. These methods, of course, are only applicable to the milder degrees of mental deficiency.

One of the commonest and most important defects occurring in these children concerns the faculty of *attention*. In children of the inert, placid type, spontaneous attention is often lacking, and the child remains unmoved and indifferent, whatever happens. This condition results from a diminished nervous excitability, and it is remedied by a vigorous bombardment of the sensorium through every afferent pathway. On the other hand, the restless, unduly motile, hyperexcitable type are usually characterized by a want of voluntary attention and concentration. Though seemingly so vivacious, they can settle down to nothing, and almost every conscious sensation or every thought distracts them from their task. The only way in which concentration and useful work can here be obtained is by presenting the child with something which is interesting. In fact, the keynote to attention is interest, and the psychological principles for developing the power of attention may be expressed in the following three maxims : *First*, the pupil's occupations must be those in which he has an interest naturally (and it may be remarked that the child whom *nothing* will attract is in a very parlous state) ; *secondly*, his interest must be enlarged by the introduction of new occupations closely allied to, and leading out of, those in which he is naturally interested; *thirdly*, an artificial or derived interest must be created for those subjects which are not attractive in themselves, or, as Ribot says, they must be "rendered attractive by artifice." Rewards of various kinds form useful attractions.

The process of *association* is of paramount importance in mental action. By its means all the varying impressions received through the senses are again connected, so as to produce a complex picture or a sequence of ideas. Defective power of association means not only crudeness of the individual mental images, but often paucity of images and ideas generally. In training this function, the method is the opposite of that employed in teaching discrimination. There sensations were presented singly, here they are presented simultaneously; the law of association being that impressions which are simultaneously received by the brain tend to acquire functional connexions. For example, let the child handle, bite, note the form and colour and learn the name of, a shilling. The subsequent auditory sensation "shilling" will call up a mental picture composed of its associates. Object-lessons are also of great value in training association.

Memory is largely dependent upon the power of association, and in proportion as we develop this so we cultivate memory. It is very useful to encourage the child's power of recall by getting him to give an account of the things seen or done upon returning from a walk or at the end of the day. Exercises in repeating poetry, quotations, and the like, help the child to remember the particular things repeated, but it is a mistake to imagine that they do anything towards cultivating the "faculty" of memory in general.

The capacity for *forming thoughts, judging* and *reasoning*, is best stimulated and encouraged by individual contact with that teacher who knows how to present to the deficient mind in an easily assimilable form the simple facts of nature and everyday life. What are called *object-lessons* are here of the greatest value, but their value consists, not so much in the matter, as the manner in which they are presented. A good teacher will know how to turn almost anything to account, although most benefit will result from those objects in which the child has a natural interest. It is of the highest importance that he should be carefully questioned and encouraged to ask questions, and the teacher must ensure that everything is in the concrete, and that the ideas presented to the child have their visible, tangible, and material counterparts.

Speech.—The mechanism concerned in speech, and the chief anomalies present in the mentally deficient, have been described in a previous chapter. In some of these children speech is absent in consequence of a lesion of the motor centre, and these cases are probably incurable. In others intractable deafness is the cause, and then occasionally (but very occasionally where mental defect is present), speech may be acquired by means of lip imitation. Other children of the lower grades apparently never speak because they have no ideas to express, or because it is easier for them to voice their feelings by grunts, screeches, and inarticulate noises. In the majority of the milder aments, however, there is some ability to speak, but speech is faulty and imperfect in consequence of conditions which, if not entirely curable, are at least in great part ameliorable by treatment.

There are two chief causes of these defects: First, anatomical abnormalities of the end-organs concerned in speech-production or in the perception of sounds; secondly, deficient muscular action and inco-ordination. The former of these consist of adenoids, enlarged tonsils, cleft palate, suppurating otitis, etc., and are chiefly responsible for thickness, indistinctness, and alterations of tone. These must be attended to by the surgeon before systematic instruction is attempted. Muscular inco-ordination gives rise to stammering, stuttering, inability to pronounce certain consonants, and the habit of substituting easy sounds for those which are difficult. The essence of speech training consists in discovering the nature and cause of the particular faults, and remedying them by the appropriate methods.

Where muscular action is defective, which may be but part of a general inertia as seen in the stolid type of aments, it may be cultivated by encouraging the child to make use of his lips and tongue in blowing a toy trumpet or whistle. But in cases where muscular inco-ordination is the chief fault this is unnecessary, although such children, including stutterers and stammerers, will be benefited by a course of lip and tongue gymnastics and breathing exercises. In many cases where the faculty of speech lingers music is a great help. As Dr. Shuttleworth says, " Such children will frequently hum tunes that take their fancy before they are able to articulate words ; but if attractive tunes set to words containing repetitions of simple sounds (such as the ' Ba-ba, black sheep,' of our old nursery rhymes) are constantly repeated to them, the probability is that, after a time, first one word and then another will be taken up by the pupil, till the rhyme as well as the tune is known."

In cases of slurring, word-clipping, and consonantal defects, the fault generally lies in a want of synergic action, and the only remedy is for the teacher to demonstrate with his own articulatory apparatus how the defective sound should be produced, until the child is able to imitate it. This requires considerable patience of both teacher and pupil, and it is essential that the latter should carefully watch the teacher's mouth and lips the while. It is useful to remember that many consonants which cannot be pronounced at the beginning of a word can be produced in the middle, and thus the desired sound may often be forthcoming if it is preceded by one the child knows.

Writing naturally follows speech, and the first steps consist in the making of strokes upon the ruled slate. Much of the difficulty experienced by defective children is the result of imperfect co-ordination, which only practice and patience will overcome, and many of the imbeciles never do overcome it. In any case it will be necessary for the teacher to guide the child's hand in his initial attempts at making vertical, horizontal, and oblique lines, and this may have to be kept up for weeks. Some children learn to make rough drawings more easily than to write, probably because the task is more interesting, and the practice of tracing pictures which underlie a piece of framed frosted glass is sometimes of assistance to writing. The imbecile who, after repeated coaxing, is unable to make any attempt at tracing, and whose only result is a meaningless scribble, is probably incapable of being taught.

Reading.—Few imbeciles acquire the power of reading, but the majority of the feeble-minded, as a result of years of training, learn to read books of simple words and short sentences. Many of the higher types, indeed, become good readers. Probably the best method of teaching is the word method, in which short words are read " at sight " before any attempt is made to teach the alphabet ; but time and patience rather than any particular method are the chief essentials.

Arithmetic.—Number is usually a great stumbling-block to aments, although there are some feeble-minded persons who have an extraordinary affection for dates, and occasionally ability to calculate. The reason of their difficulty seems to be their inability to appreciate the abstract, and it is essential, in teaching number, that concrete examples should always be made use of. This is done by means of beads, counters, the abacus, or by graduated wooden rods. The cultivation of the child's faculty of discriminating *size* and *weight* through his muscle sense, in the manner previously described, is a useful prelude to teaching him number. An excellent form of concrete instruction is afforded by the " shop lesson." Having mastered the principles of addition and subtraction by means of actual objects, the less defective pupils may be initiated into the mystery of the numerical symbols, but progress with these will usually be very laborious.

Industrial Training.

Hitherto we have been concerned with the chief means by which the intellectual and nervous functions of the mentally deficient child may be stimulated and brought into orderly use— with *education* in its general sense. We now pass to technical instruction. It is not to be assumed, however, that the two are really separate, or that this latter has no educational value. On the contrary, technical or industrial training is not only a continuation, and the natural outcome, of many occupations and exercises which have formed part of the general training ; but in itself it is of distinct educational value. It is a well-recognized fact that the mentally deficient child learns more with his hands than with his head ; whilst his future is far more a matter of manual than of mental dexterity. Industrial and technical training, therefore, is at once an educational factor of considerable importance, as well as the only means of turning these unfortunate children to practical account. It has been shown that, as a result of this training, a considerable number of the milder aments become capable of remunerative work ; and even where the social position is such that this is unnecessary, it is still of the greatest use in providing them with employment. The teaching of a definite occupation, then, should never be omitted, and should, if possible, be begun during childhood or adolescence. One cannot but feel that in many instances there is a tendency to allow school-training to go beyond its real purpose—that of cultivating intellectual and nervous action generally—and to make it too scholastic.

The nature of the industrial training must be determined by the particular characteristics of the individual, regard being paid, of course, to sex and social position, and to the probable environment in after-life. Where possible, an outdoor occupation should be selected, and particularly so in the case of those whose coarsely formed hands stand in the way of any manual dexterity—such, for instance, as the Mongolians. But care must be taken to protect those so engaged against the inclemency of the weather, and it must be remembered that there may be many days when this will absolutely prevent outdoor work. Gardening, whether of flowers, fruit, or market produce, is particularly suitable, and the child's taste for this may be developed, as well as a certain amount of useful information imparted, by practical object-lessons in growing seeds, plants, etc., in the schoolroom. The strong and sturdy type may be usefully employed in the dairy or on the farm.

Where regular outdoor work is impossible, either on account of the physical condition of the patient or for lack of accommodation, there are many useful and remunerative indoor occupations which may be taught. Amongst these may be mentioned, for males, boot-making, tailoring, carpentry, basket-weaving, mat and brush making, chair-caning, book-binding, and such-like. For females there are cookery, laundry work, dressmaking, hand and machine sewing, knitting, and even embroidery and fine-art needlework. In all well-equipped institutions a considerable amount of the making, mending, and general domestic work of the establishment—even the printing—is performed by the inmates, under supervision. Instruction in these various occupations is, of course, given by skilled master hands.

Moral Training.

The training of the child's moral or ethical sense is by no means the least important of the teacher's duties ; indeed, if this is not carefully attended to, the education of his intellect may simply result in an increased power for ill, and cause him to be, not merely useless, but actually dangerous to society. Moral education, therefore, forms an essential part of the home and school training of the mentally deficient child. It has for its general object the repression of antisocial tendencies and the inculcation of habits or principles which will enable the child to adapt his conduct to the laws of his society and the well-being of his fellow-creatures. It is entirely removed from, and, from the physician's standpoint, is of greater importance than, religious education. If the condition of the child permits, the elementary principles of a religious doctrine may be added, and in some cases Christian ideals may exert a considerable effect upon the moral behaviour. The question of religious education, however, is the domain of the ecclesiastic, and beyond the scope of this work.

The bulk of aments are rather *a*moral than *im*moral, and their defect of ethical sense stands in the same relationship to that of the normal child as does their defect of general intelligence, requiring also special means for its development. There are, however, three types specially prone to the commission of immoral acts, and the training of these must be the object of particular care.

These are, first, those who are readily induced to commit antisocial acts, at the instigation of unscrupulous persons, because of their extremely " facile " disposition. Impressionable, susceptible, and readily swayed, utterly incapable of withstanding the suggestions, good or bad, of their companions, the only safeguard is to keep them away from temptation, and to ensure that their social atmosphere shall be good. It is possible that in course of time this atmosphere may to some extent lead to the formation of an active moral sense, and that the persistent inculcation of moral precepts may make impressions capable of influencing their conduct ; but, in my opinion, this can never be relied upon, and the only safe course with regard to this class is to keep them under permanent supervision. They are simple and confiding beings, and many of them are industrious workers.

The second group consists of those persons whose nervous constitution is so unstable and explosive that the most trifling occurrence serves to produce a violent storm. In this they will commit a grave breach of discipline, an offence against law and society, or even a serious crime. The attacks in many ways resemble the motor storms of the epileptic; in fact, the condition may well be termed one of psychic epilepsy. In such cases some degree of control is frequently acquired as the result of regular occupation, careful supervision, and firm discipline. Medicinal treatment in the form of the bromides is often also a valuable adjunct, and by these means considerable improvement, or even cure, may be brought about.

The third group consists of the so-called *moral imbeciles*. In these there seems to be an absolutely ineradicable propensity to the commission of every kind of offence, and these persons will lie, steal, burn, destroy, and assault, without being influenced in the slightest by persuasion, threat, or punishment of any description. Again and again have I known the offence repeated almost whilst the words of contrition were hot upon the tongue. I believe that this condition is practically incurable, and that the only safeguard lies in strict and permanent detention.

Passing now to the ordinary type, in which there is neither a specially facile disposition, a predisposition to emotional storms, nor deeply ingrained immoral and criminal tendencies, we have to consider the manner in which the latent ethical sense may be sufficiently developed to lead the child to shape his conduct in accordance with the manners and customs of good society. If this be not so developed, it is tolerably certain that the age of puberty, if not earlier, will see the assertion of many animal instincts which the weakened capacity of control will be powerless to overcome.

It was stated by John Stuart Mill that the foundation of the moral principle lies in *utility*. The mentally normal child may be taught to be moral through a gradual recognition of this. By being made to suffer the natural consequences of his own breaches of discipline, he is gradually brought, through his intellect, to appreciate that virtue is attended with pleasurable, and vice and wrongdoing with unpleasant, consequences. To a certain extent this may be made use of in the mentally deficient child, but his defect is often such that he cannot be made to appreciate the natural consequences, the utility or futility, of every act he commits, and this result can only be attained by a system of arbitrary rewards and punishments.

There are many rewards for good conduct which appeal to these children. In the lower types the promise of a toy, a sweetmeat, or some little treat in the shape of an entertainment, will often prove a useful incentive to good behaviour. Many mentally defective school-children attach great value to the little cardboard medal pinned upon their breast by the teacher, and at a later stage the commendation alone of the instructor to whom they have grown attached will suffice. Similarly with punishment. The deprivation of some favourite article of food, such as the withholding of pudding for dinner, the denial of the entertainment which the child's companions are allowed to enjoy, the reproof of the teacher—all these may be made use of to impress upon the child that wrongdoing is unpleasant, and that it is wisdom to be good.

It is very important that the whole demeanour of the teacher should be kind and sympathetic, gentle but firm, and that all petting and spoiling should be rigorously avoided. Approbation, if earned, should be bestowed ungrudgingly, and will be found a powerful incentive to further progress and factor in moral training. Disapprobation, if consistently expressed, is often equally efficacious as a deterrent.

With regard to the infliction of corporal punishment opinions are somewhat divergent. My own feeling is that it should be avoided wherever possible. But in cases of wilful and flagrant breaches of discipline or open defiance of authority it is not only justifiable, but beneficial; in fact, it is often the only means by which the child may be taught that respect for others which is the essence of morality.

In the task of implanting good habits and the developing of the ethical sense, the faculty of imitation, often so marked in these children, must never be lost sight of, since it may readily be turned to good or bad account. It is extraordinary how mild and gentle girls, brought up in an atmosphere of refinement and care, will suddenly, and upon the slightest provocation, give vent to a torrent of the most disgusting and obscene abuse which they may have heard by chance on some solitary occasion. It is of the highest importance that the surroundings and the tone of mentally deficient persons should be well ordered from the very beginning, and there is no doubt that the home environment of early life exercises a most potent influence in after-years. We cannot expect these children to become affectionate, sympathetic, and generous unless these qualities are evident in the lives of those about them, and a rigorous censorship of the entire social atmosphere, even with regard to pictures and entertainments, is an absolute necessity. If we are to ensure truthfulness, honesty, and uprightness, it is essential that parents, teachers, and physician should be truthful, just, and straightforward in all their dealings with these children. Reward and punishment must be deliberate, and apportioned in such a manner as not only to fit the crime, but to establish its relationship in the mind of the child. Otherwise it will result in more harm than good, and will inevitably lead to a complete alienation of confidence and affection. By the judicious imposition of punishment or reward which the child recognizes as being related to his fault or virtue, we shall be in no danger of losing his love and affection or violating his sense of justice. We shall develop, rather than perplex, his reasoning power, and we shall cultivate his moral sense and control just as we developed his intellectual capacity.

CHAPTER XX

CONCLUSION

IN the preceding pages we have attempted to give an account of the prevalence, causation, pathology, and clinical characteristics of amentia, as well as of the abilities and disabilities of persons suffering from this condition, and the manner in which their social relationship is thereby affected. There are a few matters arising out of this account to which we may refer in conclusion.

With regard to *training*, it might be argued—indeed, it is sometimes argued—that, since we can never *cure* these persons or make them really self-dependent, the expenditure of time and money upon their education is unjustifiable. This is a fallacy. I fully recognize that we must avoid the danger of their training becoming a fashionable fad, and being carried to an extent out of all proportion to the results likely to be achieved—that, in fact, not only must the ament be sheltered from the neglect or adverse competition of society, but that society and the ratepayer must be protected against the ament. I believe, however, that both these ends are best attained by suitable training, and that the withholding of such is not only injurious to the individual ament, but constitutes a danger to the State; moreover, it is an economic blunder.

It has been shown that a considerable number of these persons possess habits and propensities which render them a decided menace to society. These are partly inborn, but they are also to a great extent the result of neglect, and there can be no doubt that judicious and systematic training would do much to prevent their development. I do not say that such training would entirely prevent crime and insanity in these persons, but

I do think that it would do very much to diminish these conditions.

But education not only results in a lessening of evil; it is attended with a positive good. Although self-dependence may never be attained, it has now been amply shown that, in consequence of proper training, a considerable proportion of the milder aments become capable of useful and remunerative work. In the case even of persons of good social position, this is a decided advantage; for employment adds greatly to their happiness, as well as diminishes their possibilities for mischief; whilst in the case of persons whose circumstances are such that they must be supported by the public, this is an economic consideration of great importance.

Many imbeciles, even, may be trained to help in the routine work of the institution or home, whilst in the idiots the power of self-help and cleanliness which may by this means be acquired is not to be despised.

These facts are now generally recognized, and there are few civilized countries entirely lacking in laws and institutions for the training of the mentally deficient. It must be admitted, however, that in many cases the accommodation provided falls short of the demand, and in this country it is at present woefully inadequate.

But training alone is not sufficient. No one, of course, would expect an idiot or imbecile to be capable of taking care of himself; but a large number of people do think that the merely feeble-minded youth or girl—the educated product of the special school—ought to be able to do so, and the neglect, accordingly, to subsequently provide adequate *supervision* or *after-care* often results in a complete undoing of all the good that has been done.

The fact is, that although training will certainly do much to repress the growth of vicious, criminal, and insane tendencies, and will render the mildest grades of defect capable of remunerative employment, or even of earning a living, this can only be so " under favourable circumstances." Competition with the normal population is impossible, and, as a result of the Workmen's Compensation and Employers' Liability Acts, employment is becoming more and more difficult to obtain for these persons. Not only must work suited to their capacity be found for them, but in the great majority of cases the wages so earned must be laid out, and a general supervision exercised over their whole behaviour, just as in the case of children. Provided this be done, the time and money spent on training will be well repaid, and will result in the transformation of useless, and even dangerous, individuals into useful, happy, and contented members of society. Failing this supervision, however, aments, whether trained or otherwise, will certainly degenerate, and will inevitably swell the population of our asylums, prisons, and workhouses. In the case of females, it is tolerably certain that even before this can happen the blight will have been passed on to a new generation.

The question arises as to what form this supervision should take. At present, as we have seen, the majority of feeble-minded persons in this country, who are not at home, where often the supervision is far from adequate, are (excluding criminals and lunatics) resident in workhouses or in charitable institutions of various kinds. In each of these cases there is the grave disadvantage that detention cannot be enforced, but is entirely subject to the will of the patient; the majority of workhouses suffer from the additional disadvantage that they provide no remunerative or systematic employment.

It would be beyond the purpose of this work to enter into any discussion on this matter, and undoubtedly the nature of the provision must vary with, and be dependent upon, the habits, propensities, capacity, and character of the individual. Any method of administration which does not take these into account, and which attempts to provide for mental defect in the abstract, cannot be an economic success. Briefly, we may say that to be satisfactory the provision for each individual must be of such a nature as to (1) adequately safeguard the interests of society against the special peculiarities of the ament; (2) protect the ament against the evil suggestions and pernicious influence of certain sections of society, and at the same time ensure him kindly treatment; (3) utilize his working capacity to the fullest and most remunerative extent, so that the cost of provision falls as lightly as possible upon an already overburdened ratepayer. In general, these three conditions will best be fulfilled by compulsory detention in suitable colonies or institutions.

With regard to the *prevention of propagation* by these persons, two methods have been proposed—namely, the restriction of their marriage, and their sterilization by operation.

In America, *sterilization* or *asexualization* has been performed upon some hundreds of patients, both male and female, and it is contended that this method has an additional advantage in that, by its means, many depraved habits and bestial propensities have been cured and the general behaviour much improved. But it can never take the place of segregation, and it is a method which is at present decidedly repugnant to English feeling. My own opinion is that, given proper training, followed by adequate supervision, it should rarely be necessary. Where, in the judgment of the physician, it is definitely indicated, and likely to be attended with advantage to the patient, I do not think the parents or guardians would withhold their consent; but it is a grave matter to advocate its legalization for any and every case of mental deficiency.

The question of *marriage* is, of course, one of very great importance, not only as applying to those who are actually mentally deficient, but in regard to those who, non-defective in themselves, are yet the descendants of a neuropathic or otherwise diseased stock, and likely to beget amentia or other morbid mental and physical conditions.

There are some persons of whom it may be said with certainty that they will transmit disordered or enfeebled conditions of mind or body to their children; such, of course, should never marry. Others, again, would probably only do so if conjoined to a person of like tendencies. In yet others a slight existing taint might, by suitable marriage, be diminished, and, with further selection, finally eradicated. Although it generally happens that the child bears a greater resemblance to one particular parent, it is nevertheless a mixture of both, and this is one of Nature's means for bringing about modifications and variations in the human race. The result of any union is a step either in an upward or a downward direction.

The effect upon any community of the continued propagation of the unfit is simply a question of mathematics. As soon as that stage is reached at which there is a preponderance of persons suffering from diminished moral, intellectual, and bodily vigour, that community is inevitably doomed ; and history shows that this has repeatedly happened to the civilizations of the past, although *Mankind* undoubtedly continues, and will continue, to progress. Whether the account of Noah and the Ark be considered literally true or not, it contains a world of meaning for the thoughtful student of human evolution.

The importance of the question of marriage, therefore, and particularly the marriage of the " unfit," cannot be too strongly urged. It is far too often entered upon without any thought beyond the convenience or taste of the contracting parties, and, indeed, not always with even that amount of consideration ; but sooner or later we shall be compelled to consider its effect upon future generations. Considering the amount of attention which is bestowed upon the breeding of our horses, cattle, dogs, and even our vegetables, it is surely not too much to ask that a little thought should be given to the breeding of our race.

In some of the States of America legislation towards this end has actually been adopted, the marriage of epileptic, imbecile, and feeble-minded persons being prohibited by law ; but what may be the practical effect of these regulations I have been unable to ascertain.

I see no reason why such restrictions with regard to persons suffering from mental deficiency should not be made in this country, although at present they are hardly likely to be passed with reference to any less pronounced conditions. But the relation of the sexes cannot be entirely controlled in this compulsory way, and it seems to me that it is chiefly to the education of public opinion and the gradual development of the conscience of the community that we must look for improvement in this matter of the responsibilities attaching to marriage. The Church has peculiar opportunities of rendering incalculable service to future generations by pointing out the important issues of the marriage tie ; whilst it is at once the solemn duty and privilege of the Medical Profession to speak on this subject in authoritative and unmistakable terms. Unfortunately, the tendency of recent legislation has often been in a contrary direction. It has aimed at quantity rather than quality, and, by diminishing in many ways the responsibilities of parents for their offspring, it has certainly not contributed to the development of home life and of that grit and sturdy independence of character of which we English were formerly so proud.

So long as we are content to raise no voice against the marriage of the diseased, the degenerate, the criminal, and the pauper, and are willing to educate, feed, clothe, and ultimately pension as many offspring as these persons see fit to produce ; so long as legislation is permitted a free hand in doing everything calculated to diminish parental and social responsibility and to strike at the very root of any incentive to labour ; so long as our lawmakers and would-be philanthropists are blind to the folly of transferring the burdens and penalties inevitably following carelessness, improvidence, indifference, drunkenness, and unlimited selfishness, from the shoulders of those upon whom they should rightly fall to the careful, provident, and industrious members of the State : then so long will these classes (and these qualities) continue to be perpetuated, and their numerical ascendancy is simply a question of time.

Finally, we have to consider how this disease may be prevented, and this can only be accomplished by dealing with its prime cause. The origin of mental disease is intimately connected with the origin of disease in general, but, as we have seen, there are certain factors which appear to have a particular influence in initiating that nervous instability whose final culmination is mental defect. To-day the chief of these are chronic alcoholism, tuberculosis, mental worry and anxiety, and the hurry and scurry, with all their attendant excesses and dissipations, of modern life. Possibly in other ages other causes have predominated, but at any period they have been *excesses* of some kind or other which have entailed an undue demand upon the bodily structure.

According, therefore, as we diligently seek out and conform to the laws of health, and as we improve the manner of living, the moral, mental, and physical fibre, and the general well-being of our people, so shall we be successful in preventing disease of the mind.

APPENDICES

[redacted]

APPENDIX I

A TABLE OF NORMAL DEVELOPMENTAL DATA

Age and Sex.		Weight.	Height.	Chest Circumference.	Cranial Circumference.	Brain Weight.	Dentition.	Mental.
		Pounds.	Inches.	Inches.	Inches.	Grammes.		
7 days	M.	7½	20½	13½	14	330	—	Sucks vigorously. Distinguishes between sweet and bitter laces placed on the tongue. Eyes often follow a light.
	F.	7⅛	20½	13	13½	283	—	
1 mth.	M.	8¼	—	—	14½	—	—	dirs nds. Will notice difference in temperature of milk.
	F.	7¾	—	—	14	—	—	
2 mths.	M.	10½	—	—	15	—	—	
	F	10	—	—	14½	—	—	
3 mths	M.	12½	23	15	16	602	—	Lifts up lead, and will turn head in direction of sounds.
	F.	12	22½	14½	15½	560	—	Grasps lijects voluntarily.
4 mths	M.	13¾	—	—	16½	—	—	
	F.	13¼	—	—	16	—	—	Recognizes voice of parents. Tactile sensation present all over body.
5 mths.	M.	14¾	—	—	16¾	—	—	
	F.	14¼	—	—	16¼	—	—	
							TEMP ARY.	
6 mths	M.	15¾	25½	16½	17	712	2 loer central incisors	Begins to notice and recognize objects.
	F.	15½	25	16⅛	16½	670		Able to sit erect for several minutes at a time.
9 mths	M.	17½	—	—	17½	—		
	F.	17	—	—	17	--		Attempts to stand.
12 mths	M.	20½	29	18	18	916	4 upper incisors	
	F.	19¾	28½	17½	17½	816		Able to stand alone.
18 mths.	M.	22¾	30	18½	18½	—	12 teeth are present	Begins to walk. First words.
	F.	22	29½	18	18	—		Runs about freely.
2 years	M.	26½	32½	19	19	990	16 teth are present	Able to say short baby sentences of two or three words.

4 years	M.	35	38	20¾	19¾	—	—	
	F.	34	38	20½	19½	—	—	
5 years	M.	41	41½	21½	20¼	—	—	Knows letters, and able to count.
	F.	39½	41½	21	20	—	—	
6 years	M.	45	44	23¼	20½	—	PERMANENT. 4 molars	Can read, spell, and write simple words of one syllable.
	F.	43½	43¾	22¾	20¼	—	—	
7 years	M.	49½	46¼	23¾	20¾	1,138	—	
	F.	48	46	23¼	20½	1,135	Incisors	
8 years	M.	54½	48	24½	—	—		Can do Standard I. work.
	F	53	48	23¾	—	—	—	
9 years	M.	60	50	25	—	—	—	Can do Standard II. work.
	F.	57½	49½	24½	—	—	Bicuspids	
10 years	M.	66½	52	25¾	21	—		Can do Standard III. work.
	F.	64	52	24¾	20¾	—	—	
12 years	M.	80	56	27	21½	—	—	Can do Standard IV. work.
	F.	81½	57	26½	21¼	—	Canines	
14 years	M.	99	61	28¾	21¾	1,301		Can do Standard VI. work.
	F.	100	60¼	29¼	21½	1,154	2nd molars	
15 years	M.	110¾	63	30	21¾	—	—	
	F.	108½	61½	30¼	21½	—	—	
16 years	M.	123¾	65¾	31¼	—	—	—	
	F.	113	61¾	30¾	—	—	—	

This ble is pil ed from Holt's "D as of Infancy," the bis of R. Boyd, the wrk of W. Per, and a thr of bis by the author. The body-weights l bow five ags of age are without clothing; the bave that age ide ordinary cl ing. The object of the ble is to provide data regarding the development of the al hild in a mint form for me; but it s, of course, to be rid that the figures are iply the man ags of a large ies of aes, and that the idal vis in me as may be ble. This is ily the case with regard to iht, ht, chest circumference, and the eruption of the th. In the folding of the ntal ts ble vis alo ar, but the cranial fence in the mal hild is mh me uniform. This, al th aritions in any ne of the particulars may be of little diag tic ance, this in everal par tilars are indicative of al als and are of geat significance

APPENDIX II

METHOD OF ESTIMATING THE TOTAL NUMBER OF AMENTS IN ENGLAND AND WALES

ALTHOUGH the local investigations of the Royal Commission of 1904 only relate to eleven areas, having an aggregate population of 2,321,567, nevertheless, provided certain corrections are made, it is possible to calculate from these returns the total number of aments in England and Wales with tolerable accuracy.

Two corrections are necessary, for the following reasons: (1) The areas investigated may not be a fair sample of the entire country; (2) the returns do not include such aments as are certified under the Lunacy Acts.

CORRECTION I.—The only means of ascertaining whether the areas investigated are a fair sample of the whole country is to take some similar condition, the total incidence of which is known; the only one available being insanity. As remarked in Chapter II., there are slight differences in the relative incidence of amentia and insanity as a result of environment, but, on the whole the incidence of the one is directly proportionate to that of the other. Considering the close etiological relationship of these two conditions, I think we may assume that the same holds good throughout the country, or at all events sufficiently so for our present purpose. As we have seen (see p. 8), the incidence of insanity in the eleven areas examined is 3·15 per 1,000 population, whereas the incidence of insanity in England and Wales is 3·42 per 1,000 population. This can only be due to the fact that the eleven areas contain a relatively greater proportion of districts in which insanity (and consequently amentia) is of low incidence, the co-efficient of incidence being

$$\frac{3\cdot 42}{3\cdot 15} = 1\cdot 085.$$

CORRECTION II. *Aments Certified under the Lunacy Act.*—A considerable number of idiots and imbeciles are detained in ordinary lunatic asylums, etc., and their number is very difficult to calculate, for the reason that the proportion varies in different localities. From the Report of the Lunacy Commissioners, which, however, does not give the actual figures, idiots and imbeciles would appear to comprise about 5 or 6 per cent. of the asylum population. I am convinced, however, that this estimate is much too low. From information kindly placed at my disposal by the medical superintendents of the asylums of Manchester, Birmingham, Somersetshire, Wiltshire, Carmarthen, and Northumberland, as well as from my own examination of a number of workhouses and the asylums of the London County Council, I have come to the conclusion that if the "notified insane" of the county and borough asylums, the Metropolitan District asylums, the workhouses, and the outdoor paupers, be considered in the aggregate, they will contain about 10 per cent. of idiots and imbeciles, in the proportion of one idiot to three imbeciles. The number of the above classes throughout the country is 112,702;[*] there are consequently 11,270 aments certified under the Lunacy Act.

But this is not the whole of the certified aments. As a result of personal inquiries, I am of opinion that at least another 5 per cent. of the inmates of county and borough asylums are feebleminded. Many of these owe their incarceration to epilepsy or insanity, but the real condition is mental deficiency, and I think that they should be classed with the aments rather than the insane. Their number may be stated approximately as 4,450.

[*] The figures given in the Sixtieth Annual Report of the Lunacy Commission are as follows:

In county and borough asylums	89,342
In workhouses	11,151
In Metropolitan District asylums	6,591
Outdoor paupers	5,618
	112,702

Mental Deficiency

Consequently the total number of aments in England and Wales is approximately as follows:

$$\left\{ \frac{\substack{\text{Aments ascertained in areas} \\ \text{investigated.} \\ 8{,}079} \times \substack{\text{Pop. England and Wales,} \\ 1901. \\ 32{,}525{,}716}}{\substack{2{,}321{,}567 \\ \text{Pop. of areas.}}} \times \substack{\text{Coefficient of} \\ \text{incidence.} \\ 1 \cdot 085} = \substack{\text{Uncertified.} \\ \mathbf{122{,}809}} \right\}$$

$$\div \left\{ \substack{\text{Idiots and imbeciles.} \\ 11{,}270} + \substack{\text{Feeble-minded.} \\ 4{,}450} = \substack{\text{Certified.} \\ \mathbf{15{,}720}} \right\}$$

$$= \mathbf{138{,}529} \text{ Total Aments.}$$

It is necessary to point out that in the Report of the Royal Commission the total number of "mentally defective persons" (apart from certified lunatics) in England and Wales is estimated at 149,628. In making this calculation the Commissioners assume that the statistics ascertained regarding the districts investigated are applicable to England and Wales generally, and consequently their total estimate should be less, and not more, than that arrived at by myself. This increase in the estimate of the Royal Commission appears to be due to the inclusion of sane epileptics, and since, in my opinion, these should not be classed as aments, and since also I believe that the results of the local investigations are not strictly applicable to the whole country, I have thought it advisable to make an independent calculation. It will, of course, readily be understood that no calculation of this kind can be other than approximate, and even were a house to house visitation practicable it is doubtful whether the statistics would be absolutely accurate.

With regard to the *total number of aments in England and Wales who are urgently in need of provision at the present time* (for reasons which have been stated on p. 286), there are, inclusive of feeble-minded ("mentally-defective") children. according to my estimate 61,525, or, according to the estimate of the Royal Commission, 66,509. These numbers, again, are only approximate, but they are sufficiently near for practical purposes.

The areas in Scotland and Ireland which were investigated by the Royal Commission are not sufficiently numerous to enable a corresponding estimation to be made regarding those countries;

it may be stated, however, that in Glasgow there were ascertained to be present 1,614 mental defectives, equivalent to 0·26 per 1,000 population ; whilst in the four areas examined in Ireland there were 1,527 mental defectives, equivalent to 0·57 per 1,000 population. But it is impossible to conclude that these figures are applicable to these countries as a whole, and, therefore, as the Commissioners remark, they are merely given for what they are worth.

APPENDIX III

THE LAW OF ENGLAND CONCERNING AMENTIA

THE law of England regarding the care and control of persons suffering from amentia is at present very far from satisfactory. It was, in fact, to a great extent the recognition of this which led to the appointment of the Royal Commission of 1904, " to consider and report upon the existing methods of dealing with idiots and epileptics, and with imbecile, feeble-minded, or defective persons not certified under the lunacy laws."

The Commissioners have now furnished their Report, and their conclusions and proposals are set forth in eighty-nine recommendations.* These are based upon a voluminous mass of evidence, a series of careful local investigations conducted by medical men, and the personal visits of several of the Commissioners to institutions in America and on the Continent. The conclusions are formulated with conspicuous care and ability, and there can be no doubt that as a whole they are extremely sound, and that their adoption would do very much indeed to solve the pressing problem of the mentally deficient of this country. It is therefore earnestly to be hoped that the Legislature will not long delay giving effect to them.

In view of this report, the effect of which would be materially to alter the present methods of dealing with aments, I feel that any lengthy account of the law as it stands to-day is unnecessary. I shall therefore confine myself to a brief outline of the existing law and a short sketch of the main modifications proposed.

* Report of the Royal Commission on the Care and Control of the Feeble-Minded, 1908. Vol. viii.

Appendix III

The Present State of the Law.

Idiots and Imbeciles.—" Idiots " come within the provisions of two statutes—viz., the Lunacy Act of 1890 and the Idiots Act of 1886. " Imbeciles " come within the latter only.

1. According to the Lunacy Act of 1890 [53 Vict., ch. 5], " ' lunatic ' means an idiot or person of unsound mind ;" hence *idiots* may be certified and committed to care in precisely the same manner as " lunatics " as ordinarily understood.

2. Under the Idiots Act of 1886 [49 and 50 Vict., ch. 25], " an *idiot or imbecile* from birth or from an early age may, if under age, be placed by his parents or guardians, or by any person undertaking and performing towards him the duties of a parent or guardian, and may lawfully be received into, and until of full age detained in, any hospital, institution, or licensed house registered under this Act . . . upon the certificate in writing of a duly qualified medical practitioner."

This certificate, which is accompanied by a statement of particulars signed by the parent or guardian, is in a prescribed form, and is to the effect that the person " is an idiot (*or* has been imbecile from birth, *or* for . . . years past, *or* from an early age), and is capable of receiving benefit from [the institution (describing it)]." The person is, on this certificate, detained until he is of full age. If he has been so detained, he may, with the consent of the Commissioners in Lunacy, be retained after he is of full age. If, on the other hand, he be of full age at the time of application, he may be admitted on the same certificate and statement.

All institutions for the care of idiots have to be registered by the Commissioners in Lunacy, and are inspected by them. They are educational and custodial, and admission is obtained by payment of fees by relatives or public bodies, by election through votes, or in some cases by a combination of both these methods.

Idiots and imbeciles may also be taken into the workhouse, or receive outdoor relief from the Poor Law guardians ; not, however, on the ground of their deficiency, but on account of being paupers, in precisely the same manner as may non-defective paupers. But the father of an idiot or imbecile child who is in this way relieved by the Poor Law loses the Parliamentary franchise.

Feeble-Minded Adults.—If a feeble-minded person cannot be certified as " of unsound mind " or " imbecile " under either of the preceding statutes, he is not, *qua* mental defect, amenable to any existing law. If insane, he may be committed to care in a lunatic asylum in precisely the same way as an ordinary lunatic. If a pauper, he may be granted indoor or outdoor relief by the Poor Law guardians on account of his pauperism. Or he may be found incapable of managing his affairs, and his property safeguarded by proceedings in Chancery. There are, moreover, a number of *voluntary* homes and training establishments to which feeble-minded persons may be sent, and some of these homes are certified by the Local Government Board as institutions suitable for the reception of applicants sent by the Boards of Guardians. But there is no legal machinery by which feeble-minded persons may be detained in these establishments against their will.

Feeble-Minded (" Mentally-Defective ") Children.—Under the Elementary Education (Defective and Epileptic Children) Act of 1899 [62 and 63 Vict., ch. 32], the local education authorities are empowered (but not required) to make educational provision for " what children in their district, not being imbecile and not being merely dull or backward, are defective—that is to say, what children by reason of mental or physical defect are incapable of receiving proper benefit from the instruction in the ordinary public elementary schools, but are not incapable by reason of such defect of receiving benefit from instruction in such special classes or schools as are in this Act mentioned."

Where this Act has been adopted and special classes or schools established, the attendance of feeble-minded children can be compelled between the ages of seven and sixteen years. After that age the education authority has no further jurisdiction. Where this Act has not been adopted and there are no special schools, the guardians may, if they see fit, place the child in such a school in another district, and maintain him there out of the rates. Up to September 30, 1906, the Act had been adopted by 87 local education authorities in England and Wales, and on August 1, 1907, special accommodation existed for a total of 9,082 children, of whom 4,946 were in London. The total number

Appendix III

of these feeble-minded children in England and Wales, it will be remembered, has been estimated at 50,665, thus leaving 41,583 (or, according to the estimate of the Royal Commission, 35,662) at present unprovided for.

Recommendations of the Royal Commission.

The general tenor of the proposals of the Commissioners will be evident from the following summary of their " Principles Adopted in Dealing with the Problem of the Mentally Defective " :

1. That persons who cannot take a part in the struggle of life owing to mental defect, whether they are described as lunatics, or persons of unsound mind, idiots, imbeciles, feeble-minded or otherwise, should be afforded by the State such special protection as may be suited to their needs.

2. That the mental condition of these persons, and neither their poverty nor their crime, is the real ground of their claim for help from the State.

3. That, if the mentally defective are to be properly considered and protected as such, it is necessary to ascertain who they are and where they are, and to bring them into relation with the local authority.

4. That the protection of the mentally defective person, whatever form it takes, should be continued as long as is necessary for his good. This is desirable, not only in his interest, but also in the interest of the community. It follows that the State should have authority to segregate and to detain mentally defective persons under proper conditions and limitations, and on their behalf to compel the payment of contributions from relations who are able to pay for their support ; or should itself provide such care and accommodation as may be necessary, either directly or through the local authority.

5. In order to supervise local administration of this nature, a central authority is indispensable.

6. That in regard to the protection of property all mentally defective persons should have like privileges.

7. It is essential that there should be the closest co-operation between judicial and administrative authorities—in this case the Chancery Division of the High Court and the Central Authority.

Mental Deficiency

The manner in which it is proposed to apply the foregoing principles is briefly set forth in the following extracts from the Commissioners' Recommendations and Report:

I. That there be one central authority—to be known as "The Board of Control" for the general protection and supervision of mentally defective persons, and for the regulation of the provision made for their accommodation and maintenance, care, treatment, education, training, and control.

[Recommendations I. and V.]

II. That there be placed under the general protection and supervision of this central authority—

(1) *Persons of unsound mind.*
(2) *Persons mentally infirm.*
(3) *Idiots.*
(4) *Imbeciles.*
(5) *Feeble-minded.*
(6) *Moral imbeciles.*
(7) *Epileptics.*
(8) *Inebriates.*
(9) *Deaf and dumb, or blind* } Who are also mentally defective.

[Recommendation IV.]

NOTE.—(1) corresponds to "lunatics" and "insane" as ordinarily understood. (2) corresponds to the various forms of "dementia." (3), (4), (5), (6), (7), (8), (9), comprise the several forms, varieties, and degrees of "amentia" which have been described in this book, and of which definitions have already been given (see Chapter V., "Classification").

III. That the providing of the necessary educational and custodial care shall be in the hands of the local authorities (County Borough, and County Councils acting through a statutory ("Committee for the Care of the Mentally Defective"), who shall be under obligation to make directly or indirectly suitable and sufficient provision for the manual, industrial, and other training of all mentally defective children, as well as for the care and control by institutions, homes, or houses, or in observation or reception wards, or under family guardianship, or in any other way of which the Board of Control shall approve, of all such other sufferers from mental defect within their district as come within the terms defined in Section II.

These local "Committees for the Care of the Mentally Defective" would therefore take over the work of the Education Committees, the Asylum Visiting Committees, and the Poor Law Guardians, in so far as these are concerned with the mentally defective.

[Pars. 532-534 of Report and Recommendations XXVIII-XXXIV., XLVI., LXXIV.]

IV. With regard to feeble-minded ("mentally defective") children, the Commissioners advocate a system of record and limited notification, but, believing that the Defective Children's Education Act of 1899 by itself "cannot meet the needs of the mentally defective," they recommend that the education and training of these should pass from the Board of Education to the "Board of Control," the local authority being empowered to contract with the educational authority for the supply of schools and classes or other suitable measures, but being responsible that suitable control and training is supplied.

The Commissioners insist upon continuity of control as a fundamental principle, and justly urge that the childhood and schooling of mentally defective children cannot rightly be treated apart from their after-life, and that no age can be fixed in their case as separating school-time from supervision and after-care.

[Par. 23 of Report and Recommendations LXXII.-LXXXVI.]

V. In order to bring certain classes not now certifiable (notably feeble-minded and moral imbeciles) under efficient care and control, the Commissioners recommend that the procedure under the Idiots Act be extended so that not only idiots and imbeciles whose parents or guardians desire to obtain for them admission to an idiot asylum may be admitted on a single medical certificate, *but also that feeble-minded persons, moral imbeciles, and such inebriates, epileptics, and blind or deaf and dumb persons, as are mentally defective, and of any age, may be admitted to suitable institutions in the same way.*

Mental Deficiency

Further, that the Idiots Act and the Lunacy Acts be remodelled and drafted in the form of a single statute, which should contain all regulations for procedure, certification, and the supervision of institutions, which it may be necessary to insert in an Act for the care and control of the mentally defective.

[Par. 27 of Report and Recommendations LXVIII.–LXXI.]

INDEX

ABNORMAL nerve signs, 111
    in mentally defective children, 130
Abstract ideas, 107
Achondroplasia and cretinism, 257
Act, Defective and Epileptic Children (Education), 124, 372
    Employers' Liability, 358
    Idiots, 371
    Lunacy, 371
Action, deliberate, 112
    impulsive, 112
    reflex, 112
    spreading, 130
    volitional, 112
Adenoids in Mongolism, 187
Adenoma sebaceum, 88
Æsthetic sense, 293
After-care, necessity for, 358
Age at which training should begin, 339
    of aments at death, 92
    of feeble-minded in workhouses, 282
    of parents as a cause of amentia, 24
Agenesis corticalis, 70
Agnes Halonen, the case of, 267
Alcohol as a cause of amentia, 18, 37
    effect of, upon eggs, 19
    susceptibility of aments to, 300, 313
Alimentary system, anomalies of, 89
Allegations, unfounded, by aments, 134, 316
Allowance, Poor Law, to aments, 284
Amaurotic family idiocy, 249
Amentia accompanied by porencephaly or hemiatrophy, 220, 221
    acquired, 15, 71

Amentia, brain cells in, 56
    causation of, 14
    clinical varieties of, 72 *et seq.*
    congenital, 15, 71
    cretinoid, 182, 253
    definition of, 2
    degrees of, 74 *et seq.*
    delayed primary, 47, 72
    developmental, 47, 72
    diagnosis of, 324
    due to asphyxia neonatorum, 213
        birth injury, 212
        blindness, 265
        cerebral disease, 196
            lesions, 202
        deafness, 264, 275
        defective cerebral nutrition, 251
        isolation, 263
        malnutrition, 261
        sense deprivation, 263
        sunstroke, 216
        toxic lesions, 218
        trauma, 31, 203, 214
        traumatic epilepsy, 214
    eclampsic, 201
    epileptic, 197
    forms of, 71
    hydrocephalic, 235
    hypertrophic, 229
    incidence of, 4 *et seq.* See also Incidence
    inflammatory, 202
    myxœdematous, 253
    pachydermic, 253
    paralytic, 211
    prevention of, 362
    primary, 37, 56, 71, 173. See also Primary
    prognosis in, 327
    rachitic, 262
    sclerotic, 224 *et seq.*

Index

Amentia, secondary, 47, 64, 71, 194.
 See also Secondary
 " sporadic," 45
 syphilitic, 240
 toxic, 202
 varieties of, 73, 173, 194
 vascular, 202
 with hemiplegia, 212, 214
  moral deficiency, 293
  motor aphasia, 218
  paralysis, 166, 192, 204, 211
  paraplegia, 215
Aments and crime, 298
 and society, 281
 in cottages, 288
 in workhouses, 282, 289
 insane, 310
 location of, 12, 281
 needing provision, 286
 number of, in England and Wales, 7, 368; method of estimating, 366
 pauper, 282
 propagation by, 288
 receiving Poor Law relief, 282
 sane, 310
 sex of, 13
Andriezen, Dr. L., 19
Anomalies, anatomical, 65, 80, 82, 129
 of labour, 27, 29, 46
 physiological, 82, 89, 130
Aphasia, motor, in amentia, 218
Appearance of mentally defective children, 129
 of primary aments, 148, 160, 166, 171, 194
 of secondary aments, 194, 210
Aristotle on temperaments, 109
Arithmetic in idiots savants, 274
 teaching of, 351
Arndt and Sklarek, 67
Articulation in aments, 117
Asexualization, 360
Ashby, Dr. H., 120, 130
Asphyxia neonatorum causing amentia, 28, 46, 203, 213
Association, capacity for, in aments, 105
 law of, 348
 systems, 58, 62
  cultivation of, 348
Asylums, feeble-minded in, 284, 367
 idiots and imbeciles in, 284, 367
Atavism and microcephaly, 174
Athetosis, 117, 192
 correction of, 346

Athyroidea, 252
Atrophic sclerosis, 226
Attention, cultivation of, 347
 in aments, 103, 161, 167
 in mentally defective children, 132
 spontaneous, 103
 voluntary, 104
Audry, 66
" Aztecs," the, 180

Baer, Dr., 296
Baillarger, 174
 line of, 58
Barr, Dr. M. W., 272
Beach, Dr. Fletcher, 21, 123, 176, 229
 and Shuttleworth, Drs., 16, 18, 20, 23, 27
Becker, Helene, case of, 180
" Bird man," case of, 180
Birth lesions causing amentia, 27, 203, 208, 212, 215
 premature, causing amentia, 30, 46
Births, number of, to a marriage, 39
Bischoff, Professor, 180
Blindness, congenital, causing amentia, 265
Blood in cretins, 256
Bolton, Dr. J. S., 38, 62, 198, 263, 311
Bourneville, Dr., 18, 19, 60, 90, 223, 226
Boyd, Dr. R., 51
Brachycephaly in Mongolism, 185
Brain, atrophy of, 70
 in sclerosis, 225
 bloodvessels of, 61
 cells of, in amentia, 56
  in dementia, 64
  imperfect development of, 57
  irregular arrangement of, 56
  numerical deficiency of, 56
Brain cells, pigmentation of, 58
 cortex of, 58, 61
 development of normal, 51
 hæmorrhage into, 69
 hemiatrophy of, 66, 220, 221, 223
 hypertrophy of, 60, 229
 in amentia, 65
 in cretinism, 255
 in criminals, 296
 in dementia, 70
 in microcephaly, 176

Index

Brain, in Mongolism, 184
  in sclerosis, 59, 234
  inflammation of, 69, 202
  malformations of, 66
  membranes of, 70
  morbid anatomy of, 65
  regions of, affected in amentia, 62
  situation of changes in, 61
  size of, and intelligence, 176
    range of normal variation in, 176
  weight of normal, 176, 364
    in hemiatrophy, 220, 223
    in hypertrophic amentia, 229
    in microcephaly, 176
    in Mongolism, 184
  in porencephaly, 220, 223
Bridgman, Laura, case of, 266
Broca, Professor, 52
Brothers and sisters of aments, condition of, 38
Brunet, Dr. D., 229

Caldecott, Dr. C., 16, 92, 93, 96, 188, 259, 273, 275
Cappelletti, Dr., 323
Cardiac lesions in Mongolism, 187
Cardona, Dr. F., 180
Care, inadequate, aments under, 286, 368
Caswell, Oliver, case of, 267
Catarrhal affections in Mongolism, 188
Causation, factors of, acting after birth, 31; before birth, 25; during birth, 27
  age of parents, 24
  alcoholism, 18, 37
  consanguinity, 22
  convulsions, 32, 196
  diseases of nervous system, 16, 37
  ecbolics, 26
  environmental, 16, 24, 47
  epilepsy, 16, 32, 197
  extrinsic, 16, 24, 47
  gross cerebral lesions, 55
  heredity, morbid, 15, 34
  intrinsic, 15, 16, 35
  illegitimacy, 26
  injuries, 27, 31
  in regard to local variations of incidence, 48
  malnutrition, 33
  maternal impressions, 26
  plumbism, 22, 25

Causation, factors of, premature birth, 30, 46
  primogeniture, 30
  rickets, 33, 262
  slum life, 48, 127
  sunstroke, 32, 216
  syphilis, 21
  toxic, 31
  tuberculosis, 20, 37
  of primary amentia, 37
  of secondary amentia, 47
Cells of brain, development of, 52
  in amentia, 56
  in dementia, 64
Cerebellum, atrophy of, 234
  in hydrocephalus, 235
  in Mongolism, 184
  lesions of, in amentia, 67
Cerretti, the brothers, 180
Character in the feeble-minded, 149
Charitable institutions, aments in, 12, 288
Charts of family histories, 41-45
Children born during insanity of mother, 27
  dull and backward, 141
  dull owing to disease, 144
  epileptic, 145
  feeble-minded, 123
  insane, 145
  mentally defective, 123
  of delayed mental development, 143
Choking, liability of idiots to, 167
Chorea in aments, 117, 191
Choreiform movements, 212
Circulation in Mongolism, 187
Civil incapacity of aments, 309
Classification of amentia, 71
  table of, 77
Clinical varieties of primary amentia, 173
  of secondary amentia, 194
Clothing of aments, 334
Clouston, Dr. T. S., 86, 87
Colour-blindness in aments, 84
  discrimination, cultivation of, 342
Commission, Lunacy, 8
  of Legislature of Connecticut, 16
  Prison, 299
  Royal, on care and control of feeble-minded (of 1904), 4, 125, 147, 281, 288, 299, 368, 373
  Royal, of Sardinia on cretins, 253

Index

Commission, Scottish Lunacy, 290
Committee, Anthropometric, 296
    Departmental, of Board of Education, 124
Common sense, lack of, in aments, 158
Compensation of neurones in cerebral lesions, 206
Complications of primary amentia, 190
Consanguinity as a cause of amentia, 22
Consecutive lesions of brain, 67
Consonantal defects in aments, 121
Contemporaries of aments, 38
Contractures in paralytic aments, 211
    in sclerotic aments, 226
Control, defect of, in aments, 115, 133, 299
    influencing responsibility, 306, 307
    inadequate, 286, 287
Convulsions (see also Epilepsy) as a cause of amentia, 32, 196, 201
    as a cause of death, 96
    in amaurotic family idiocy, 250
    in amentia due to cerebral disease, 211
    in epileptic amentia, 199
    in hydrocephalus, 237
    in mentally defective children, 138
    in microcephalics, 179
    in Mongolism, 189
    in primary amentia, 190, 191
    in sclerotic amentia, 225, 226, 230, 233
    in syphilitic amentia, 243
    Jacksonian, 211
    predisposition to, 201
    acquired, 202
Co-ordination, defects of, 115
    development of, 345
Coprolalia, 121
Corporal punishment, 355
Corpus callosum in aments, 55, 67
Cortex cerebri, 56, 62
    in sclerosis, 234
Cottages, aments in, 288
Country, employment of feeble-minded in, 283
Craniectomy in amentia, 332
Cranium, anomalies of, in aments, 70, 84
    in criminals, 296
    artificial compression of, 29

Cranium, in hydrocephalus, 235, 237
    and rickets, 237
    in hypertrophic aments, 229
    in microcephalics, 177
    in Mongolism, 185
    mensuration of, 85
    oxycephalic, 177
    premature synostosis in microcephaly, 174
    " sugar-loaf," 177
Cretinism, 251
    endemic, 251
        description of, 252
        incidence of, 252
    sporadic, 253
        causation of, 253
        description of, 255
        differential diagnosis in, 257
        pathology of, 254
        prognosis, 331
        treatment and its result, 258
Cretinoid idiocy, 182
Criminal actions in feeble-minded persons, 157, 298
    aments, 298
        and insanity, 300, 314
        number of, 299
        responsibility of, 305
        types of, 299
    responsibility, 305
Criminals, habitual, antecedents of, 297
    mental characteristics of, 297
    physical characteristics of, 296
    potential, 295
    relation of, to aments, 295
Crocker, Dr., 89
Crothers, Dr., 18
Crowley, Dr. R., 128
Cruelty of feeble-minded children, 134
    of idiots, 169
Cunning of aments, 134, 301, 302
Cunningham and Telford-Smith, Drs., 181
Cure of mental deficiency, 127, 328
Cutaneous sensation, 101
    system, anomalies of, 88
Cuvier, brain of, 176

Dahl, Dr. Ludwig, 17
Dalton, Dr., 181
Darenth asylum, 22, 28
Darwin, Dr. G., 23

Index

Deaf-mutism causing secondary amentia, 264; cases of, 264-267, 303, 304
  in primary amentia, 193
Deafness, cause of, 81, 100
  causing amentia, 264
Death, age at, in amentia, 92
  in Mongolism, 188
  causes of, in amentia, 94, 96
Definition of amentia, 2
  of feeble-mindedness, 75
  of idiocy, 76
  of imbecility, 76
  of mentally defective child, 75
  of moral deficiency, 76
  of "normal" mind, 2
Degeneracy, stigmata of, anatomical, 80
  in aments, 78, 194
  in criminals, 296
  physiological, 89
Degeneration of brain cells, 64
Degrees of amentia, description of, 74
  prognosis in, 331
Delisle, Dr., 30
Delivery, instrumental, as a cause of amentia, 29
Delusional insanity, 316
Delusions in aments, 300, 314
Dementia, condition of brain in, 62
  distinguished from amentia, 1, 3
  in epilepsy, 197, 317
  in insanity, 317, 319 et seq.
  in primary amentia, 317
  in syphilitic amentia, 242
Dentition in aments, time of, 90, 364
  in cretins, 255
Deprivation, amentia due to, 263
Destructiveness in idiots, 169
Developmental anomalies in aments, 65, 80, 89, 194
  in criminals, 296
  data, normal, 364
  or delayed a amentia, 47
Development, delayed, 128
  in children, 129, 143
  imperfect, of nerve cells, 57
  of normal brain, 51
Diagnosis of amentia, 324
  of cretinism, 257
  of feeble-mindedness, 158
    in children, 138
  of hydrocephalus, 237
  of hypertrophy and hydrocephalus, 229

Diagnosis of idiocy and imbecility, 171
  of mentally defective children, 138
  of syphilitic amentia, 243
Dietary in amentia, 334
Disposition in amentia, 109, 134, 150, 162, 168
  due to cerebral lesions, 210
    hydrocephalus, 236
    hypertrophy, 230
  in cretins, 256
Dobson, Dr. M. B., 235
Donaldson, Dr. H. H., 266
Down, Dr. J. Langdon, 19, 20, 21, 23, 24, 47, 86, 87, 91, 181, 185, 210, 274, 329
Down, Dr. R. Langdon, 187, 188, 271, 273
Drawing, capacity for, in mentally defective children, 137
  in idiots savants, 272
Drugs in amentia, 332
Dugdale, Dr. R. L., 298
Dull and backward children, 141
Dullness, mental, due to disease, 144
Duncan, Dr. Matthews, 24
Dunces compared with aments, 141

Ear, anomalies of, in aments, 80
  in criminals, 81
  in insane, 81
  and hearing, 100
  disease of, 100
Earlswood Asylum, particulars regarding mortality in, 92 et seq.
  the Genius of, 275
Earnings of feeble-minded persons, 284, 285
Ecbolics as a cause of amentia, 26
Echolalia, 122
Eclampsia and epilepsy, 202
  as a cause of amentia, 33, 202
"Eclampsic" amentia, 201, 218
Edinger, Professor, 236
Educability of aments, 339
  of mentally defective children, 132
Education Act regarding defective and epileptic children, 124
  Board of, report of Departmental Committee, 124
  of aments, general principles, 335
    home, 339
    industrial, 351

Education of aments, intellectual, 347
    moral, 353
    objects of, 335
    religious, 353
    school, 341
    technical, 351
    value of, 358
Ego, perversion of the, 310
Eichler, Professor, 55
Ellis, Dr. Havelock, 296, 297
Emotion in feeble-minded persons, 155
    in mentally defective children, 133
    in primary aments, 110, 168
    in secondary aments, 210
Employment of feeble-minded persons, 151, 155, 358
    in country districts, 283
    in workhouses, 283
    vagrants, 285
Encephalitis causing amentia, 217
    pathology of, 68
Enteric causing amentia, 203
Enumeration of aments, 4 et seq., 366
Enuresis, treatment of, 334
Environment and heredity, relative importance of, 34
    and mentally defective children, 127
    factors of, causing amentia, 24, 47. See also Causation
Epicanthus, 84
Epilepsy, acquired predisposition to, 202. See also Convulsions
    and eclampsia, 202
    as a cause of amentia, 16, 32, 198
    as a cause of dementia, 197
    exciting factors of, 202
    in children, 145
    in feeble-minded persons, 191
    in gross cerebral lesions, 190
    in idiots, 167, 191
    in imbeciles, 160, 191
    in microcephalics, 179
    in primary amentia, 117, 190
    Jacksonian, 211
    predisposition to, 202
    psychic, 62, 354
    relations of, to amentia, 196, 204
    traumatic, causing amentia, 214

Epilepsy, treatment of, 334
"Epileptic" amentia, description of, 197
    illustrative cases of, 199
    prognosis in, 331
Epileptic insanity, 318
Erotic tendencies in aments, 180, 290
Esquirol, Dr., 75, 118
Ethnic types of amentia, 73
Examination of mentally defective children, 139
Excitement determining insanity, 313
    in aments, 155, 162, 168, 300
Exhaustion of mother as a cause of Mongolism, 183
Expression in mentally defective children, 130
Extent of lesions in secondary amentia, 207
Extrinsic factors causing amentia, 24, 47
Eye, anomalies of, 84. See also Vision
    drill, 346
Eyes in Mongolism, 187

"Facile" aments, 290, 299
Factors of causation in regard to local variations of incidence, 48
Fagge, Dr. Hilton, 253
Family history charts, 41-45
Farr and Newsholme, Drs., 40
Fatty tumours in cretinism, 256
Fecundity of neuropaths, 39
Feeble-minded adults, 147
    character of, 149
    description of, 148
    illustrative cases of, 151, 156
    incapacity of, 154
    in charitable institutions, 12
    in lunatic asylums, 12, 284
    in Poor Law institutions, 12, 282
    number of, 9, 147
    of stable mental equilibrium, 150
    of unstable mental equilibrium, 155
    receiving parish relief, 282, 283
    sex of, 148
    children, 123
        abnormal nerve signs in, 130

Index

Feeble-minded children and slum life, 127
  clinical varieties of, 137
  " cured," 127
  definition of, 75, 124
  description of, 128
  grades of, 134
  incidence of, 125, 126
  in special schools, 135, 372
  mental condition of, 131
  number in England and Wales, 125, 373
  physical condition of, 129
  scholastic acquirements compared with ordinary children, 135
  sex of, 128
  social status of, 128
  stigmata of degeneracy in, 129
  criminals, 298
  insane, 311
  persons, 147
  vagrants, 285
Feeble-mindedness, definition of, 75
Fennell, Dr. C. H., 186
Fenwick, Dr. Soltau, 259
Féré, Dr., 19
Fibres of cortex cerebri, 58, 63
Fingers in Mongolism, 187
Flechsig, Professor, 62
Fœtus, injuries to, 27
Forceps, use of, as a cause of amentia, 29
Fournier, Dr. E., 21, 241
Fraser, Dr. Alec, 220
" Freddy," the case of, 181
Fright, as a cause of amentia, 26
  determining insanity, 313
Freud, Dr. S., 55, 69, 204, 207
Fundus oculi in amaurotic family idiocy, 250

Gambetta, brain of, 176
Games, use of, in training, 346
Garrod, Dr. A. E., 187
General paralysis in aments, 317, 323
  in syphilitic amentia, 242, 244 et seq.
  morbid heredity in, 241
Generative organs, anomalies of, 89, 90
" Genetous " idiocy, 73
Genius, the, of Earlswood Asylum, 275
Germ plasm, how influenced, 35, 36

Gestation, importance of mother's condition during, 45, 183, 184
Giacomini, Professor, 174
Gill, Dr., 289
Gliosis, 59. See also Sclerosis
Goitre in endemic cretins, 252
  in sporadic cretins, 253
" Goose man," the, 180
Gowers, Sir W. R., 33, 38, 198
Gradenigo, Dr., 80
Grandoni, Antonia, 180
Gray, Dr., 307
Grenzer, Dr., 87
Grimacing in aments, 114
  in Mongols, 188
Grinning in aments, 114
Gross lesions causing amentia, 55, 202

Habits and tricks, 114, 346
Hæmorrhage, cerebral, 61, 69
Hair, growth of, in aments, 88
  in cretins, 255
  in microcephalics, 177
Hallucinations in aments, 314
Hammarberg, Dr., 56
Hands in Mongols, 187
Hauser, Kaspar, the case of, 268
Head-nodding, 114
Hearing and attention, 104
  cultivation of, 344
  defects of, 81, 100, 264
  in amaurotic family idiocy, 250
  in cretins, 252, 256
  in hydrocephalus, 236
  in idiots savants, 271
Heart, anomalies of, in aments, 89
  in Mongolism, 187
Helin, Dr. Aug., 267
Hemiatrophy of brain, 66, 220
Hemiplegia and amentia, 212, 214
Heredity, alcoholic, 18
  and environment, relative importance of, 34
  morbid, and consanguinity, 23
    importance of, as a cause of amentia, 34
    modus operandi in causation of amentia, 35
  neuropathic, 16, 17, 20
    in criminals, 297
    in general paralysis, 241
    in sporadic cretinism, 253
    in syphilitic amentia, 241
  syphilitic, 21
  tuberculous, 20

Heubner, Dr. O., 227
High-grade amentia, 75
Hirsch, Dr., 244
Histology of primary amentia, 56
    of secondary amentia, 64
Hjorth, Dr. B., 183
Holt, Dr. E., 69
Home training of aments, 339
Homes, voluntary, for feeble-minded, 12, 372
Horsley, Sir Victor, 333
    and Sturge, 19
Howe, Dr., 18, 266, 274
Huschke, Dr., 184
Hutchison, Dr. R., 258, 259
Huth, A., 23
Hybernation of aments, 91
Hydrocephalic amentia, description of, 235
    and cretinism, 257
    and hypertrophy, 229
    illustrative cases of, 238
Hydrocephalus, acute, 236
    and hypertrophy, 229
    arrested, 236
    cause of, 68
    causing amentia, 235
    cure in, 236
    in microcephalics, 235
    in primary amentia, 192
    pathology of, 68
Hypertrophic sclerosis, 229
    and cretinism, 257
    amentia due to, 229
Hypertrophy of brain and hydrocephalus, 229
    amentia due to, 229
    pathology of, 60

Ideation in aments, 106, 149, 151, 167
Idiocy, absolute, complete or profound, 171
    amaurotic family, 249
    and crime, 298
    apathetic and excitable, 168
    by sense deprivation, 263
    definition of, 76
    description of, 166
    diagnosis of, 171
    differentiation from imbecility, 165
    illustrative cases of, 169
    maniacal excitement in, 169
    mental and nervous characteristics of, 167
    partial or incomplete, 166
    physical characteristics of, 166
Idiots, number of, in England and Wales, 9, 165
    receiving Poor Law relief, 284
    savants, 270 et seq.
    sex of, 166
Illegitimacy as a cause of amentia, 26
Illegitimate children of aments, 288, 291
Ill-health of mother during pregnancy, 25, 183, 184
Imagination in aments, 106, 161, 167
    in mentally defective children, 133
Imbeciles and mentally defective children, 145
    insane, 318
    in schools, 284
    number of, in England and Wales, 9
    receiving Poor Law relief, 284
    sex of, 159
Imbecility, 159
    and crime, 298
    definition of, 76
    description of, 159
    diagnosis of, 171
    differentiation from idiocy, 165
    illustrative cases of, 162
    mental and nervous characteristics of, 160
    physical characteristics of, 160
Imitation in aments, 106, 161, 355
Imperfect development of nerve cells, 57
Improvement in amentia due to cerebral lesions, 210
    limitation of, 339
Incapacity, civil, of aments, 309
    of feeble-minded persons, 154
Incidence of amentia, 4 et seq.
    in urban and rural districts, 49, 50, 126
    relative to insanity, 11, 49; to sex, 13
    of insanity, 11
    of mentally defective children in schools, 126
    of the respective degrees of amentia, 9, 50
Inco-ordination, 115
    correction of, 346
Industrial training, 351
Infantile cerebral degeneration, 249
Inflammation of brain, 69
Inflammatory amentia, 202. See also Vascular

Injuries. See Trauma
Insanity, alternating, 316
    anatomical basis of, 62
    and amentia, 3, 310, 311, 314
    and crime, 300, 314
    and dementia, 3, 317
    and town life, 49
    antecedent, as a cause of amentia, 16
    delusional, 316
    epileptic, 318
    in children, 145
    incidence of, relative to amentia, 11
    in feeble-minded, 311
    in idiots and imbeciles, 318
    in mother, effect upon children, 27
    predisposition to, in aments, 300, 311
    recurrences in, 316
Instability of feeble-minded persons, 155, 300, 312
Institutions, aments in, 12, 282, 284
Instrumental delivery as a cause of amentia, 29
Intellectual sense, 293
Intelligence and size of brain, 176
    training of, 347
Interest, arousal of, 337
    importance of, in training, 347
Ireland, Dr. W. W., 19, 20, 72, 87, 229, 236, 253, 290
Irregular arrangement of nerve cells, 56
Isolation, amentia due to, 263 et seq.
Itard's wild boy, 101

Jacksonian convulsions, 211
Jaws, anomalies of, 88
Jendrassik, 60
Jews and amaurotic family idiocy, 249
"Joe," the case of, 181
Johnson, Samuel, 29
Joints in Mongolism, 187
Judgment in aments, 107, 149, 161, 167
Juke family, the, 298

Kaes, Professor, 53
Kalmuc variety of amentia, 181
Keen, Dr., 333
Keller, Helen, case of, 267
Kerlin, Dr., 18, 20, 23
Kind, Dr., 18

Kindergarten occupations in training, 337, 346
Kingdon and Russell, Drs., 249
Kleptomania, 308
Klob, Dr., 55
Knowledge of wrong, and criminal responsibility, 306
Koch, Dr. J. L. A., 16
Kolk, Schroeder van der, 298
Korosi, Dr., 24
Kundrat, Professor, 66, 221

Labour, abnormalities of, as a cause of amentia, 27, 29, 46
"Lalling," 120
Lamination, cortical, in amentia, 58, 61, 63
    in sclerosis, 234
    normal, 52
Lankester, Dr., 26
Lannelongue, Dr., 333
La Page, Dr., 84, 86, 120, 129
Law of England concerning aments, 370
Lead-poisoning causing amentia, 22, 25
Legal responsibility of aments, 305
Lesions, cerebral, and amentia, 202-207
    age at occurrence, 205
    initial symptoms of, 208, 209
    nature of, 207
    paralysis in, 208, 209
    prognosis in, 209, 330
    situation and extent of, 207
    consecutive, of encephalon, 67
    of motor cortex, effect of, 207
Lewis, Dr. Bevan, 57, 61
Lips, anomalies of, 84
Little, Dr., 29
Location of aments, 12, 281, 286
    needing provision, 287
Lock wards, aments in, 289
Logical sense in aments, 293
Lombroso, Professor, 179, 180, 296
Looft, Dr. Karl, 18
Low-grade amentia, 76
Lucon, Dr., 19
Lunatics, potential, 157. See also Insanity

Malar flush in Mongolism, 187
Malnutrition as a cause of amentia, 33, 261
Mania in aments, 314, 318 et seq.
Marie, Dr., 60

Marriage of aments, 288, 360
   restriction of, 360
Marro, Dr., 298
Masturbation in aments, 162
Maternal impressions, 26
Maternity wards, aments in, 289
Maudsley, Dr. H., 274, 297
McDowall, Dr. T. W., 177
Measles as a cause of amentia, 203
Meat diet, 334
Medium-grade amentia, 76
Melancholia in aments, 314
Melland, Dr., 283, 289
Membranes of brain, condition of, 70
Memory, cultivation of, 348
   in aments, 105, 161, 167
   in idiots savants, 272
   in mentally defective children, 132
Meningitis causing amentia, 219
Meningo-encephalitis causing amentia, 218
   pathology of, 68
Menstruation in aments, 90
Mental characteristics of aments, 98, 103
   deficiency, literal meaning of, 1
   development, arrested, 262, 268
      delayed, 262
      normal, 51, 251, 335
   instability in the feeble-minded, 155, 300
   stability in the feeble-minded, 150
Mentally defective children, 123. See also Feeble-minded children
Mercier, Dr. C., 307, 309, 310
Meystre, case of, 267
Microcephalic amentia, 173
   and atavism, 174
   and cranial synostosis, 174
   brain in, 176
   causation of, 174
   definition of, 173
   description of, 177
   intelligence in, 178
   morbid heredity in, 175
   pathology of, 175
   prognosis in, 329
Microgyria, 66
Microkinesis, 111
Mill, J. Stuart, 354
Mimicry in microcephalics, 179
   in Mongols, 189
Mind, disease of, 3
   normal, definition of, 2
      development of, 51, 251, 335

Mind, normal, range of, 1
   types of, 293
   relation of, to nerve cells, 54, 62
Mind, Gottfried, case of, 272
Mingazzini, Professor, 181
Modesty in aments, 290
Mongolian amentia, 181
   amelioration of bodily signs in, 188
   and cretinism, 189
   and syphilis, 22, 182
   causation of, 182
   description of, 185
   mental and nervous characterstics of, 188
   pathology of, 184
   physical characteristics of, 185
   prevalence of, 182
   prognosis in, 329
   semi-, 182
Moon, Dr. R. O., 202
Moral deficiency, 293
   and amentia, 295
      latent, 295
         and criminals, 295
   imbecility, 76, 354
   sense, 110, 133, 168, 293
   training, 353
Morel, Dr., 19
Mortality after craniectomy, 333
Mortality of aments, 91-97
   of cretins, 257
Motor aphasia with amentia, 218
   cortex, lesions of, 207
   functions in aments, 111
   cultivation of, 338
   in idiots savants, 270
Mott, Dr. F. W., 21, 221, 241
Movements, automatic, 114, 169
   co-ordinated, 111
   deficient, 113
   deliberate, 112, 115
   development of, 345
   excessive, 113
   imitation, 116, 346
   impulsive, 112, 115
   inco-ordinated, 115
   instinctive, 112
   irregular, 114
      correction of, 346
   reflex, 112
   training of, 345
   transfer, 116, 346
   spontaneous, 111
   volitional, 112, 115
Müller, Professor Max, 121

Index

Mumbray, Miss N., 135, 344
Murray, Dr. G. R., 258
Muscle sense, 101
    cultivation of, 343
Muscles, anomalies of, 88
    atrophy of, in amaurotic family idiocy, 250
    condition of, in "paralytic" aments, 211
    sensations from, 343
    weakness of, in cretins, 256
        in sclerosis, 226, 230
Music, fondness for, in idiots savants, 274
    in Mongols, 189
    value of, in training, 344, 350
Mutilations, transmission of, 35
Myxœdema and cretinism, 254

Napoleon, brain of, 176
National Vigilance Society, 290
Nerve cells, development of normal, 52
    in amentia, 56, 61, 63
    in dementia, 63, 64
    in sclerosis, 61
Nerve fibres in amentia, 58, 63
    in dementia, 63
    normal, 53, 63
    signs, abnormal, 111, 130, 324
Nervous characteristics of amentia, 98
Neurasthenia in children, 145
Neuroblasts in amentia, 57, 64
    in normal brain, 52, 62
Neuroglia, condition of, 59, 224
    contraction of, 225
Neuropathic heredity. See Heredity
Newsholme and Farr, Drs., 40
Nicholson, Dr., 297
Nobiling-Jolly, 55
Norman, Dr. Conolly, 220
Nose, anomalies of, 84
    in Mongolism, 186
Number of aments in England and Wales, 9, 368
    inadequately cared for, 287, 368
    method of estimating, 366
Numerical deficiency of nerve cells, 56
Nystagmus, 117

Object-lessons, value of, in training, 348
Occupation of aments, 151, 283, 285

Occupations suitable for aments, 352
Offences committed by aments, 300, 301
Operative treatment of amentia, 333
Optic atrophy in amaurotic family idiocy, 250
    in hydrocephalus, 236
Organic sensations in aments, 102
Osseous system, anomalies of, 84
Otitis as a cause of amentia, 203
Otorrhœa in aments, 100
Outdoor relief, aments in receipt of, 282–284, 286
Oxycephalic skull, 177

Pachydermic idiocy, 253
Pain, appreciation of, 102, 169
Palate, anomalies of, 86, 87
    causation of, 87
    cleft, 87
    saddle-shaped, 87
    V-shaped, 87
Palpebral fissures in Mongols, 185
Paralysis, general. See General paralysis
    in amentia, 166, 179, 192, 204, 211, 237
    nature of, in "paralytic" aments, 211
"Paralytic" aments, 211
Paraplegia in aments, 215
Parasyphilitic conditions, 241
Parents' disparity in age as a cause of amentia, 24
Parry, Dr., 289
Parturition, anomalies of, 27
Pathology of amentia, 54 et seq.
Paul, Dr. C., 22
Pauper aments, 281 et seq.
Peacock, Dr., 52
Pearce, Dr. F. H., 92, 96
Pearse, Dr., 289
Peruvians, ancient, 176
Petersen, Dr., 86, 271
Phthisis. See Tuberculosis
Physical characteristics of amentia, 78 et seq.
Physiological anomalies of amentia, 89 et seq.
Pigmentation of nerve cells, 58, 64
Pituitary gland, administration of, in Mongolism, 190
Play, use of, in training, 337, 346
Plumbism. See Lead
Pneumonia "aspiration," 334
    as a cause of death, 96

Index

Polio-encephalitis of Strümpell as a cause of amentia, 203
Poor-Law institutions, aments in, 12, 282, 284
Porencephaly, 66
  as a cause of amentia, 55
  double, 222
  in primary amentia, 192
  in secondary amentia, 220
  pseudo-, 67, 221
  symptoms of, 220
Potential criminals, 295
  lunatics, 157
Potentiality of cerebral development, 205
Potts, Dr. W. A., 283, 289
Powell, Dr. E., 128
Pregnancy, abnormal condition of mother during, 25, 45
Premature birth as a cause of amentia, 30, 46
  synostosis in microcephalics, 174
Pressure, sense of, 102
Primary amentia, causation of, 37
  clinical varieties of, 73, 173
  complications of, 190
  pathology of, 56
Primogeniture, 30
Pringle, Dr., 89
Prisons, aments in, 12, 299, 300
Progeny of aments, 289, 290
  of insane mothers, 27
  of neuropaths, 39
Prognosis in amentia, 327-331
    due to cerebral lesions, 209
    cretinism, 258
    epilepsy, 199
    sense deprivation, 331
    sclerosis, 225
    syphilis, 245
Pronunciation, defects of, 102
Propagation by aments, 288
    prevention of, 360
Prostitutes, 289, 290, 292, 299
Provision, number of aments in need of, in England and Wales, 287, 368
  nature of, required, 359
Puberty, mental changes accompanying, 149, 169
  retardation of, in aments, 90
  in cretins, 252, 256
  in syphilitic aments, 242
unishment, effect upon aments, 109, 301, 355

Pupils in special schools, 135, 372
  in syphilitic amentia, 242
Purkinje's cells, 234

Quatrefages, 19

" Rabbit man," the, 180
Rage, attacks of, in hypertrophic aments, 230
" Raphael, Der Katzen-," 272
Rational type of mind, 293
Reading, teaching of, 350
Reasoning in aments, 107, 149, 161, 167
  cultivation of, 348
Recommendations of Royal Commission on the Feeble-minded, 373
Recurrences in insanity, 316
Reflexes in paralytic aments, 211
Regions of brain affected in amentia, 62
Registrar-General, 39, 40, 97
Relations of amentia to insanity, 311
  of epilepsy to amentia, 196
Religious education, 353
  sense, 293
  in aments, 110, 134
Rennert, Dr., 25
Respiratory system, anomalies of, 89
Responsibility, conditions of, 309
  of aments, 305
Rewards, use of, in training, 355
Rhinitis in amentia, 203
Ribot, Dr., 348
Rickets and cretinism, 257
  and hydrocephalus, 237
  as a cause of amentia, 33, 262
Ross, Dr., 222
Rossi, Dr., 297
Rumination, 167
Russell and Kingdon, Drs., 249

Sabatier, 19
Sachs, Dr., 69, 70, 249
Sailer, Dr. J., 60, 234
Sander, Dr., 176
Sangford, 266
Saulle, Legrand du, 27
Savage, Dr. G. H., 198, 310
Scalp in hydrocephalics, 237
  in microcephalics, 177
Scarlet fever as a cause of amentia, 203
Scholastic acquirements of imbeciles, 161

Scholastic acquirements of mentally defective children, 134
Schools, imbeciles in, 284
  special, description of children attending, 135
  training, 341
"Scissor-legs," 166
Sclerosis, contraction in, 225, 234
  diffuse, 59
  hæmorrhage in, 61, 234
  hypertrophic, nodular, or tuberous, 60
  in amentia, 193, 224
  localized, 59
  origin of, 60
  pathology of, 59
Sclerotic amentia, 224
  diffuse, 225
    atrophic form, 226
    hypertrophic form, 229
    localized, tuberous, or nodular, 233
  prognosis in, 331
Secondary amentia, causation of, 47
  clinical varieties of, 73, 194
  pathology of, 64
  prognosis in, 330
Séguin, Dr. Édouard, 271, 274, 327, 336
Sensations, importance of, to mental development, 98, 263
Sense deprivation, amentia due to, 263
Senses, four chief, in normal mind, 293
Sensory functions, abnormal development, in idiots savants, 271
  cultivation of, 338, 342
  in aments, 98, 131, 160, 167
  in cretins, 256
  in mentally defective children, 131
Sentiment in aments, 110
Sex of aments, 13
  of idiots savants, 270
  of mentally defective children, 128
Sexual instincts, 102, 167, 290, 298
Shuttleworth, Dr. G., 21, 91, 123, 181, 189, 330, 350
  and Beach, Drs., 16, 18, 20, 23, 27
Siege of Paris, 27
Sichard, Dr., 298

Simple variety of amentia, 73, 173
Situation of aments, 12, 281, 286, 287
  of brain changes in primary amentia, 61
  of lesions in secondary amentia, 207
Skeleton, anomalies of, 88
Skin, anomalies of, in aments, 88
  in cretins, 252, 256
  in Mongols, 187
Skull in amentia, 70, 84. See also Cranium
Sleep in aments, 113
Slums, effect of, in causation of amentia, 48, 127
Small-pox as a cause of amentia, 203
Smell in aments, 101, 271
  cultivation of, 344
Smith, Dr. F. J., 248
Society and the ament, 281
Sollier, Dr., 75, 90
Speech, consonantal defects, 121
  cultivation of, 349
  in aments, 117
  in cretins, 255
  in idiots, 168
  in idiots savants, 272
  in mentally defective children, 131
  in savages, 120
  in syphilitic amentia, 242
  nervous mechanism of, 117
  retardation of, 90
Spiegelberg, Dr., 30
Spiller, Dr. W. G., 206
Spinal cord in amentia, 67
  in microcephaly, 175
  secondary sclerosis of, 234
Spontaneity, 111, 335
  deficient, 113
  development of, 337
  excessive, 114
Stammerers, 349
Stature of aments, 88, 194
  of cretins, 255
  of criminals, 296
  of mentally defective children, 130
  of microcephalics, 178
Stephen, Sir FitzJames, 306, 309
Sterility in cretins, 256
  in idiots, 167
Sterilization of aments, 360
Stigmata of degeneracy in criminals, 296
  in insane, 312

Stigmata of degeneracy in mentally defective children, 129
　in primary aments, 78, 80, 82
　in secondary aments, 194
Still-births in neuropaths, 39
Strümpell, Professor, 60
Stupor in aments, 315
Stutterers, 349
Sugar-loaf cranium, 177
Suicide in aments, 110, 314, 315
Sunstroke as a cause of amentia 32, 203, 216
Suspicion in aments, 210, 300
Sutherland, Dr. G. A., 22, 182, 185, 187, 258
Sutures, cranial, in microcephaly, 174
Synostosis, premature, in microcephaly, 174
Syphilis as a cause of amentia, 21, 241, 243
　　Mongolism, 22, 182
Syphilitic amentia, 240
　　and general paralysis, 242
　　description of, 242
　　diagnosis of, 243
　　treatment in, 244, 332
　　toxæmia, 241

Talbot, Dr. E., 81, 87, 89
Talents, special, in aments, 270
Talipes in paralytic aments, 211
Taste, cultivation of, 344
　defects of, 101
Tay, Mr. Waren, 249
Taylor, Dr. F. R. P., 226, 228
Teeth, anomalies of, 88
Telford-Smith, Dr., 187
Temperament of aments, 108
Temperature, appreciation of, 102
　effect of, upon aments, 91
　in amentia due to cerebral disease, 209
　in cretins, 256
Thirst in aments, 102, 167
Thompson, Dr. J. Bruce, 296
Thomson, Dr. John, 87, 115, 186, 254, 255, 258
Thymus gland, effect of, in Mongolism, 190
Thyroid gland, administration of, in cretinism, 258
　in Mongolism, 190
　condition of, in cretinism, 252, 253
　secretion, effect of, upon brain, 254

Thyroid secretion, temporary arrest of, 260
Tongue, anomalies of, 84
　in cretins, 252, 255
　in Mongolism, 186
　sucking, 186
Touch, sense of, 101
　cultivation of, 343
　in idiots savants, 271
　in paraplegia, 216
　painful, 344
Toxæmia, syphilitic, 241
Toxic amentia, 202
　conditions causing amentia, 32
Tracey, Mr. Justice, 305
Tracheotomy, necessity for, in aments, 167
Training, age at which to begin, 339
　effect of, in amentia due to lesions, 206
　　sense deprivation, 263
　general principles of, 335
　home, 339
　industrial, 351
　intelligence, 347
　moral, 353
　of movement, 344
　of senses, 342
　of speech, 349
　school, 341
　value of, 358
Train-wrecking by aments, 303, 304
Trauma as a cause of amentia, 27, 31, 203, 214
Treatment, 332
　in cretinism, 258
　in epileptic amentia, 201
　in syphilitic amentia, 244
　medical, 332, 334
　surgical, 332, 334
Trélat, Dr., 274
Tremor in amentia, 192, 211
　in sclerosis, 225, 226, 228, 230
　in syphilitic amentia, 242
Tricks and habits, 114
　correction of, 346
Tuberculosis, antecedent, as a cause of amentia, 20, 37
　as a cause of death, 96
Tuke, Sir J. Batty, 2
Tuke, Dr. Hack, 123
Turgenieff, brain of, 176

Ultimate result of cerebral lesions, 203
Umbilical hernia in cretins, 256

Umbilication of sclerotic nodules, 225, 234
Unstable type of feeble-minded, 155
Urinary organs, anomalies of, 89
Uterine exhaustion as a cause of Mongolism, 183

Vagrancy, 285
Vanity in imbeciles, 162, 278
Vaquez, Dr., 256
Varieties, ethnic, 73
   of mental action, 109
   of mentally defective children, 137
   of mind, 294
   of primary amentia, 73, 173
   of secondary amentia, 73, 194
Vascular, toxic, or inflammatory amentia, 202
   causes of, 203
   illustrative cases of, 212 *et seq.*
   initial symptoms of, 208, 209
   mental condition in, 210
   physical condition in, 208
   prospects of improvement in, 210
Vessels of brain, 61, 65, 203
Vision, cultivation of, 342
   defects of, and cortical development, 263
   in amaurotic family idiocy, 250
   in amentia, 100
   in hydrocephalus, 236
   in idiots savants, 271
   in Mongolism, 187
   in syphilitic amentia, 242

Vitality of aments, 91
Vocabulary of normal child, 118
Vogt, Professor C., 174
Voisin, Dr. Félix, 176
   Dr. Jules, 18, 23, 90, 271

Walking, age at, in aments, 90, 255
Warner, Dr. Francis, 111, 116, 123, 140, 344, 346
Watson, Dr. G., 243
Weight of brain in aments, 176, 184, 220, 223, 229
   of criminals, 296
   of mentally defective children, 130
   normal, 176, 364
Weismann, Professor, 35
Wey, Dr. H., 296
Whooping-cough as a cause of amentia, 203
Wilbur, Dr., 179
Will in aments, 110, 161, 168, 306
Wilmarth, Dr., 59, 184
Wilson, Dr. G., 296
Winslow, Dr. Forbes, 273
Witnesses, aments as, 309
Wizel, Dr., 274
Work, capacity of aments for, 136, 149, 151, 156, 161, 189, 283
Workhouses, feeble-minded in, 282
   idiots and imbeciles in, 284, 288
   maternity wards, aments in, 289
Works of the Genius of Earlswood Asylum, 276
Writing, teaching of, 350
Wyllie, Dr., 120

Ziegler, Professor, 55, 66

THE END